The New Politics:
Polarization or Utopia?

The New Politics: Polarization or Utopia?

Robert T. Golembiewski

Charles S. Bullock, III

Harrell R. Rodgers, Jr.

Department of Political Science
University of Georgia

McGraw-Hill Book Company
New York, St. Louis, San Francisco, Düsseldorf,
London, Mexico, Panama, Sydney, Toronto

The New Politics: Polarization or Utopia?

Library of Congress Catalog Card Number 75-128787

23678

1 2 3 4 5 6 7 8 9 0 M A M M 7 9 8 7 6 5 4 3 2 1 0

This book was set in Univers and Press Roman by Visual Skills, Inc., and printed on permanent paper and bound by The Maple Press Company.
The designer was Visual Skills, Inc.
The editor was James Mirrielees. Annette Wentz supervised production.

TO
Peggy, Fran, and Judy

We would like to express thanks to our research assistants Kitty Griffin, Earl Benson, and Larry Braddy for toiling many long hours in the library Xeroxing articles and tracking down fugitive facts and figures. Mrs. Sigrid Sanders handled the other frustrating task, securing permissions with patience and persistence. Mrs. Jackie Hall typed the various drafts of the manuscript and tolerated three guys who kept touching up the finished product for several months. We also wish to thank Judy Rodgers and Barbara Gilbert for helping with the typing and in securing permissions.

Robert T. Golembiewski
Charles S. Bullock, III
Harrell R. Rodgers, Jr.

CONTENTS

PART FIVE
Taking On the Fuzz:

Introduction

This volume has two major points of departure. First, it attempts to highlight some significant contemporary challenges to our political institutions and traditions. We believe we have identified these significant challenges with tolerable precision, and that we have spotlighted at least the major actors in the diverse confrontations that these challenges involve. Some of the confrontations are more directly political than others, but their common characteristic is that they all require political action.

Hence, we entitle this volume: *The New Politics*. Political institutions and traditions will adapt to today's challenges, or they will break before them. In more direct language, these significant challenges all relate to questions of who is to get what, where, when, and how. As Lasswell emphasized long ago, these are the classical political issues. Confrontation and reaction are the warp and woof of efforts to resolve these basic political issues.

Second, we are not at all clear whether adaptation or dissolution of our political institutions and traditions will be the probable outcome of today's challenges. Too much evidence is unavailable and too many trends are still developing. Hence, the many question marks both literal and figurative that are sprinkled throughout the following text. The lack of evidence also motivates this volume's subtitle: *Polarization or Utopia?* Today's political challenges may lead to such extreme polarizations as to rend the social fabric into tatters. Or they may usher in a new era of expanded pluralism, with significantly more people unprecedentedly influencing public policy through a growing number of increasingly sensitive representational devices.

These two points of departure give a particular flavor to this volume. We are tentative about predictions. At the same time, we believe it is abundantly clear what the major issues are, how big the stakes are, and which major alternative

1

resolutions of today's political challenges are more or less probable. This volume, therefore, is at once timid and bold.

These dual emphases characterize this volume, and expose it to dual criticisms. We are bold in describing what we see as major political challenges, as well as in identifying the major participants in the confrontation induced by the challenges, and are vulnerable to the criticism of being too bold, or of flirting with simplification. Oppositely, we are leery of predictions regarding how contemporary dynamics will evolve. And this emphasis leaves us open to charges of neglecting empirical analysis or of copping out in the face of moral choices. So be it.

FIVE CHALLENGES OF THE NEW POLITICS

What are these "significant political challenges" of which we write? We have isolated five major themes for the purpose of organizing this volume. The classification of themes is useful, even if it is artificial; they do interact and commingle. Moreover, the same interests or people may be important actors in several of the five issue areas that are carved out below. The artificiality of organizing this book around the five issue areas in this case, however, is not deemed too great; the reader can help reduce that artificiality by making those numerous connections that we have left implicit.

Introducing the vitals of this book will be done in two basic ways. First, the major challenges around which this volume is organized will be briefly described and the issues they raise will be sketched. Second, the major actors in the political confrontations generated by each of these challenges will be identified briefly.

The first major challenge to our institutions and traditions goes to the heart of the quality of our political life. The core question is starkly clear and momentous. What degree of involvement in political issues can we expect in the future, and in what styles will that involvement appear? To simplify, will our politics be characterized by a fervent new involvement and an activist citizenship? This style constantly seeks to bring more and more issues into the political arena, while at the same time innovating representative vehicles that permit more and more people to influence the evolution of public policy. Perhaps, in addition, this new maxipolitics will have to provide more room for disturbance or violence, as cathartics that temporarily reduce the emotional fever induced by having so many issues and interests up for explicit political judgment.

Alternatively, or even simultaneously, we may see efforts to reduce the scope and intensity of political issues, or perhaps even a significant movement toward a kind of highly localized tribalism. In either case, more and more issues would be defined as outside political institutions and traditions as we understand them today. Both cases also imply an antipolitics of variable degree, a devaluation of power as an instrument and an aversion to attempting to control large political aggregates of people. Such an antipolitical tendency is perhaps best illustrated by the growing number of hippie communes. Hippies substitute love for power in their ideology, and ask only to do their own thing rather than to set policy for large political aggregates, or rather than to have policy set for them by larger political units.

Two tentative guesses seem appropriate. The probability is that we will get bewildering combinations of both antipolitics and maxipolitics in the future, which must somehow be accommodated to one another. Moreover, the danger is that maxipolitics and antipolitics will encourage mutual escalation into polarized positions with which our political institutions and traditions deal so poorly. To explain, maxipolitics prescribes the use of even violent confrontation to radicalize the "inert masses." But these techniques of maxipolitics might only turn off the masses at first, and later induce them to lash out in reactionary ways. The self-heightening cycle is plain: increasingly more inflammatory techniques that lead to increasingly harsh repression which encourages even more inflammatory techniques. The progressively tolerant political community cuts off such escalating sequences early in the game.

The readings in the first section attempt to sensitize the reader to the complex of issues and actors involved in the politics of the future. Our convenient focus is on the relatively intense political involvement surrounding the 1968 Democratic National Convention in Chicago, as well as on the more cerebral activities of the "libertarians." They illustrate approaches to maxipolitics and antipolitics, respectively.

The second contemporary challenge to our political institutions and traditions involves classical and tormenting issues. That is, how does a relatively tolerant society respond to any significant part of its membership which at once rejects some of the prevailing ground rules but yet cannot induce relatively peaceful change in those ground rules? And what are the consequences of various ways of dealing with such rejecting interests? In its classic form, the question involves the kind of treatment appropriate for a person who refuses to defend his political community, or for a person in a simple society who demands to be fed but who refuses to help till the soil.

The contemporary versions of this second challenge are more subtle than the classic form. But they imply similar issues, and their significance can hardly be overestimated. On the one hand, the danger is that a tolerant society becomes so intolerant of individuals and groups that are seen as deviant that it develops repressive traditions and institutions. Such a society digs its own grave while seeking to protect itself. Unfortunately, creating a stagnant and intolerant society seems all too easy, to judge by the track record of man's written history. All societies need a substantial degree of protection and stability, for a society must continue to exist in order to innovate and develop.

Hence, the issues are inevitably joined, and there are no easy resolutions today. Perhaps the slogans of individualism versus collectivism sufficed to provide answers in simpler days. Today's questions seem more complex. Suppose an individual decides to do his own thing, and thereby deprives his community of some needed skill, actual or potential? Most of us would find this acceptable. But suppose his life style implies health hazards or welfare burdens or problems of law enforcement? The balance may begin to shift somewhat, and at various points for different people specific behavior or attitudes are seen as so deviant as to be unacceptable. Moreover, deviant practices by a handful of people may be acceptable and even charming, but the same behavior by one or five percent of the population may be seen as unbearable. "How much and by how many" are crucial judgments, and there are only historical standards to go by. Clearly, we are testing both limits today, and the associated questions tend to get posed in more and more extreme forms. Who will make those crucial judgments is a critical issue of the new politics.

The second set of readings focuses on three varieties of confronting by dropping out. Their common core is a rejection of square society in diverse degrees in reaction to its perceived repressiveness. The focus encompasses: the hippie movement, the use (or misuse) of drugs, and resistance to the draft. These three varieties of challenging a society deemed unjust illustrate the issues raised by a broader family of ways of reacting against or rejecting existing social and/or legal ground rules.

The third major challenge is posed by those who basically seem to accept the broad framework of institutions and traditions, but who also feel disadvantaged by existing political processes. Such interests occupy a curiously central role. Proponents of intense maxipolitics see such people as finking out, as wanting only a bigger piece of the pie rather than as desiring drastic changes in political institutions and processes. The common strategy of the intense politicos is to encourage such interests to express their concerns and dissatisfactions in some organized form. Beyond this point, their strategy can take several routes. For example, the intense politicos can attempt to capture the leadership of any such movement that gets off the ground so as to turn it to revolutionary purposes. In one variation, they also seek to prevent any satisfaction of the underlying concerns, using their leadership to guarantee failure and increase frustration, in the short run. The hoped-for consequence in the long run is a radicalization of some of the accepting-but-disadvantaged. This will add to the number of revolutionary shock troops.

From the point of view of square society, the accepting-but-disadvantaged are also central. Generally, if their needs cannot be met, any square society really intent on an expanding pluralism will have to admit failure, and, over the long run, can properly anticipate that additional radicals will have been created in the process who must be reckoned with later. Therefore, it is the public purpose of representative systems to develop a kind of expanding pluralism which provides avenues through which more and more interests can make their demands effectively heard. The limiting conditions include scarcity of resources, as well as an unwillingness of the haves to share with the have-nots in a degree and at a time acceptable to the latter.

A third set of readings uses two categoric groups to illustrate the issues associated with confrontations involving the accepting-but-disadvantaged, teachers and the poor. Not all teachers nor all poor people fit within the broad and ill-defined category, of course. In terms of central tendencies, however, most confrontations involving teachers and the poor seem to be based on their willingness to accept existing political institutions and traditions. Both are attempting to unionize in order to express their concerns more effectively, but within the context of more or less accepted avenues of political expression. Thus, picketing and strikes—long acceptable techniques in industrial unionism, and variously defined and circumscribed by law and tradition—are coming into extensive use by teachers and the poor; testing available means for expressing their concerns, and not yet rejecting them. They want more of the good things that the system provides, not destruction of that system.

The fourth major challenge involves the expression of concern or discontent in violent ways. Obviously, political institutions and traditions in any representative policy must somehow be capable of defining the prohibited with increasing precision, while gaining broad support in the process. And those institutions and traditions must also prove capable of coping with violent expressions. The ways in which this defining and coping are accomplished will go far toward determining whether a political community can preserve and expand a relative tolerance, or whether it will degenerate step by step into a war of all against all.

The fourth set of readings focuses on three aspects of the new politics, via uncivil acting out—by students, blacks, and urbanites. Sometimes one person fits in all three categories, sometimes not. Students and blacks and urbanites alike reflect a broad range of confronting behavior, ranging from minor expressions of concern to peaks of violence. The readings direct attention to that range, and help isolate the complex factors that determine the degree to which expressions of concern can be escalated into violence.

The fifth major challenge to our political institutions and traditions involves a confrontation between the classic right and left, between the defenders of what exists and the proponents of what they would like to exist. Every political society reflects this tension between stability and change, and perhaps contemporary America does so in especially acute forms. Overall, the resolution of that tension between stability and change is a delicate and significant one, and involves complex and shifting sets of actors. Too much movement in one direction causes a political community to become moribund and inelastic, while too much movement in the other direction can lead to a chaos of rootlessness and normlessness.

The final set of selections illustrates the basic right/left confrontation in two ways. First, the opposition of the liberal intellectuals to the police is described. The two categoric groups represent the New Order and the Establishment, although there no doubt are cases in which the same persons can be classified as both law enforcement officials and liberal intellectuals. Second, the extremes of this confrontation are also illustrated by selections that deal with the leftist urban guerillas and with those rightist organizations that propose to save the Republic by violently augmenting the peace-keeping capacities of civil and military authorities.

SOME NOTES ON STYLE

Our approach to directing attention at these five major challenges in which the new politics is embroiled has a deliberate and distinctive style. Overall, we have tried to frame classical political issues in modern garb to encourage discussion about them in contemporary terms. The all-too-common tendency is to look at today's political issues as being radically new, thereby forfeiting valuable and available insights and understanding.

Relatedly, we have tried to keep the selections descriptive, rather than analytical or theoretical. Our intention is that the readings be suitable for supplementing diverse analytical and theoretical approaches; a basic set of resources, to be enriched by instructors and students with divergent views of the political issues and distinct preferences for ways of analyzing them. For example, users can approach the materials below through various theoretical frameworks, which include pressure group analysis, systems theory, power as a focus, or the "great issues" of classical political analysis.

Moreover, this volume attempts to be with it but not necessarily of it. It raises many New Left issues, without implying that we editors share or intend a New Left persuasion. Our intention is to approach the five challenges from more than one vantage point. When limitations of space do not allow us to include articles illustrating all the major perspectives from which these problems can be viewed, we have broadened the range of views represented by briefly discussing some materials not reprinted here. Additional insights and perspectives can be generated in the thrust and parry of classroom discussions and lectures.

Through it all, one constant remains. Our hope is that the selections will induce an exchange of ideas between students and instructors about topics that are stimulating, critical, relevant, and sometimes neglected.

PART ONE

A.
A Basic Dilemma

B.
The Libertarians: true radicalism
or nostalgic yearning for a simpler world?

C.
The New Politicos: intense involvement
or determined alienation?

Psyching Out the Future:

A New Involvement or the Death of Politics?

A decade ago, the national sport among intellectuals was to find new ways in which to deplore the political apathy of American youth. After a glowing description of the keen political interest displayed by foreign students, the typical writer would proceed to color the American student gray. Authors pleaded with students to swerve from their pursuit of security long enough for one good protest. The silent generation paid little heed.

Times have changed. Today young Americans are probably more active politically than any previous generation has ever been. They provide the manpower in political campaigns, they march for peace, sit in for civil rights, boycott for improved working conditions, and rally around a multitude of challenges to the establishment. The overall impression is one of action. Even if only a small percentage of youth is involved, their numbers are unprecedentedly great and growing.

If this is the turned-on generation, politically speaking, it is not altogether clear what directions its new political consciousness will take. We make no bold predictions, and seek only to provide a broad framework that reflects major contemporary notions. Attention will be focused on:

> The Libertarians: true radicalism or nostalgic yearning for a simpler world?

> The New Politicos: intense involvement or determined alienation?

A. A BASIC DILEMMA

The new political consciousness of the turned-on generation has found diverse expressions, which complicate making predictions about the future. Specifically, perhaps the basic dilemma in governance is the issue of the balance between individual needs and collective requirements. The expressions of the new political consciousness suggest only that some polarization is occurring in attitudes about what constitutes a desirable balance. Hence, the future probably will bring a greater emphasis on collective requirements, laced with increasingly insistent demands for individual self-determination. Similarly, the future probably will see a new involvement in politics, but we can also expect stronger pressures toward the death of conventional politics. Modern political life reflects strong tendencies toward polarization, that is, out of which either new institutions may evolve or old society may devour itself.

Three specific expressions of the new political consciousness suggest the diverse ways in which we can expect the dilemmas of governance to be approached in the future. These expressions polarize those who work within the existing system from those who would destroy it; and they polarize those playing the political game from those who say they reject that game. These three expressions of the new political consciousness emphasize, in turn:

> *reform by seeking marginal changes while working within the going system.* Examples of this kind of change include the passage of new civil rights acts, the nomination of a liberal candidate, and the establishment of a more equitable means for carrying out the work of government.

> *reform by destroying the present governmental, economic, and social organization and by replacing it with organizational forms more responsive to today's problems.* In this tradition, for example, are those on our nation's campuses who seek to destroy our universities as a first skirmish with the Establishment. These people want an across-the-board change in all existing institutions that control their behavior.

> *reform by a radical libertarianism,* which disdains acquiring and wielding political power. There are traces of this expression in such diverse sources as Barry Goldwater's abortive presidential campaign and the antics of the Yippies. From the perspective of radical libertarianism, the two preceding approaches are reactionary and authoritarian in that they only seek to *revise* who will acquire and wield political power and how that will be done. Radical libertarianism seeks to *reduce* or *eliminate* the institutions that permit or require the very exercise of political power.

B. THE LIBERTARIANS: TRUE RADICALISM OR NOSTALGIC YEARNING FOR A SIMPLER PAST?

Libertarianism is a kind of antipolitics that, at most, seeks to gain political power only to do away with it. As such, it may seem an unlikely approach to our future politics, or rather the future death of politics in conventional terms. But the libertarian expression of today's new political consciousness cannot be written off as a mindless bleating for a long dead and simpler past. In various diluted forms, we are likely to see many future expressions of this form of antipolitics.

Karl Hess, a Goldwater speechwriter in 1964, describes the libertarian position in "The Death of Politics." He states that the only way to free man is to severely curtail the powers of government. This was an important motive behind Goldwater's campaign against Johnson, a method that seemed political suicide.

All popular approaches fail his crucial test, Hess notes. For example, Hess goes to great pains to demonstrate the overriding philosophical similarities between today's liberals and conservatives. Both camps are hung up with the need for a strong government. They differ only on the minor questions; those concerning what governmental power is to be used for and who is to use it. Conservatives want a government strong enough to protect the present distribution of goods in society, such as wealth and licenses for television stations. Liberals desire a government which will force changes such as integration, new welfare programs, and so forth. Both philosophies find the concept of a true laissez-faire society with unrestricted political and economic activity intolerable. As Hess says: "Political parties and politicians today—all parties and all politicians—question only the forms through which they will express their common belief in controlling the lives of others." Hess even rejects the contention that the participatory democracy of today's "radicals" is a new form of politics. He points out that many of the new leftists, including Tom Hayden of the Students for a Democratic Society, envision only a different elite in charge of the same old powerful state.

Hess goes George Wallace one better, as it were. Where the White Knight of Dixie said there was not a dime's worth of difference between Republicans and Democrats, Hess includes the Wallaceites as well as the New Leftists and reduces the ante to a nickel. Hess calls for a government which would have power to insure neither freedom from discrimination nor freedom from economic competition. "Such a state would have as its purpose (probably supported exclusively by use taxes or fees) the maintenance of a system to adjudicate disputes (courts)," he explains, "to protect citizens against violence (police), to maintain some form of currency for ease of commerce, and as long as it might be needed because of the existence of national borders and differences, to maintain a defense force."

C. THE NEW POLITICOS: INTENSE INVOLVEMENT
OR DETERMINED ALIENATION?

Whatever the impact of libertarianism, without question the future belongs to the new politicos. Their common focus is on acquiring and wielding political power, but they pursue that prize in two distinct ways that have profoundly different implications. Some of the new politicos reflect an intense involvement within the present system; and some profess a determined alienation that can be satisfied only by destroying our political institutions and by evolving others that are somehow more responsive. Which camp emerges as most influential will surely make a profound difference in American politics.

The future balance of involvement/alienation by the New Politicos is uncertain, but some observers already see signs of an evolving new citizenship that will improve our political life. For example, Christian Bay's "Life or Justice?" sketches the outlines of a more dynamic citizenship being built on the foundations of the activity and commitment of today's young. This new citizenship is similar to the "participatory democracy" of the new left, and the price of admission is active concern for their less fortunate neighbors. If Bay's vision of the future is more or less accurate, we can expect some lively politics. For example, these new citizens can legitimately resort to "creative disorder" or civil disobedience to protest the unrepresentative nature of existing institutions. Indeed, the new citizen may have a moral responsibility to make his views heard in such ways. Current student questioning of myths long accepted as truisms is the kind of healthy inquiry which Bay encourages and foresees.

A constant infusion of young, well-educated idealists is needed to achieve the new citizenship, Bay notes. Their task is dual: to free themselves and others from unreasoning commitment to dead laws, defined as the rationalizations for our inequities; and to move toward a justice in which the government works to expand the rights enjoyed by all citizens. The required soldiers of justice will come from our colleges and universities. They will come on the political scene with no a priori bondage to existing institutions. They will be free to pledge their prime loyalty not to the system but to their fellow men. These new citizens will work to improve the lot of their neighbors, especially the deprived. These are the goals of the new politics foreseen by Bay.

Other perspectives on the new politicos encourage a less sanguine view of the future. Consider the youthful protesters at the 1968 Democratic National Convention. These uninvited "delegates from the masses" were all hyperactive politically, but differed in that one group was content to work within the system while another was determined to destroy that system. Senator Eugene McCarthy's "crusaders" demanded extensive changes, for example, but they were eager and willing to work within the existing system. This willingness and eagerness lasted even though the convention system beat them. By the time of their arrival in Chicago, many McCarthy supporters knew that their political Pied Piper had lost his magic. Nonetheless some of the youthful exuberance typical of the McCarthy campaign still showed in Chicago, a spirit vividly captured in Charles Heckscher's "The Children's Crusade." Heckscher recounts how McCarthy's anti-hero personality and forthright policy stands, especially opposition to President Johnson and the war in Vietnam, kindled a fierce loyalty in many young Americans. Heckscher speaks for millions of young people who experienced a crescendo of hope as their candidate moved along the primary trail by winning in New Hampshire, Wisconsin, Oregon, and New York. Their hope was shattered upon the anvil of practical politics. McCarthy's poetry and erudite repartee did not generate sufficient energy to fuel a political machine seeking to capture the presidential nomination. Some McCarthy supporters expect the youth movement to recover from Chicago, but their faith in the viability of existing political institutions was certainly shaken.

The SDSers and their allies could have told the crusaders how it would be. They made some of the same demands as the McCarthy campaigners, but they saw the system as too ossified to enact essential reforms. They wanted to force the uptight establishment "up against the wall," to destroy it. To try to modify the system was to cop out. Nothing short of revolutionary change was acceptable. Unlike some McCarthyites who were disheartened and alienated after the convention, the second group came to Chicago not to nominate a president but to show the congenital flaws of the system. They left the city satisfied that the activities of the Chicago police demonstrated not only the viciousness of the establishment's guardians but also the general corruption of contemporary politics.

The type and intensity of political activity among the alienated dissenters at the Chicago convention is mapped in detail by Gary Wills in "Convention in the Streets." He describes how the Yippies prepared for the hoped-for riot, a preparation whose unevenness is consistent with the basic creed of the hippie movement—do your own thing. It is surprising as well as frightening to contemplate the disruption wrought by those "doing their own thing." Had the Yippies and other demonstrators been as well organized as the ideal Communist cell, a staggering havoc might have been wreaked upon Chicago.

Only the future will tell whether or not a substantial number of McCarthy's crusaders will take their cue from those who despair of working within existing political institutions. To the degree that they do, the future balance of American politics will shift further toward a determined alienation among the New Politicos. The resulting consequences are hard to predict, but they will be crucial.

1

THE DEATH OF POLITICS

Karl Hess

This is not a time of radical, revolutionary politics. Not yet. Unrest, riot, dissent and chaos notwithstanding, today's politics is reactionary. Both right and left are reactionary and authoritarian. That is to say: Both are political. They seek only to revise current methods of acquiring and wielding political power. Radical and revolutionary movements seek not to revise but to revoke. The target of revocation should be obvious. The target is politics itself.

Radicals and revolutionaries have had their sights trained on politics for some time. As governments fail around the world, as more millions become aware that government never has and never can humanely and effectively manage men's affairs, government's own inadequacy will emerge, at last, as the basis for a truly radical and revolutionary movement. In the meantime, the radical-revolutionary position is a lonely one. It is feared or hated, by both right and left—although both right and left must borrow from it to survive. The radical-revolutionary position is libertarianism and its socioeconomic form is laissez-faire capitalism.

Libertarianism is the view that each man is the absolute owner of his life, to use and dispose of as he sees fit; that all man's social actions should be voluntary; and that respect for every other man's similar and equal ownership of life and, by extension, the property and fruits of that life, is the ethical basis of a humane and open society. In this view, the only—repeat, only—function of law

Reprinted from Karl Hess, The Death of Politics, *Playboy,* 16, no. 3, pp. 102-104, 178-185 (March 1969).

or government is to provide the sort of self-defense against violence that an individual, if he were powerful enough, would provide for himself.

If it were not for the fact that libertarianism freely concedes the right of men voluntarily to form communities or governments on the same ethical basis, libertarianism could be called anarchy. . . .

Libertarianism is rejected by the modern left which preaches individualism but practices collectivism. Capitalism is rejected by the modern right—which preaches enterprise but practices protectionism. The libertarian faith in the mind of man is rejected by religionists who have faith only in the sins of man. The libertarian insistence that men be free to spin cables of steel as well as dreams of smoke is rejected by hippies who adore nature but spurn creation. The libertarian insistence that each man is a sovereign land of liberty, with his primary allegiance to himself, is rejected by patriots who sing of freedom but also shout of banners and boundaries. There is no operating political movement in the world today that is based upon a libertarian philosophy. If there were, it would be in the anomalous position of using political power to abolish political power.

Perhaps a regular political movement, overcoming this anomaly, will actually develop. Believe it or not, there were strong possibilities of such a development in the 1964 campaign of Barry Goldwater. Underneath the scary headlines, Goldwater hammered away at such purely political structures as the draft, general taxation, censorship, nationalism, legislated conformity, political establishment of social norms, and war as an instrument of international policy.

It is true that, in a common political paradox, Goldwater (a major general in the Air Force Reserve) has spoken of reducing state power while at the same time advocating the increase of state power to fight the Cold War. He is not a pacifist. He believes that war remains an acceptable state action. He does not see the Cold War as involving U.S. imperialism. He sees it as a result only of Soviet imperialism. Time after time, however, he has said that economic pressure, diplomatic negotiation, and the persuasions of propaganda (or "cultural warfare") are absolutely preferable to violence. He has also said that antagonistic ideologies can "never be beaten by bullets, but only by better ideas."

A defense of Goldwater cannot be carried too far, however. His domestic libertarian tendencies simply do not carry over into his view of foreign policy. Libertarianism, unalloyed, is absolutely isolationist, in that it is absolutely opposed to the institutions of national government that are the only agencies on earth now able to wage war or intervene in foreign affairs.

In other campaign issues, however, the libertarian coloration in the Goldwater complexion was more distinct. The fact that he roundly rapped the fiscal irresponsibility of Social Security before an elderly audience, and the fact that he criticized TVA while speaking in Tennessee, were not examples of political naïvete. They simply showed Goldwater's high disdain for politics itself, summed up in his campaign statement that people should be told "what they need to hear and not what they want to hear."

There was also some suggestion of libertarianism in the campaign of Eugene

McCarthy, in his splendid attacks on Presidential power. However, these were canceled out by his vague but nevertheless perceptible defense of government power in general. There was virtually no suggestion of libertarianism in the statements of any other politicians during last year's campaign.

I was a speechwriter for Barry Goldwater in the 1964 campaign. During the campaign, I recall very clearly, there was a moment, at a conference to determine the campaign's "farm strategy," when a respected and very conservative Senator arose to say: "Barry, you've got to make it clear that you believe that the American farmer has a right to a decent living."

Senator Goldwater replied, with the tact for which he is renowned: "But he doesn't have a right to it. Neither do I. We just have a right to try for it." And that was the end of that.

Now, in contrast, take Tom Hayden of the Students for a Democratic Society. Writing in *The Radical Papers,* he said that his "revolution" sought "institutions outside the established order." One of those institutions, he amplified, would be "people's own antipoverty organizations fighting for Federal money."

Of the two men, which is radical or revolutionary? Hayden says, in effect, that he simply wants to bulldoze his way into the establishment. Goldwater says he wants, in effect, to topple it, to forever end its power to advantage or disadvantage anyone.

This is not to defend the Goldwater Presidential campaign as libertarian. It is only to say that his campaign contained a healthy element of this sort of radicalism. But otherwise, the Goldwater campaign was very deeply in hock to regular partisan interests, images, myths and manners.

In foreign policy, particularly, there arises a great impediment to the emergence of a libertarian wing in either of the major political parties. Men who call upon the end of state authority in every other area insist upon its being maintained to build a war machine with which to hold the Communists at bay. It is only lately that the imperatives of logic—and the emergence of antistatist forces in eastern Europe—have begun to make it more acceptable to ask whether the garrison state needed to maintain the Cold War might not be as bad as or worse than the putative threat being guarded against. Goldwater has not taken and may never take such a revisionist line—but, among Cold Warriors, his disposition to libertarian principles makes him more susceptible than most.

This is not merely a digression on behalf of a political figure (almost an *anti*political figure) whom I profoundly respect. It is, rather, to emphasize the inadequacy of traditional, popular guidelines in assessing the reactionary nature of contemporary politics and in divining the true nature of radical and revolutionary antipolitics. Political parties and politicians today—all parties and all politicians—question only the forms through which they will express their common belief in controlling the lives of others. Power, particularly majoritarian or collective power (i.e., the power of an elite exercised in the name of the masses), is the god of the modern liberal. Its only recent innovative change is to suggest that the elite be leavened by the compulsory membership of authentic represen-tatives of the masses. The current phrase is "participatory democracy."

Just as power is the god of the modern liberal, God remains the authority of the modern conservative. Liberalism practices regimentation by, simply, regi-mentation. Conservatism practices regimentation by, not quite so simply, revela-tion. But regimented or revealed, the name of the game is still politics.

The great flaw in conservatism is a deep fissure down which talk of freedom falls, to be dashed to death on the rocks of authoritarianism. Conservatives worry that the state has too much power over people. But it was conservatives who gave the state that power. It was conservatives, very similar to today's conservatives, who ceded to the state the power to produce not simply order in the community but *a certain kind of order.*

It was European conservatives who, apparently fearful of the openness of the Industrial Revolution (why, *anyone* could get rich!), struck the first blows at capitalism by encouraging and accepting laws that made the disruptions of in-novation and competition less frequent and eased the way for the comforts and collusions of cartelization.

Big business in America today and for some years past has been openly at war with competition and, thus, at war with laissez-faire capitalism. Big business supports a form of state capitalism in which government and big business act as partners. Criticism of this statist bent of big business comes more often from the left than from the right these days, and this is another factor making it difficult to tell the players apart. John Kenneth Galbraith, for instance, has most recently taken big business to task for its anticompetitive mentality. The right, meantime, blissfully defends big business as though it had not, in fact, become just the sort of bureaucratic, authoritarian force that rightists reflexively attack when it is governmental.

The left's attack on corporate capitalism is, when examined, an attack on economic forms possible only in a collusion between authoritarian government and bureaucratized, nonentrepreneurial business. It is unfortunate that many New Leftists are so uncritical as to accept this premise as indicating that all forms of capitalism are bad, so that full state ownership is the only alternative. This thinking has its mirror image on the right.

It was American conservatives, for instance, who very early in the game gave up the fight against state franchising and regulation and, instead, embraced state regulation for their own special advantage. Conservatives today continue to re-vere the state as an instrument of chastisement even as they reject it as an instrument of beneficence. The conservative who wants a Federally authorized prayer in the classroom is the same conservative who objects to Federally au-thorized textbooks in the same room.

Murray Rothbard, writing in *Ramparts,* has summed up this flawed conser-vatism in describing a "new, younger generation of rightists, of 'conserva-tives' . . . who thought that the real problem of the modern world was nothing so ideological as the state *vs.* individual liberty or government intervention *vs.* the free market; the real problem, they declared, was the preservation of tradition, order, Christianity and good manners against the modern sins of reason, license, atheism and boorishness."

The reactionary tendencies of both liberals and conservatives today show clearly in their willingness to cede, to the state or the community, power far beyond the protection of liberty against violence. For differing purposes, both see the state as an instrument not protecting man's freedom but either instructing or restricting how that freedom is to be used.

Once the power of the community becomes in any sense normative, rather than merely protective, it is difficult to see where any lines may be drawn to limit further transgressions against individual freedom. In fact, the lines have not been drawn. They will never be drawn by political parties that argue merely the cost of programs or institutions founded on state power. Actually, the lines can be drawn only by a radical questioning of power itself, and by the libertarian vision that sees man as capable of moving on without the encumbering luggage of laws and politics that do not merely preserve man's right to his life but attempt, in addition, to tell him how to live it.

For many conservatives, the bad dream that haunts their lives and their political position (which many sum up as "law and order" these days) is one of riot. To my knowledge, there is no limit that conservatives would place upon the power of the state to suppress riots.

Even in a laissez-faire society, of course, the right to self-defense would have to be assumed, and a place for self-defense on a community basis could be easily imagined. But community self-defense would always be exclusively defensive. Conservatives betray an easy willingness to believe that the state should also initiate certain *offensive* actions, in order to preclude trouble later on. "Getting tough" is the phrase most often used. It does not mean just getting tough on rioters. It means getting tough on entire ranges of attitudes: clipping long hair, rousting people from parks for carrying concealed guitars, stopping and questioning anyone who doesn't look like a member of the Jaycees, drafting all the ne'er-do-wells to straighten them up, ridding our theaters and bookstores of "filth" and, always and above all, putting "those" people in their place. To the conservative, all too often, the alternatives are social conformity or unthinkable chaos.

Even if these were the only alternatives—which they obviously aren't—there are many reasons for preferring chaos to conformity. Personally, I believe I would have a better chance of surviving—and certainly my values would have a better chance of surviving—with a Watts, Chicago, Detroit, or Washington in flames than with an entire nation snug in a garrison.

Riots in modern America must be broken down into component parts. They are not all simple looting and violence against life and property. They are also directed against the prevailing violence of the state—the sort of ongoing civic violence that permits regular police supervision of everyday life in some neighborhoods, the rules and regulations that inhibit absolutely free trading, the public schools that serve the visions of bureaucracy rather than the varieties of individual people. There is violence also by those who simply want to shoot their way into political power otherwise denied them. Conservatives seem to think that greater state police power is the answer. Liberals seem to think that more preferential state welfare power is the answer. Power, power, power.

Except for ordinary looters—for whom the answer must be to stop them as you would any other thief—the real answer to rioting must lie elsewhere. It must lie in the abandonment, not the extension, of state power—state power that oppresses people, state power that tempts people. To cite one strong example: The white stores in many black neighborhoods, which are said to cause such dissatisfaction and envy, have a special, unrealized advantage thanks to state power. In a very poor neighborhood there may be many with the natural ability to open a retail store, but it is much less likely that these people would also have the ability to meet all the state and city regulations, governing everything from cleanliness to bookkeeping, which very often comprise the marginal difference between going into business or staying out. In a real laissez-faire society, the local entrepreneur, with whom the neighbors might prefer to deal, could go openly into business—selling marijuana, whiskey, number slips, books, food or medical advice from the trunk of his car. He could forget about ledgers, forms and reports and simply get on with the business of business, rather than the business of bureaucracy. Allowing ghetto dwellers to compete on their own terms, rather than on someone else's, should prove a more satisfying and practical solution to ghetto problems than either rampages or restrictions.

The libertarian thrusts away from power and authority that marked the Goldwater campaign were castigated from the left as being "nostalgic yearnings for a simpler world." (Perhaps akin to the simplistic yearnings of the hippies whom the left so easily tolerates even while it excoriates Goldwater.) Goldwater's libertarianism was castigated from the right—he received virtually *no* support from big business—as representing policies that could lead to unregulated competition, international free trade and, even worse, a weakening of the very special partnership that big business now enjoys with Big Government.

The most incredible convolution in the thinking that attacked Goldwater as reactionary, which he isn't, rather than radical, which he is, came in regard to nuclear weapons. In that area he was specifically damned for daring to propose that the control of these weapons be shared, and even fully placed, in the multinational command of the North Atlantic Treaty Organization, rather than left to the personal, one-man discretion of the President of the United States.

Again, who is reactionary and who is radical? The men who want an atomic king enthroned in Washington, or the man who dares ask that that divine right of destruction become less divine and more divided? Until recently, it was a popular cocktail pastime to speculate on the difference between the war in Vietnam under "Save-the-world-from-Goldwater" Johnson, or as it might have been under wild Barry, who, by his every campaign utterance, would have been bound to share the Vietnam decision (and the fighting) with NATO, rather than simply and unilaterally going it alone.

To return to the point: The most vital question today about politics—not *in* politics—is the same sort of question that is plaguing Christianity. Superficially, the Christian question seems simply what kind of religion should be chosen. But basically, the question is whether any irrational or mystical forces are supportable, as a way to order society, in a world increasingly able and ready to be rational. The political version of the question may be stated this way: Will men continue to submit to rule by politics, which has always meant the power of some men over other men, or are we ready to go it alone socially, in communities of voluntarism, in a world more economic and cultural than political, just as so many now are prepared to go it alone metaphysically in a world more of reason than religion?

The radical and revolutionary answer that a libertarian, laissez-faire position makes to that question is not quite anarchy. The libertarian, laissez-faire movement is, actually, if embarrassingly for some, a civil rights movement. But it is antipolitical, in that it builds diversified power to be protected against government, even to dispense with government to a major degree, rather than seeking power to protect government or to perform any special social purpose.

It is a civil-liberties movement in that it seeks civil liberties, for everyone, as defined in the 19th Century by one of Yale's first professors of political and social science, William Graham Sumner. Sumner said: "Civil liberty is the status of the man who is guaranteed by law and civil institutions the exclusive employment of all his own powers for his own welfare."

Modern liberals, of course, would call this selfishness, and they would be correct, with intense emphasis on self. Many modern conservatives would say that they agree with Sumner, but they would not be correct. Men who call themselves conservatives, but who operate in the larger industries, spend considerable time, and not a small amount of money, fighting government subsidies to labor unions (in the form of preferential tax and legal considerations) or to people (in the form of welfare programs). They do not fight *direct* subsidies to industries—such as transportation, farming or universities. They do not, in short, believe that men are entitled to the exclusive employment of their own powers for their own welfare, because they accept the practice of taxing a good part of that power to use for the welfare of other people.

As noted, for all the theoretical screaming that sometimes may be heard from the industrial right, it is safe to say that the major powers of government to regulate industry were derived not only from the support of businessmen but actually at the insistence of businessmen. Uneconomical mail rates are cherished by businessmen who can profit from them and who, significantly, seem uninterested in the obvious possibility of transforming the postal service from a bureau into a business. As a business, of course, it would charge what it costs to mail things, not what is simply convenient for users to pay.

The big businessmen who operate the major broadcast networks are not known for suggesting, as a laissez-faire concept would insist, that competition for channels and audiences be wide open and unregulated. As a consequence, of course, the networks get all the government control that they deserve, accepting it in good cheer because, even if censored, they are also protected from competition. It is notable, also, that one of the most fierce denunciations of pay TV (which, under capitalism, should be a conceptual commonplace) came not from the *Daily Worker* but from the *Reader's Digest,* that supposed bastion of conservatism. Actually, I think the *Digest* is such a bastion. It seems to believe that the state is an institution divinely ordained to make men moral—in a "Judaeo-Christian" sense, of course. It abhors, as does no publication short of William Buckley's *National Review*, the insolence of those untidy persons who today so regularly challenge the authority of the state.

In short, there is no evidence whatever that modern conservatives subscribe to the "your life is your own" philosophy upon which libertarianism is founded. An interesting illustration that conservatism not only disagrees with libertarianism but is downright hostile to it is that the most widely known libertarian author of the day, Ayn Rand, ranks only a bit below, or slightly to the side of, Leonid Brezhnev as an object of diatribe in *National Review*. Specifically, it seems, she is reviled on the right because she is an atheist, daring to take exception to the *National Review* notion that man's basically evil nature (stemming from original sin) means he must be held in check by a strong and authoritarian social order.

Barry Goldwater, during his 1964 campaign, repeatedly said that "the government strong enough to give you what you want is strong enough to take it all away." Conservatives, as a group, have forgotten, or prefer to ignore, that this applies also to government's strength to impose social order. If government can enforce social norms, or even Christian behavior, it can also take away or twist them.

To repeat: Conservatives yearn for a state, or "leadership," with the power to restore order and to put things—and people—back in their places. They yearn for political power. Liberals yearn for a state that will bomb the rich and balm the poor. They too yearn for political power. Libertarians yearn for a state that cannot, beyond any possibility of amendment, confer any advantage on anyone; a state that cannot compel anything, but simply prevents the use of violence, in place of other exchanges, in relations between individuals or groups.

Such a state would have as its sole purpose (probably supported exclusively by use of taxes or fees) the maintenance of a system to adjudicate disputes (courts), to protect citizens against violence (police), to maintain some form of currency for ease of commerce, and, as long as it might be needed because of the existence of national borders and differences, to maintain a defense force. Meanwhile, libertarians should also work to end the whole concept of the nation-state itself. The major point here is that libertarians would start with no outstanding predispositions about public functions, being disposed always to think that there is in the personal and private world of individuals someone who can or will come along with a solution that gets the job done without conferring upon anyone power that has not been earned through voluntary exchange.

In fact, it is in the matters most appropriate to collective interest—such as courts and protection against violence—that government today often defaults. This follows the bureaucratic tendency to perform least-needed services—where the risk of accountability is minimal—and to avoid performing essential but highly accountable services. Courts are clogged beyond belief. Police, rather than simply protecting citizens against violence, are deeply involved in overseeing private morals. In black neighborhoods particularly, the police serve as unloved and unwanted arbiters of everyday life.

If, in the past few paragraphs, the reader can detect any hint of a position that would be compatible with either the Communist Party of the Soviet Union or the National Association of Manufacturers, he is strongly advised to look again. No such common ground exists. Nor can any common ground be adduced in terms of "new politics" versus "old politics." New or old, the positions that parade today under these titles are still politics and, like roses, they smell alike. Radical and revolutionary politicians—antipoliticians, if you will—should be able to sniff them out easily.

Specific matters that illustrate the differences would include the draft, marijuana, monopoly, censorship, isolationism-internationalism, race relations and urban affairs, to name a few.

As part of his aborted campaign for the Presidency, Nelson Rockefeller took a position on the draft. In it, he specifically took exception to Richard Nixon's draft stand, calling it the "old politics" as contrasted with his own "new politics." The Rockefeller position involved a certain streamlining of the draft, but nothing that would change it from what it patently is—forced, involuntary servitude. Rockefeller criticized Nixon for having asserted that, someday, the draft could be replaced by a voluntary system, an old Republican promise.

The new politician contended that the Nixon system wouldn't work because it never *had* worked. The fact that this nation has never offered to pay its soldiers at a rate realistic enough to attract them was not covered in Rockefeller's statement. Nor did the new politician address himself to the fact that, given a nation that not enough citizens can be attracted to defend voluntarily, you probably also have a nation that, by definition, isn't really worth defending.

The old politician, on the other hand, did not present quite as crisp a position on the draft as the new politician tried to pin him with. Nixon, although theoretically in favor of a voluntary military, was—along with the presumably even *more* conservative Ronald Reagan—opposed to trying voluntarism until *after* the Vietnam war. Throughout the conservative stance one sees a repetition of this position. Freedom is fine—but it must be deferred as long as a hot war or the Cold War has to be fought.

All should be struck by the implications of that baleful notion. It implies that free men simply cannot be ingenious enough to defend themselves against violence without themselves becoming violent—not toward the enemy alone, but to their own persons and liberty as well. If our freedom is so fragile that it must be continuously protected by giving it up, then we are in deep trouble. And, in fact, by following a somewhat similar course, we got ourselves in very deep trouble in Southeast Asia. The Johnson war there was escalated precisely on the belief that southern Vietnamese freedom may best be obtained by dictating what form of government the south should have—day by day, even—and by defending it against the North Vietnamese, by devastating the southern countryside.

In foreign relations, as in domestic pronouncements, new and old politicians preach the same dusty doctrines of compulsion and contradiction. The radical preachment of libertarianism, the antipolitical preachment, would be that as long as the inanity of war between nation-states remains a possibility, free nation-states will at least protect themselves from wars by hiring volunteers, not by murdering voluntarism.

One of the most medievally fascinating minds of the 20th Century, that of Lewis Hershey, sole owner and proprietor of the Selective Service System, has put this unpretty picture into perfect perspective with his memorable statement, delivered at a National Press Club luncheon, that he "hate[s] to think of the day that [his] grandchildren would be defended by volunteers." There, in as ugly an example as is on public record, is precisely where politics and power, authority and the arthritis of traditionalism, are bound to bring you. Director Hershey is prevented from being a great comic figure by the rather obvious fact that, being involved with the deaths of so many unwilling men, and the imprisonment of so many others, he becomes a tragic figure or, at least, a figure in a tragedy. There is no new or old politics about the draft. A draft is political, plain and simple. A volunteer military is essentially commercial. And it is between politics and commerce that the entrant into radical or revolutionary politics must continually choose.

Marijuana is an example of such a choice. In a laissez-faire society, there could exist no public institution with the power to forcefully protect people from themselves. From other people (criminals), yes. From one's own self, no. Marijuana is a plant, a crop. People who smoke it do not do so under the compulsion either of physiological addiction or of institutionalized power. They do so voluntarily. They find a person who has volunteered to grow it. They agree on a price. One sells; the other buys. One acquires new capital; the other acquires a euphoric experience that, he decides, was worth allocating some of his own resources to obtain.

Nowhere in that equation is there a single point at which the neighbors, or any multitude of neighbors, posing as priesthood or public, have the slightest rational reason to intervene. The action has not, in any way, deprived anyone else of "the exclusive employment of all his own powers for his own welfare."

The current laws against marijuana, in contravention even of all available medical evidence regarding its nature, are a prime example of the use of political power. The very power that makes it possible for the state to ban marijuana, and to arrest Lenny Bruce, is the same power that makes it possible for the state to exact taxes from one man to pay into the pockets of another. The purposes may seem different, but upon examination they are not. Marijuana must be banned to prevent people from succumbing to the madness of its fumes and doing some mischief upon the community. Poverty, too, must be banned for a similar reason. Poor people, unless *made* unpoor, will angrily rise and do mischief upon the community. As in all politics, purposes and power blend and reinforce each other.

"Hard" narcotics must be subjected to the same tests as marijuana in terms of politics versus antipolitics. These narcotics, too, are merely salable materials except that, if used beyond prudence, they can be quite disabling to the person using them. (I inject that note simply because, in my understanding, there remains at all levels of addiction the chance of breaking or controlling the habit. This suggests that a person *can* exercise a choice in the matter; that he can, indeed, be prudent or not.)

The person who uses drugs imprudently, just as the person who imprudently uses the politically sanctioned and franchised drugs of alcohol or tobacco, ends up in an unenviable position, perhaps dead. That, rationally, is his own business as long as he does not, by his actions, deprive you of the right to make your own decision not to use drugs, to assist addicts or, if you wish, to ignore them. But it is said, by right and left today, that the real problem is social and public—that the high price of the drugs leads the addict to rob and kill (rightist position), and that making drugs a public matter, for clinical dispensation, would eliminate the causes of his crime (leftist position).

These both are essentially political positions and clearly inept in a society where the line between mind-expanders such as coffee or LSD is highly technical. By choosing the economic and cultural approach rather than a political one, the antipolitical libertarian would say, sell away. Competition will keep the price down. Cultural acceptance of the root ethic, that a man's life and its appurtenances are inviolate, would justify defense against any violence that might accompany addiction in others. And what is there left for the "public" to do? Absolutely nothing—except, individually, to decide whether to risk drugs or to avoid them. Parents, of course, holding the purse strings of their children, can exercise a certain amount of control, but only individually, never collectively.

Incidentally, it is easy to imagine that, if drugs were left to economics and culture instead of politics, medical researchers would shortly discover a way to provide the salable and wanted effects of drugs without the incapacitation of addiction. In this as in similar matters—such as the unregulated competition from which it is felt people need protection—technology rather than politics might offer far better answers.

Monopoly is a case in point. To suppose that anyone needs government protection from the creation of monopolies is to accept two suppositions: that monopoly is the natural direction of unregulated enterprise, and that technology is static. Neither, of course, is true. The great concentrations of economic power, which are called monopolies today, did not grow *despite* government's anti-monopolistic zeal. They grew, largely *because* of government policies, such as those making it more profitable for small businesses to sell out to big companies rather than fight the tax code alone. Additionally, Federal fiscal and credit policies and Federal subsides and contracts have all provided substantially more assistance to big and established companies than to smaller, potentially competitive ones. The auto industry receives the biggest subsidy of all through the highway program on which it prospers, but for which it surely does not pay a fair share. Airlines are subsidized and so protected that newcomers can't even try to compete. Television networks are fantastically advantaged by FCC licensing, which prevents upstarts from entering a field where big oldtimers have been established. Even in agriculture, it is large and established farmers who get the big subsidies—not small ones who might want to compete. Government laws specifically exempting unions from antitrust activities have also furthered a monopoly mentality. And, of course, the "public utility" and "public transportation" concepts have specifically created government-licensed monopolies in the fields of power, communications and transit. This is not to say that economic bigness is bad. It isn't, if it results from economic efficiency. But it *is* bad if it results from collusion with political, rather than with economic, power. There is no monopoly situation in the world today, of which I can think, that might not be seriously challenged by competition, were it not for some form of protective government license, tariff, subsidy or regulation. Also, there isn't the tiniest shred of evidence to suggest that the trend of unregulated business and industry is toward monopoly. In fact, the trend seems in the opposite direction, toward diversification and decentralization.

The technological aspect is equally important. Monopoly cannot develop as long as technology is dynamic, which it most abundantly is today. No corporation is so large that it can command every available brain—except, of course, a corporate state. As long as one brain remains unavailable, there is the chance of innovation and competition. There can be no real monopoly, just momentary advantage. Nor does technological breakthrough always depend upon vast resources or, even where it does, would it have to depend upon a single source of financing—unless, again, only the state has the money. Short of total state control, and presuming creative brains in the community, and presuming the existence of capital with which to build even modest research facilities, few would flatly say that technological innovation could be prevented simply because of some single source enjoying a temporary "monopoly" of a given product or service. The exceptions, to repeat, are always governments. Governments can be—and usually are—monopolistic. For instance, it is not uneconomical to operate a private post-office department today. It is only illegal. The Feds enjoy a legal monopoly—to the extent that they are currently prosecuting at least one entrepreneur who operated a mail service better and cheaper than they do.

Politics is not needed to prevent monopoly. Unregulated, unrestricted laissez-faire capitalism is all that is needed. It would also provide jobs, raise living

standards, improve products, and so forth. If commercial activity were unregulated and absolutely unsubsidized, it could depend upon only one factor for
success—pleasing customers.

Censorship is another notable example in which politics, and politicians,
interpose between customer and satisfaction. The gauge becomes not whether
the customer is happy, but whether the politician (either singly or as a surrogate
for "the public") is happy. This applies equally to "public" protection from
unpopular political ideas as well as protection from pornography. Conservatives
are at least consistent in this matter. They feel that the state (which they
sometimes call "the community") can and must protect people from unsavory
thoughts. It goes without saying who defines unsavory: the political—or community—leaders, of course.

Perhaps the most ironic of all manifestations of this conservative urge to
cleanthink concerns the late Lenny Bruce. He talked dirty. He was, therefore, a
particularly favorite target of conservatives. He was also an explicit and, I think,
incisive defender of capitalism. In commenting that communism is a drag ("like
one big phone company"), Bruce specifically opted for capitalism ("it gives you
a choice, baby, and that's what it's about"). There is no traditional conservative
who is fit to even walk on the same level with Lenny Bruce in his fierce devotion
to individualism. Lenny Bruce frequently used what is for many conservatives
the dirtiest word of all: He said capitalism. When was the last time that the
N.A.M. did as much?

Lenny Bruce wasn't the only man to alienate conservatives by opening his
mouth. In 1964, Barry Goldwater alienated Southern conservatives in droves
when, in answer to a regionally hot question about whether Communists should
be permitted to speak on state-university campuses, Goldwater said, flatly and
simply: "Of course they should."

Even anti-Communist libertarians have no choice but to deny the state the
right to suppress Communists. Similarly, libertarians who are aesthetically repelled by what they deem pornography have no other course than not to buy it,
leaving its absolutely unregulated sale to producer, purchaser and no one else.
Once again, a parent could intrude—but only by stopping an individual, dependent purchaser, never by stopping the purveyor, whose right to sell pornography
for profit, and for absolutely no other socially redeeming virtue whatever, would
be inviolate. An irate parent who attempted to hustle a smut peddler off the
street, as a matter of fact, should be sued, not saluted.

The liberal attitude toward censorship is not so clear. At this point, it needn't
be. Liberals practice it, rather than preach it. The FCC's egregious power to
insist that broadcasting serve a social purpose is both a liberal tenet and an act of
censorship. In the FCC canons, social purposes are defined so that a station can
get good points for permitting a preacher free time but no points—or even bad
points—for extending the same gift of free air to an atheist.

It is partly in the realm of air, also, that differences regarding nationalism
between the old left/right politicians and the libertarian antipolitician show up.
If today's conservative has his fervent jingoism for old nations, the liberal has

just as fanatic a devotion to the jingoism of new nations. The willingness of modern liberals to suggest armed intervention against South Africa, while ignoring, even in terms of major journalistic coverage, slaughters in Nigeria and the Sudan, is a demonstration of interest only in politics—and in particular persons—rather than in human life per se.

Of course, conservatives have a similar double standard in regard to anti-Communist slaughter and anti-Communist dictatorship. Although it is not as whimsically selective as the liberal decision to be revolted or cheered by each particular blood bath, the conservative double standard can have equally tragic results. The distinct undercurrents of anti-Semitism that so obviously muddle many conservative movements probably can be traced to the horrid assumption that Adolf Hitler's anticommunism excused his other, but comparatively minor, faults. Somehow, anticommunism seems to permit anti-Semitism.

I have met in my time many anti-Communists who view communism as simply a creature of Jewish plotting for world dominion. The John Birch Society's separate chapter for Jewish members is a seriocomic reflection, I think, of such good old WASP anti-Semitism. The widely reported admiration of Hitler by the head man of the right-wing Liberty Lobby is a reflection, presumably, of the "you need a strong man to fight atheistic communism" school of thought. There are, of course, notable Jewish anti-Communists. And there are many anti-Communists who condemn anti-Semitism. But the operating question for most of the full-time anti-Communists that I have met is simply: Are you anti-Communist? Being also anti-Semitic is not automatically a disqualification on the right, though it usually is on the left.

Conservatives and liberals alike hold in common the mystical notion that nations really mean something, probably something permanent. Both ascribe to lines drawn on maps—or in the dirt or in the air—the magical creation of communities of men that require sovereignty and sanction. The conservative feels this with exaltation when he beholds the Stars and Stripes. The liberal feels this with academic certitude when he concludes that Soviet boundaries must be "guaranteed" to prevent Soviet nervousness. Today, in the ultimate confusion, there are people who feel that the lines drawn by the Soviet Union, in blood, are better than the lines drawn, also in blood, by American foreign policy. Politicians just think this way.

The radical and revolutionary view of the future of nationhood is, logically, that it has no future, only a past—often an exciting one, and usually a historically useful one at some stage. But lines drawn on paper, on the ground or in the stratosphere are clearly insufficient to the future of mankind.

Again, it is technology that makes it feasible to contemplate a day in which the politics of nationhood will be as dead as the politics of power-wielding partisanship. First, there is enough information and wealth available to ensure the feeding of all people, without the slaughtering of some to get at the possessions of others. Second, there is no longer any way to protect anything or anybody behind a national boundary anyway.

Not even the Soviet Union, with what conservatives continue to fear as an "absolute" control over its people, has been able to stop, by drawing lines or executing thousands, the infusion of subversive ideas, manners, music, poems, dances, products, desires. If the world's pre-eminent police state (either us or them, depending upon your *political* point of view) has been unable to protect itself fully behind its boundaries, what faith can or should we, the people, retain in boundaries?

It is to be expected that both liberals and conservatives respond to the notion of the end of nationhood with very similar shouts of outrage or jerks of reaction. The conservative says *it shall not be.* There will always be a U.S. Customs Inspector and long may he wave. The liberal says that far from ending nationhood, he wants to expand it, make it world-wide, to create a proliferation of mini- and micronations in the name of ethnic and cultural preservation, and then to erect a great superbureaucracy to supervise all the petty bureaucracies.

Like Linus, neither liberal nor conservative can bear the thought of giving up the blanket—of giving up government and going it alone as residents of a planet, rather than of a country. Advocates of isolationism (although some, admittedly, defend it only as a tactic) seem to fall into a paradox here. Isolationism not only depends upon nationhood, it rigidifies it. There is a subcategory of isolationism, however, that might avoid this by specifying that it favors only military isolationism, or the use of force only for *self-defense.* Even this, however, requires political definitions of national self-defense in these days of missiles, bases, bombers and subversion.

As long as there are governments powerful enough to maintain national boundaries and national political postures, then there will be the absolute risk, if not the certainty, of war between them. Even the possibility of war seems far too cataclysmic to contemplate in a world so ripe with technology and prosperous potential, ripe even with the seeds of extraterrestrial exploration. Violence and the institutions that alone can support it should be rendered obsolete.

Governments wage war. The power of life that they may claim in running hospitals or feeding the poor is just the mirror image of the power of death that they also claim—in filling those hospitals with wounded and in devastating lands on which food could be grown. "But man is aggressive," right and left chant from the depths of their pessimism. And, to be sure, he is. But if he were left alone, if he were not regulated into states or services, wouldn't that aggression be directed toward conquering his environment, and not other men?

At another warlike level, it is the choice of aggression, against politically perpetuated environment more than against men, that marks the racial strife in America today. Conservatives, in one of their favorite lapses of logic—States' rights—nourished modern American racism by supporting laws, particularly in Southern states, that gave the state the power to force businessmen to build segregated facilities. (Many businessmen, to be sure, wanted to be "forced," thus giving their racism the seal of state approval.) The States' rights lapse is simply that conservatives who would deny to the Federal Government certain controls over people, eagerly cede exactly the same controls to smaller administrative units. They say that the smaller units are more effective. This means that conservatives support the coercion of individuals at the most effective level. It certainly doesn't mean that they oppose coercion. In failing to resist state segregation and miscegenation laws, in failing to resist laws maintaining racially inequitable spending of tax money, simply because these laws were passed by states, conservatives have failed to fight the very bureaucracy that they supposedly hate—at the very level where they might have stopped it first.

Racism has been supported in this country not despite, but thanks to, governmental power and politics. Reverse racism, thinking that government is competent to force people to integrate, just as it once forced them to segregate, is just as political and just as disastrous. It has not worked. Its product has been hatred rather than brotherhood. Brotherhood could never be a political product. It is purely personal. In racial matters, as in all other matters concerning individuals, the lack of government would be nothing but beneficial. What, actually, can government do for black people in America that black people could not do better for themselves, if they were permitted the freedom to do so? I can think of nothing.

Jobs? Politically and governmentally franchised unions do more to keep black men from good jobs than do all the Bull Connors of the South. Homes, schools and protection? I recall very vividly a comment on this subject by Roy Innis, the national director of the Congress of Racial Equality. He spoke of Mayor John Lindsay's typically liberal zeal in giving money to black people, smothering them with it—or silencing them. Innis then said that the one thing Mayor Lindsay would not give the blacks was what they really wanted: political power. He meant that the black community in Harlem, for instance, rather than being gifted with tax money by the bushel, would prefer to be gifted with Harlem itself. It is a community. Why shouldn't it govern itself, or at least live by itself, without having to be a barony of New York City ward politics? However, I take exception to the notion of merely building in Harlem a political structure similar to but only separate from New York City's. And I may be doing Mr. Innis, who is an exceptional man, an injustice by even suggesting that that is what he had in mind.

But beyond this one instance, there is implicit in the very exciting undercurrents of black power in this country an equally exciting possibility that it will develop into a rebellion against politics itself. It might insist upon a far less structured community, containing far more voluntary institutions within it. There is no question in my mind that, in the long run, this movement and similar ones will discover that *laissez faire* is the way to create genuine communities of voluntarism. *Laissez faire* is the only form of social/economic organization that could tolerate and even bless a *kibbutz* operating in the middle of Harlem, a hippie selling hashish down the street and, a few blocks farther on, a firm of engineers out to do in Detroit with a low-cost nuclear vehicle.

The *kibbutz* would represent, in effect, a voluntary socialism—what other form could free men tolerate? The hash seller would represent institutionalized—but voluntary—daydreaming, and the engineers would represent unregulated creativity. All would represent laissez-faire capitalism in action and none would need a political officeholder or a single bureaucrat to help, hinder, civilize or stimulate. And, in the process simply of variegated existence, the residents of this voluntary community, as long as others voluntarily entered into commerce with them, would solve the "urban" problem in the only way it ever can be solved; i.e., via the vanishment of politics that created the problem in the first place.

If cities cannot exist on the basis of the skills, energy and creativity of the people who live, work or invest in them, then they should not be sustained by people who do *not* live in them. In short, every community should be one of voluntarism, to the extent that it lives for and through its own people and does not force others to pay its bills. Communities should not be exempted from the civil liberty prescribed for people—the exclusive employment of all their own powers for their own welfare. This means that no one should serve you involuntarily and that you should not involuntarily serve anyone else. This means, for communities, existing without involuntary aid from other communities or to other communities.

Student dissenters today seem to feel that somehow they have crashed through to new truths and new politics in their demands that universities and communities be made responsive to their students or inhabitants. But most of them are only playing with old politics. When the dissenters recognize this, and when their assault becomes one against political power and authority rather than a fight to gain such power, then this movement may release the bright potential latent in the intelligence of so many of its participants. Incidentally, to the extent that student activists the world over are actually fighting the existence of political power, rather than trying to grab some of it for themselves, they should not be criticized for failing to offer alternative programs; i.e., for not spelling out just what sort of political system will follow their revolution. What ought to follow their revolution is just what they've implicitly proposed: no political system at all.

The style of SDS so far seems most promising in this respect. It is itself loosely knit and internally anti-authoritarian as well as externally revolutionary. Liberty also looks for students who rather than caterwauling the establishment will abandon it, establish their own schools, make them effective and wage a concerned and concerted revolt against the political regulations and power that, today, give a franchise to schools—public and private—that badly need competition from new schools with new ideas.

Looking back, this same sort of thinking was true during the period of the sit-ins in the South. Since the enemy also was state laws requiring separate facilities, why wasn't it also a proper tactic to defy such laws by building a desegregated eating place and holding it against hell and high water? This is a cause to which any libertarian could respond.

Similarly with the school situation. Find someone who will rebel against public-education laws and you will have a worthy rebel indeed. Find someone who just rants in favor of getting more liberals, or more conservatives, onto the school board, and you will have found a politically oriented, passé man—a plastic rebel. Or, in the blackest neighborhood, find the plumber who will thumb his nose at city hall's restrictive licenses and certificates and you will have found a freedom fighter of far greater consequence than the window breaker.

Power and authority, as substitutes for performance and rational thought, are the specters that haunt the world today. They are the ghosts of awed and superstitious yesterdays. And politics is their familiar. Politics, throughout time, has been an institutionalized denial of man's ability to survive through the exclusive employment of all his own powers for his own welfare. And politics, throughout time, has existed solely through the resources that it has been able to plunder from the creative and productive people whom it has, in the name of many causes and moralities, denied the exclusive employment of all their own powers for their own welfare.

Ultimately, this must mean that politics denies the rational nature of man. Ultimately, it means that politics is just another form of residual magic in our culture—a belief that somehow things come from nothing; that things may be given to some without first taking them from others; that all the tools of man's survival are his by accident or divine right and not by pure and simple inventiveness and work.

Politics has always been the institutionalized and established way in which some men have exercised the power to live off the output of other men. But even in a world made docile to these demands, men do not need to live by devouring other men.

Politics does devour men. A laissez-faire world would liberate men. And it is in that sort of liberation that the most profound revolution of all may be just beginning to stir. It will not happen overnight, just as the lamps of rationalism were not quickly lighted and have not yet burned brightly. But it will happen—because it must happen. Man can survive in an inclement universe only through the use of his mind. His thumbs, his nails, his muscles and his mysticism will not be enough to keep him alive without it.

2

LAW OR JUSTICE? AN EMERGING CONCEPTION OF CITIZENSHIP

Christian Bay

May I propose a definition of citizenship, which may seem new if you haven't read Plato or Aristotle lately, but actually is a venerable one, if unfashionable these days, and unpalatable to all powers that be: "Citizen" should refer exclusively to *politically alive* and *responsible* participants in political contests and controversies; politically alive (as I define "politics[1]") are those and only those who care deeply about justice for the oppressed, the defenseless, and the yet unborn; politically responsible are those and only those whose concern for justice outweighs any other public allegiance, and thus, for example, consider themselves not only free to but obligated, in Socratic fashion, to violate the law or any other social institution if this should be necessary in order to promote justice, or forestall grievous injustice.

Thus, defined, citizens are only those who take on the sovereign responsibility for determining what to do with their own lives, and collectively, with their community and society, or their world. The true citizen does not wait for authorities, nor, of course, for a democratic consensus, to tell him what is right and what is wrong, what is human and what is inhuman, what is just and what is

Reprinted from a revised edition of a lecture sponsored by Stanford's Century 21 Project, presented at Stanford University on May 8, 1968, and at the American Political Science Association 1968 meeting; pp. 16-45.

[1]Christian Bay, Politics and Pseudopolitics, *American Political Science Review*, **59**, pp. 39-51, 1965.

unjust, or what to live for, or what to kill or die for. His own mind and heart and his own experience and study and reflections are his ultimate guideposts.

Let me group under four headings the kinds of trends that appear to contribute most effectively, in my judgment, toward the emergence of a new commitment to citizenship in the Aristotelian sense, on the part of young people in particular; and I shall focus on the situation in the United States: (1) Demographically, the young are relatively more numerous than before; (2) semantically, establishment control over politically potent words appears to be slipping; (3) the youngsters appear relatively far more secure in their defiance and affirmation, economically and psychologically, compared to the youngsters of the 1930s, the last previous vocal "protest generation"; and (4) the accelerated technological changes of our time have also hit the field of techniques of protest, which appear to be becoming more varied and promise increasing effectiveness.

(1) As long as there is death there is hope, someone has said. It is a fact that our population is rapidly becoming younger, with those under 25 now in the majority. In fact, people between 18 and 25 are now possibly our largest disenfranchised minority group, and there are many signs of increasing awareness of this fact on their part, along with increasing resentment. The 21-25 year olds have the vote, of course, but hardly ever can they vote for one of their own, let alone effectively help decide public policies, or corporate policies, or mass media policies. The incongruity of this state of affairs is becoming clearer with the increasing proportions of young people, who on this ground, among others, increasingly will reject the legitimacy of the political system.

Following last April's attempted assassination of Berlin student leader Rudi Dutschke, I read in an official West German government bulletin the following ostensibly reassuring statement about the future of Germany: "The older generations that speak for the German past and present, and are still mainly responsible for its future, have agreed to take more closely into their counsels those young people who abide by the rules of parliamentary democracy."[2] Remember that it is precisely the political impotence and stagnation of parliamentary democracy in West Germany, following the establishment of the coalition regime in 1966, which has inspired the leftward move among West German youth, and the emptiness even of the phrase itself becomes obvious; it is as if in Berkeley President Kerr in 1964 would have promised, as a concession in an effort to pacify the FSM, to consult more often with members of the most placid fraternities and sororities.

This kind of approach on the part of our elders and betters is natural enough; it is not substantially different from the practice of colonial powers of consulting with certain categories of native spokesmen, namely those spokesmen who against suitable rewards are willing to cast their own lot with the powers that be. Now, some of my best friends are older people, including my own

---

[2] *The Bulletin*, Press and Information Office of the German Federal Government, Bonn, p. 1, April 23, 1968.

parents—and I rejoice in their being alive and well—but this does not prevent me from thinking that the days of our gerontocratic-oligarchical system are numbered, in Europe as in America, because the absurdity of this system is fast becoming more clear to more people.

A person's stake in the future of his society does not grow but if anything decreases as he grows older, compared to the stake of those whose lives are still ahead of them. More important, in our fast-changing times our ways of thinking become obsolete and irrelevant far more quickly than they used to, so that even on the grounds of rationality, for the purpose of sheer survival of a social order—a cause certainly favored by conservatives—it becomes vitally necessary that not just pliable young people but the natural leaders among young people are given a significant influence, at least, in shaping the affairs of state and of the communities (including, of course, our academic communities).

(2) Now a word about words; about how our ruling strata have been able to utilize our most common hurrah-words and boo-words[3] as means to forestall political rationality and to cement the power of our traditional oligarchies. Perhaps the most obvious example is the rash of *required* rituals of patriotic and religious incantations, best symbolized by the loyalty oaths, which were at their peak in this country in the 1950s. Since hypocrisy comes easier as we get older and less idealistic, or less alive, this has been a useful device with which to weed out citizens of conscience from positions of influence, or even from an opportunity to earn a livelihood in some places[4]. In addition, further reinforcement was given to the general idea, particularly addressed to young people, that radical ideas on social issues must be shunned like the pox, never examined with an open mind, unless one wished to jeopardize one's future.

Nowadays loyalty oaths are all but gone, and are unlikely to become fashionable again. More insidious, because less obvious, is the establishment control over so many of our most common emotion-packed words, which are defined in ways to limit our vision. In this area a tremendous educational task remains to be done, but I think it will be done. It is a large task, but not a complicated one. I have talked already of the habit of referring to our system as "democratic" and to subjects as "citizens." Another important example is the practice of defining "freedom" as referring almost exclusively to free enterprise for the affluent and free speech for the articulate, so that in political controversy the "cause of freedom" so easily in a gullible public mind can be associated with anti-humane policies: for example, the choice of selling houses only to whites or perhaps only to Wasps becomes an exercise of freedom, while the choice of the neighborhood

---

[3]H. Mark Roelofs uses these terms, in preference to the conventional academic jargon: respectively "eulogistic" and "dyslogistic" words in, "The Tension of Citizenship: Private Man and Public Duty," Rinehart, New York, p. 8 *passim* 1957.

[4]Or, for that matter, from opportunities to indulge in conventional leisure activities. For one example, New York City in 1957 required loyalty oaths from applicants for permits to fish in the city's reservoirs, according to *The New York Times* of May 7, 1957. At least two communists were refused fishing permits.

in which to raise one's children becomes merely a demand for racial equality;[5] for another example, Cuba is said to lack freedom because there are no opposition newspapers there, and people are in jail on political grounds, while in the slums of Rio de Janeiro and the rest of Brazil people can die of starvation and preventable diseases in the glory of freedom; and so on. "Security" automatically means "military security"; "defense" means "military defense"; billions can patriotically be spent on the most infernal weapons with which to supposedly deter supposed enemies, while mere driblets are invested from time to time to seek ways to promote the defense of the traditional values of Martin Luther King's American Dream, or our national security in a broader sense, which would aim for a world of live and let live, with *no* enemies.

I have referred to boo-words like "communist" already, which serve to rule out by definition the possibility of achieving a dialogue with our supposed enemies, and the possibility of promoting real national security and world security by way of finding a common ground with the communists, or at least an agreement to compete politically instead of planning to annihilate one another. Through the 1950s our elders and betters on both sides have kept on escalating that deadly deterrence game, with all its self-fulfilling prophesies of mutually reinforced enmity to feed the paranoia so often found among the influentials on each side—take James T. Forrestal, the Alsop brothers, and Dean Rusk as conspicuous examples on our side of the fence.

A massive educational task remains to be done against the tyranny of such words, but it is being tackled; witness the growing campus political unrest and the wide following won by the new McCarthy in all the better universities, and indeed in many states. Yet as a final commentary on establishment semantics let me refer to the ways of characterizing and of studying student unrest. I remember that a few years ago at Stanford, while I was working with the Institute for the Study of Human Problems, we once received a request from an organization of deans; we were asked to propose an approach to the study of student political activism, and it fell on my lot to draft a reply. I suggested that the behavior of protesting students as well as the behavior of university administrators interacting with them ought to be studied simultaneously, without building into the study an a priori assumption that one side in such conflicts behaves rationally and the other one does not. You guessed what happened next: nothing at all. Our reply was never even acknowledged.

But this should have been expected. For political radicalism in America has as a general rule been studied mainly in psychodynamic terms, unlike conventional voting behavior and all the pseudopolitical special pleading that is termed interest group behavior, which by establishment definition are examples of perfectly rational behavior. "Acting out" is something that radical students do, never university administrators. This, too, is an example of the usual establishment

---

[5] In the 1964 campaign in California for "Proposition 14," which would constitutionally bar state fair housing legislation, this was the main line of the argument advanced by the organized state realtors and their allies.

control of the terms of our political discourse. But I think, as I have said, that these means of control are slipping; young people are becoming less scared of the boo-words,[6] less taken in by the hurrah-words, and more cognizant of the increasingly horrible results, abroad and at home, of the traditional American way of leaving the responsibilities of politics in the hands of the legal profession and their corporate clients.

(3) To their own parents, and many others in my generation, the spirit of defiance of many youngsters is far more visible than the spirit of affirmation of values of their own. The rejection of many middle class standards by the hippies has been given much publicity; but the glare of that confrontation has made it possible for millions of less bold, more square youngsters to assert themselves in more limited rebellions, say limited to matters of sex, or politics, or smoking preferences. The burning of an American flag by black students on the Stanford campus, which would have been almost unthinkable ten years ago, was taken in its stride by the university's disciplinary authorities, who perhaps would rather have a flag than a building burnt; and judging by letters to the *Stanford Daily,* only the least mature, least literate members of the community were shook up by the incident (possibly the censor may have blocked some juicy alumni letters about this event).

Where some see only a spirit of defiance, however, many of us, I am sure, also see a profound spirit of affirmation in the present youth rebellion, here and abroad. In the hippie movement the message affirmed is often inarticulate, to be sure, and as in any genuine movement there are hangers-on without any moral concerns; but the central positive themes of love and nonviolence are unmistakable, along with an insistence on the right and obligation to choose one's own values and to respect individualities and differences. The true hippies endeavor to rise above the narrowmindedness and the hypocrisy of much of the "square world," which talks of morality and condemns pornography and adultery while exonerating the use of napalm and torture; which intones about freedom but stands ready to condemn people on the basis of haircuts and the clothes people wear.

In the recent burning of an American flag I see a profound and clear affirmation of American principles: that all men should be treated as if created equal, and that the use of the American flag as a cloak for the continuing oppression of American Negroes must no longer be tolerated. The incident is, I think a harbinger of the new—and old—conception of citizenship in which our loyalty to people, first of all to the most oppressed among us, will take precedence over our show of respect for symbols associated with the established order; when we ask, not what can we do for our country, but what can we do to build a better country, which will be worth the loyalty of humane men and women, and will be secure in the readiness of its citizens to defend it, and the values for which it stands. The burning of a flag can be a good thing if it brings home to unthinking

---

[6]The late and lamented Lenny Bruce, a saintly martyr in his crusade against middle class hypocrisy, deserves a share of the credit for this.

patriots, brought up to accept the conventional wisdom, the fact that there *is* defiance among the oppressed and among the just, and that there *is* affirmation of values that take precedence over the inherited but frequently misused and thereby impoverished symbols of conventional patriotism.

Now, a growing spirit of defiance—and of affirmation of moral alternatives to conventional politics—can be ascertained. I have said; but this is hardly a sufficient basis for prognostications about social change. Young people, most prone to defiance as well as idealistic affirmation, are notorious in their tendency to grow older, and more pragmatic-minded, and more accepting of the system and of its conventional wisdom. Are those now in their twenties or late teens likely to be different from their forebears, say the student radicals of the 1930s?

I think so. Not genetically, of course, but in their economic and psychological situation and in the social technologies at their disposal. Let me first suggest a few characteristics of present student rebels in the United States, and subsequently (4) speak very briefly to the issue of changing technologies of social action.

While student radicalism in the 1930s in large part was a response to the Great Depression, and therefore often subject to being cured by relative affluence,[7] contemporary student rebellions in the United States are the product of personal affluence, or at any rate of a personal sense of economic security, in the context of blatant social injustice and of alienation from an immobile political system. There is a wealth of evidence to show that it is the strongest students, from the most secure family circumstances, in the best universities, who are most highly represented among the student activists.[8]

Now, insecure young people are often very easily subjected to being trained and molded into pliable role players, satisfied with life if their acquired skills can earn them a livelihood while their work and career serve other people's purposes, and who stand always ready to salute the flag, sign loyalty oaths, obey the law; in short, to do and die, never asking why. It is mainly the secure who can become *educated*, as distinct from becoming merely trained and molded. By "educated" I mean capable of, indeed insisting on, asking the fundamental questions on what life is all about, and letting the answers they find actually influence the course of their lives, or at least the moral and political standards by which they judge their own lives and those of their fellows.

Families, schools, colleges, mass media, churches and most other institutions that help socialize young people have this in common, that they seek to mold and to train but to prevent real education, real independence of mind. Parents, school administrators, professors, bureaucrats, indeed most older people have this much in common, that we like attentiveness, not defiance, in young people;

[7]See Seymour Martin Lipset, Student Opposition in the United States, *Government and Opposition*, I, 1966.

[8]See Richard Flacks, The Liberated Generation: An Exploration of the Roots of Student Protest, *Journal of Social Issues,* 33, pp. 52-75, 1967.

we like young people to affirm the right values, our values, not theirs; we like young people with desirable ideas and attitudes, not with independent intellects.

And here is where the significance for the future of current student radicalism is most apparent: this is *not* an imitation of older people's radicalism; student radicals are not flocking into the old leftwing parties as they did in the 1930s; they are not uncritical in their admiration even for a Staughton Lynd, a Paul Goodman or a Herbert Marcuse; nor are they uncritical of one another. Sheldon Wolin and John Schaar have remarked on how wrong the University of California administrators were in thinking they could stem student discontent by way of barring "outside agitators" or suspending "*the leaders*"; real communities of politically able intellectuals had developed in Berkeley, so that there always were scores of effective militants to take over the leadership whenever one batch of leaders was incapacitated by suspensions, expulsions, arrests or graduation.[9] In short, the confrontations between student militants and university administrators had been very educational; they had created politically and morally conscious citizens out of students who without this experience might have been destined for subject-status in the continuing service of established institutions, heading for the quiet conventional lives in the suburbs. Many young citizens at Columbia University, in West Germany and in Paris have no doubt been similarly reclaimed for intelligent citizenship in recent weeks.

The great thing about real education, as distinct from mere training, molding, or polishing, is that it is likely to be a lifelong process, once it has really started. You can't become uneducated again once you have seen the light and have achieved self-determination—*unless*, of course, you find that you have to sell your mind for a mess of pottage. Now,.in the 1930s, with the fear of dismal poverty, many would do that. In the late 1960s there is virtually no fear of this kind among our student militants—and there is every reason to believe that the economic security among the well-educated will keep increasing, as our society's complexity and dependence on people with vision as well as skills keep on increasing.

(4) Our society is in many ways at the mercy of technological change, which keeps accelerating. For example, our privacy is threatened by the new techniques for gathering and assembling enormous quantities of information at incredibly low cost. We may all be suddenly wiped out by nuclear or bacteriological-chemical weapons, or more slowly poisoned or made to suffocate by the pollution of our air and water supplies. It seems quite clear that our private enterprise system, or our pluralist political system, so easily dominated by the private corporate interests, is quite unsuited to contribute significantly to the task of increasing the odds for human survival on this earth. But the clearer argument for urgent, long overdue political reforms in the public interest, the bigger has been the private investment in emotional slogans and myths in support of the status quo.

[9]See their, The Berkeley Crisis, *New York Review of Books*, March 11, 1965.

At the same time, however, the technology of protest and of social counter-coercion has kept developing, too. Our only chance of turning mankind away from our drift to nuclear war and other global disasters may well be in rebellions against the established systems, within the great powers—especially in the most lethal of them all—but this is no mean hope. As political-economic systems become more complex they also become less adaptable, less flexible, more subject to cracking and to breaking down. It is worth recalling the confusion that resulted when the lights went out in New York City a few years ago, or the uproar caused in New York City in 1964 when extremist rent-strikers took to dumping garbage on the Triborough Bridge.[10]

Now, I am not an advocate of turning off lights or of dumping garbage in the wrong places. I simply want to illustrate how dependent we all are on the innumerable conveniences of our modern technological civilization. Monstrosities like our ghetto poverty or the war in Vietnam are possible, as Martin Luther King often said, not just because some people do evil but because most people do not care enough to resist the evil that hits their fellow men. But these "most people" do care about some things, invariably—namely their own habitual routines and conveniences. As R.V. Denenberg has written about the tactics the New York rent-strike extremists, just referred to, in an illustrious but now defunct publication called the *Stanford Challenger*:

> But, although certainly exasperating, what these demonstrators did was, in fact, not dangerous—the traffic slowdown probably saved a few lives that evening—and quite efficient. Had these few demonstrators instead stalked the streets that night, committing ten random murders and pinning CORE STRIKES AGAIN notes to the bodies of the victims, those motorists on the bridge would probably not have paid much attention as they scanned the headlines the next morning; murders occur every day. But could they endure the terror of being caught on the Triborough for 45 minutes every day? If demonstrators came back evening after evening to block the roads, stricken motorists would soon be dispatching pleading letters to their legislators asking what those fellows in Harlem are so upset about and telling them to please, in a hurry, do something about it.[11]

Within the rules of the so-called democratic game—rules developed by lawyers for the convenience of those who favor law and order and are opposed to social change—permanent minorities have been permanent prisoners of whatever indifferent majorities can be brought to accept and defend. Reference has been made to the youth in West Germany—how that section of the youth which is willing to accept the rules of the parliamentary game now supposedly will at some future date be listened to by their elders, who are responsible for Germany's past, present and future, and who will respectfully vote the young people down.

---

[10] R.V. Denenberg, The Loneliness of the Long-Distance Agitator, *Stanford Challenger,* pp. 57-59, February 1965.

[11] *Ibid.,* p. 59.

American Negroes, too, have been exhorted by their legislators to work for and hope for changes accomplished within the system. And the legendary white liberals, again, have worked optimistically for the day when *within* our system the righteous and just would outvote the greedy and the privileged.

What is becoming clearer to more people every day, in my judgment, is that the kind of citizenship orientation that is prepared to act only within the system is ineffective at best, or merely playing at politics, sabotaging the real pressures toward change at worst. For if you work only within the system, then you are powerless to change things; the smug majority will always find reasons for voting you down. Those who are basically unconcerned about social and racial justice are always in the majority; this cannot change until most people either become truly educated—a distant prospect—or truly scared. And it is to accomplish the latter that we must cultivate the field of extralegal social action.

Mind you, if you scare people too much, you may be worse off than you are if you stay inside the rules of the game. Violence breeds counterviolence, and the government and the police and the rightwingers are both far more ruthless and far better armed, always, than the people who favor righteousness and social justice. The crucial task is to develop relatively or absolutely nonviolent ways of bringing about, in Arthur I. Waskow's phrase "creative disorder." Mahatma Gandhi was a great inventor in this field. His innovations have been drawn upon in this country, particularly by SNCC and SCLC in the days of the integrated, nonviolent civil rights movement, and in the days of the pacifist-dominated peace movement.

Subsequently, as we all know, the peace movement has become less peaceful, and the Nonviolent Coordinating Committee has become less nonviolent. I am not happy about this development; it would have been nice if consistently nonviolent action outside the system would have proved sufficient to change it, and thus accomplish what working inside the system couldn't achieve. Yet there is nothing logically absurd, as some liberals seem to believe, in a peace movement resorting to violent means, whether the violence is directed against persons or property; the magnitude of the violence that our peace movements oppose is such that if it can be stopped by modestly violent disorder in the streets at home, the total amount of bloodshed saved could still be enormous. Yet I must emphasize that I am not advocating or welcoming violence in the streets; on empirical grounds it is extremely doubtful whether in fact it can lead to a de-escalation in military uses of violence, while it is almost certain to lead to escalation in police violence. And I detect a frightening amount of romanticism about revolutionary violence among many young people on the left, who appear to have done little hard thinking about precisely how or why good things will follow after shooting across barricades in the streets.

Looking ahead, I fear that these romantic hopes about anticipated blessings of revolutionary violence will set back the task of changing the system, and that many lives will be lost quite needlessly. Other, more sober citizens will, I believe, draw the political conclusion that what is needed is a third way, neither inside the law nor involving violence against people—namely essentially nonviolent but militant civil disobedience, politically creative disorder, which inconveniences and perhaps scares people, perhaps destroys property, but always seeks to avoid bloodshed if possible.

When you consider that those who are conscious of being unjustly oppressed, or of others being unjustly oppressed, constitute a small minority, given our neglect of education as distinct from molding and training, then it should become clear, first, that to play the democratic game means being voted down, almost always; and secondly, that to build barricades and to shoot means being decimated by the nonthinking but conventionally patriotic majority. The only way we can make up our lack of numbers on the humanistic left is by capitalizing on the fact that the stouter hearts and the better minds and the greater willingness to endure inconvenience as well as danger probably are on our side. Beyond a certain point of inconvenience—even the traffic jam category of inconvenience—the otherwise satisfied majority, whose behavior can be studied and predicted, perhaps more readily than ours, will be in a mood for concessions. This is how victories have been won in the race relations field. Even the dramatic withdrawal of President Johnson's name from the Presidential race, along with his announcement of being ready for peace talks, responded to an accumulation of frustrations and anxieties on the part of millions of Americans who see nothing wrong in killing Vietnamese but who are upset by the increasingly bitter, often violent divisions among Americans, including the intense generational conflict about the war, and about race—and it all is connected, given the present priorities in government spending, for one thing.

The biggest challenge on the left perhaps is not so much the achievement of victories by way of carefully planned campaigns of creative disorder, as it is the consolidation and cumulation of victories without loss of purpose or loss of determination. This is the task of political education within our own ranks. There always comes a point when political results achieved are a temptation to complacency—the Scandinavian labor movements have been a case in point; the only way around this is continual political dialogue in which the youngest adults take part as equals, so that the vision of social justice can be ever renewed. Every conservative social organization, every stagnating society is gerontocratic, ruled by old people; for the first time we have an opportunity to experiment with institutionalizing full and equal participation by young people in political action. For all the ugliness of the American scene today, with the bloody oppression at home and abroad, this is the great promise of America; excepting Cuba, I can think of no other country in which the prospects seem brighter for a rapidly growing influence on the part of young people, young people in the universities and in the social movements. Where the fathers and mothers have been subjects, the sons and daughters are, by the thousands, becoming citizens in a full sense, alive and responsible human beings, determined to live morally and politically meaningful and useful lives.

Now let us discuss some implications and consequences of the emergence of citizens, by the thousands, on the American scene—in the universities and outside, among whites and blacks.

Enlightened liberals and progressives often have expressed despair about the prospects for creating a more humane society on the ground that so few people seem to care; most people are much too busy earning a living to develop any strong concern about other people's bad luck, let alone other people being permanently oppressed and disfigured by the economic system. I share this despair about the common indifference to man's inhumanity to man, but I am less pessimistic regarding prospects for change. In my view it will not be necessary to wait till "most people" care about establishing a more just society; it will suffice if and when determined minorities of real citizens do.

Here is where I in principle part company with most liberal democrats, who really do believe, it would seem, that majorities rule, and make the laws, and that it will take new majorities to change the laws. The secret of the stability of our social system—its almost total invulnerability to structural change, up to now—is precisely, I believe, in this democratic illusion, which has held liberals as well as conservatives in its grip: that our laws reflect the will of the sovereign majority, and that if you want the laws to change you have to first educate the majority to desire that the laws be changed. Just and brave democrats have fought manfully for political sanity and humanity since the beginning of the Republic—I think of the venerable democratic socialist, Norman Thomas, as the archetypical example—and they have succeeded in establishing many benefits that have improved the lot of the least fortunate among us. What they have not and could not bring about, within the system, are structural changes that would make the private corporate powers subservient to the state or to the public interest.

A small minority of economically powerful men and their lawyers are governing this country, I have argued; the majority of so-called citizens behave like subjects or parochials, finding their places within the system without questioning its justice or even its future viability in our fast-changing world; they pay their taxes, serve in the military forces, root for the flag no matter what uses the flag has been put to, and so on; and stand ready to boo and hiss at whomever the government or forces further Right wish to label "subversive." With our present economic and educational system, no majority can be mobilized, with which to dislodge this all-powerful minority.

But a counter-minority is emerging, we have seen, which is well trained and is becoming well educated, and which above all else liberated from the conventional subject-status associated with the majoritarian myth. This counter-minority is predominantly young, and knows that it has no legitimate power within the system; it draws the conclusion that the system itself is illegitimate, at least to the extent that it claims to be representative. This counter-minority is bold, because it knows that the democratic myth imposes real constraints on the means with which it can be repressed. And it is strong, at least in a psychological sense, because it is inspired by simple ideals with a powerful appeal: ideals of justice, brotherhood, equality, freedom for all. As Gandhi saw, such ideals not only strengthen your own side but also weaken the other side; there is something in every man that responds to them. And we have seen that the complexity of our modern society has made it possible to experiment with many new techniques of creative civil disorder, all aimed at inconveniencing enough people sufficiently to make them wake up to social facts and choose to go along with demands for changes, or for redress of grievances, so that disorder may cease, at least on their doorsteps.

Now, nobody in his right mind engages in civil disobedience without very compelling reasons. For the criminal and the delinquent, breaking the law may be a matter of convenience or possibly necessity, but the aim is personal gain and the method is concealment. I know that Mr. J. Edgar Hoover has difficulties with this distinction but it isn't that hard: the civil disobedience activist by definition violates the law in public, and for a moral purpose, not for personal gain—the law itself and its enforcement agencies see to that (looting during riots cannot be called acts of civil disobedience, even if desire for hitting back at the white man or at the system may well be the principal motive in many cases, rather than a desire for merchandise).

Philosophically speaking, the new kind of citizen is an existentialist, or at least ought to be one, in my view: he recognizes no a priori moral commitments imposed on him by the system, not only because the system is illegitimate but most basically because he insists on choosing his own basic moral commitments. Embedded in man's own human nature, unless he is harried or sick, is, as Aristotle saw, a sense of justice; and the young, articulate, new citizens will therefore naturally be on the left in their politics, to the extent that they are sufficiently liberated from traditional mores and taboos to start from existentialist first principles.

Now, every society requires its laws, and obedience to its laws, as a general habit on the part of most people. On the other hand, complete obedience to every law would mean complete stagnation, if such a state of affairs could be imagined. And it certainly would mean an end to even the pretense of justice. But the existentialist citizen will tend to define the law in logical positivist fashion, much as Max Weber does: "Law exists when there is a probability that an order will be upheld by a specific staff of men who will use physical or psychical compulsion with the intention of obtaining conformity with the order, or of inflicting sanctions for infringement of it."[12] In other words, the law exists as a set of facts and probabilities, not as a moral arbiter.

But with this conception of the nature of the law, there can be no a priori duty to obey it. Civil obedience becomes a matter of prudence, and for the moral person prudence can never be the only concern. In the interest of justice, or in the interest of saving lives, he willingly places his sense of moral obligation ahead of his prudence; he places justice above the law, whenever there is an important conflict between the two.

But what is the nature of the citizen's ultimate moral commitment? On this issue the pluralist liberal is of very little help. Merriam refuses to go beyond the

[12] cf. Max Weber, "Essays in Sociological Theory," ed. H.H. Gerth and C. Wright Mills, p. 180, Oxford University Press, New York, 1946.

conventional acceptance of our established system, as we have seen. And so does Roelofs, a quarter-century later. In pluralist fashion, he sees our ultimate commitment not in terms of substantive humane values but in terms of the tangle of procedural and substantive values associated with his concept of democracy; paraphrasing and reciting the beginning of the Declaration of Independence he propounds (with my italics) "We hold to these propositions *as a result of* our commitment *to the often contradictory values* of the democratic way of life—that all men . . . are . . . to be respected as moral agents . . . are private men with public duties . . . ."[13] *Because* we by tradition believe in "the democratic way of life," whatever that means (and clear deductions from "often contradictory values" are a logical impossibility) we are to respect men as moral agents! This seems to me precisely the kind of moral obfuscation that in fact (unintentionally, I am sure) serves the defense of the established order. Moreover, Roelofs explicitly rejects the eighteenth century vision of a universal community of men, receding instead to the notion of "a Brotherhood of Man under the kingship of the Christian God."[14] In fact, to Roelofs the idea of a common humanity in all men is judged and found wanting as a "satisfactory transcendant community for democrats." Citizens of many benighted countries, we are told flatly, "do not share our basic values and would deny us our present opportunities of allegiance to them if they dared or could."[15] This reads like a page right out of a cold war manual—particularly when one recalls the author's insistence that the democratic values to which we should all be committed are "often contradictory values." In the last analysis, then, it seems that his ultimate political commitment is to "our traditions," or in effect to "our team," with our best, most Christian, foot forward.

But this strikes me as another example of the usual pluralist liberal failure to think radically, to the root of the questions, when it comes to issues of citizenship and political obligation. Every stable state, it would seem, has so far always in fact been serving to protect the strong and the privileged against the demands of social justice. If this is true, then in the last analysis every conscientious citizen is faced with a choice between a commitment to man and a commitment to a particular social system. Roelofs' pluralist commitment in this book is clearly to the system; the "democratic way of life" is the ultimate value; even when he stresses the value of individualism in our traditions of citizenship he makes no distinction between the individualism of the strong and of the weak.

My own basic commitment, and I think the commitment of increasing numbers, is emphatically to man first, and therefore only contingently to any system. Politics, like medicine, should in my scheme of values serve to establish and protect the sanctity of life; to protect life and health, with a clear priority

---

[13] Roelofs, p. 241.

[14] Roelofs, pp. 235-236.

[15] *Ibid.*, p. 236.

for those who are oppressed and endangered; it should matter little whether lives are wasted or stymied in the name of democracy or some other ism. Democracy, too, is only an ism; the merits and defects of democratic procedures should no more be beyond dispassionate inquiry than those of other isms, say communism or liberalism or capitalism. The only substantive commitment ought to be to the sanctity of human life itself, with its freedom to grow and find expression of its individuality, regardless of social class, or nation, or generation.

Citizenship anchored in this fundamental norm will have to treat *all* other loyalties as contingent. Americanism, Christianity, democracy, the Constitution, even motherhood are then no longer intrinsic but extrinsic values, deserving a hearing but subject to free acceptance or rejection on the basic of their utility in the promotion of life; or more precisely, in the promotion first of all of a sheltered life-space for the least privileged, least favored lives, in each society, at each time.

The task of the Supreme Court, for example, can then no longer be construed as a concern with merely interpreting, say, the Bill of Rights. Its task is to work to gradually *expand* the range of rights to be protected, as widely as empirically possible, for the protection of life in liberty and enjoyment of rights is *the* purpose of civilized government. If civil disobedience can help demonstrate to the Supreme Court, or other authorities, that rights are in fact being violated, or that an expansion of protected rights is possible, or indeed overdue, then this should be done, and be rendered morally legitimate, perhaps morally obligatory.

Now, the instrumentalities by which politics and legislation and judge-made law can serve to protect life, liberties and human rights are manifold, as we have seen, and developments in the technologies of demonstration and protest are accelerating. Gone forever is, hopefully, the myth that the rich and the poor are in fact, in our time, treated equally under the law; but not, hopefully, the aspiration that the poor must be given *at least* equal treatment by our police and courts and legislatures and administration, from now on until poverty disappears. It is now widely realized that institutions of formal equality often are in fact instruments of accelerating substantive inequality. As T.B. Bottomore convincingly argues, "equality of opportunity" in a traditionally unequal society is at best a contradiction in terms, positing permanent inequality, and at worst a cloak for accelerating degrees of inequality.[16]

The necessity of divorcing the right to consume, or the right to economic security, from the opportunity to hold a productive job, in an increasingly automated and job-scarce industrial society, has rapidly become more widely recognized, and this recognition is by no means confined to writers on the left.[17] Milton Friedman, a leading conservative economist, has for years

[16] T.B. Bottomore, "Elites and Society," Penguin Books, London, last chapter.

[17] See Donald G. Agger *et al.*, The Triple Revolution, *Liberation*, April, 1964; and Robert Theobald, "The Guaranteed Income: Next Step in Economic Evolution?" Doubleday, New York, 1964.

championed the principle of the Negative Income Tax, albeit as a substitute for most other welfare programs.[18]

It would be good if issues like these could be discussed dispassionately, and be subjected to openended empirical research, without the distracting influence of emotion-packed terms like "socialism," "free enterprise" and the like.

This is, in my view, what we have universities for; which brings me to my concluding remarks on the future of citizenship. Academic citizenship is an ideal which I would like to superimpose upon the concept of citizenship already developed. Being professors or students in universities with a wide freedom of speech and of inquiry opens a range of possibilities and perhaps of responsibilities beyond the range accessible to many other people. True, students are still treated as subjects, indeed as objects, in virtually every major university, while the influence of faculty members varies enormously from one institution to another—from Europe's universities, typically governed by small faculty gerontocracies to the other extreme, still not uncommon in this country, of an entirely corporate structure with absentee government by businessmen and with faculty as hired hands.

Yet in no other type of community is democracy as feasible as in the modern university. No other population is as potentially able to govern its own affairs responsibly, as is the community of scholars, senior and junior. Some of us attempted here at Stanford to take over this university a couple of years ago, by way of a Stanford Association of University Scholars, which we hoped, or some of us at least, would eventually become the legitimate seat of sovereignty at Stanford; if in demonstrable fact representing the Stanford academic community, eventually, it should from then on have been for us to hire or fire members of the administration, and of the Board of Trustees. The time was not ripe for us then, evidently, but the idea that student and professors should be self-determining and self-governing citizens, ultimately responsible for the government of their own institutions, seems to me just as self-evidently valid as the idea in the opening statement in the Declaration of Independence has seemed to many generations of Americans: it expresses a principle bound to become realized sooner or later. Not this week, it appears, but surely within the next ten years, surely here at Stanford, surely at Columbia and Berkeley and Wisconsin and in all the most enlightened university communities, public and private.

The university of the future will, I think, be the repository not only of man's knowledge of the natural world and of the human body, but also, to the same extent *and with the same freedom from foreign influences,* it will be the repository of social knowledge, as well as the stage for a continuing rational and

[18]See his "Capitalism and Freedom," University Press, Chicago, 1964 (1962), Chapter XII. More recently, a committee of national business leaders, appointed by New York Governor Nelson Rockefeller, has called for negative income tax payments to 30 million impoverished Americans, according to *The New York Times* of April 30, 1968.

therefore radical intellectual and political dialogue. The reputable university will never again be an ivory tower, in which anemic scholarship remote from social issues, or theoretically and methodologically complex apologies for the status quo, dominate in the average social science department; it will be the seedbed for plans for bold, constructive experimentation with novel social, political, and economic reform schemes.

In our present pluralist social order, in which private interests bargain and compete, and politicians get elected by appealing mainly to fears and money interests, rather than to reason and the forecasts about the public interest, the universities are the only major centers capable of becoming, some day, dedicated to work for the study of, the clarification of, and the promotion of the public interest. Today, dependent as most university presidents think they are on the support of the government and the corporate interests, the notion of the multiversity, the service station for existing powers, is predominant in North America. However, since modern governments and corporations in fact are at least equally dependent the other way, on the collaboration of the major universities, I believe the present concept of the university is bound to change, so that the way will soon be clear for self-governing universities, free to and indeed obligated to study and promote the public interest, and thus the interest of the future of mankind.

Eventually I believe that all citizens will in some way continue to belong to universities or to other kinds of academies of excellence in innumerable fields of human effort. All individuals need to aspire to excellence of some kind, and to belong to lasting communities in which such individual efforts are nourished and appreciated. But there is one area of study and aspiration to which enlightened and free, self-governing academies are vital not only to individual welfare but to the very preservation of mankind, let alone its present and future collective well-being. That is the political realm, in the Aristotelian sense; i.e., the realm of concern with the public interest, with *summum bonum.*

Those of us who share deeply in this concern, and as professionals are dedicated to the study of politics, must aspire first of all to become participating citizens of our societies and of the world, but must in addition aspire to full citizenship also in our much smaller but strategically important academic communities; the future quality of politics in our larger society probably will depend in no small measure on the freedom of our academic communities from anti-intellectual, anti-radical, and other anti-rational pressures. Or, much more strictly speaking, on the inclination and ability to stand up to such pressure in our academic communities.

I have nothing against lawyers per se, but I think our prospects for liberty and social justice are dim unless we stop being placid subjects under their *de facto* rule, on behalf of themselves and their corporate clients. Perhaps democratic rule is a distant prospect, outside our close-knit academic communities. If so, then I hope that in the meantime social scientists will at least cut into the influence of lawyers—especially social scientists with continuing ties with democratically

governed universities, continually partners in political dialogue, continually subject to intelligent criticism and if need be exposure by their own free-spirited
students and colleagues; academics who are citizens in their teaching-and-
learning communities as well as in their society, and citizens of the world as well.

But, to paraphrase Aristotle, taking certain liberties, social scientists divorced
from community with radical students who will challenge the relevancy or morality of what they are doing can become the worst of political animals. Professors need students to keep them honest, just as students need professors to make
them worldly-wise; and society needs very badly free and concerned universities,
governed by professors and students together, working in the public interest,
working to build a more humane civilization. Without viable academic communities to show the way, I doubt that enlightened democracy will ever triumph
anywhere else. Without responsible Aristotelian citizenship, inside and outside
the unversities, I fear that oppressive law and other violence will continue to
triumph over justice everywhere, for the duration of the human experiment.

3

THE CHILDREN'S CRUSADE

Charles Heckscher

Professional politicians and other practical people have been hard-put to account for the role of young people in politics last summer. Countless analysts have been puzzled over the transformation of Senator McCarthy's Children's Crusade into a powerful fighting force. But they can hardly be more surprised than the crusaders themselves; for at first we were far from being the tight-knit band of idealists which the press later depicted. The transformation was a slow and complex process for each of us. Certainly none of us imagined, in New Hampshire, that our effort was to go so far and become so serious.

The snows of New Hampshire are a legend now, even to those who were there to brave the chill of the weather and the inhabitants. We poured into the unsuspecting state from hundreds of schools, driven by the flimsiest of reasons (for many it was the boredom of school in midwinter) and united only by the vaguely felt necessity to protest the policies of the hated Johnson Administration. No one knew anything about McCarthy, but as we discussed the war and the President far into the morning hours, we began to learn something about the man for whom we worked.

Personal loyalty to McCarthy developed only slowly. When we first heard him speak, most of us were puzzled by his lack of fire; in the wind-blown streets his voice seemed to wander, aimless and confused. But the words remained; and as we came to realize that the man was saying that the war was *immoral*, and as we

Charles Heckscher, The Children's Crusade, *Commonweal,* 87, pp. 12-14, October 4, 1968.

began to divine the philosophy that underlay his words, we knew we could trust him to express our profound dissatisfaction with the attitudes of the Government. "We are the only great nation in history," McCarthy said, "to look upon its role primarily as a defensive one. The time has come to make mistakes, if we must make them, on the side of trust rather than on the side of mistrust, on the side of hope rather than on the side of despair." Gradually we saw that we were working not just to stop the war, or to jettison the President; we were trying for a much deeper change, whose extent we did not yet realize.

Meanwhile we were being initiated into the methods of politics. Only a few knew anything about canvassing techniques or the organization of a campaign, and the confusion of the storefronts reflected our ignorance. I myself, too shy normally to ask a stranger the time of day, found myself that first afternoon on a street corner in suburban Concord with the assignment of persuading several hundred families that an unknown Senator was a better man than the nation's President. My panic was not much relieved by the people I spoke to: the inhabitants of New Hampshire are a defensive lot, and it takes considerable charm to get a foot in the door. For days the gaunt faces, narrowed eyes, and stiffly poised bodies of those I spoke to haunted me; when they chased me away, with shotguns or a curt remark, I took it as a personal affront.

But we soon learned guile and acquired thicker skins. When a voter said how much he admired McCarthy's brother Joe, we would enthusiastically agree that it was a fine family. To hawks we spoke of welfare reform and the high cost of the war; with old people we emphasized Medicare. More important, we learned to convey our enthusiasm to total strangers and to talk to people we would never have met ordinarily. We were becoming seasoned politicians.

The astonished excitement of primary night is hard to recapture. We were all near collapse from exhaustion and lack of food; as the night wore on no one could quite believe that our hopes and wildest predictions were being realized. It was more plausible to think we were suffering from a mass hallucination. "My God," people muttered, hesitantly at first, then with greater and greater elation, "My God, he just might win this." By the early hours of the next morning, with the figure of 42 percent coming into view, the headquarters was a madhouse of sheer joy. When we thought of where we had started, of what we had done, that we had brought low the President of the United States, our emotions were uncontrollable.

The success in the primary abruptly changed the whole tenor of our involvement. Suddenly the effort had become serious; we now had a very real chance to alter the conditions we so hated. As McCarthy, in his quiet way, challenged us to accept the full responsibility of our beliefs, most of us understood that we were not through yet, that we must stay with the fight as long as it lasted.

Some had a struggle of conscience when Kennedy entered the race. A few switched to him, arguing that he stood for the same things as McCarthy did and had a better chance. But most of us had begun to glimpse the philosophical depth of McCarthy's positions. He himself put it with characteristic clarity in Indiana: "We are no longer fighting over Vietnam, but over who is best qualified to be President." On that basis, because we knew he understood the full extent of the needed change, we stayed with McCarthy.

Indiana was my next stop on the primary trail; already the nature of the campaign had changed. In New Hampshire we had been fighting a symbol but in Indiana we were opposed by a very real and active candidate, backed by a professional staff and inexhaustible finances. Everything about the Kennedy headquarters seemed efficient and well-planned; they had banks of phones manned by banks of self-assured young people. When we managed to put up one poster in a neighborhood, it would immediately be covered with ten Kennedy posters while a sound truck broadcasting Bobby's voice went merrily by. It was, as McCarthy said, like wading through an endless snowdrift.

If the citizens of New Hampshire were cold, the people of Indiana acted as if they were part of a separate country. Governor Branigan, the favorite son, campaigned to "Keep Indiana for the Hoosiers" and blasted the "outsiders" who had invaded the state. Nowhere else did I receive such reactions from those I canvassed: "I've made up my mind and I don't want anyone to change it"; or "I've been voting for sixty years, young man, and I don't need your advice." I came to prefer canvassing the ghettos, where we were at least well received, but even there we heard again and again: "I know Kennedy. I know what his brother did for us. I never heard of McCarthy until this week."

In the end we found few who made the effort to understand McCarthy, and he went down to clear defeat. Yet the atmosphere, at the Claypool Hotel headquarters that night was far from discouraged; we felt like a battle-hardened army ready to fight again.

THE WINDS SHIFT

I will never quite forgive myself for missing the Oregon primary. It seemed a personal loss to be deprived of the spoils of such a victory. But success again shifted the tenor of the campaign to a higher level and strengthened us for the California contest.

By then most of us were hardened professionals. We went about our work with quiet efficiency, although we retained our underdog mentality. We had hopes for victory, but we accepted our narrow defeat with Stoic resolution. . . .

The California campaign was overshadowed by the tragedy which marked its end. I had come during the primaries to like Bobby Kennedy rather more than at first. I shared with many a distaste for his methods—his appeals to special interests and his unscrupulous use of money—and I remember thinking that if it was necessary to use such methods to win, the political system needed serious reform. But it became apparent that the man himself was not the ruthless opportunist often portrayed. The cold efficiency seemed to come from his staff; Kennedy himself seemed an intensely emotional and introspective man. McCarthy was a President, but Kennedy was a kind of Hotspur of politics.

The New York primary was almost an anticlimax. We still worked late into the night and talked even later, but politically we were no longer innocent. We knew the techniques of argumentation; we could gather a crowd for a rally on a day's notice. Even the stunning victory—more than five times Humphrey's delegate count, and the upset triumph of Paul O'Dwyer for the Senatorial nomination—was taken in stride. Almost before it was over we were looking forward to the next stage of the campaigns—the delegate hunting, which was to prove our Waterloo.

A shrewd observer of the New York state committee meeting at the end of June could easily have foreseen the rock on which we were to founder. In the election a week before we had won more than half the elected delegates; the committee was to appoint a slate of 60 more at-large delegates. With the simple logic of idealists, we argued that we should get about half the representation on the slate. But the party leaders are not logicians; they play the political game. The members of the committee, Charles Dickens' caricatures come to life—fat, impassive, with heavy faces and large cigars—listened unmoved to fervent pleas for justice by Eleanor Clark French and Allard Lowenstein; then they proposed a slate, agreed on beforehand, which gave McCarthy less than a quarter of the delegates.

Filled with righteous indignation, we stalked from the hall, 300 strong, with Paul O'Dwyer in the lead. For four hours we picketed outside, chanting "The Hacks Must Go" and "Gene, Not the Machine." Meanwhile, the committee endorsed their slate and left quietly by a back door.

DESCENT TO CHICAGO

That was the story of our efforts. For the rest of the summer we wrote thousands of letters to delegates, held massive rallies, collected hundreds of thousands of names of McCarthy supporters—without any apparent effect. The machine rolled on and we would not stoop to work the levers. We were, McCarthy told us at a banquet in June, testing the process; as far as we were concerned, we would beat the machine honestly, through popular pressure, or not at all.

There was one young man in our office who might be called a "politico": he had been in politics since the age of 11, had worked for O'Connor and Beame, and knew the ways of the professionals. He frequently devised plans for putting pressure on delegates, but we scornfully rejected them as "dishonest." He became a kind of outcast, shunned because he was willing to adopt impure means to noble ends.

As the convention approached, it became clear that we were beating against a stone wall. And our anger, which had originally been directed against Johnson, but which McCarthy had channeled constructively, began to rise again. The dislike we had always felt for Humphrey's backroom methods, fueled by our frustration, grew into a personal hatred for the Vice President. As we watched him run smiling among the party bosses, indignantly defending President Johnson, vacillating on the war, preaching his vacuous message of joy, we began to look on him as representative of the worst in American politics. When he came to town, we picketed and booed him. It was all we could do.

As our anger grew, the extraordinary unity of purpose which we had achieved began to disintegrate. Frustration does not lead to constructive plans. Thus, some said they would give up on politics and retreat to ivied walls; some would take to the streets; some would work within the party for people like O'Dwyer, who gave some hope of change. Even before the convention it was apparent that the "McCarthy youth" could not hold together without their leader. We went to Chicago with no hope and with a cold fury growing within us. We were determined to see the effort through to the end, but no one dared think beyond Wednesday night when, we knew, the effort of months would be crushed.

There is not much that can be said about Chicago. We were ready for defeat, but not for the incredible brutality of it, psychological and physical, inside and outside the convention hall. All we could do was scream at the television set, scream at the immovable, unthinking, impassive machine—and when it was all over, take to the streets to register in the only way we had left our rage at what had been done, there to be gassed and clubbed along with the others.

Back in New York I heard one young black talking to another: "You know why they nominated Humphrey?" he said. "Because they knew the young people were for McCarthy—and they hate the young people."

Let there be no mistake: Chicago did not teach us to play the political game. It was the first battle of open warfare. As they gave us no quarter at the convention, so we will give them none; we seek nothing less than the destruction of the political machinery which proved so unresponsive this year. We will dedicate ourselves now to breaking the grip of the old men, the defensive, frightened men who hate all change.

These old men tried to stop the movement of the young in Chicago, but the pressure for change which has been building for so long cannot so easily be turned off. The party leaders are on the defensive; and they, who refused to listen to a poet among politicians, might do well to listen to the poet of our generation:

"You know there's something happening
But you don't know what it is.
Do you Mr. Jones?"

4

CONVENTION IN THE STREETS

Garry Wills

THE KIDS

From a high hotel window at the Republican National Convention, one saw only a restive rather dirty edge of the Atlantic—slide of one color across another, with tattered-lace slaps of grey lather, moving in festooned with nets of weed toward the smelly mini-beaches. At the Democratic Convention, a window similarly high looked over the green fretted apron of Grant Park and Lake Michigan's garish blue. The scene had the too-real brilliance of a big Kodak ad, lit from behind, in Grand Central Station. The lakefront museums showed massive through their clumps of trees. Sailboats leaned tactically in and out of the narrow gap in a long thin breakwater. And, on the grassy apron, a game seemed to be in progress, bowling on the lawn but with no click as the balls hit—all muffled, lazy movement. It seemed crazy, but these were human beings being bowled, rolled, lifted, dragged in a genial mingle of people, as at a county fair.

But when I went down into this pastoral scene, its aspect changed from county fair to gypsy rally. The people wore rags, but rags deliberately chosen for their gay cut or color. Despite the festive laughing, there was a tightness of purpose in people's talk and movements. A street theater was demonstrating to one crowd, by means of a long barnyard parable, that support for Gene McCar-

Garry Wills, Convention in the Streets, *National Review,* **20,** no. 38, pp. 952-960, September, 1968.

thy was just a way of perpetuating the System. This particular group of actors has a glow of celebrity about it, since the troupe is fresh from performances at The Oleo Strut, pacifist coffee house for GIs near Fort Hood, where, everyone is telling each other, some black soldiers have been put in the guard house because they would not board planes for riot service in Chicago.

Further into the Park, the bowling goes on—teams attack children, throw them, beat them in pantomime with clubs of air, kick, drag and carry them to imaginary paddy wagons. It is done with enthusiasm and good humor, by young people who were up all last night singing and chanting in the Park, newly won by them, and who now enjoy their quarters as a prize of battle—while they sharpen toward the next clash. Bystanders criticize each prisoner's conduct; debate the fine points; offer alternative views. All are agreed that the thing to do when grabbed is prepare for clubbing—fall into a fetal position, knees drawn up high to protect the stomach from kicks, arms up around the face. But should one put *hands* over the head, spreading a fan of fingers over the cranium like one of the old ridged-leather football helmets of twenty years ago (which, in fact, one young boy is wearing as he watches the drill)? This gives the face good protection, from one's forearms; but fingers make a brittle cage, easily broken themselves and not cushioning the pigstick's blow. Better perhaps (much sage nodding at this) to put forearms over the skull and squeeze one's elbows in over face and nose as far as possible (bystanders try it and blunder around in weird peek-a-boo poses).

Then there is the question of when to go limp—clearly when lifted and carried (otherwise, if there is any suspicion of rigidity meant as resistance, the beating is resumed); but what if one is dragged? Tight, fetal clump, or in a draggle of limp arms and legs? There are pros and cons, posed and contradicted, ending always with the one directive that takes precedence over other instructions at this open-air school—do it *your* way. It's your thing. A teen-age girl skips up, let-me-try, light and laughing as the mock pigs grab and twirl her like a top (she is from the kind of family that sends cops lumbering out to find her lost tops and toys, how quaint to be manhandled by them). No ghetto kid here, with hatred of pigs engrained all through a bitter childhood. When the police stopped seeming benevolent to her, they gave off a whiff of Keystone—as does this whole scene. All "street theater." She will still be half-surprised when her game becomes reality. But now she laughs, curls up, goes limp, tossed from one boy to another. It looks like a merry scene of play amid the haystacks, something left on the cutting floor after editing *Tom Jones.*

All very jolly. And yet serious. It is amazing that clubs could swing so much so hard in the days ahead, and yet no one was killed, or even seriously maimed. Part of the answer was being acted out here, on Tuesday afternoon, in the bright sun, on the too-real green grass, Kodak shots. These were kids who knew how to be beaten. And how to joke. All glue-and-paint sparkle in the sun, a vision of the Military paraded by, toy planes on his epaulettes, toy gold rockets cross-crossed on his MacArthur brim for its "scrambled eggs." He introduces himself as General Waste-More-Land, and inveighs in parody against traitors who would draft beer rather than boys.

One of the General's friends tells me how they came, in a caravan of Volks-wagen buses and cars, from California. This friend, Morris Kight, is well over thirty; but he has a safety pass written all over him. The kids instinctively know he is one of them. Though he wears the inverted-V soft military hat of the Vets for Peace, he explains that he chose his present life of protest long before the Vietnam issue arose. "I was a hotel man and, if I do say so myself, a rather successful one—I owned seven hotels. But I dropped out ten years ago to stop the madness." What was the madness then? "Pollution of the air, the triumph of the machine; the cold war and the arming. We are in the midst of three major revolutions. First, the social one: we now realize that we cannot mistreat those of another color, or of another religion; cannot mistreat our behavioral minori-ties (like the youth). Second, the cybernation revolution, by which machines do mankind's work, making mankind obsolete. Third, the weapons revolution, which puts terrible new weapons in the hands of a small number of unqualified men." What does one do about the machines, destroy them? "No, make them work for man, not against him. Let them make it possible for man to return to the soil. Make them *clear* the air, rather than foul it. . . ."

The kids live easily, here in Grant Park, having gained it yesterday. They seem to need little food or sleep, each snatched in small amounts as occasion arises; no booze (though cigarettes, straight and loaded). They move around with packs strapped to them; soft ones, of course—things they can lean against, lie on, use for bedding.

The Park was gained only with difficulty. For almost a week kids had been expelled, in growing numbers, from Lincoln Park, three miles to the north. Things escalated Sunday night, the first time I joined the kids. After eleven, the time when the Park is officially closed, large crowds were settled here and there. Police cars and motorcycles moved slowly through them, unsettling them, get-ting them up, on their feet, on the move. The trunk cycles (with three wheels) moved by squadrons, taking over an area, then one by one peeling off, occupy-ing new sites—the kids all the while being crowded to one corner of the park, then edged across the street, some blazing with anger, others just troubled, with frightened young faces (milk in a cup blown across)—but no one fighting. It is a slow, effective process. Soft war.

Lincoln Park was originally chosen by Abbie Hoffman's "Yippies" as a place for a Festival of Life. If the cops had let them have the area, Hoffman's group would probably have remained separate (as he clearly wanted them to) and irrelevant—as they were at the Pentagon March, where they tambourined an elaborate "exorcism." Other groups had, for the most part, made provision to stay in churches and gymnasiums, or doubled up in rooms and private homes. But as, every night, the Yippies get displaced and need shelter, two things happen, both caused by Mayor Daley's untenable first-line toughness. First, other kids, sensing this is the first battleground, flock north and swell the Yippie ranks toward nightfall. Second, the Yippies and their allies, driven out after eleven, start heading south toward the Loop, looking for lodging, and for trouble.

So, on Sunday night, one of the first groups to be edged over the street gathers numbers and courage at a gas station, then heads south with vague thoughts of the Amphitheatre in their heads but ready to settle for the Hilton. At first, standby prowl cars scatter the kids in the street, still moving slowly, the electronic come-and-go of their new-style sirens slowed from scream (mreem-mreem) to purr (meeyown-meeyawmp). Each car is swiveling, now its one male-volent blue eye, which seems to have a hypnotic effect on the kids. When they turn into a block and see that one blue eye at the other end, they swerve instantly and try a new route. The cops are like cowboys bending and turning a stampede, but with this important difference: they have no place to herd these cattle *toward*. Their orders are to disperse the crowd, and the framers of this edict seem to think that means dissolving the kids in thin air. Dispersing a crowd has, as its final objective, the scattering of people back to their homes. But these kids have no homes, at least not in Chicago; and they cannot be eternally "kept moving" as isolated bums are harried from park bench to bus station and back. . . .

KEEPING UP WITH IT

The kids spill into Wells Street, the self-proclaimed "Village" of Chicago; boutiques tinkly with love beads, backyards turned into mewses with cutsie names. The "swinging" shopowners, one step behind the kids' fashions, have looked with some suspicion on the Yippies in Lincoln Park—and with good reason. Wells Street is commercializing yesterday's fads—psychedelic posters as big business; strobe lights, instead of candles, in the dining room. The prize exhibit in the Wax Museum is Hugh Hefner under glass—blobby on the floor before his typewriter, with a waxen bunny-Muse standing near to inspire his blobs of prose. (And which Hugh is the real Hugh?) The kids know the routine—bubbly matrons twisting and jerking and frugging, fresh from Arthur Murray, in expensive disco-teques. It is hard for the kids to stay even one step ahead—which makes that one step all-important. Fall behind an inch, lose the argot, the nuance, blunder into yesterday's "in thing," and you are out of the action—the action being, at any moment, an enclosed totality, the right beat, beads, color, noise, words. Only someone who gives it his full time can keep current—and who gives full time to being kids except kids?

No wonder, then, the middle-aged mods, mini-skirted, frugging, fly-eyed, turned blank faces outward as the kids go by, faces stiff as the wooden shutters they would nail on their windows next day. For the kids broke windows as they went down Wells Street. For several nights, these would be the only windows they had broken. Better be in front of them than one step behind.

HALLOWE'EN—AND AFTER

On Monday, the gay soapy-scented windows, with fake paper tiffany lamps, were covered with the tell-tale modern sign of riot, protective plywood; and one shop hung out an angry sign: "Destroying property on Wells St. is a total cop-out which we equate to marching around your own room. What you apparently fail to realize is that the shopowners and the community share many of the same views about the way things are being run in this country. May we suggest that if you were to unite with the National Mobilization, Peace and Freedom Party and the Black Panthers your voice might be heard." The sheer ignorance of the sign shows that nothing increases the generation gap like attempts, on the part of adults, to join what they will insist on calling "the now generation."

It was a lark. The very young are soon in the lead, distancing all those near the fatal thirtieth year. Girls with white petal faces under limp Grampa McCoy hats, with flapping pants and wilted boots, the very picture of floating innocence, so many Giulietta Massinas scampering along in the street, turn those white petals up toward the street lamps and bay their brave new chant, "Cops eat shit." Dodging the blue police-car blink, splitting off and running together like crushed quicksilver, the kids thread their way back toward the lakefront and reunite on Michigan, coursing south. In the process, cars are stranded in the stream of runners. The kids demand, from drivers quickly rolling windows up, the V-for-Victory Peace Sign—given readily or grudgingly, by most; otherwise the kids bang hoods, hammer windows, kick the doors. Bearded kids with huge cameras hang on a careening car: the Movement records its own achievements with total immediacy. The big metal wicker-work-type trashcans of Chicago are rolled out onto the street, their contents scattered. The camera car makes the kids move cans back so it can get through; then they are rolled once more into the path of "straight" traffic. The thing had an atmosphere of Hallowe'en—until the widely-spaced front runners reached the Chicago River.

The Chicago police are justly proud of their communications system. On the second floor of the State Street Police Station, a vast room—all wires underneath, with neat little pick-up squares to get at the nervous system—has 24 big illuminated consoles, three to a zone, flashing the location of police vehicles, receiving all radio and phone calls from that zone. There are overflow, backup, and coordinating consoles; a whole room devoted to taping calls; an elaborate quick-check system of couriers and computers. Over each console, red and amber lights blink to summon higher officers or messengers. Orlando Wilson, the progressive police leader, cooperated with Motorola to pioneer a new kind of police readiness. And so, as the kids ran, radio reports informed men at the green consoles where they were. They had to be cut off before they reached the Hilton. The Sheraton Chicago could not be protected now; the best line of defense was the bridge over the Chicago River, which—if the worst comes—can be lifted. The dots begin to converge on the scene: police cars. Meanwhile, at a staging area, rented city buses are being filled with the powder-blue riot helmets.

As the first kids came in sight of the bridge, there, on the far side—consoled, blinked, computered into place—were Jimmy Riordan and his First District cops (they handled daily marches two summers ago, and have dealt with innumerable demonstrations in the Loop area). Battle-ready, right?

Wrong. These cops have known two things—"marches," arranged beforehand, tense with the possibility of trouble, but in a predictable way; or looters, a lone one or a few, sprung free in the Loop (run them down). But what did they see now? Some fat, winded photographers and reporters trying to keep up with idiotically grinning boys and girls at a dead run. At sight of the sullen car-blinks across the bridge, most of the kids slow down, look back for support, unwilling still to attack a police car, but with no more side streets they can duck down (the police have chosen well). The very front runners do not slow down, however—two teen-age girls unwinded after three miles; one, wearing buckskin, goes forward with the semihiant singultus of her anticipated political defloration. The nightsticks are raised; the girls are ready, they have been anticipating this (fall *limp*). But the cops merely turn them around and shove them back. They use their clubs only once—on a photographer who tries to get a picture of them manhandling the buckskin girl.

The police advance across the bridge, lower the gates that block traffic for the raising of the drawbridge, and slowly work the crowd back. Riordan is on the bullhorn, threatening to use tear gas if the crowd—perhaps two hundred kids—does not disperse. A Yippie shouts, "Great! I get a high on that stuff." Tear gas is still a joke. There is a certain amount of muttering, but no real resistance. Clumps of kids shout "We want *pig*meat." But the cops ignore them and huddle, out in the center of the street, confiding information to their walkie-talkies—a cluster of antennaed heads, the aerials sticking out at all angles, a quiet insect orgy. People fall back and mill beside Colonel McCormack's huge cathedral (in the window are straw hats with headbanks for all the candidates—including John Connally, Lester Maddox, and R. Sargent Shriver).

Then the big dots move on the consoles and five—count 'em, five—busloads roll, open, lazily disgorge their contents. This is Riordan's technique, always—flood the area, discourage the hotheads before anything happens, make the numbers prohibitive. The buses come from the city's transit company, whose black drivers are on strike. There are Gilbey's Vodka ads on the side, with cossack dancers. The sludgy flow of blue helmets out along each sidewalk splits the kids, edges them off, turns them around—peaceably, as in the Park. Round One to the police.

But a Pyrrhic victory. A half-hour later, I went back north toward the Park. There are no signs of the kids. Where had they gone? Back at the consoles, the policemen must have been wondering the same thing. The cops had bumped the Yippies out of the Park, only to drive them into the Loop—and into the arms of the better-organized, more militant Mobilization. The kids see in the whole process a vivid symbol of the fact that the System has no place for them. And they are ready to turn this "defeat" to their advantage. The third of the daily bulletins put out by SDS exulted: "We are learning. We are learning how to move together. Learning the City . . . Pretty soon, brothers and sisters. We are learning targets, targets where the rich buy their things." Mayor Daley had given his police something to think about, at the consoles.

THE PROS

The National Mobilization Committee Against the War in Vietnam is the group that, under David Dellinger, organized the 1967 March on the Pentagon. They had planned two major events for Chicago—on Tuesday, an Unbirthday Party for LBJ (meant to run in sinister counterpoint to the real birthday scheduled for Soldiers Field) and, on Wednesday, a protest march on the convention site (the Chicago Amphitheatre). Every morning Dellinger's group held a press conference, announcing many smaller activities. The Mobilization, known as Mob (pronounced Mobe), worked out of an office and a storefront in the Loop, coordinating activities of other groups, finding places for people to stay, recruiting and training marshals and medics for the Wednesday march, and maintaining the tragicomic personal bulletin boards of the Movement ("Your parents may have called you—check the board").

Chicago is the home of SDS (Students for a Democratic Society), which takes a harder line than Mob (as in its veiled invitation to loot "targets where the rich buy their things"). The SDS meeting at Michigan State, earlier this summer, studied ways to use local or national issues on each campus in order to "politicize" the nonpolitical student and "radicalize" the politically interested. Tom Hayden, a founding father of SDS, in a prescient article written for the underground New York *Rat*, looked ahead to Chicago as the kickoff of this fall campaign on all campuses. After describing the seminal role of events like the Pentagon March, he wrote: "Chicago promises to fill the same mood-creating function for the Movement at the beginning of the school year."

Hayden and Rennie Davis became local project directors for Mob—i.e., young field guerrillas of the Movement, out on the streets or in hiding, when they were not in jail. The first time I went to the Mob's office, a girl in charge pointed at two large young men, just leaving, who wore immaculate short-sleeved turtleneck sweaters; "Rennie's tail—they lost him, so they came up to ask where he is. Can you imagine?" How do you know they are policemen?" "Tattoos! Can you *imagine*?" While Hayden and Davis handled the street leadership, Dellinger took over the task of voicing "responsible protest." Every morning at his ten o'clock press conference, he would make much of the fact that the Mayor had not only refused to issue a march permit; he refused even to see representatives of the demonstration. At first, no one in his office would see them. On Monday, after the kids' Sunday-night run to the bridge, Dellinger reported two main atrocities —the "brutalization of newsmen" (i.e., the photographer whose camera was smashed on the bridge), and the deception by which Dellinger was shunted off, Sunday afternoon, to meet the Deputy Mayor's deputy, rather than the Deputy

Mayor himself. But *this* afternoon, he continued, he meant to get some action at City Hall. By the time Dellinger arrived for his afternoon meeting with David Stahl (the Deputy Mayor was available now), there was a new grievance—the arrest of Tom Hayden, on state and city charges, for letting air out of a police car's tires. Dellinger has brought along with him some other respectable figure-heads—men like Dr. Sidney Peck, Associate Professor of Sociology at Case Western Reserve. They want Hayden's release, a march permit, and—what dooms this whole elaborate game of negotiation—"withdrawal of the troops." The Deputy Mayor temporizes with them for an hour and says nothing, so they emerge (at 4:30) angry and prepared to escalate. Professor Peck says he is interested in the situation as a sociologist, a student of collective behavior (tie, coat, objective manner, no Yippie here): "With a high degree of predictability, anger will build up and begin to vent itself. The repressive actions of the city are inciteful"—yes, he *is* a sociologist—"inciteful to violence."

Then it is Dellinger, middle-aged, high-voiced, mild in manner, quivering with indignation: "We charge Mayor Daley with dereliction of duty. He invited the Democratic Convention here, and then refused to see those who inevitably came along with it. He is available to the bosses in the back room, and to those carrying on the war in Vietnam, but not to the constituents in the street." Dellinger has, unconsciously, the gift of the extremist (deliberately cultivated by the Yippies) for self-caricature. But even more disturbing, he has a point: Daley did invite to his town a party, some of whose leading candidates have used the rallying of kids as a political instrument. In many ways, the Democratic Party *had* called the kids there. And now Daley pretends they do not exist; gives them no place to stay and demonstrate peacefully; chases them down toward trouble, exacerbates their edgy drive toward "confrontation"; and, to cap it all, refuses to discuss the crisis with any of the kids' representatives. Though Dellinger mimes a righteous anger, he is undoubtedly pleased as possible. This is just what the Mob wants—in fact, just what Tom Hayden predicted in his optimistic sce-nario for Chicago: the System will put itself on the weakest possible grounds, and excuse beforehand the scuffles that are bound to occur.

But enough of responsibility. Another participant in the City Hall press con-ference moves up to the microphone—Marilyn Katz, a tiny leader of the Marshals Squad, dressed in sneakers, sweatshirt, and slacks. "If there is trouble now, the City must be held responsible. They have given the jails and streets and skies to the military, and left no place to the kids, who have come to fight for freedom. The streets are theirs." How old are you, Miss Katz? "Twenty-three—seven years from the cut-off point."

ALWAYS THE SYSTEM

The press conference breaks up as news goes around that the kids are marching from Lincoln Park to the police station (*beyond* the Hilton, heading south), where Hayden is being held. I catch a ride with Miss Katz, who takes the parking ticket off her car and casually tears it up: "They're always pestering us." Marilyn feels hunted. "Doesn't that make you feel good?" she says with a wave at the police helicopter patrolling Michigan Avenue. Marilyn is rather plain and boyish, but with the fuzzy-eyed jerky charm of a Shirley MacLaine (who is hard at work on the floor of the *other* convention). Marilyn is even smaller, though—a mini-MacLaine. When she turns her eyes defiantly up toward the helicopter, they spread wide, after a lashy blink like some flower opening—not pretty, but with a moist unfocused look disarming as sudden beauty.

The System is everywhere, but it cannot fool her. "We even found the unmarked office of the CIA in the Federal Building, and one of our people put 'CIA sucks' on the door. The major TV networks were there to photograph the scene, but they weren't allowed to use it." What stopped them? The obscenity? Eyes wide at my innocence (who cares about *that*?)—"The CIA, of course. Or maybe the FBI." The System.

When we get to the station, the marchers have already gone by; from this vantage point, they turned back up toward the Hilton, which they finally reach. Marilyn tries to go inside the station with me, but she has no police or press credentials. Just then a Corporation Counsel (i.e., assistant city attorney) comes out and, in a sudden rage (real or feigned, exaggerated either way), screams "Don't let that girl in. She has been arrested at least fifteen times." "You big liar," she shouts back, just as wild. Another Counsel, a smooth-voiced black man, comes out and is friendly: "How did your trial go?" Wry MacLaine grimace: "Probation and a fine. Big lecture on the sacredness of property." I asked her what she was arrested for. "And it was just once! I was helping organize welfare workers, and we did a sit-down protest in the welfare office. They got us for criminal trespass."

Marilyn, even more than formal leaders like Dellinger, is the new revolutionary, one who is engaged in a total running guerrilla warfare with the System. I would meet many of these guerrillas during the week, veterans of Columbia, of the Pentagon, of the Poor People's Campaign; even—some of the older ones—of the freedom rides and sit-ins. The kids had taken Grant Park, and, in the wake of the Hayden protest, refused to head north for a planned Hippie love-in at the North Beach. The Park, so carefully guarded last night at the bridge, is seized now from the rear, with only minor battling—a boy pulled off the statue of General Logan as the crowd moved up Michigan from the station. As usual, the firstline intransigence of the cops became silly as, day after day, General Logan wore ragged kids and flags in all his metal apertures. The police had refused to give an inch, yet soon after gave a mile; they interdicted Lincoln Park, miles away from the delegates, and so found themselves having to surrender Grant Park, just across from the convention hotel-headquarters. So, that night, the chants went on till dawn; the Guard made its first appearance, to spell the totally mobilized cops. Mild-mannered General Dunne put a human barricade of brown before Grant Park, not to prevent kids, now, from entering, but to keep them from leaving the Park and crossing Michigan to the Hilton. . . .

Lincoln Park has been lined, for nights, with cars from all over America. I watched the boys and girls, at nightfall, put their expensive Nikons, their hand-held bulky movie cameras, their tape recorders, inside and lock the doors (they had to scramble for them Sunday when the run began), then flop sandal-happily over to the Park. These are the middle-class rebels, despised by the proletariat (which is made up—poor Marx—of the crustiest defenders of the *status quo*). Cabdrivers and bartenders were the people you heard attacking the "hippies." In one bar I stopped at, late one night, the men scrubbing the floor—blacks included—cheered when TV showed kids beaten and thrown into vans.

Mayor Daley's apologists tried to separate the demonstrators in Chicago into "professional revolutionaries" and "duped idealists." His police still thought in those categories. At one point, while the Wednesday march was stalled and had flopped down on the lawn in one long sinuous line, thirty men, ranging from six-foot-one up towards the neighboring tree tops, came clumping over to the line, "plainclothes" stamped all over their open collars and suburban lounging sweaters. It gave the kids something to enjoy, as everyone spotted them, pointed, jeered, but made way for the relentless stalking advance. Why on earth be plainclothesmen, I wondered, and yet advertise one's presence? So I followed. They were "the red squad" out Commie-hunting. When they saw one, they would cluster round, peer at "the subject," dwarfed as a football in this huddle of linebackers, and say things like: "We thought we'd see you here. We're ready when the trouble starts. You'd better not let us find you in the vicinity." The act lent itself too readily to parody by bystanders. The jolly square giants even stopped to scowl and growl at Frances Gabow, irrelevantly islanded by her middle-aged escorts. Peter Pramm of SDS also got the huff-and-puff treatment. So did Chris Bernard, of the Radical Organization Committee.

An exercise in anachronism. These are not the leaders. They are panting along behind the kids, trying to catch their coat tails, catch a ride. There were professed rebels out there—Tom Hayden and Rennie Davis. . . .

These kids are mobile; money is no problem for them; they know what they are in for. If anything, the organizers tend to scare off the innocents who do not realize what the game is all about. The Mob gave out arrest slips everywhere, to be filed for use by volunteer lawyers if the kids ended up in the pokey; they went through the Park with grease pencils, printing the legal-aid number on everybody's forearm.

The picture the Chicago police tried to project was of an "agent" taking his orders from Moscow, and manipulating the kids into town by the thousands. It is a much more satisfying conception than the reality. By police thinking, all one has to do is catch the agents, and the dupes will be disillusioned. But no one duped these kids here. The few people who had been to Cuba or who pal around with the Vietcong are not mesmeric enough to cause this kind of reaction. Whatever triggering mechanism launched the kids simultaneously from a hundred cities is one that no one controls in Moscow, or Havana, or Hanoi. Or even in America.

Indeed, the problem of the Movement (which is the reality behind and embracing all the various segments, variously named, of "the New Left") is that it is ridiculously anti-organizational. Not only is the System evil; all systems are. Only doing one's thing is safe. Logically, this leads to the exuberant irrelevance of the Yippies—or, rather the Hippies. Even Yippism is an accommodation to the reality of politics. The trouble with doing one's thing is that it does not, in isolation, overthrow (or even affect) the System that stands in the way of one's-thingism. So, in some manner, one must organize even to overthrow Organization. One needs leaders to publish the tracts, rent the buses, collect the *money* to rent the buses, get the lawyers for those in jail, get the medics for those who are clubbed.

McCARTHY, ON THE RIGHT

So the Mob comes along, and SDS, and—out on the "right wing" of the anti-Establishment forces (so far to the right that most of those in Mob would call them "Establishment," the supreme insult)—Al Lowenstein's "Coalition," which was totally without effect in Chicago, and Marcus Raskin's "New Party," which promises to be equally ineffective. Lowenstein and Raskin (and, by extension, Gene McCarthy) fall between two stools—neither Establishment nor anti-Establishment.

But even the purists of anti-Establishmentarianism have to resort to dodges. How does one oppose the System with a simple lack of system? Rhetorically, of course, it is easy. One of the kids told me "The answer to the War is no war. The answer to the draft is no draft. The answer to the System is no system." What that means, in the myth of the New Left, is that one can be simply "issue-oriented." The very reality of things will throw up a spontaneous opposition, shaped only the the exigencies of the moment, not by leaders (not, at least, by any who are *necessary*), and not by party organizations ("structures," perhaps, but only those that are grown, not put together by planning). At the SDS meeting in Lansing, where the Columbia rebellion clearly set the pattern for all workshops, Mark Rudd would have been a commanding presence if there had not been a deliberate effort, apparently supported by Rudd himself, to prevent this. The cult of personality is hated by the kids, not for old Marxist reasons (as a romantic distraction from historical Process), but because it lures one back into the System's game of candidates and parties, not "issues."

One must do some planning of course—flunky work, hire the buses. But one hopes that events will supersede any other more extensive plans. That is what Hayden hoped for in his prophetic article on Chicago: "There will be no way to mobilize action at the time without major initiative from below. . . . The growing consciousness of the Movement—its justified distrust of organized leaderships, its creation of 'revolutionary gangs' or 'affinity groups,' its experience with the police and the streets—is sure to be a controlling force of some kind over the loose official hierarchies."

And so it was. The planned events lost all their importance as improvised violence developed its own logic. For the Hippies, *the* event was to be the love-in at North Beach, intended as a "Free Huey Newton" bash; but the kids had gone south and gained Grant Park by that time; why retreat back north and lose ground? The Mob's two major efforts were to be the party for LBJ, which lost a good deal of its steam when the real birthday party evaporated (the President couldn't risk an appearance, so Mayor Daley forgot about Soldiers Field); and, second, the March, which never took place at all. The police, luckily for the kids, gave "spontaneous opposition" its chance to prove itself. All the important activities were reactions to Daley's intransigence: by taking no strategic initiative of his own—by not trying to deal with the demonstrators, or define their actions with permits; by forswearing diplomacy and propaganda—Daley let his cops fend for themselves, trying to treat the kids as outlaws or nonbeings. And this, in turn, let the kids release all their grievances, act out the purely "anti-world' system of opposition to the System. The New Politics, anti-personal and anti-organizational, is unworkable in the long run; but Daley made it work, beautifully, in Chicago. Just as Hayden had hoped.

UP AGAINST THE WALL

They even hoped Humphrey would win. McCarthy's nomination would have been a disaster. So Hayden wrote: "when McCarthy began his campaign he hoped it would give young people a conventional and effective alternative to the politics of alienation. He obviously has attracted the support of a great many ambitious white middle class people who want to "save the System." And he has corrupted many young people into believing that by 1972 they can and should 'take over' the Democratic Party... If radicals really believe that President McCarthy could not solve America's problems but only reveal the limits of liberalism, then McCarthy is even a better establishment figure to pressure and expose than Humphrey." If one is against the System, then trying to save it is the worst crime. The aim of the kids is, simply, to force the System "up against the wall."

The amazing—and terrifying—thing is the ease with which they did it. Their numbers were nowhere near what they had predicted. Their scheduled activities misfired. No major rioting developed (the kind that has led to deaths like those in Detroit—or to any deaths at all). Yet the kids commanded instant, almost total sympathy from the press and from many politicians. They made a major impact on the convention; on this year's politics; perhaps on the election itself. They drew the eyes of the world to them, and discredited their country in those eyes. We have all heard that universities are easy to disrupt. But the kids, in fairly small numbers and with primitive planning, disrupted a major city and a political convention; tied up eleven thousand police and the whole Illinois national guard; made any further threat from the ghetto almost unthinkable in its consequences. After this, any campus must seem a knockover. Hayden was right: Chicago sets the mood for the campus this fall—and for the election. The kids have obviously struck an Achilles heel of some sort in our society. We seem to have no defense against them. Certainly Daley had none. They have money, position, and sympathy the black rioters do not command. The campus problem may well overshadow for a while what is euphemistically called "the urban problem." And in what is taking shape as the greatest problem of all—the question whether this country will be governable during the next President's tenure —the kids might hold the crucial cards. If that turns out to be the case, then the convention in the streets may have been of more lasting importance than that held in the Amphitheatre. (*Up against the wall!*)

PART TWO

Turning On and Dropping Out:

Rejecting the American Dream or Neglecting Reality?

If the character of the new politics is not altogether clear at this time, there seems no doubt that massive social forces are trending toward fundamental change. Witness the various forms in which square society is being taunted today, which suggests that many are rejecting the tenets of the American Dream; that our social institutions are (if not perfect) as good as any that man has fashioned. We look here at three ways of putting down the squares: the hippie movement, drug-taking, and draft resistance. The concern is whether these put-downs will help trigger necessary innovations in our institutions, or whether those participating dangerously neglect reality in their exuberance to be really with it.

Specifically, this section focuses on rejection of today's institutions by what is known today as "turning on and dropping out." The phenomenon is not a new one. In the past, for example, many people sought relief from a society they perceived as unjust by retiring to a monastery or a cloister. They were "turned on" by God's grace, as it were, and they "dropped out" of society to serve Him. The phenomenon today is a secular one, and stresses the gratification of personal needs rather than service to a divine call. But the similarities are still there.

Although turning on and dropping out appears in various forms and strengths in modern society, this section considers only three variants. The range of this section is broad, as the following headings reflect:

Hippies: loving or loutish?
Drugs: expanding consciousness or blowing minds?
The Draft: a new morality or an old story?

The impact of these variants of dropping out on political institutions and traditions is both diverse and significant. In a narrow sense, the various forms of dropping out imply more or less serious demands on a governmental service such as law enforcement. As the last section shows, the police are already chronically lagging in their major task—fighting crime and criminals. The role of law enforcement is difficult even when there is general agreement on the limits of permissible behavior. The various forms of dropping out attempt to test and extend those limits. Hence, they place stress on a wide array of institutions and traditions, for good or ill, and put conventional wisdom to a grievous test. For example, conventional wisdom has it that the use of marijuana leads to reliance on "harder" drugs. Therefore, stamping out the supply of marijuana by public agencies seems indicated. But it is also possible that a lack of marijuana will force the use of harder drugs, which argues for caution in restricting the supply. This illustrates the action dilemmas created when dropping out confronts political institutions and traditions.

The various forms of dropping out also raise broader challenges for any political community. Those dropping out may intend broad consequences, or they may be disinterested or unaware. But square society is likely to be preoccupied with a wide range of possible consequences. Consider the view of President Nixon's task force on drug taking. "Persistent use of an agent which serves to ward off reality," the report notes with particular reference to adolescents, "is likely to affect adversely the future ability of the individual to cope with the demands of a complex society." Broad derivative social dangers are clear to members of the task force. "At least some users," their report continues, "show evidence of a loss of conventional motivation. They seem to prefer a non-goal-oriented life style, which emphasizes immediate satisfactions to the exclusion of ambition and future planning."[1] Even the possibility of such consequences clearly relates to the entire climate of life, for good or ill, and, hence has profound political impact.

A. A BASIC DILEMMA

Turning on and dropping out, in whatever form and time, confronts societies with a nagging dilemma. Consider only two extreme positions. Those dropping out may only signal the corruptness of the society around them, a signal with the power to innovate a new and more satisfying life style. On the other hand, dropping out may seriously weaken a society that is threatened. A classic case is the way that a nonauthoritarian society deals with conscientious objectors; those who will not help defend their society against an aggressor. The issues become involved when the criteria for dropping out are less strict than those historically applied to conscientious objection, such as a deep religious conviction about the immorality of war or other forms of physical violence. The resultant problems are perhaps the thorniest in all classical political theory. Resolving those problems is particularly delicate when social dropouts are nu-

[1]Quoted in *Newsweek*, p. 37, September 29, 1969.

merous. Each age, in effect, must gropingly determine the percentage of drop-outs which its institutions and traditions can "safely" permit at any point in time. Many eggs are typically cracked in making that particular omelette.

The basic dilemma raised by turning on and dropping out is this, then: societies must innovate or they will die, but they also must live in order to innovate. Dropping out may foster innovation, but it may also threaten existence; finding a satisfactory balance is a difficult matter. This will receive detailed counterpoint from three perspectives, which can be introduced briefly. The hippie movement illustrates an extreme case of turning on and dropping out. Some of the literature on drugs will introduce the reader to one way of turning on. And consideration of resistance to the draft provides a case study of a particular kind of selective dropping out.

In all three cases, the same basic questions apply. Does the explicit rejection of the American Dream reflect any progress toward a more humane society? Or is the dropping out merely a way of attempting to avoid harsh aspects of reality which can only be neglected but not avoided? Or is it a little bit of both?

B. HIPPIES: LOVING OR LOUTISH?

Perhaps some half-million people have adopted the "hip life" to a degree that reflects their massive dissatisfaction with American society.[2] Hippies reject what they see as the major hang-ups of modern society: status-seeking, materialism, and conformity. The movement stresses "doing your own thing," with the specific goals of turning on, tuning in, and dropping out. Thousands of young people have tried all three. They have fled to hippie meccas such as Haight-Ashbury in San Francisco or the East Village in New York City. In these communes, young men and women typically live in squalor, many beg what food they eat, most experiment with sex and drugs, and some even plan a new society. They have more or less totally disengaged from square society, voluntarily.

Hippies are seen as loving or loutish, as specific objects identified by dress, speech, and manners, or as complex personifications of pervasive social changes among youth. Few reactions fall in between. The following sections provide support for both extremes, but we prefer to suspend judgment in order to determine whether hippiedom is generating a viable alternative to the American Dream. Several questions guide our interest:

Does the hippie movement have an ideological orientation?
What types of change do the hippies want in modern society?
What are their chances of instituting changes in American society?
What is the probable impact of hippies on modern society?

As John Howard establishes in "The Flowering of the Hippie Movement,"

[2] Lewis Yablonsky, "The Hippie Trip," p. 36, Pegasus, New York, 1968.

some evidence implies that at least some hippies are working toward a new society. Howard has good credentials to support his insights. He views the movement both as a sometime participant and as an anthropologist. The hippie culture, he explains, seems to affirm a set of core values rather than to deny the relevance of all values. For example, the culture prescribes that man has both a right and a responsibility to determine his own destiny. To permit this, war and violence must be abolished. The long-run goal is that all people will ultimately live as brothers in peace.

A variety of evidence permits speaking of hippies as working toward a new society. Like all other societies, the hippie culture has a differentiated membership. Howard distinguishes four basic types: visionaries, freaks and heads, midnight hippies, and plastic hippies. The categories permit real insight into the hippie culture.

The visionaries are the gurus of hippiedom. They are the serious hippies who wish to develop alternatives to our present social values and institutions. The directions chosen by the visionaries will be critical in determining whether the hippie movement develops viable social alternatives or tragically neglects them.

The freaks and heads are heavy drug users who are too severely incapacitated to attempt social reform. They are suffered to overdo their own thing, somewhat like mischievous children in an indulgent family. As the sociologist Yablonsky reports, the 'Meths" or "speed freaks" are seen by true hippies as being in a self-destructive phase, a phase necessary to free them from the bag that was laid on them by the plastic society and from which they are trying to escape.[3] Most hippies turn on with drugs to varying degrees with various kinds. Use of drugs by hippies seems related to their effect on the user, however, not to the severity of the laws regulating their use. Thus, marijuana is heavily used and will continue to be, Howard notes, although that use violates the law. Heroin and speed are employed less and this would be so even if they were legal.

Midnight hippies are older individuals who are integrated into the straight world, but whose sympathies become clear when they join the hippie culture after normal work hours. Midnight hippies can be very useful in introducing the best of the hippie world into square society, and by financial support or various other services.

The plastic hippies are generally young people who affect hippie baubles, bangles, and beads, but whose interest in the movement is only faddish. They normally have little understanding of its ideology. Indeed, plastic hippies might be repelled by that ideology. But the hippie costumes are so attractive and so much "in" that many adopt the external signs without receiving the inward grace, as it were. Even the most blatant plastic hippie, however, may in time develop strong identification with the philosophic hip life.

The visionaries attempted to set up their first experimental society in Haight-Ashbury, in 1967. Reality won this first collision with hippie idealism.

[3] *Ibid.,* pp. 34, 243-244.

The experiment failed because of external pressure and certain conspicuous internal contradictions in the hippie philosophy. If everyone were allowed to do his own thing and to avoid doing anything that did not groove them, no viable organization to meet hippie needs was possible. And voluntarism could not feed, clothe, or protect the experimental colony from disease or raids by toughs and exploiters.

External pressure and contradictions in the hippie philosophy tend to come to a single consequence in urban attempts to develop hippie societies. Consider Haight-Ashbury. Very quickly, square society moved in on all fronts, humane, exploitative, and repressive. Often the police were involved because the hippies included many young "missing persons." Furthermore, such great crowds of the curious came to Haight-Ashbury that many fly-by-night businesses were set up to service or fleece squares and hippies alike. Moreover, one close and gentle observer estimates that perhaps as many as 10 to 20 percent of the hippie movement is composed of disturbed young people who have found in the hippie community a refuge and personal immunity from square society's ways of dealing with their emotional disturbances or psychoses.[4] Such elements imply the explosiveness of the mix of hippiedom and square society. Intervention by police and other authorities was predictable, and probably inevitable.

Although the Haight-Ashbury experiment failed, large numbers of hippie communes have sprung up in California. Experimentation with developing a new society continues, particularly in rural settings where hippies have more freedom to do their thing in small groups. Their intention is to avoid drawing rubber-necking crowds and the human exploiters attracted by them, both of which increase the chances of official intervention. Howard cautions that the hippie movement must not be thought of as just another type of youth rebellion. The movement represents a concerted effort to change adult society, not merely to mock it, and must not be taken lightly.

Indeed, the hippie movement seems to attract a growing number of recruits, with the nation's colleges and universities serving as a major locus of hippie recruitment and socialization. For example, Geoffrey Simon and Grafton Trout[5] report that the entering college student usually goes through several stages before he is accepted into the more established hippie groups. The process seems to be accelerating. But even the most ambitious adolescent usually takes a couple of semesters to become a "skuzzie" or a "political," that is a freak or a visionary. And most recruits seem to progress no further than the plastic hippie stage, perhaps later to swell the ranks of the midnight hippies.

Some argue that the socialization of hippies is love's labor lost, whether in the commune or on the campus. "Challenge to the Hippies," for example, charges that the movement is useless and dead. Perhaps the notice of death is premature. But the question of uselessness is a nagging one. What good comes from drop-

[4] Ibid., pp. 294-295.

[5] Geoffrey Simon and Grafton Trout, Hippies in College: From Teeny-Boppers to Drug Freaks, *Trans-action*, 5, pp. 27-32, December 1967.

ping out of one society to create another based on self-indulgence, when the social ills of America patently require the dedicated efforts of its talented youth? The hippie response is predictable. They reject integration into the mainstream of American society, because even its liberal goals are seen as not worth achieving. Other worthy goals—like the elimination of poverty, war, and crime—are seen as defying solution within the American political structure which they believe is dominated by decadent men and institutions. Thus one observer notes:

> The hippie movement beneath the surface carnival is a valiant attempt by a segment of American youths to achieve an intense condition of human creativity and LOVE. That their aspirations fall far short of their lofty goals may be more of a commentary on the spiritual poverty of the society in which the effort is taking place than on the feeble attempts at love acted out by the young affluent participants in the movement.[6]

The issue is joined, then. If the leaders of American society wish to utilize the resources of many hippie youths, it will be necessary to gain their acceptance of some goals for social action, and to demonstrate that progress toward those goals is possible. Success in engaging the energies of hippies will require both a re-evaluation of American values and a full-scale, unflagging assault on the social ills of American society.

Hippies can also be misused, by neglecting their potential or (as some observers fear) by persecuting them as offensive deviants. From significant perspectives, indeed, the hippie phenomenon is heretical. "It is a heresy," Michael E. Brown concludes, "in a society that eschews the primary value of intimacy for the sake of impersonal service to large and enduring organizations, a society that is essentialist rather than existentialist, a society that prizes biography over interactive quality."[7] And heresy is a risky business, given a society that is unsure of itself. The outcomes are unclear, but the stakes are enormous.

C. DRUGS: EXPANDING CONSCIOUSNESS OR BLOWING MINDS?

If the number dropping out is still limited it is growing; Americans in huge numbers are at least turning on. We stress only one way of turning on among many; the use of drugs which cuts across all strata of American society. Hippiedom has provided a major early market for drugs, of course, but illegal drug usage is a national phenomenon.

Our focus is on the abuse of drug-taking, which involves the basic issue of defining "abuse." The issues are subtle, so, to begin, we take refuge in generali-

---

[6] Yablonsky, *op. cit.,* p. 287,

[7] Michael E. Brown, The Condemnation and Persecution of Hippies, *Trans-action,* **6**, p. 39, September 1969.

ties. The purpose of drug usage is to somehow augment man's inadequacies or capabilities or sensitivities. Some drug-taking is patently necessary, sometimes for survival, and some is often useful. The price of expanding one's consciousness or capabilities may be paid for by blowing one's mind, however. It is a matter of drawing a major line.

Public attention has been centered on young people but, with the exception of the very young, drug use knows no age limit. In "Drugs: The Mounting Menace of Abuse," Roland Berg surveys American drug use and sees an epidemic. "No one," he says, "is immune." We use drugs with abandon to achieve such diverse ends as sleep and activity, calm and alertness. The campus, the high school, and the executive boardroom have all become centers of drug abuse. Berg provides a classification of the types of drugs most frequently used abusively, and explains why so many people have turned to drugs. Berg's typology classifies drugs as either hallucinogens, stimulants, depressants, or narcotics. He gives their slang names, explains where the drugs come from, what effects they normally have on the user, and the harm they can cause. Reasons suggested for drug use include efforts to escape middle-class pressures, psychic experimentation, rebellion, and kicks. In the final analysis, says Berg, "drug abuse is a health and social problem, not a police problem . . . . The solution is education, not punishment."

Students of drug usage tend toward agreement on some issues. One psychiatrist describes the typical user as "usually younger, more intelligent, better educated, and from the so-called privileged class." Moreover, the effects of drugs are variable. For example, research on marijuana has shown that for it "to produce pleasurable effects often requires a great deal by way of social learning and social support."[8]

Use of drugs far exceeds agreement about it; the dangers of drugs are heatedly disputed. Almost all researchers agree that LSD can be a very dangerous drug even though it is not addictive. Marijuana is considered by some to be harmless, and by others as dangerous. "Marihuana and Society" by the American Medical Association and the National Research Council takes the latter position. The AMA-NRC report also concluded that legalization of marijuana would create a serious abuse problem, that penalties for violation of the laws are often harsh and unrealistic, and that additional research and education should be undertaken.

Joel Fort, M.D., challenges the AMA-NRC conclusion in his "The AMA Lies About Pot." Fort does not maintain that marijuana is harmless, but he finds fault with the AMA-NRC's research techniques, which he feels are inadequate to permit labelling the drug as dangerous. In addition, he notes, given "the undeniable evidence of the danger of alcohol and nicotine consumption, the AMA-NRC anti-marijuana campaign seems surreal and its puritan tone hypocritical." The applicable law also limps badly. Under Federal law possession of marijuana is a

[8]William Simon and John H. Gagon, Children of the Drug Age, *Saturday Review,* p. 62, September 21, 1968.

felony, for example, while possession of the much more potent LSD is a misdemeanor.

Whether the law is changed or not, the evidence suggests that the use of marijuana will not only continue but that it will increase. Official warnings concerning the drug have little effect because users seem to believe that their own experiences establish that the drug is not harmful.[9] Injunctions to "keep off the grass" go unheard, and a common argument maintains that legalization of marijuana is only a matter of time—the "time it will take to educate conservatives."[10]

D. THE DRAFT: A NEW MORALITY OR AN OLD STORY?

American society is characterized by selective dropping out as well as massive turning on. Resistance to the draft has reached substantial proportions, and all signs suggest that the present resistance represents only the first pebbles of an oncoming avalanche. The resistance movement is based in large part on opposition to the Vietnam War, which has increased in all sectors of American society since the late 1950s. Today, disappointment with the war may well be characteristic of a majority of the American population.[11] Many of the nation's most influential newspapers and magazines, and even past war heroes have become critics of the war.[12]

The resistance to the draft no doubt has multiple sources. On the one hand, we may be seeing a new morality at work. Allen Guttman has noted that protests against the draft often come from those who believe the war to be illegal and/or immoral. Much of the opposition has come from the more articulate, educated youth on college campuses. On the other hand, resistance to the draft may reflect an older pattern, that many prefer not to interrupt their careers or risk their lives if they can possibly avoid it. James Reston predicted in 1967 that if the government tried to draft the college-educated members of our society, we would have the most massive and disruptive dissent yet. Early in 1968 President Johnson withdrew deferments for graduate students (except for medical and dental students), and Congress failed to enact any of numerous reforms recommended for the draft. Perhaps as a direct consequence, resistance to the draft increased considerably.

Some observers reflect only puzzlement at resistance to the draft. John Keats' "The Draft Is Good for You" argues that military service is good for young men and that they should cease and desist their resistance. Keats' essay illustrates the generation gap. His philosophy is to go along with the crowd; the philosophy of

[9] Ibid., p. 63.

[10] Keep Off the Grass, The New Republic, p. 5, June 17, 1967.

[11] Allen Guttman, Protest Against the War in Vietnam, The Annals of the American Academy of Political and Social Science, p. 57, March 1969.

[12] Ibid.

the younger generation is to do your own thing. "No one," he says, "is lucky to escape the common experience of his time." At least some of his student audience seeks individual fulfillment, and can be pardoned for not hearing.

But resistance it has been, whether or not potential draftees know what is good for them. "Hell No, We Won't Go" deals with the extent and type of draft resistance. "As of January of 1968, some 15,310 men had not responded to calls or correspondence from their draft boards." Some draft resisters are malingerers, the report finds, but most are not. Mr. Davidson corroborates other research which has found that some men become draft evaders because they cannot qualify for conscientious objector status under present laws, even though they oppose the Vietnam War on moral grounds.[13] Others who qualify under the law as conscientious objectors are turned down by local boards, who consider anyone opposed to war as a matter of conscience to be a coward, a communist, or worse.

The draft laws attract massive opposition on two grounds. First, the Vietnam War makes the draft especially objectionable to some. Robert Brown, a Stanford Professor of Religion, is one example. He explains, in an article not included here, why he feels morally compelled to counsel his students to avoid the draft. A middle-class establishment-type, Professor Brown decides on resistance because he believes that "one has to oppose evil even if one cannot prevent it."[14] "Our country," says Brown, "is committing crimes so monstrous that the only thing more monstrous would be continuing silence or inaction in the face of them."[15] If America was really in danger in a just war, Brown probably would argue, many of his moral objections would disappear. But Vietnam is not such a war for Professor Brown.

Second, the draft has been under attack from a widening number of persons who—Vietnam War or no—see it as unfair, uncertain, and inconsistent. Statistical evidence shows that the draft system is unfair inasmuch as it discriminates against lower-class persons who are more likely to be inducted and consequently more likely to be killed or wounded in battle. Morris Janowitz points out that during the Korean War "the lower income groups had four times the casualty rate of the highest groups, while Negro casualties were proportionately twice as numerous."[16] College deferments and the holding of exempt jobs seem to protect many middle-class youths from the draft. Moreover, under present application of the draft laws, a man is susceptible to induction until his 26th birthday. Since the average draftee has been 24 years old, this means that the bulk of them

[13] See Conscience and the War, *The New Republic,* pp. 7-8, April 15, 1967; and James W. Davis, Jr. and Kenneth M. Dolbeare, "Little Groups of Neighbors," pp. 108-110, Markham Publishing Co., Chicago, 1968.

[14] Robert McPfee Brown, In Conscience, I Must Break the Law, *Look,* 31, pp. 48ff, October 31, 1967.

[15] *Ibid.*

[16] Morris Janowitz, American Democracy and Military Service, *Trans-action,* p. 8, March 3, 1967.

have lived five years under the shadow of conscription. In addition, the old draft system proved to be inconsistent since each local draft board was free to exercise considerable discretion over who was drafted. Since there are some 4,000 local boards, we might have had 4,000 different sets of standards.

Proposals to reform the draft system have centered around three basic designs: a national lottery (which was enacted in late 1969), a volunteer army, and a system of national service. Selections emphasizing the last two designs will be introduced below. The national lottery design can be sketched briefly, in the form suggested by Senator Edward Kennedy in a 1968 legislative proposal. Basically his bill included six parts:

1. a lottery to select draftees
2. a uniform national standard for classifying and drafting men
3. young men would be called first instead of last as under the present system
4. broader grounds would be permitted for conscientious objection
5. an alternative national service would be considered
6. the term of the Director of the Selective Service would be limited to six years

The lottery that Kennedy proposed was designed to allow each local draft board to fill its quota by a method in which each individual would have an equal chance of being selected. For example, each month the Director of Selective Service would randomly pick several days of the month. The local board would then take those men in their jurisdiction whose birthday fell on those dates, and randomly select their quota from these names.

President Johnson recommended a lottery system to Congress in 1968. No action was taken on Johnson's bill, however, and in May of 1969 President Nixon proposed a similar plan. Nixon had earlier gone on record as supporting a voluntary army, but evidently he decided that the lottery would best provide the men needed for the Vietnam War. Nixon's plan was more restrictive than Kennedy's. It provided that 19-year-olds be first in eligibility for the draft, and attempted to set uniform national standards for local boards to apply in drafting men. It also limited a man's vulnerability, except in time of national emergency to one year, either at age 19 or when he completed his undergraduate education. Over the summer of 1969 Congress failed to act on the bill. In his September response, Nixon threatened to alter the draft process by executive decree if Congress continued to stall. At the same time, Nixon suspended the draft for three months while Congress continued its deliberation. In November of 1969 Congress passed Nixon's bill, and the first lottery under the new bill was held on December 1, 1969.

Prior to the drawing the expectation was that, for two-thirds of those in the draft pool, uncertainty as to likelihood of induction would be eliminated. Those with the first 122 birth dates drawn could count on induction while those drawn after number 244 would escape service. Only the intermediate third would be uncertain as to their status. Early indications are, however, that the rejoicing of the last third drawn was premature. Through the first three months of 1970 many draft boards have been unable to fill their quotas within the limits imposed by the Selective Service of 30 numbers per month.

Senator Mark Hatfield in "The Draft Should Be Abolished" argues for a volunteer army, and against the lottery system. He argues that with a good pay scale, fringe benefits, and a progressive recruitment program, a volunteer army can be assembled. He argues that such a scheme would neither produce a mercenary army nor an army of blacks, and that the plan is economically feasible in the long run.

Morris Janowitz's "American Democracy and Military Service" proposes a much more comprehensive plan based on the concept of national service. Under this plan 18-year-olds would be given three choices:

1. volunteer for the military service (a lottery would be used to fill quotas if there were not enough volunteers)
2. volunteer for some type of alternative national service
3. apply for exemption on the basis of being a conscientious objector

Alternative national service might be the Peace Corps, Vista, Police Cadet Corps, or some other program designed to train or serve individuals. An incentive plan would be used to help fill the least desirable jobs. For example, G. I. Bill benefits to help finance college educations could be provided for those who served in the military. Janowitz believes that this plan would give each individual more freedom of choice. It would also provide persons of low educational background with a means of gaining job skills in military or alternative national service. Finally, it would deal more leniently with conscientious objectors.

In whatever way we provide manpower, other serious issues related to military service will also need attention. Consider the issue of disobeying a military order. Don Duncan and J.A.C. Dunn provide a poignant examination of the plight of a military officer whose conscience forbids him to follow military orders, in "Notes Toward a Definition of the Uniform Code of Military Justice, as Particularly Applied to the Person of Captain Howard Levy." Although the Allies at the Nuremburg trials would not accept the argument that following legitimate orders was viable defense for those accused of war crimes, this general principle was not applied in Captain Levy's case. His problems began when he refused to teach Special Forces medics the basics of dermatology. The Army decided to "throw the book at him" rather than reassign him. The authors, in reconstructing the trial of Captain Levy, show what can happen when individual conscience conflicts with the orders of administrators of a national policy who fear exceptions and perhaps self-examination.

The issue can be sketched in sharp terms. Failure to provide a clear place for conscience in such matters will force some individuals to drop out, to reject as unjust those institutions which sacrifice individual needs to some purported collective good. Conversely, how far can our institutions be accommodated to individual needs without undercutting the institutions themselves? In short, how close will reality allow us to approach a laudable ideal in today's world?

5

THE FLOWERING
OF THE HIPPIE MOVEMENT

John Robert Howard

This article is written for people who, in future years, may want to understand something of the hippie movement. To that end, I have (1) described the hippie scene as an anthropologist might describe the culture of a South Sea island tribe, (2) reviewed some of the more prominent "explanations" for the movement, and (3) advanced what seems to me to be a useful theory of the hippie phenomenon.

The data for this article were drawn from literature by and about hippies and other Bohemians in American society, and from extensive informal participation in the hippie movement. . . .

"Hippie" is a generic term. It refers to a general orientation of which there are a number of somewhat different manifestations. In the following section, I shall discuss four character types commonly found on the hippie scene: (1) the visionaries, (2) the freaks and heads, (3) the midnight hippies, and (4) the plastic hippies.

THE VISIONARIES

The visionaries gave birth to the movement. It lived and died with them in Haight-Ashbury. Let us attempt here to understand what happened.

Reprinted from John Robert Howard, The Flowering of the Hippie Movement, *The Annals of the American Academy of Political and Social Science,* 382, pp. 44-55, March 1969.

The hippies offered, in 1966 and 1967, a serious, though not well-articulated, alternative to the conventional social system. To the extent that there was theory of change implicit in their actions, it might be summed up by the phrase "transformation by example."[1] Unlike political revolutionaries, they attempted no seizure of power. Rather, they asked for the freedom to "do their thing," that is, to create their own social system. They assumed, implicitly, that what they created would be so joyous, so dazzling, so "groovy" that the "straight"[2] would abandon his own "uptight" life and come over to their side. A kind of anti-intellectualism pervades hippie thinking; thus, their theory of change was never made explicit.

The essential elements in the hippie ethic are based on some very old notions—the mind-body dichotomy, condemnation of the worship of "things," the estrangement of people from each other, and so on. Drastically collapsed, the hippie critique of society runs roughly as follows: Success in this society is defined largely in terms of having money and a certain standard of living. The work roles which yield the income and the standard of living are, for the most part, either meaningless or intrinsically demeaning. Paul Goodman, a favored writer among the young estranged, has caught the essence of this indictment.

> Consider the men and women in TV advertisements demonstrating the product and singing the jingle. They are clowns and mannequins, in grimace, speech, and action. . . . What I want to call to attention in this advertising is not the economic problem of synthetic demand . . . but the human problem that these are human beings working as clowns; and the writers and designers of it are human beings thinking like idiots. . . .

> > "Juicily glubbily
> > Blubber is dubbily
> > delicious and nutritious
> > —eat it, kitty, it's good."[3]

Further, the rewards of the system, the accouterments of the standard of living, are not intrinsically satisfying. Once one has the split-level ranch-type house, the swimming pool, the barbecue, and the color-television set—then what? Does one, then, measure his progress in life by moving from a twen-

---

[1] Interestingly, Martin Buber, in "Paths in Utopia," suggested that the example of the *kibbutz* might transform the rest of the society. The values of the *kibbutzim* and those of the hippie movement are not dissimilar.

[2] We shall have occasion to speak frequently of "straights." The derivation of the word is even more obscure than that of "hippie." At one time, it had positive connotations, meaning a person who was honest or forthright. "He's straight, man" meant that the referent was a person to be trusted. As used in the hippie world, "straight" has a variety of mildly to strongly negative connotations. In its mildest form, it simply means an individual who does not partake of the behavior of a given subculture (such as that of homosexuals or marijuana users). In its strongest form, it refers to the individual who does not participate and who is also very hostile to the subculture.

[3] Paul Goodman, "Growing Up Absurd," pp. 25-26, Vintage Books, New York, 1960.

ty-one-inch set to a twenty-four-inch set? The American tragedy, according to the hippies, is that the "normal" American evaluates himself and others in terms of these dehumanizing standards.

The hippies, in a sense, invert traditional values. Rather than making "good" use of their time, they "waste" it; rather than striving for upward mobility, they live in voluntary poverty.

The dimensions of the experiment first came to public attention in terms of a number of hippie actions which ran directly counter to some of the most cherished values of the society. A group called the Diggers came into existence and began to feed people free in Golden Gate Park in San Francisco and in Constitution Park in Berkeley. They themselves begged for the food that they prepared. They repudiated the notion that the right of the people to satisfy their basic needs must be mediated by money. If they had food, one could share it with them, no questions asked. Unlike the Salvation Army, they did not require prayers as a condition of being fed; unlike the Welfare Department, they did not demand proof of being without means. If a person needed lodgings, they attempted to make space available. They repudiated the cash nexus and sought to relate to people in terms of their needs.

Free stores were opened in Berkeley and San Francisco, stores where a person could come and take what he needed. Rock groups such as Country Joe and the Fish gave free concerts in the park.

On the personal level, a rejection of the conventional social system involved dropping out. Given the logic of the hippie ethic, dropping out made sense. The school system prepares a person for an occupational role. The occupational role yields money and allows the person to buy the things which society says are necessary for the "good life." If society's definition of the good life is rejected, then dropping out becomes a sensible action, in that one does not want the money with which to purchase such a life. By dropping out, a person can "do his own thing." And that might entail making beads or sandals, or exploring various levels of consciousness, or working in the soil to raise the food that he eats.

They had a vision of people grooving together, and they attempted to remove those things which posed barriers—property, prejudice, and preconceptions about what is moral and immoral.

By the summer of 1968, it was generally felt by those who remained that Haight-Ashbury was no longer a good place. "It's pretty heavy out there on the street," a former methedrine addict remarked to me as we talked of changes in the community, and his sentiments were echoed in one of the underground newspapers, *The San Francisco Express Times*: "For at least a year now . . . the community as a common commitment of its parts, has deteriorated steadily. Most of the old crowd is gone. Some say they haven't actually left but are staying away from the street because of bad vibrations."

In those streets, in the summer of 1968, one sensed despair. Significantly, the agencies and facilities dealing with problems and disasters were still very much in evidence, while those which had expressed the *élan* and hope of the community either no longer existed, or were difficult to find. The Free Clinic was still there, as was the shelter for runaways, and the refuge for persons on bad trips; but free food was no longer served in the parks, and I looked for several days before finding the Diggers.

Both external pressures (coercion from the police and various agencies of city government) and internal contradictions brought about the disintegration of the experiment. Toward the end of this paper, I shall discuss external pressures and why they were mounted. At this point, I am analyzing only the internal contradictions of the hippie ethic.

Stated simply, the argument is as follows. The hippies assumed that voluntarism (every man doing his thing) was compatible with satisfying essential group and individual needs and with the maintenance of a social system in which there was an absence of power differentials and invidious distinctions based on, for example, wealth, sex, or race. That assumption is open to question. Voluntarism can only work where the participants in a social system have a sufficient understanding of the needs of the system to be willing to do things which they do not want to do in order for the system to persist. Put somewhat differently, each system has its own needs, and where voluntarism prevails, one must assume that the participants will both understand what needs to be done and be willing to do it.

Let me clarify by way of illustration. I asked one of the Diggers why they were no longer distributing food in the park.

> Well, man, it took a lot of organization to get that done. We had to scuffle to get the food. Then the chicks or somebody had to prepare it. Then we got to serve it. A lot of people got to do a lot of things at the right time or it doesn't come off. Well, it got so that people weren't doing it. I mean a cat wouldn't let us have his truck when we needed it or some chick is grooving somewhere and can't help out. Now you hate to get into a power bag and start telling people what to do but without that, man, well.

By refusing to introduce explicit rules designed to prevent invidious power distinctions from arising, such distinctions inevitably began to appear. Don S., a former student of mine who had moved to Haight-Ashbury, commented on the decline of the communal house in which he had lived.

> We had all kinds of people there at first and anybody could stay if there was room. Anybody could crash out there. Some of the motorcycle types began to congregate in the kitchen. That became *their* room, and if you wanted to get something to eat or a beer you had to step over them. Pretty soon, in a way, people were cut off from the food. I don't mean that they wouldn't give it to you, but you had to go on their "turf" to get it. It was like they had begun, in some very quiet and subtle way, to run things.

In the absence of external pressures, the internal contradictions of the hippie ethic would probably have led to a splintering of the experiment. Significantly, many of the visionaries are trying it again outside the city. There are rural communes throughout California. In at least some of them, allocation of task and responsibility is fairly specific. There is the attempt within the framework of their core values—freedom from hang-ups about property, status, sex, race, and the other furies which pursue the normal American—to establish the degree of order necessary to ensure the persistence of the system within which these values are expressed.

The visionaries used drugs, but that was not at the core of their behavior. For that reason, a distinction between them and more heavily drug-oriented hippies is legitimate. The public stereotype of the hippie is actually a composite of these two somewhat different types.

Let us now discuss the heavy drug users.

FREAKS AND HEADS

Drugs are a common element on the hip scene. The most frequently used are marijuana and hashish, which are derived from plants, and Lysergic Acid Diethylamine (LSD) and methedrine, which are chemical derivatives. Much less commonly used are opium and heroin. The plant derivatives are smoked, while the chemicals are taken orally, "mainlined" (shot into a vein), or "skin-popped" (injected under the skin). To account for the use of drugs among hippies, one must understand something of the mythology and ideology surrounding their use.

Marijuana is almost universally used by the hip and by hippies.[4] For some, it is simply a matter of being "in"; others find it a mild euphoriant. A subgroup places the use of drugs within a religious or ideological context.

Both freaks and heads are frequent users of one or more psychedelic agents; the term "freak," however, has negative connotations, suggesting either that the user is compulsive in his drug-taking, and therefore in a "bag," or that his behavior has become odd and vaguely objectionable as a result of sustained drug use. The mild nature of marijuana is suggested by the fact that, among drug users, one hears frequent mention of "pot heads" but never of "pot freaks." LSD and methedrine, on the other hand, seem to have the capacity to induce freakiness, the "acid freak" and the "speed freak" being frequently mentioned.

In 1966 and 1967 in Haight-Ashbury, the drug of choice for those who wanted to go beyond marijuana was LSD. An elaborate ideology surrounded its use, and something of a cult developed around the figure of Dr. Timothy Leary, the former Harvard professor who advocated it as the answer to the world's problems.

[4] Marijuana, also known as "weed," "pot," "grass," "maryjane," and "reefers," has not been proven to be physically addictive. It is one of a number of "natural" hallucinogens, some of which are found growing around any home: Jimson weed, Hawaiian wood roses, common sage and nutmeg, and morning-glory seeds. There are claims in Haight-Ashbury that the dried seeds of the bluebonnet, the state flower of Texas, have the same property. In California, the bluebonnet is called "Lupin" and grows wild along the highways, as does the Scotch broom, another highly praised drug source.

The LSD ideology

The major tenets of the ideology may be summed up as follows.

(1) LSD introduces the user to levels of reality which are ordinarily not perceived.

The straight might speak of "hallucinations," suggesting that the "acid" user is seeing things which are not real. The user admits that part of his trip consists of images and visions, but insists that part also consists of an appreciation of new and more basic levels of reality. To make the straight understand, some users argue that if a microscope had been placed under the eyes of a person during the Middle Ages, that person would have seen a level of reality for which there was no accounting within the framework of his belief system. He possibly would have spoken of "hallucinations" and demanded that microscopes be banned as dangerous.

Some users speak of being able, while on a trip, to feel the rhythm and pulse of the earth and to see the life within a tree. They contend that the trip leaves them with a capacity to experience reality with greater intensity and greater subtlety even when not high.

(2) LSD develops a certain sense of fusion with all living things.

The tripper speaks of the "collapse of ego," by which he means a breakdown of the fears, anxieties, rationalizations, and phobias which have kept him from relating to others in a human way. He also speaks of sensing the life process in leaves, in flowers, in the earth, in himself. This process links all things, makes all things one.

The ideology can be expanded, but these are some of its essential elements.

Three things account for the decline of "acid" use in Haight-Ashbury: (1) personal disillusionment on the part of many people with Timothy Leary, (2) a rise in the frequency of "acid burns" (the sale of fake LSD), and (3) the rise of methedrine use.

Let us deal with the decline and fall of Timothy Leary. Leary was, in a sense, the Johnny Appleseed of LSD. He was hailed by some as a new Christ. When the unbelievers began to persecute him, however, he had need of money to fight various charges of violation of drug laws which carried the possiblity of up to thirty years in jail. Possibly for that reason, he embarked upon what was, in essence, a theatrical tour. His show (billed as a religious celebration) was intended to simulate the LSD experience. It was bad theater, however, and consisted mostly of Leary sitting cross-legged on the stage in front of candles and imploring his audience, which might have had to pay up to $4.00 apiece, to commune with the billion-year-old wisdom in their cells. Leary's tour coincided in time with the beginning of his decline among hippies, and probably contributed to it. Additionally, the increased demand for LSD brought on traffic in fake "acid," the unsuspecting would-be tripper possibly getting only baking soda or powdered milk for his money.

In 1967 methedrine replaced LSD as the major drug in Haight-Ashbury. There is no evidence that marijuana is physically harmful. The evidence on LSD is open to either interpretation. Methedrine, on the other hand, is a dangerous drug. It is a type of amphetamine or "pep" pill and is most commonly referred to as "speed." Taken orally, it has the effect of a very powerful amphetamine. "It uses up body energy as a furnace does wood. . . . When it is shot [taken in the blood stream] it is said to produce an effect of watching the sun come up from one hundred miles away. And the user is bursting with energy." In an interview which I conducted in July 1968, a former "speed freak" discussed the effects of the drug.

> You're really going. You know you can do anything when you're high on speed. You seem to be able to think clearer and really understand things. You feel powerful. And the more you drop the stuff the more you feel like that. It kills the appetite so, over time, malnutrition sets in. You're in a weakened state and become susceptible to all kinds of diseases. I caught pneumonia when I was on speed. But I couldn't stop. I was falling apart, but it was like I was running so fast I couldn't hit the ground. It was a kind of dynamic collapse.

From 1966 through 1968, there was a discernible pattern in drug use in Haight-Ashbury, a pattern which has relevance in terms of the effectiveness of drug laws. I would advance as a proposition that the volume in use of a drug is determined not by the laws, but by the effects of the drug. If a drug is relatively harmless (as with marijuana), its use will spread, irrespective of severe laws. If it is harmful, its use will be limited, despite more lenient laws (as with methedrine). That heroin, cocaine, and the like have not penetrated Haight-Ashbury can probably be explained in terms of the fact that their deleterious effects are well known. Methedrine was an unknown, was tried, and was found to be dangerous; thus, one frequently hears in Haight-Ashbury the admonition that "speed kills."

In summary, then, the pattern of use probably reflects the effects of each drug. Marijuana, being relatively mild, is widely used. LSD is much more powerful; a person may have a good trip or a very bad one; thus, its pattern of use is checkered. Methedrine is dangerous; consequently, powerful sentiment against it has begun to form. Hippies, then, are very much predisposed to go beyond tobacco and alcohol in terms of drug use, and if what has been said here is correct, the pattern of use should be seen as a realistic response to the effects of the drugs available to them.

THE PLASTIC HIPPIE

Everybody is familiar with the story of King Midas who turned whatever he touched into gold. Ironically, this faculty eventually brings tragedy to his life and, with it, some insight into the nature of love. In a strange kind of way, the story of Midas is relevant in terms of the hippie movement. The hippies repudiate the values of conventional society, particularly as these relate to work and commerce. They decry the consumption mania—the ethic and passion which compels people to buy more and more. They grieve that so many people are locked into the system, making or selling things which other people do not need, and buying from them equally useless things. The system is such that every man is both victim and victimizer.

Their repudiation of conventional society brought notoriety to the hippies, and, ironically, they themselves became a marketable item, another product to be hawked in the market place. And the more they defamed the commercial process, the more they became a "hot" commercial item.

Those who used the hippie phenomenon to make money appealed in part to an audience which wanted to be titillated and outraged by revelations about sex orgies and drug parties, and in part to adolescents and young people who were not inclined to drop out, but who viewed wearing the paraphernalia of the hippie—love beads, headbands, Benjamin Franklin eyeglasses, leather shirts, and the like—as daring and exciting. These were the plastic hippies.

Any movement runs the risk of becoming merely a fad, of being divested of substance and becoming mostly style. Symbols which might at one time have powerfully expressed outrage at society's oppression and absurdity become merely fashionable and decadent. By the spring of 1968, the plastic hippie was common in the land, and leather shirts and trousers sold in Haight-Ashbury shops for more than $100. Some of the suits at Brooks Brothers did not cost as much.

In April of 1968, I interviewed Deans of Students at four Bay Area colleges— San José State College, Stanford University, Foothill Junior College, and the College of San Mateo. The research, financed by the United States Office of Education, focused on students who dropped out of school to live the hippie life. Uniformly, the deans indicated that, despite appearances, there were very few hippies on campus. Despite long hair and beads, most of their students were as career-oriented and grade-conscious as ever. They wore the paraphernalia of the outsider, but were not themselves outsiders.

The plastic hippies have, unintentionally, had an impact on the hippie movement. First, in one important respect, their behavior overlaps with the core behavior of the true hippie—many are users of marijuana. By the summer of 1968, the demand for "grass" had become so great that there was a severe shortage in the Haight-Ashbury area. Beyond the obvious consideration of price, the shortage had two consequences. The number of "burns" increased, a "burn" being the sale of some fraudulent substance—alfalfa, oregano, ordinary tobacco, and the like—as genuine marijuana. And a synthetic marijuana was put on the market.

The "pot squeeze" and the resulting burns, along with persistent but unsubstantiated rumors that "the Mob" (organized crime) had moved in and taken over the lucrative trade, contributed to what was, by the summer of 1968, an accelerating sense of demoralization in the Haight-Ashbury community.

THE MIDNIGHT HIPPIE

Most hippies are in their teens or early twenties. There are a significant number of people, however, who share a whole complex of values with hippies, but who are integrated into the straight world to the extent of having families and careers. Most of these people are in their thirties. They were in college during the 1950's and were nonconformists by the standards of the time. Journalists and commentators of the 1950's decried the apathy of youth and spoke of a "silent generation." These people were part of that minority of youth who were not silent. They were involved, even then, in civil rights and peace and the other issues which were to engage the passions of youth in the 1960's.

There was no hippie scene into which these people could move. They could have dropped out of school, but there was no Haight-Ashbury for them to drop into. Consequently, they finished school and moved on into the job world. Significantly, many are in professions which can accommodate a certain amount of Bohemianism. They teach in colleges and universities and thus avoid working the conventional nine-to-five day, or work as book salesmen on the college and university circuit. Relatively few are in straight occupations such as engineering or insurance or banking. They are in jobs in which there is some tolerance for new ideas and which facilitate trying out various styles of life.

The midnight hippie provides an important link between straight society and the hippie world. The straight finds hippies strange, weird, or disgusting. Therefore, he views any action taken against them as justified. The midnight hippie, on the other hand, looks straight. He has a straight job, and does not evoke the same immediate hostility from the straight that the hippie does. The midnight hippie's relative social acceptance allows him to articulate and justify the hippie point of view with at least some possibility of being listened to and believed.

HIPPIES, BEATS, AND THE "LOST GENERATION"

How may we account for the hippie phenomenon? Is it simply the traditional rebellion of youth against parental authority, or does it have more profound implications for the society and greater consequences for those who take part in it?

I am inclined to view it as more significant than previous youth movements. Hippies differ in important ways from the beats of the 1950's or the "lost generation" of the 1920's, two groups with whom they have often been compared. In attempting to account for the movement, I have developed a theory of social deviance which identifies its unique features and yields certain predictions with regard to its future.

VERTICAL AND LATERAL DEVIANCE

The literature of sociology is rich in theories of deviance. Some focus on "cause," as, for example, the delinquency theories of Cloward and Ohlin which suggest that lower-class boys, in the face of inadequate opportunities to realize middle-class goals, resort to various forms of unlawful behavior. Others deal with the process whereby a person learns to be a deviant, Howard Becker's paper "Becoming a Marijuana User" being a major example.

In the approach taken here, neither cause nor process is the focus. Rather, I identify two types of deviance: vertical and lateral. The dimensions of each type seem to be useful in differentiating the hippies from earlier Bohemians, and in reaching conclusions about their future.

Vertical and lateral deviance occur in the context of social systems in which differentiations according to rank exist, that is, officer-recruit, teacher-student, adult-child, boss-employee, or guard-convict. Inevitably, certain privileges and prerogatives attach to the superior rank. That is one of the things which makes them superior. Adults can smoke, consume alcoholic beverages, obtain drivers' licenses, vote, and do a host of other things which are denied to children or teen-agers.

Vertical deviance occurs when persons in a subordinate rank attempt to enjoy the privileges and prerogatives of those in a superior rank. Thus, the ten-year-old who sneaks behind the garage to smoke is engaging in a form of vertical deviance, as is the fourteen-year-old who drives a car despite being too young to get a license and the sixteen-year-old who bribes a twenty-two-year-old to buy him a six-pack of beer. They are attempting to indulge themselves in ways not deemed appropriate for persons of their rank.

Lateral deviance occurs when persons in a subordinate rank develop their own standards and norms apart from and opposed to those of persons in a superior rank. Thus, the teen-ager who smokes pot rather than tobacco is engaging in lateral deviance, as is the seventeen-year-old girl who runs away to live in a commune, rather than eloping with the boy next door. Lateral deviance occurs in a context in which the values of the nondeviant are rejected. The pot-smoking seventeen-year-old, wearing Benjamin Franklin eyeglasses and an earring, does not share his parents' definition of the good life. Whereas value consensus characterizes vertical deviance, there is a certain kind of value dissensus involved in lateral deviance.

Let us explore the implications of these two types of deviance.

Where vertical deviance occurs, power ultimately remains with the privileged. The rule-breaker wants what they have. They can control him by gradually extending prerogatives to him in return for conforming behavior. They have the power to offer conditional rewards and, in that way, can control and shape the deviant's behavior. The sixteen-year-old is told that he can take the car if he behaves himself at home. Where lateral deviance occurs, the possibility of conditional rewards being used to induce conformity disappears. The deviant does not want what the privileged have; therefore, they cannot control him by promising to let him "have a little taste." From the standpoint of the privileged, the situation becomes an extremely difficult one to handle. Value dissensus removes a powerful lever for inducing conformity. The impotent, incoherent rage so often expressed by adults towards hippies possibly derives from this source. A letter to the Editor of the *Portland Oregonian* exemplifies this barely controlled anger.

> Why condone this rot and filth that is "hippie" in this beautiful city of ours? Those who desecrate our flag, refuse to work, flaunt their sexual freedom, spread their filthy diseases and their garbage in public parks are due no charitable consideration. The already overloaded taxpayer picks up the bill.
>
> If every city so afflicted would give them a bum's rush out of town, eventually with no place to light, they might just wake up to find how stupid and disgusting they are. Their feeling of being so clever and original might fade into reality. They might wake up and change their tactics.[5]

The second implication follows from the first. Being unable to maintain control via conditional rewards, the parent, adult or other representative of authority is forced to adopt more coercive tactics. This, of course, has the consequence of further estranging the deviant. What constitutes coercion varies with the situation, and can range all the way from locking a teen-age girl in her room to setting the police on anyone with long hair and love beads. Lateral deviance has a certain potential for polarization built into it. To the extent that polarization takes place, the deviant becomes more committed to his deviance.

The third implication follows from the first two and allows us to differentiate hippies from earlier Bohemians. Bennett Berger, the sociologist, contends that the Bohemians of the 1920's and the hippies of the 1960's are similar as regards ideology. Borrowing from Malcolm Cowley's *Exile's Return*, he identifies a number of seemingly common elements in the thinking of the two groups, and, following Cowley, suggests that Bohemians since the mid-nineteenth century have tended to subscribe to the same set of ideas. The ideology of Bohemianism includes: the idea of salvation by the child, an emphasis on self-expression, the notion that the body is a temple where there is nothing unclean, a belief in living for the moment, in female equality, in liberty, and in the possibility of perceiving new levels of reality. There is also a love of the people and places presumably still unspoiled by the corrupt values of society. The noble savages may be Negroes or Indians or Mexicans. The exotic places may be Paris or Tangier or Tahiti or Big Sur.[6]

---

[5] Letter to the Editor, *Portland Oregonian,* p. 22, July 31, 1968.

[6] Bennett Berger, Hippie Morality—More Old Than New, *Trans-action,* **5**, no. 2, pp. 19-20, December, 1967.

I would dispute Bennett Berger's analysis and contend that the differences between the hippies and the lost generation are quite profound. The deviant youth of the 1920's simply lived out what many "squares" of the time considered the exciting life—the life of the "swinger." Theirs was a kind of deviance which largely accepted society's definitions of the bad and the beautiful. Lawrence Lipton contrasted values of the lost generation with those of the beatniks, but his remarks are even more appropriate in terms of the differences between the lost generation and the hippies.

> Ours was not the dedicated poverty of the present-day beat. We coveted expensive illustrated editions and bought them when we had ready cash, even if it meant going without other things. We wanted to attend operas and symphony concerts, even if it meant a seat up under the roof in the last gallery or ushering the rich to their seats in the "diamond horseshoe. . . ." We had disaffiliated ourselves from the rat race . . . but we had not rejected the rewards of the rat race. We had expensive tastes and we meant to indulge them, even if we had to steal books from the bookstores where we worked, or shoplift, or run up bills on charge accounts that we never intended to pay, or borrow money from banks and leave our cosigners to pay it back with interest. We were no sandal and sweatshirt set. We liked to dress well, if unconventionally, and sometimes exotically, especially the girls. We lived perforce on crackers and cheese most of the time but we talked like gourmets, and if we had a windfall we spent the money in the best restaurants in town, treating our friends in a show of princely largess.[7]

Could they have been more unlike the hippies? The lost generation was engaging in vertical deviance. They wanted the perquisites of the good life but did not want to do the things necessary to get them. They were a generation which had seen its ranks severely decimated in World War I and, having some sense of the temporal nature of existence, possibly did not want to wait their turn to live the beautiful life. Their deviance was at least comprehensible to their elders. They wanted what any "normal" person would want.

From 1957 through 1960, the beat movement flourished, its major centers being the North Beach section of San Francisco and Greenwich Village in New York. The beat movement and the hippie movement are sufficiently close in time for the same individual to have participated in both. Ned Polsky, writing about the Greenwich Village beat scene in 1960, indicated that "the attitudes of beats in their thirties have spread rapidly downward all the way to the very young teen-agers (13-15)."[8] It is not unlikely, then, that some hippies began as beats. There are several reasons for suggesting beat influence on the hippie movement. The beat indictment of society is very much like that of the hippies.

---

[7]Lawrence Lipton, "The Holy Barbarians," p. 284, Grove Press, New York, 1959.

[8]Ned Polsky, The Village Beat Scene: Summer 1960, *Dissent,* 3, no. 3, p. 341, Summer, 1960.

Lipton recounted Kenneth Rexroth's observations on the social system and its values:

> As Kenneth Rexroth has put it, you can't fill the heads of young lovers with "buy me the new five-hundred-dollar deep-freeze and I'll love you" advertising propaganda without poisoning the very act of love itself; you can't hop up your young people with sadism in the movies and television and train them to commando tactics in the army camps, to say nothing of brutalizing them in wars, and then expect to "untense" them with Coca Cola and Y.M.C.A. hymn sings. Because underneath . . . the New Capitalism . . . and Prosperity Unlimited—lies the ugly fact of an economy geared to war production, a design, not for living, but for death.[9]

Like the hippie a decade later, the beat dropped out. He disaffiliated himself, disaffiliation being "a voluntary self-alienation from the family cult, from moneytheism and all its works and ways." He spoke of a New Poverty as the answer to the New Prosperity, indicating that "it is important to make a living but it is even more important to make a life."

Both the hippie and the beat engage in lateral deviance. Their behavior is incomprehensible to the square. Why would anyone want to live in poverty? Given the nature of their deviance, they cannot be seduced back into squareness. Lipton recounts the remarks of a beat writer to the square who offered him an advertising job: "I'll scrub your floors and carry your slops to make a living, but I will not lie for you, pimp for you, stool for you, or rat for you."[10]

The values of beats and hippies are virtually identical: the two movements differ principally with regard to social organization. Hippies have attempted to form a community. There were beat enclaves in San Francisco and New York, but no beat community. The difference between a ghetto and a community is relevant in terms of understanding the difference between the two movements. In a ghetto, there is rarely any sense of common purpose or common identity. Every man is prey to every other man. In a community, certain shared goals and values generate personal involvement for the common good. Haight-Ashbury was a community in the beginning but degenerated into a ghetto. Significantly, however, more viable rural communities have been established by hippies in response to the failure of urban experiment. The beats had neither any concept of community nor any dream of transforming society.

Given their attempt to establish a viable community, the hippies will probably survive longer than the beats, and should have a more profound impact upon the society. As has been indicated, if a society fails to seduce the lateral deviant away from his deviance it may move to cruder methods (police harassment, barely veiled indictments to hoodlums to attack the deviants, and the like). A functioning community can both render assistance to the deviant in the face of

[9]Lipton, *op. cit.* p. 150.
[10]*Ibid.*

these assaults and sustain his commitment to the values which justify and explain his deviance.

The beats, then, have influenced the hippies. Their beliefs are very similar, and there is probably an overlap in membership. The hippies' efforts to establish self-supporting communities suggest, however, that their movement will survive longer than did that of the beats.

In summary, the hippies have commented powerfully on some of the absurdities and irrationalities of the society. It is unlikely that the straight will throw away his credit cards and move to a rural commune, but it is equally unlikely that he will very soon again wear the emblems of his straightness with quite so much self-satisfaction.

6

CHALLENGE TO THE HIPPIES

On August 22, Haight-Ashbury, the national campus of the hippie cult, came alive for millions. CBS-TV's Harry Reasoner was exploring the "Who, What, When, Where and Why" of the hippie subculture. Some viewers came to jeer; others to learn. Most shared the concern of program producer Warren Wallace. Of this dropout group he noted fearfully: "The hippies are a sympton of something that is terribly wrong with us and what we offer young people. Their answer in soft drugs can mean a higher price on their health than they ever would have expected." Still, a first impression of these young people (despite a militant unwashedness) is how young and good-looking they are—or were.

Viewers had questions and impressions. Is a hippie a young kid with long hair, goofy clothes, a string of beads, a sprig of flowers—painted or real? Not exactly, although such accessories, along with love-buttons, make hippies easy to spot in any crowd. Oldsters looked beneath the decorations and saw only the Bohemians of the 1920's. Youngsters heard only a bongo of altruism.

The hippie message was clear. Hippies reject material goods and gain, and to prove it they leave suburban homes (garaged cars and grilled steaks) to seek peace of mind, peace of life—and peace, brother, peace. Their live-and-let-love philosophy disturbs parents and society, but even more disturbing is the way they go after truth. When they want to find God or discover Self while floating on a cool sea of warm jello, they smoke pot, travel on LSD, and sample instant

Reprinted from Challenge to the Hippies, *America*, p. 216, September 2, 1967.

relief drugs. Suddenly, the world is, like, beautiful, and maybe real—hangover, hospitalization and all.

Yet the hippies are in trouble. William I. Nichols, publisher of *This Week* magazine, thinks they have had it. He gives three reasons: 1) many are committing suicide through massive physical self-abuse; 2) with original hippies "graduating back" into the adult world, ex-hippies now abound; 3) race riots make the hippies seem "silly, irrelevant and strangely out of date."

Nichols has a point. The race riots have silenced bongo beats with a human noise. Somehow body-painting and toilet-paper throwing don't fit the mood of a nation to be rebuilt. There is plenty of real action to go around and this leaves no time for being bored.

Admittedly, hippies "just don't dig the civil rights movement," because "Negroes are fighting to become what we have rejected." But ghetto statistics and living conditions can't be rejected—even by a hippie with "love buttons." Talking about love is good; doing something about it is better. How? They could try, says Nichols, identifying with their favorite hero, St. Francis of Assisi, who rejected riches and left home to preach love. St. Francis didn't just sit there, he did something. He founded a religious order to serve the poor and the sick— including lepers.

If it gets pretty boring just to sit there and be nothing but a Nothing Person, they might remember that VISTA at home and the Peace Corps abroad are understaffed. There is no call for Nothing Persons now.

7

DRUGS: THE MOUNTING MENACE OF ABUSE

Roland H. Berg

An epidemic of drug abuse is sweeping the nation. The contagion, centered on college campuses, also infects high-school students and adults in our cities, suburbs and small towns. No one is immune.

We are a drug-dependent society. At its peak is the small, perhaps diminishing, group of narcotic addicts: urban, poor, colored. At its base are the millions of Americans who can't sleep, wake up or feel comfortable without drugs. Most of these are white and affluent. The kids smoke marijuana and pop in hallucinogens; the parents swallow medicines that may be needless, self-prescribed or harmful: barbiturates, amphetamines, laxatives, pain-killers and tummy soothers. They don't know—or won't admit—they are "hooked" on drugs. Their habits create no social stigma. With the exception of marijuana, STP and LSD, their drugs have accepted medicinal uses and can be found in most bathroom cabinets. The trouble lies not in the pills, but in the people.

Drugs are no longer only a slum problem. Some experts even feel that addiction among people living in the hope-killing ghettos is decreasing. They see them rejecting the heroin retreat, not wanting to stay where they are, but get out. Heroin boxes them in.

Reprinted from Roland H. Berg, Drugs: The Mounting Menace of Abuse, *Look*, 31, no. 16, pp. 11-16, August 8, 1967.

Meanwhile, serious drug problems sweep through white America: Junction City, Kans.; Pagedale, Mo.; Woodford, Va.; Plymouth, Mich.—places with apple-pie smells and wind-snapped flags. No one knows how many middle-class Americans are involved. The problem is too new for an accurate head count. But there are indicators. There are 12 billion amphetamine and barbiturate tablets and 50 million tranquilizers manufactured in the U.S. About half of these are diverted into the illegal market. In many communities, police report, arrests for the sale of illicit drugs are up 400 percent this year. Drug arrests in wealthy Westchester County, N.Y., for example, jumped from 309 in 1965 to 700 in 1966. Dr. Jean Paul Smith, of the U.S. Bureau of Drug Abuse Control (BDAC), concludes: "In the middle class, we are seeing much more drug use and abuse than ever before."

Police officials estimate that between 15 and 50 percent of the teen-agers in *any* suburban community may be experimenting with marijuana. In one West Coast town, 15 high-school kids got arrested for using the drug. One father, a church deacon, was the supplier. This spring, at least five New England prep-school boys got busted for drug use; one of them was the son of a U.S. congressman. A 1967 survey of 2,800 students in upper-middle-class Great Neck, N.Y.'s two high schools showed that eight percent admitted smoking marijuana; six percent took barbiturates without a doctor's prescription; two percent used LSD or DMT. Nassau County DA William Cahn puts the figure higher. He says that one kid out of every six (about 60,000) in his county is experimenting with barbiturates, amphetamines and marijuana. In a night-long sweep through Ventura County, Calif., last April, cops netted 50 people, ages 15 to 32, and found marijuana, LSD, pills and heroin. The raid was the largest in the county's history and hit high-income neighborhoods. Two weeks earlier, the same police arrested 14 other suspects, including two 12-year-olds accused of selling marijuana to teen-agers. Burnell H. Blanchard, supervisor of the Southern California branch of the state's Bureau of Narcotics, says that he is finding more "major peddlers" in high schools. Not long ago, two high-school boys were arrested for selling marijuana by the kilo (2.2 pounds). Last year, a 14-year-old girl tried to make a ten-kilo sale in Northern California. "Our undercover agents," Mr. Blanchard reports, "are being offered marijuana in ton lots." Arrests don't always enlighten parents. When 22 teen-agers got busted in Queens, N.Y., for selling or possessing LSD, marijuana, barbiturates and amphetamines, one anguished mother told the New York *Times*: "I'm still in shock, he was never deprived of anything. Do you know what this does to us? We'll have to move. We live in a small community."

LSD and marijuana use, the major problem on the college level, reaches from pot-smoking midshipmen at the U.S. Naval Academy to acid heads in Berkeley. Harvard's freshman class may be "the hippiest ever." John H. Finlator, director of the Bureau of Drug Abuse Control, which tracks down illicit pill and LSD markets, told LOOK: "Colleges don't talk to them today. So they listen to Leary and Ginsberg tell them, 'Light up the candles, let's tune in, turn on, take off.'"

Adults may be the biggest drug abusers, a fact hard to check and easy to hide. They can pay others to take their risks: Some women have their maids sneak in their pill supply while they're in the hospital taking the cure. Police and doctors are reluctant to report cracks in the pillars of their communities.

Who are the affluent drug takers? They are the 30-year-old architect in Atlanta who drank and took pills and now can't work. Or the construction engineer who got into debt and took pills for two years to calm his nerves. He can't stop. Or the insurance salesman who drank all the time, and his wife thought the big thing to do was take pills and get high with him. Or the Detroit, Mich., lawyer who took amphetamines to keep him alert through a tough real-estate problem that lasted several weeks. He couldn't stop taking them. He had to use barbiturates to sleep. Over a two-year span of increasing dependence, he couldn't appear in court or work, he got disbarred, his marriage fell apart.

Detective Paul McKenna, head of the Morris County (N.J.) Prosecutor's Narcotics Bureau, tells about suburban housewives who get started on amphetamines to lose weight. "We have husbands call in and say, 'My wife is getting such-and-such a drug from this doctor. Can you stop this?' " Sometimes they can. Who are the drug abusers in affluent Morris? A pregnant nurse using codeine, a pregnant wife on amphetamines, a husband and wife on narcotics for ten years (the neighbors never knew). One matron had teen-age pill parties and got the kids running burglaries. A woman phoned her pharmacy, posing as a nurse, to get Doriden. A chemist rigged up his own lab and started making mescaline.

Dr. Vernelle Fox, an Atlanta, Ga., psychiatrist, sees middle-income, middle-aged patients with problems of alcoholism *and* pill abuse. They start drinking and find that pills help the hangovers. A dangerous cycle begins: drink; pills to calm the hangover; pills to pep them up; drink to relax. Dr. Fox also sees the spree-drinking businessman with his little box of Librium or Doriden. Other drug abusers are in the over-65 group, who turn to pills to blur the fears of old age.

Middle-class people are afraid to admit they depend on drugs. Although they are using pills, many may not realize they've got a problem. Some may not even know they are taking them. Dr. Jerome Levine, of the National Institute of Mental Health (NIMH), says: "There are a great many unknown addicts; they are unknown to themselves and to the community." One Georgia physician had been drinking heavily and using amphetamines. He told his psychiatrist that he had only a drinking problem. But the psychiatrist went to his home and found pills scattered all over the rooms and furniture.

Most of these drug takers get their pills from a legal source—a doctor or pharmacist. The affluent user becomes proficient at talking doctors into writing prescriptions. He studies medical journals and relates lengthy medical histories that call for the drug he wants. Or he tells the physician about the wonderful relief he got from a drug his former doctor prescribed.

Some users go from doctor to doctor, collecting prescriptions, taking them to different drugstores. They go back and tell the pharmacist they lost the pills; he means well and refills the prescription too soon. Few people challenge drug abuse among steady bill payers.

The more desperate steal prescription pads, forge prescriptions, alter amounts and dosage, or impersonate a doctor and telephone prescriptions to a pharmacy.

There are also doctors who do nothing but write prescriptions—300-400 a day at $5 a head. Others, nearing retirement, let their names be used for mail-order prescriptions. Last March, an Owingsville, Ky., doctor and a gas-station operator from Salt Lick, Ky., who had been working together, were sentenced to a year and a $1,000 fine for selling amphetamines. The BDAC agents who testified said the doctor had ordered 756,000 tablets from New York and Philadelphia drug companies. "Enough," said Judge Mac Swinford, who heard the case, "to supply the whole state of Kentucky."

These middle-class drug abusers live in a chemical world that may be more dangerous and harder to escape than their old one. Barbiturates, hallucinogens, amphetamines and certain tranquilizers are dangerous and sometimes addictive.

Essentially, all drugs are harmful. Even when used medically, they do their good deeds by unnaturally altering the function or chemical structure of various organs in the body. A physician weighs carefully potential harm against potential good. The nonmedical, unsupervised use of drugs holds no safeguards, only dangers.

LSD is a case in point. More and more users, taking LSD in city apartments and off-campus houses, are ending up in hospitals with psychoses. Early, inconclusive reports indicate that LSD may also damage chromosomes—the cells that dictate our inherited characteristics. Hard-core acid heads are injecting LSD into their veins—mainlining—for a faster high (the drug takes 15 to 45 minutes when swallowed). They are suffering the needle-induced diseases of the heroin and amphetamine mainliner: local abscesses, phlebitis, hepatitis, endocarditis and pulmonic foreign-body reactions.

A new, more powerful drug, STP, appeared last month in Greenwich Village, San Francisco, and San Bernardino, Orange and Riverside counties in California. At least 12 persons have been hospitalized after swallowing blue-spotted, white STP capsules. The drug, dubbed a "mega-hallucinogen" and "the caviar of the psychedelics," takes a user on a three-to-four-day drug "trip." (LSD lasts eight to twelve hours.) There are two dangers already known about STP: (1) It may cause atropine poisoning, with respiratory paralysis. (2) The tranquilizer chlorpromazine, used to calm down LSD "trippers," can't be taken because it heightens the effects of STP. The letters may come from a motor-fuel additive named STP which means scientifically treated petroleum.

The case against marijuana isn't clear. Many authorities testify that smoking pot is no more injurious than smoking tobacco—which is not without harm. Physiologically, that's true. Marijuana has been wrongfully indicted as a narcotic. But there may be other dangers in the user's growing indifference to society.

The hang-up on stimulants, depressants and tranquilizers often begins with the physician prescribing the medication for legitimate need. The dangers grow from there. Tranquilizers and amphetamines may induce psychic or emotional dependence. Amphetamines stimulate a feeling of well-being. They pep you up. But they can also cause permanent, organic brain damage or serious psychiatric disorders.

Barbiturates are depressants that help in illness and insomnia. But abused—as they are on a large scale—they have become a major drug menace. Heavy use makes a person stagger, slur his speech, become uncoordinated. An excess can paralyze the breathing center of the brain and cause death. Each year, some 3,000 Americans take a fatal dose, many accidentally. Barbiturates lead all other drugs as a cause of death.

It is easy to take an overdose. The drug confuses thinking, and the body builds tolerance, requiring larger and more dangerous doses to achieve the desired effect. The heavy barbiturate user will suffer the agonies of withdrawal, usually far more dangerous than a narcotic addict's. Barbiturate withdrawal, unless under a physician's supervision, may take as long as three weeks and can result in convulsions and death.

An added danger is that the average physician seldom recognizes a case of true barbiturate abuse. Dr. Sherman Kieffer of NIMH told LOOK: "It's quite true doctors in some suburban areas don't know barbiturate addicts or how to treat them. This is a very serious gap."

Why do we take these drugs? The pressures and demands of society may become too much for adults to bear. They may have family and job problems and anxieties, the feeling of being trapped by split-level existence. They find artificial ways to escape from hard realities. "But more than this," says Dr. Fox, "they are unable to adjust to middle-class adulthood—its mores, hang-ups and pressures. They escape into drugs. This is the insidious kind of thing: They take pills to sleep and pills to stay awake, pills to calm down and pep up. They take drugs to keep going through life."

College and high-school kids are different. They are just starting life. Why do they take drugs?

Dr. Kenneth Keniston, associate professor of psychiatry at Yale University, goes beyond the pat explanations—rebellion, kicks, etc.—to add a new theory. At a Drug Education Conference held in Washington, D.C., he claimed that today's youths who seek an answer to the traditional cry, "Who am I?" face special problems that yesterday's adolescents didn't confront.

Dr. Keniston believes it takes more knowledge to get ahead nowadays, and modern youth is crawling into an inner shell to avoid being overstimulated by the discordant sights and sounds of modern living. The here and now, Dr. Keniston says, have become overly important. How the inner self expands and responds to the immediate experience is all-important. Anything that promises—however falsely—to enlarge the parameters of the mind, is sought after eagerly.

Research psychologist Richard H. Blum, at Stanford University's Institute for the Study of Human Problems, went to the source to learn who takes drugs and why. His findings illuminate Dr. Keniston's. Dr. Blum and his associates interviewed at random 200 persons, young and old, living in the San Francisco Bay area. Their interviews painted a revealing composite of the kind of people who are heavy drug users.

They are more often white than Negro, and they are better educated, divorced more often, earn more money and have fewer political ties than the average person. Also, they rebel against authority and frequently express dislike of their parents, themselves and their work. Heavy users reveal strong likes and dislikes, are compulsive about their activities and show numerous signs of inner conflicts. They use drugs for religious motives or for self-analysis. As a group, they told of frequent use of medicinal drugs during childhood.

Dr. Blum concludes that those students and adults who turn to LSD, marijuana and pills are "inner" people; those who do not abuse drugs, he calls the "outer" people. Inner people concentrate on the thoughts that swirl within their heads. Outer people look to external experiences, what's happening around them.

Contrary to claims of indescribable delights by some drug takers, most people abuse drugs to relieve anxiety. They're not pursuing pleasure, they just hurt less on drugs. This is true also of hard-narcotic users. A heroin addict told a reporter, "You don't even know what I'm talking about; you feel okay all the time. Me, it costs me $100 a day just to stop hurting so much."

Fundamentally, drug abuse is a health and social problem, not a police problem. Stopping the hurt isn't easy. The solution is education, not punishment. We are a pill-oriented society, conditioned to find happiness through chemistry. If any "crash" program is needed, it should call for more knowledge and understanding of the role of drugs. It should focus on the kids who are trying drugs today on college campuses and in hippy hangouts. They have the most to lose from drug abuse.

We must make the outside world more attractive than the inner. Arresting people and putting them behind bars is no better than letting them hide behind a chemical curtain. Either way, they are in prison.

A DIRECTORY OF DRUGS: WHAT THEY DO, WHERE THEY COME FROM, THE HARM THEY CAUSE

Drug	Slang Names	Description	Medical Use	Risks of abuse
HALLUCINOGENS				
Marijuana *Cannabis sativa*	pot grass boo	Flowering, resinous top of female hemp plant	None	Altered perceptions. impaired judgment
Peyote *Lophophora williamsii*	cactus	Dried cactus buttons containing mescaline. Chewed or brewed	Some experimental study	Visual hallucinations, anxiety, paranoia, possible psychosis
LSD *Lysergic acid diethylamide*	acid hawk the chief	Synthetic chemical 400 times more powerful than mescaline	Some experimentation	Visual and auditory hallucinations impaired judgment, possible psychosis
DMT *Dimethyltryptamine*		Synthetic chemical similar to mushroom alkaloid psilocybin	Some experimentation. Chemical warfare	Possible psychotic reaction
STP *Unidentified*	none	Atropine-like synthetic	None	Same effects as LSD, but more intense and lasting 3-4 days
STIMULANTS				
Cocaine *Erythroxylon coca*	coke corinne happy dust snow	Isolated alkaloid of coca leaf	Anesthesia of eye and throat	Loss of appetite, irritability, weight loss, insomnia
Benzedrine *Amphetamine sulphate*	A bennies (pep pills)	Synthetic central-nervous-system stimulant	Treatment of obesity, narcolepsy, encephalitis, fatigue, depression	Nausea, hypertension, irritability, confusion, delirium, aggressiveness
Dexedrine *Dextroamphetamine sulphate*	A dexies copilots (pep pills)	Same as above	Same as above	Same as above
Methedrine *Methamphetamine hydrachloride*	A crystals (pep pills)	Same as above	Same as above	Same as above

DEPRESSANTS

Nembutal *Pentobarbital sodium*	yellow-jackets	Barbituric acid derivative	Sedation, treatment of insomnia	Incoherency depression, possible respiratory arrest, addiction with withdrawal symptoms including vomiting, tremors, convulsions
Seconal *Secobarbital sodium*	red birds	Same as above	Same as above	Same as above
Luminal *Phenobarbital*	purple hearts	Same as above	Same as above	Same as above
Amytal *Amobarbital sodium*	blue heavens	Same as above	Same as above	Same as above
Miltown and Equanil *Meprobamate*		Non-barbiturate sedatives	Same as above	Same as above
Doriden *Glutethimide*		Same as above	Same as above	Same as above
Librium *Chlordiazepoxide*		Tranquilizer	Treatment of anxiety, tension, alcoholism, neurosis	Blurring of vision, confusion, possible severe depression when combined with alcohol

NARCOTICS

Opium *Papaver somniferum (plant)*		Dried, coagulated milk of unripe opium-poppy pod	Treatment of pain, severe diarrhea	Loss of appetite, temporary impotency or sterility. Painful withdrawal symptoms
Morphine	M miss Emma	10-1 reduction of crude opium	Treatment of severe pain	Same as above
Heroin	H horse junk smack	Converted morphine	None	Same as above

8

MARIHUANA AND SOCIETY

American Medical Association and
National Research Council

After careful appraisal of available information concerning marihuana (cannabis) and its components, and their derivatives, analogues and isomers, the Council on Mental Health and the Committee on Alcoholism and Drug Dependence of the American Medical Association and the Committee on Problems of Drug Dependence of the National Research Council, National Academy of Sciences, have reached the following conclusions:

1. Cannabis is a dangerous drug and as such is a public health concern.

For centuries, the hemp plant (cannabis) has been used extensively and in various forms as an intoxicant in Asia, Africa, South America, and elsewhere. With few exceptions, organized societies consider such use undesirable and therefore a drug problem, and have imposed legal and social sanctions on the user and the distributor.

Some of the components of the natural resins obtained from the hemp plant are powerful psychoactive agents; hence the resins themselves may be. In dogs and monkeys, they have produced complete anesthesia of several days' duration with quantities of less than 10 mg/kg.

American Medical Association and National Research Council, Marihuana and Society, *Journal of the American Medical Association*, **204**, no. 13, pp. 91-92, June 24, 1968.

Although dose-response curves are not so accurately defined in man, the orders of potency on a weight (milligram) basis are greater than those for many other powerful psychoactive agents, such as the barbiturates. They are markedly greater than those for alcohol. In India, where weak decoctions are used as a beverage, the government prohibits charas, the potent resin, even for use in folk medicine. In many countries where chronic heavy use of cannabis occurs, such as Egypt, Morocco, and Algeria, it has a marked effect of reducing the social productivity of a significant number of persons.

The fact that no physical dependence develops with cannabis does not mean it is an innocuous drug. Many stimulants are dangerous psychoactive substances although they do not cause physical dependence.

2. Legalization of marihuana would create a serious abuse problem in the United States.

The current use of cannabis in the United States contrasts sharply with its use in other parts of the world. In this country, the pattern of use is primarily intermittent and of the "spree" type, and much of it consists of experimentation by teenagers and young adults. Further, hemp grown in the United States is not commonly of high potency and "street" samples sometimes are heavily adulterated with inert materials.

With intermittent and casual use of comparatively weak preparations, the medical hazard is not so great, although even such use when it produces intoxication can give rise to disorders of behavior with serious consequences to the individual and to society.

And, while it is true that now only a small proportion of marihuana users in the United States are chronic users and can be said to be strongly psychologically dependent on the drug, their numbers, both actual and potential, are large enough to be of public health concern.

If all controls on marihuana were eliminated, potent preparations probably would dominate the legal market, even as they are now beginning to appear on the illicit market. If the potency of the drug were legally controlled, predictably there would be a market for the more powerful illegal forms.

When advocates of legalizing marihuana claim that it is *less harmful* than alcohol, they are actually comparing the relatively insignificant effects of marihuana at the lower end of the dose-response curve with the effects of alcohol at the toxicity end of the curve—ie, the "spree" use of marihuana vs acute or chronic "poisoning" with alcohol. If they compared both drugs at the upper end of the curve, they would see that the effects on the individual and society are highly deleterious in both cases.

Admittedly, if alcohol could be removed from the reach of alcoholics, one of the larger medical and social problems could be solved. But to make the active preparations of cannabis generally available would solve nothing. Instead, it would create a comparable problem of major proportions.

That some marihuana users are now psychologically dependent, that nearly all users become intoxicated, and that more potent forms of cannabis could lead to even more serious medical and social consequences—these facts argue for the retention of legal sanctions.

3. Penalties for violations of the marihuana laws are often harsh and unrealistic.

Persons violating federal law with respect to possession of marihuana are subject to penalties of from 2 to 10 years imprisonment for the first offense, 5 to 20 years for the second offense, and 10 to 40 years for additional offenses. Suspension of sentence, probation, and parole are allowed only for the first offense. Many of the state laws provide comparable penalties. With respect to sale, penalties are even more severe.

Laws should provide for penalties in such a fashion that the courts would have sufficient discretion to enable them to deal flexibly with violators. There are various degrees of both possession and sale. Possession ranges from the youngster who has one or two marihuana cigarettes to an individual who has a substantial quantity. Sale may range from the transfer of a single cigarette to the disposition of several kilograms of the drug.

While persons should not be allowed to become involved with marihuana with impunity, legislators, law enforcement officials, and the courts should differentiate in the handling of the occasional user, the frequent user, the chronic user, the person sharing his drug with another, and the dealer who sells for a profit.

Of particular concern is the youthful experimenter who, by incurring a criminal record through a single thoughtless act, places his future career in jeopardy. The lives of many young people are being needlessly damaged.

For those persons who are chronic users of the drug, and are psychologically dependent on it, general medical and psychiatric treatment, plus social rehabilitative services, should be made readily available. Such persons should not be treated punitively for their drug abuse alone any more than are persons dependent on other drugs, such as narcotics or alcohol.

Furthermore, if the purpose of imposing penalties is to deter acts which might injure the individual and disrupt society, then equitable penalties, insofar as they enhance respect for the law, can contribute to effective prevention.

4. Additional research on marihuana should be encouraged.

Only recently has an active hallucinogenic principle of cannabis been exactly identified and synthesized. Sufficient time has not elapsed to obtain a substantial body of pharmacologic and clinical evidence concerning its effects. There are no carefully controlled clinical studies of long-time effects of cannabis on the central nervous or other organ systems. These and other considerations point to the importance of ongoing research in this area.

It must be emphasized, however, that the issue which faces the United States today is not whether we know all there is to know about marihuana scientifically. Obviously every effort should be made to correct the deficiencies in our knowledge. The issue is whether we can ignore the experiences and observations established over centuries of heavy use of hemp preparations in various societies. A current solution to the problem does not relate to what is not known, but to those facts which are known about cannabis and its preparations. There is extensive experience in its use in all of its forms, including the effects of the potent natural resins which contain the active biological principles.

5. Educational programs with respect to marihuana
should be directed to all segments of the population.

Educational material, based on scientific knowledge, should point out the nature of marihuana and the effects of its use. Such material should be an integral part of a total educational program on drug abuse.

Primary and secondary schools, as well as colleges and universities, should establish such programs.

The communications media should disseminate authoritative information to the general public.

Physicians, as professional practitioners and concerned members of the community, should call attention frequently and forcibly to the problems of drug abuse and drug dependence.

An informed citizenry, in the final analysis, is the most effective deterrent of all.

9

THE AMA LIES ABOUT POT

Joel Fort, M.D.

With their dramatic new report on the alleged dangers of marijuana, the American Medical Association and the National Research Council have dimmed the hopes for a liberalization of the drug laws. The AMA-NRC pronouncement also seems to have frightened many laymen who take a doctor's word as sacrosanct. It is important to note, therefore, that the report brought to light *no* new findings and was compiled *not* by research physicians but by men who move in the remote worlds of administration, academics and medical politics.

At the press conference announcing publication of the report in the June 24 Journal of the American Medical Association, its spokesmen—a University of California pharmacologist and a Harvard psychiatrist, neither of whom has done research on marijuana or has had sustained contact with users—stressed that there was "danger" in the drug. The taking of any drug, of course, or any biologically active substance, always involves some danger. This goes for aspirin and antibiotics as well as mind-altering substances like marijuana and alcohol.

The "new" research on which the AMA and the NRC based their conclusion was completed many months ago—and has already been covered in the national press. At the federal hospital in Lexington, Kentucky, a small number of former narcotics addicts were given varying oral doses of an extract of crude marijuana,

Reprinted from Joel Fort, M.D., The AMA Lies About Pot, *Ramparts,* 7, no. 5, pp. 12-16, August 24, 1968.

ordinary smoking marijuana, and a recently synthesized sub-component of tetrahydrocannabinol (THC), the active principle in marijuana. With low doses of each of these substances, the subjects experienced the same "high" that follows social marijuana smoking. With larger doses of either the synthetic THC or the concentrated crude extract, most of the subjects showed marked perceptual changes or abstractions, labeled "hallucinations" by the experimenter and "psychotic reactions" in the AMA-NRC report. What this shows, of course, is that higher doses of a drug bring about stronger responses—an axiom of pharmacology.

Another axiom borne out in the recent study is that the same dose will have a different effect on different individuals. At a cocktail party, for instance, if people of the same age range and background consume like quantities of alcohol in the same time period, they may behave in vastly different ways, ranging from passivity to aggressiveness, impotence to satyromania. With marijuana, as with other mind-altering drugs, the effect depends upon a complex interaction between the dose taken, the social setting, and, most important, the personality of the drug user, including his or her state of mind, attitudes and expectations.

When an individual consumes alcohol, barbiturates, amphetamines, marijuana, LSD or another such substance, he is apt to experience an illusion (a misinterpretation of an actual sensation) or an hallucination (a perception arising internally but felt by the perceiver to have originated in the environment). There is also a finite possibility that underlying emotional instabilities or already existing psychoses will come to the fore; i.e., that a disintegration of the personality and loss of contact with reality will occur. The chances of this happening increase with the dosage. The most common example of psychosis in connection with the drugs listed is the permanent breakdown caused by excessive use of alcohol, which accounts for about 20 percent of the patients in U.S. mental hospitals.

In contrast, there have only been a small number of fleeting "psychotic" reactions reported in U.S. professional literature in association with marijuana use—an infinitesimal number in view of the millions of users. I have seen a few instances of this kind of reaction, each lasting about eight to twelve hours.

From countries where marijuana use is widespread there have come occasional reports of "cannabis psychosis," and these are widely cited by U.S. foes of the drug. Visits to the institutions from which these reports emanate show that they are anecdotal, uncontrolled and unverifiable. In parts of India, Morocco, Egypt and Nigeria where cannabis use is widespread, it is standard practice at mental hospitals (where there may be only one psychiatrist for several thousand patients) to attribute most non-specific psychoses to cannabis, even though the proportion of hospitalized citizens who regularly use it is often lower than the proportion of users in the total population.

Given the undeniable evidence of the dangers of alcohol and nicotine consumption, the AMA-NRC anti-marijuana campaign seems surreal and its puritan tone hypocritical. There are more alcoholics in the San Francisco Bay Area than there are narcotics addicts in the entire United States. Six million Americans have an unshakable dependency on alcohol. It leads to some 25,000 deaths and a million injuries on the highway each year. Fifty percent of our prison population committed their crimes while drunk.

Some 60 million Americans smoke cigarettes, which contribute to hundreds of thousands of deaths and disabilities each year from lung cancer, heart disease, hypertension, emphysema and bronchitis. Sedatives, stimulants and tranquilizers are used by about 20 million, most of them in the middle and upper classes, most over thirty. An estimated 200,000 are or are becoming barbiturate addicts or victims of amphetamine psychosis. Millions of law-abiding people use narcotics prescribed by their doctors—morphine, codeine, Percodan and Demerol—for temporary relief of coughs and pains. Countless others take caffeine in coffee, tea and Coca-Cola, and use pseudo-sedatives such as Compoz.

America is the most drug-ridden society in history. The average "straight" American adult consumes from three to five mind-altering drugs a day. With such adults as role-models, it should not surprise us that so many young people accept with equanimity the wide range of opportunities for the alteration of their livers and lives. From infancy onward, children are directly and indirectly taught by parents, television, movies and advertising that every time they have a pain or a problem, they should "solve" it by taking something. The alcohol, tobacco and pill industries spend hundreds of millions of dollars annually to encourage and promote maximum use of their products, each associating its drug with youthfulness and happiness.

The cigarette industry has taught our society that it is desirable to stick a dried plant leaf in one's mouth, set it on fire and inhale its fumes. One legacy of this mass inculcation is that Americans have tried smoking various leaves, including the leaves of the female cannabis sativa plant: *marijuana.* It does not, as its most zealous advocates claim, quickly produce creativity, insight, happiness and sexual prowess. Nor does it, as its detractors insist, transform contented, socially responsible individuals into murderers, rapists, heroin addicts and psychotics. The fact is that for most users there is no mind-altering effect.

A special technique of smoking must be learned, the effects of the drug must be perceived and related to the drug, and what is perceived must come to be subjectively interpreted as pleasurable if a person is to become a regular user. It is a process of learned behavior not much different from learning to use alcohol. Relaxation, euphoria, increased sociability, heightened awareness, quietude, perceptual changes, thirst and hunger, anxiety—each or all of these can occur within ten minutes of smoking, increasing over the next 30 to 45 minutes, and lasting up to several hours. With more than minimal doses, as with alcohol, coordination and reaction time are slowed. With excessive doses, whatever joyful effects the user has learned to feel are usually dissipated, and thus most users are content with perhaps a half a cigarette at a time. Heavy use on one single occasion produces gross intoxication or "drunkenness" with drowsiness or sleep. But even heavy use over many years produces no known damage to the liver, brain or other body organs.

What is it about our society, then, that proscribes this one drug and prescribes the others? In the mid-1930's a small group of underemployed former prohibition agents led by Harry J. Anslinger, head of the Federal Bureau of Narcotics, began lobbying for tougher anti-marijuana laws. At that time marijuana was a little known substance used chiefly by Mexican-Americans in the Southwest, some urban Negroes, jazz musicians and other outcasts of society. Congress held hearings on the drug at Anslinger's urging, and in 1937 the Marijuana Tax Act was passed. No medical, scientific or sociological evidence was introduced at the hearings, and it was Anslinger himself who testified as to the drug's alleged effects. To enforce the Marijuana Tax Act and the state laws which followed and made it a crime to sell the leaf without remunerating the government, Anslinger built an intricate system of national, state and local "drug police." He has now retired from the Narcotics Bureau, which has been made a branch of the Department of Justice.

The present federal laws impose sentences of two to ten years in prison for a first conviction for possessing even a small amount of marijuana; five to 20 years for a second conviction; and ten to 40 years for a third. The usual discretion that judges are given to grant probation or suspended sentences for most real crimes is taken from them by the laws for most pot offenses. For any sale—regardless of the amount and no matter whether from friend to friend or from "pusher" to "victim"—the federal penalty for a first offense conviction is five to 20 years, ten to 40 for a second.

As sociologists and criminologists have repeatedly pointed out, laws directed against status crimes, or crimes without victims (sex, drugs, gambling), in addition to creating a new crop of criminals by definition, drive the trade underground, making it profitable to organized crime. Thus, marijuana came to be supplied by the same operators who supplied heroin, and an individual growing up in an urban ghetto came into contact with both drugs from the same source at the same time. In actual fact, there is no inherent or causal relationship between marijuana use and any other drug, in the United States or in any other country—such as India, where millions regularly use cannabis in beverage or smoking forms but where heroin use is nonexistent.

As the "stepping stone" myth has been demolished, a new worry has been created: "psychological dependence." The concept is identical with that of "habituation," and it means becoming so used to something psychologically that when the thing is absent, one becomes ill at ease and irritable. Indeed, this does occur with some marijuana users, just as it occurs with some alcohol, caffeine and nicotine users—and with some television viewers when the tube suddenly burns out. It is a perfectly valid charge against marijuana—and a perfectly hypocritical one.

It is apparent that marijuana has assumed symbolic values far beyond its actual importance as a drug both for those who wish to use it and those who wish to restrict its use. Indeed, it is probably the main symbol of the widening generation gap. How we deal with it in the next few years will have implications reaching far beyond the drug laws.

Marijuana and the laws relating to it play a major "smoke screening" role in American society, enabling police, politicians and the mass media to hide real drug, health, criminal and social problems which are difficult, embarrassing and interwoven with powerful interests. There is also an important scapegoating function: marijuana laws provide leverage for attacking youth, Negroes, Spanish-Americans, dissenters and intellectuals who might otherwise succeed in changing the status quo. Pot serves the purposes of those in power so well that they are evidently willing to pay the price of keeping it illegal: rapid manufacture of tens of thousands of criminals through the imprisonment of otherwise well-adjusted people; the breeding of disrespect for laws and police; the waste of tens of millions of tax dollars for ineffective—and often harmful—narcotics agencies, jails, court costs; the sustaining of organized crime; and the deployment of police away from dealing with the rapidly increasing crimes of violence.

Although spelled out as a basic goal in our Declaration of Independence, the pursuit of happiness is somehow looked upon as immoral and unacceptable by a considerable number of Americans who are able to rationalize alcohol and tobacco use, television watching and extramarital sex so as not to be uncomfortable. Marijuana use and youth are both attacked by an attitude of puritanism well defined by H. L. Mencken: "The haunting fear that someone, somewhere may be happy."

10

THE DRAFT IS GOOD FOR YOU

John Keats

Many a draftee looks forward to military service with about as much enthusiasm as he would to a jail term that could end in wounds or death. Having spent four years in the Army myself, I must say that this is indeed what a military career in large part resembles. Therefore, whenever a young man tells me he was lucky to have escaped the draft, or that he hopes to escape it, or that he finds the Vietnam war to be immoral and says he does not want to go to it, I find his attitude entirely understandable—but absolutely wrong.

The whole truth of the matter must surely include these three facts:

First, we are moving whether we like it or not, through the most murderous century in all recorded time, and we are at the center of world affairs.

Second, a tour of duty can be the best thing that ever happened to a young man. Granted, it can injure him, or at the very least waste years of his youth and delay his career—as it did for some 15 million men of my generation. Yet, in many ways that civilian life cannot, a military experience can also give a young man good reason to believe in himself and a realistic view of himself with respect to others around him.

Third, no one is lucky to escape the common experience of his time. Somewhere inside him, a man will always know that he has missed something

Reprinted from John Keats, The Draft Is Good for You, *Saturday Evening Post,* **241,** No. 3, pp. 8-9, February 10, 1968.

important that everyone else has shared, and he will always wonder how he would have done, had he been there.

I think it necessary to keep these three facts in mind if we are to tell our sons anything sensible about the draft that awaits them.

I think we should begin by reminding them that history is so replete with wars as to make peace seem to be anomalous. War has been almost constantly with us throughout the 190 years of this Republic, and in just the last 25 years we have been involved in three major wars. Meanwhile, we have had to send troops to various parts of the world to tamp down several minor wars, and to prevent still others from erupting. Whether all of our wars have been either necessary or just ones may certainly be argued, but the fact that they occurred cannot be debated, and I would think that any reflection on the state of the world today would indicate that we are going to have to maintain a large standing Army for some years to come, and that this Army will probably be to great extent an army of conscripts, composed of your son and mine, and the boy next door. In sum, the world has been an exceedingly dangerous place since time began, and all these young men will have to take their turns at defending their nation.

I do not wish to sound like a recruiting sergeant, but the problem does exist, and our sons will be called upon to deal with it. If an 18-year-old boy thinks he can best defend the nation by being a conscientious objector, I have no quarrel with him as long as his objection is indeed conscientious and reasoned, and as long as he is willing to spend what would have been his draft term in an alternate service that is in the public interest. But one way or another, I think the boy must realize that he has a civic obligation. (The boys for whom I have no use—and I have met several of them—are those who deny that they owe any sort of debt to their parents or to the nation that has so far provided them with a fairly fat life, and whose only objection to the draft is that they fear it would interrupt their pleasures.)

Now what happens to a boy when he is drafted? Today's Army, the one that my son entered, is basically no different from the one I entered at the time of Hitler's war, nor from the one my father entered during the Kaiser's war, and the first impressive thing about it is that it is a citizens' army, almost entirely composed of young men who almost certainly would rather be somewhere else. On his way to the induction center, the recruit is bound up in the kind of camaraderie that obtains in a pitching lifeboat, slowly pulling away from a steamer sinking in a storm.

The mood of the incoming recruits abruptly changes to that of prisoners, however, beginning at the barbershop. The Army shears your scalp. You become part of a line of naked men to be examined, measured, fingerprinted, and inoculated against all manner of diseases. In the course of this shearing and stripping, the Army destroys all barriers between you and all the other men in the line; wipes away all your pasts and former conditions; does away with thoughts of college, jobs, aimless drifting, girls, worries, doubts, fears, ambitions. Then the Army thrusts you all beneath the level of manhood by dressing you in fatigue uniforms, and clad like jailbirds, you can only aspire to something better. A profound truth begins to emerge: It is the Army, and not whatever nation the Army happens to be fighting when you enter it, that is the first enemy of the soldier. You have entered an authoritarian society, insistent on its own peculiar needs, wherein all members of the society have only functional significance. Listening to the Uniform Code of Military Justice, you are struck by the repetition of the phrase, "shall be punished by death, or such other punishment as a court-martial may direct."

This is sobering. You, the recruit, are immediately confronted with the problem of personal survival—of survival as an individual. Civil life is too full of bypaths and hiding places, of protective families and friends, to provide the root-hog-or-die kind of confrontation the Army presents. As nowhere else in our society, you are truly on your own. As a very wise drill sergeant put it to my group of infantry recruits, shivering in a Georgia sleet storm at four in the morning, "So far as I'm concerned, every one of you is equal until he proves himself different." This is not at all like school, where the teacher will try to find for every child some task at which the child can succeed. Instead, it is much more fair. You and all the other recruits with hair as short, dressed alike, and equally ignorant of the new world you have entered, are given an equal opportunity to show what sort of men you are. You are set at common tasks. If you want to establish your difference from the men around you, it will be up to you, and you alone, to try it.

It is just here that you can, perhaps for the first time in your life, look around you to see how you measure up in honest competition with all other men. No parents are going to send you to a better school than other children attend; no one is going to give you a better job because of the influence of your father. You now have an opportunity to demonstrate your character, or lack of one. I will not say that you might not be given a chance to do so in civil life, but only that the Army gives you this chance in the bleakest possible way, and that you are extremely fortunate to be given this kind of opportunity on the very threshold of manhood.

Perhaps more fairly, and more desperately than in civil life, the Army searches for competence and rewards it by every means it can. After all, complex as the modern Army is, and comparatively few as its combat soldiers are, the Army is organized for the purposes of battle, and it is not anxious to trust incompetents with responsibility when failure to carry out that responsibility can cost not just money, but your life, or the life of the boy next door. The Army does not care about you personally, but it does care about the security of the Army in which you are an anonymous cipher. I will not say the Army never makes mistakes about those whom it places in responsible positions, but I do say that if you prove yourself to be a better man than those around you, the Army will certainly promote you.

Promotion in the Army often gives you command of other men, and this can mean that you, only a year or two out of high school, can be given greater responsibilities and experience in handling other men than you could ever hope to be given in civil life at your very early age. Let us think about the 18-to-22-year-old age group for a moment. Labor unions do not want them in the job market, employers do not want them, and we do not want them hanging around the house. In fact, almost nobody wants them unless they are bright, and if they are, then we say that college is the only socially acceptable place for them. The other place, we say, is in the Army. We do not really reflect on whether college is necessarily the best place in the world, or whether the Army is some kind of junk heap, and few of us realize that the Army has lessons to teach that cannot be taught so well anywhere in civil life. I should say that one of the things the Army proves is that a 20-year-old man, if he is a man, can handle a platoon, whereas civil life seldom gives anyone that young a comparable opportunity no matter how much of a man he may be.

The Army's standards are its own, of course, and therefore you will have to do what the Army wants you to do instead of what you might want to do. In a way this is limiting, and you may find it oppressive, even stupid. But I am reminded that Robert Frost described writing free verse as being akin to playing tennis with the net down, which is to say that art implies performance within form. Military discipline and military rules comprise a very arbitrary form, and many a young man seems to be rather badly in need of some form within which to practice the art of growing into a mature person. I have seen too many confused college boys not to know how difficult they find the free-form civilian world to be, and I know too many parents who are thankful for what the Army has done for their sons not to know that discipline can be a kindness. Perhaps only after you have left the Army do you realize what it was all about. Perhaps some men never do understand this, but I should say that he who has undergone discipline will be better able to discipline himself.

But lest this sound too much like a recruiting poster, let us hear an enemy of armies speak. The voice is that of a Quaker, who, like all of his sect, believes that all wars are immoral and is opposed to all forms of coercion, including military life:

"I think we all must admit that the Army is a creator of equality in our national life. It is, for example, one place, where the Negro has a full, free and equal chance to move ahead, on the basis of his abilities, to middle-class status. It serves as a melting pot, bringing rural boys from the South together with boys from Wisconsin and Wyoming and the northern cities. It can be a kind of giant international-exchange program, in a sense, giving GI's and their wives and children a chance to live in another country in which they can learn to respect another people and culture.

"It is a place where lost kids can find themselves, and I will say I have seen young men, who were lost before they went in, come out of the service after a couple of years and go booming into civil life, full of drive and self-confidence they never had before."

Having served myself, I certainly do not believe that everything about the Army is good. For the most part I found my years in the Southwest Pacific boring, and I am sure that my son found his years in Oklahoma, Texas and Korea equally so. But I do know that it is a great source of satisfaction to learn that you can do what millions of men your age have done before you, and to have taken part in the events of your time. I also know that if you should be the one soldier in 10 who is told to fight, you will meet nothing on the battlefield that can be more hideous than anything other men have encountered before you. It is neither necessary nor possible for you to do better than the men who fought, say, at Gettysburg: You will merely be asked to do as well, and it is entirely likely that you will.

This is what I would tell any boy of draft age; this was what I told my son when it came his turn to decide just what his obligation to his country was. Much as I might agree with my Quaker friends as to the nature of wars and armies, I am more impressed by the fact that we are citizens of a great power living in a time of wars, and that maintenance of an Army is a sad necessity that has been thrust upon us. I am sorry about that, as an Army man would say. But that is the way it is. We need an Army, and someone must serve in it. Looking at any boy of draft age, I should ask him, "Why should it not be you?" I know what I am asking of him, but I also know that I am asking no more than has been asked of youth by any nation in time of war. And I know, too, that if he takes his turn in serving in the ranks, the Army, in its own relentless, uncaring and impersonal way, can be of service to him by giving him an opportunity to be himself, and that he will return to civil life more sure of himself, and feeling more certain of his right to citizenship, than anyone who has not served.

11

HELL NO, WE WON'T GO

Bill Davidson

A big interstate bus noses into the checkpoint on the Canadian border near Rouses Point, N.Y. Canadian customs officials come aboard, accompanied by two FBI men. The agents have fugitive warrants in their pockets, and they are looking for young Americans of draft age trying to flee the country. They tap one boy on the shoulder. . . .

It's 10 a.m. in the offices of a big utility company in Chicago. Two FBI men and two federal marshals enter a supervisor's cubicle and ask to speak with a young clerk. The youth is called out into the corridor, and the agents put him under arrest for violation of the Selective Service Act. They snap handcuffs on the young man's wrists. . . .

A Pfc. is standing at attention in the orderly room of a quartermaster company at Ft. Knox in Kentucky. A reservist, he is wearing civilian clothes. His company commander says to him, "I'm giving you a direct order to put on your uniform and report for duty." The young soldier says, "I cannot for reasons of conscience." The company commander orders the soldier taken to the post stockade, where he is stripped and put in a steel isolation cell. . . .

Two FBI men are working their way up Avenue A in New York City's East Village hippie colony. They are asking about a boy named Johnson who failed to register for the draft in his hometown, Sacramento, California, and then disap-

Reprinted from Bill Davidson, Hell No, We Won't Go, *Saturday Evening Post*, **241,** no. 2, pp. 21-26, January 27, 1968.

peared. They walk right past Johnson without knowing it. Johnson hasn't been Johnson for a long time. Hiding out with the hippies in San Francisco, Los Angeles, Chicago, and New York, he has used half a dozen names. In the East Village he is known simply as Scuby....

Across the country such scenes are taking place nearly every day. "Open resistance to the draft," says columnist Clayton Fritchey, "is greater than at any time since the Civil War."

The anti-draft demonstrations last month in New York and elsewhere, part of a series of draft protests planned for this year and next, were merely the noisiest and most noticeable signs of the defiance. Less obvious but considerably more significant is the exodus of young Americans to Canada. According to the private groups in Canada that assist the exodus, some 10,000 men have slipped across the border to evade the draft, choosing to live as aliens and to cut themselves off from friends and family and all things familiar; if they return to the United States, they face jail sentences of up to 15 years. The Justice Department says that only 200 men have been indicted for fleeing to Canada, but the government figures are misleading. With the ponderous legal machinery of Selective Service, it takes nearly a year to get an indictment and a fugitive warrant through the courts, and the greatest flow to Canada has come in the past few months.

Altogether the Selective Service System lists 15,310 "delinquents," men who have not responded to calls or correspondence from their draft boards. Some 2,000 of these belong to a loose national federation of draft-defying groups—the one in Chicago is called CADRE (Chicago Area Draft Resisters). The members have pledged themselves to go to prison rather than into the Army; they have turned in their draft cards and are awaiting indictment. Slowly, but with increasing speed, the Government is obliging them. In the fiscal year 1966, some 650 young men were indicted for violations of the Selective Service laws; in fiscal 1967 the number doubled. Convictions have doubled too—from 372 in 1966 to 748 in 1967. Last month the Justice Department, declaring that prosecutions were "at an all-time high," said it was forming a "special unit" to prosecute more vigorously.

There is still another factor in gauging the resistance: More than 22,000 men (not counting veterans) have won classification as conscientious objectors. The rate of conscientious objection is 70 percent greater than it was during World War II. The Selective Service people attempt to soften this by pointing out that there are only 1.7 conscientious objectors for every 1,000 registrants, and they add that only four men in every 10,000 registrants are delinquent. The key word here is *registrants.* By measuring the resisters against all *registrants,* the Government manages to disguise the magnitude of the phenomenon. The nation's 35 million registrants include all men in the United States between the ages of 18 and 45, most of whom are overage, disabled or deferred—that is, not eligible for the draft anyway.

But even if one accepts the official figures at face value, the problem is still a serious one. The Selective Service System, like most operations of our Government, relies to a large degree on voluntary cooperation; compulsion can go just so far. Now, for the first time in living memory, a sizable number of Americans are refusing to cooperate. Some, of course, are merely cowards trying to save their skins. And some are so intemperate in their opposition that they may be passed off as chronic misanthropes. "The FBI," says Stuart Byczynski, a draft dodger now in Toronto, "is the new Gestapo, and the country is becoming a vast concentration camp." But many reveal a strength of conviction that is hard to scorn. "This is my country, and I love it," says Richard Boardman, who is waiting in Chicago to be prosecuted for draft evasion, "and I will stay here and go to jail if necessary to help correct its mistakes. I accept the general framework of the law, and I accept the penalties for breaking the law."

The draft evaders, or "non-cooperators," as some call themselves, vary tremendously in background. There are simple Mennonite farm boys as well as scholars with Ph.D.'s. There are Negroes from the ghetto and boys from America's richest families. Politically, they range from Maoists to Bobby Kennedy Democrats to Goldwater Republicans. It is possible, however, to group these diverse young men in six major categories.

The first is composed of those men who have gone to prison for their anti-conscription activity. These are the elite of draft-dodger society, the folk heroes of the resistance movement. Typical of them is Fred Moore Jr., who was back on the anti-war picket lines just two days after completing his two-year sentence at the Allenwood Federal Prison Camp near Lewisburg, Pa. Moore, a slight, cleancut 26-year-old from Arlington, Va., is a Quaker and a follower of Mahatma Gandhi. He regards himself as an out-and-out pacifist and says he would not even defend himself if attacked.

In 1962 Moore's draft board classified him 1-A. That prompted him to apply for conscientious-objector status (classification 1-O) so that instead of soldiering he could work in a civilian hospital or a social-service agency. Normally, a youth of Moore's religious beliefs receives the 1-O classification fairly routinely, but he objected to some of the phrasing in the government form. He crossed out the words "Supreme Being" and substituted "God, which is the power of love." Moore was investigated by the FBI and had to appear before a hearing officer to explain his religious convictions. In April, 1964, he received his 1-O classification.

"I had a strange reaction to the notice," Moore says. "I had no feeling of relief or gladness. Instead, I had the feeling that I was a moral coward, and that I had ended up cooperating with the Selective Service System in order to get special status for myself." He sent his classification card back to his draft board, informing it that it was participating in "the march toward totalitarianism." He then hit the road, lecturing on peace at college campuses all over the country. He wore sandwich boards reading, LIBERTY YES. CONSCRIPTION NO, THOU SHALT NOT KILL, and DON'T DODGE THE DRAFT; OPPOSE IT.

His protesting ended in June, 1965, when two FBI men came to see him at Pendle Hill, a Quaker study center in Pennsylvania. The government agents told him that they had been sent to give him a last chance. They practically pleaded with him to go to Richmond, where he had been assigned by his draft board to do his alternative service—hospital work. Moore thanked them politely and said no. A few days later he received a registered letter ordering him to surrender himself at the United States courthouse in Alexandria, Va. He did so and went on trial for draft evasion on October 21, 1965.

On his way to the trial he picketed the White House and distributed pacifist leaflets outside the court building. Refusing court-appointed counsel and electing to defend himself, he told Judge Oren R. Lewis that he couldn't plead guilty because the draft was on trial and not he. His defense was that conscription was unconstitutional because it represented involuntary servitude, as defined by the 13th Amendment. Moore says, "The judge was hostile at first, but then he began to realize I was sincere and trying to live according to my beliefs. He even said so." The trial lasted three hours. Moore was found guilty and sentenced to two years in the federal penitentiary.

Moore today is back at the old stand, demonstrating against the Vietnam war and counseling opposition to the draft. He has gone to work as office manager for a group called Quaker Action, which dispatches boatloads of medical supplies to both North and South Vietnam, and has married Suzanne Williams, a 19-year-old peace demonstrator who has been arrested and jailed no less than seven times. Moore already has burned his new 1-O draft card, which was sent to him after he got out of jail, and he fully expects to be prosecuted a second and maybe even a third time. He says, almost casually, "I'm perfectly willing to go to jail again for my beliefs." A Justice Department official says, "This boy is either nuts or so goddamn sincere you have to respect him—but what can we do but throw the book at him again?"

Less sincere and more elusive is the second category of draft evaders, "the Underground." These are the young men, registered and unregistered, who hide out in the ghettos and hippie colonies of the major American cities. No one in the Government will even guess at how many of them there are, but the Central Committee for Conscientious Objectors in Philadelphia estimates that they probably number in the thousands. Certainly they make up a good proportion of the 15,310 Americans listed as "delinquent" by Selective Service.

Many in the Underground have been runaways and "floaters" since their late teens. The Negro youngsters wander from tenement to tenement in the ghettos, where itinerant boarders are common, and no questions are asked. The whites are hippies or disguise themselves as hippies and blend into the anonymity of "crash-pad" living.

In New York's East Village, the Underground member named Scuby was sitting in a delicatessen eating a pastrami sandwich. "Man," he said, "there are fifty of us within two blocks of here." A few minutes before, the two FBI men had passed him without recognizing him; they were showing his picture to shopkeepers and asking for him by the name of Johnson. But the picture was not recent, and Scuby now has a full, reddish beard and wears dark glasses.

He spoke of his background—he came from a "typical middle-class materialistic family," and when he first "took off," as he put it, he joined the hippie colony in Venice, Calif. Afterwards he floated to other hippie settlements around the country, leaving no trail and never once telling his family where he was. "My father's a fink," he said. "He'd turn me in to the feds."

Scuby doesn't participate in hippie demonstrations or anti-war protests. "The idea is to play it cool," he said, "and never do anything to call attention to yourself. Another thing you got to be careful about is not to get high on acid, because you might lose control and say something to give yourself away. You never know who's a fink for the feds." Scuby expressed no convictions about pacifism or the Vietnam war. He simply said, "I got better things to do than get shot at by a bunch of Viet Congs."

Many of the young men in the third major category of draft resisters—those who leave the country—share Scuby's nonideological, live-and-let-live attitude. This reporter encountered a high percentage of misfits among the fugitives in Canada. Many had records of family conflict and had moved often from one school to another. Nearly all had 2-S student deferments and hadn't thought seriously about their personal convictions until the 2-S was revoked. At least a dozen youths claimed they had considered going to jail but had decided against it on the grounds that they just weren't up to it.

Canada is a natural haven for these young men. Some flee to France or South America, but most find it simplest to cross the Canadian border, knowing that Canadians on the whole are not enthusiastic about the Vietnam war, and that Canada will extradite criminals only for offenses that are also illegal in Canada— since Canada has no draft, draft evasion is not a crime there. Vancouver is an entry point for West Coast evaders and Montreal for fugitives from the East Coast. But, except for menial jobs, employment in Vancouver is tightly controlled by the unions, and the use of French in Montreal presents a language problem for the average American. So Toronto, a cosmopolitan, English-speaking city with an American flavor, has become the center of the draft-dodger community.

One of the more impressive of the Toronto refugees is John Phillips, a tall, blond, 22-year-old Quaker from Algona, Iowa. Phillips's pacifism is founded in his religion, and ordinarily he would have had little trouble obtaining the conscientious-objector classification he applied for. But he bewildered the five farmers on his rural draft board; he was the first objector they had encountered, and they didn't know what to make of him. "They called me a coward and a Communist," Phillips says, "and when they learned I had covered the Selma, Alabama, civil-rights march as a photographer, they said, 'Oh, so you went down there to help those niggers.' I told them I'd go to Vietnam as a combat photographer, anything so I wouldn't have to kill, but they didn't believe me. For the first time in my life I broke down and cried."

Phillips filed an appeal and went so far as to report for his preinduction physical examination. He spent the night in a barracks at Fort Des Moines, where the other draftees—until they were stopped by an officer—tried forcibly to shave him from head to toe. That decided Phillips. He married his fiancée, also a Quaker, and they left immediately for Canada. Today his wife, Laura, is a social worker in the Toronto slums, and Phillips is a photographer for an agency of the Canadian Government.

Another young man who made his decision under duress is 22-year-old Michael Miller (not his real name). A student at Penn State and the City University of New York, Miller developed such strong convictions about the U.S. involvement in Vietnam that he refused to cooperate with the Selective Service —even though he has a physical disability that probably would have kept him out of the Army anyway. He decided to go to jail, and his father, a bombardier in the Army Air Corps in World War II, called him a Communist and kicked him out of his house. Then Miller's wife, who was pregnant, told him that his going to jail would be unfair to her, so they went to Canada. Miller genuinely grieves about his permanent exile from the United States. "I miss being out of the mainstream," he says. "I miss not being able to go to my parents' twenty-fifth wedding anniversary and my sister's wedding. I miss not being able to go home again."

But Miller's attitude is not a common one in Toronto. Most of the draft dodgers there have turned against their country completely. They make statements like "They ought to tear down the Statue of Liberty because it doesn't mean anything any more." The left-wing draft dodgers say they don't want to live in the United States any more because it has become a "fascist dictatorship no better than Hitler's Germany." The right-wingers say they have fled from "a collectivist tyranny no better than Soviet Russia."

Typical of the latter is 20-year-old Stuart Byczynski, a thin, intense, balding young man who wears glasses. Byczynski was born into a rigid, Catholic, New Deal-Democrat family in Parkville, Md., but was in constant revolt against his parents' religious and political beliefs. He left the Catholic Church and became a Unitarian when he was 17, and in 1964 he campaigned for Barry Goldwater and other conservative Republicans.

"I believe in the freedom of the individual," he said, "and Big Government in the United States is taking away all our freedoms. It bleeds us to death with taxes, it tells us at what age we can drink whiskey and drive a car, it spends a lot of money forcing artificial racial equality. Even while I was still in high school, I decided no government was going to tell me I couldn't pursue my chosen profession and would have to sleep on cots with a lot of other people. My sole reason for going to college was to avoid the draft as long as possible with a 2-S student deferment."

The war resisters in the fourth category do not generally enjoy the luxury of escape. These are the young men who have already entered the armed forces and then decided they couldn't fight in Vietnam. Their only recourse is to desert (which very few do), or to apply for a conscientious-objector discharge (which are rare; the Army approves less than five percent of the applications). If the young man persists, the usual result is a prison term for disobeying orders. The Department of Defense says it has about 400 C.O. applications pending. The

Central Committee for Conscientious Objectors insists, on the basis of its correspondence from servicemen seeking legal help, that the figure is much higher.

One of the most interesting cases in this category involved Michael Wittels, who now is 28 years old and a successful young artist in Philadelphia. Wittels, never a peace activist or protester during his years at Cheltenham High School and the Philadelphia College of Art, joined the Army Reserves and was assigned to a quartermaster company in 1962. His six months of active duty at Fort Knox, Ky., were uneventful. He was a good soldier and was promoted to squad leader when the company took heavy weapons training at Fort Polk, La. "But suddenly," Wittels told me, "the whole thing jumped up and hit me in the face. An instructor was demonstrating a new rifle, and he said, 'This weapon can tear a hole the size of a fist in a man.' At that moment I knew I could never kill—that I was a conscientious objector at heart."

Wittels finished his active duty, but he continued to brood about his convictions, even while faithfully attending his reserve meetings. Finally, in June, 1965, he sought legal advice from the Friends Peace Committee and learned that he could apply for a conscientious-objector discharge. He painstakingly filled out the complicated application, and on August 25, 1965, he turned it in to his company commander.

Six months went by and Wittels heard nothing about the application, though he kept writing to all the higher reserve echelons. In January, 1966, he stopped going to reserve meetings and returned his Army pay checks. In March, the application was turned down. Then he was demoted from Pfc. to Private and, as a punishment, was ordered to report to Fort Knox for 45 days of active duty. He did so, arriving in civilian clothes. He explained his position to his new company commander, a young Negro officer named Capt. Albert Thurmond. "He was very kind and polite," said Wittels, "but he didn't know what to do about me, since I told him I could not put on my uniform and serve. He sent me to see the adjutant general and two chaplains. They all tried to talk me into taking the easy way out by putting on my uniform and serving the forty-five days. They didn't even seem to listen when I told them I would not retreat from my stand."

After three days, according to Wittels, Captain Thurmond called him into the orderly room, sighed, and gave him a direct order to put on his uniform and report for duty. When Wittels respectfully refused, he was taken to the stockade, where a sergeant told him, "We've had your kind in here before, and we're going to break you." He was stripped of his shirt, shoes and socks and locked in "The Box," a 6-by-8-foot isolation cell with nothing in it but a Bible and a steel slab for a bunk. The guards kept him standing until 2 a.m., when he was sent to take a shower. When he got back to the cell, his blanket was gone. It was a cold night, but a guard said, "You don't want that blanket. It says U.S. Army on it."

Wittels says he was in "The Box" for three days, during which he was fed bread, dry cereal and cabbage. On the third day the confinement officer, a six-foot, seven-inch Negro captain named Wyatt Minton, came to see him. "Just put on the regular stockade fatigue shirt, not your uniform, and I'll let you out of here. I need the space." Wittels agreed, and was put in a 24-man cell with the general prison population. There were eight other C.O.'s in the stockade. Two weeks later he went on trial for disobeying his company commander's direct order to put on his uniform. He was found guilty and sentenced to six months at hard labor.

Wittels was returned to a solitary cell on the grounds that "he would contaminate the other prisoners." The quarantine didn't work. The other prisoners and even the guards came to admire Wittels's uncomplaining courage, and they smuggled food and books in to him. Six weeks later Captain Minton sent for Wittels. "I hear you're a damned fine artist," he said. "I'm going to let you out around the base to do paintings to decorate the stockade. All you have to do is sign a statement saying you'll obey stockade rules." Wittels signed the statement.

On February 6, 1967, the end of his sentence, Wittels was released from the stockade. He went back to his Fort Knox company where an officer again ordered him to put on his uniform and report to a duty station. Again Wittels refused, and he was returned to the stockade. This time Wittels faced a general court-martial and a sentence of five years at Fort Leavenworth. He was made a maximum-custody prisoner, often with handcuffs and an armed guard.

But without his knowledge a series of events were taking place far from Fort Knox. Wittels's mother had appealed to Congressman Richard S. Schweiker, a Republican from Pennsylvania, who demanded that the Army investigate. The Army told him it was processing Wittels's new application for a conscientious-objector's discharge. And then a hearing officer ruled that the charge pending against Wittels was unsupported. He was released to perform noncombatant duties on the base.

After 26 days Wittels was sent home. In July, 1967, he received a general discharge "under honorable conditions ... by reason of conscientious objection." Later one of the Fort Knox stockade guards wrote to him: "What you went through here took more guts than going to Vietnam."

Wittels, of course, could have avoided his ordeal if he had obtained conscientious-objector status *before* going into the Army. This type of war resistance is perfectly legal. The more than 22,000 men who have been classified as C.O.'s by their draft boards make up the fifth and sixth categories of war resisters—the two kinds of legitimate C.O.'s recognized by the Selective Service System.

One kind is the men who are classified 1-A-O. The 1-A-O's go into the Army as draftees along with the 1-A's, but they are not required to handle weapons, and they perform only noncombatant duties, usually in the Medical Corps. Members of churches such as the Seventh-Day Adventist almost automatically get 1-A-O status from their draft boards when they apply for it; others have to prove their case. All 1-A-O's—there are 4,500 of them—take their basic training in two 400-man companies in the Army Medical Training Center at Fort Sam Houston in San Antonio, Tex. They are treated the same as other soldiers, except that they get no weapons training. After training, most are assigned as medical corpsmen with Army units in the field, including Vietnam. Col. C. C. Pixley, commander of the Army Medical Training Center, says, "These people are among the best soldiers I have ever known."

Sgt. Richard Enders epitomizes the C.O. in the Army. A Seventh-Day Adventist from Longview, Wash., Enders was classified 1-A-O and sent to Fort Sam Houston. From there he went to Vietnam and was assigned to the 346th Medical Dispensary in Can Tho, the heart of the Viet Cong-infested Mekong Delta. Enders not only tended wounded GI's but consistently volunteered for expeditions on which teams of Army Medical Corps specialists go into the countryside under heavy guard and treat the civilian population in Vietnamese villages. There was only one other C.O. in Enders's outfit, but, he says, "no one thought of us as being different from anyone else."

Getting to be a 1-O, the other type of legitimate conscientious objector, is a bit more complicated. The 1-O, after he receives that classification from his draft board, does not serve in the Army but puts in two years of so-called "alternative service" as a civilian. The type of work he does is severely restricted and must be approved by the draft board. Usually it's duty of some sort in a civilian hospital or social-service agency. Although 1-O's outnumber 1-A-O's by about four to one, most draft boards are loath to give the classification. Some refuse to give 1-O's at all, even to *bona fide* members of pacifist religions; the feeling is that anyone taking such a stand is either a coward or a traitor. The conscientious objector's only recourse then is to appeal. Appeals can be expensive, and those who do not have the money often become draft dodgers even though they are anxious and willing to fulfill their obligation by doing legitimate "alternate service." An official of the American Friends Service Committee remarks that a large proportion of draft evasion is precipitated by "senile, bumbling, bigoted draft-board members."

As a Justice Department official told me, "I know most Americans wouldn't agree, and certainly the fighting men in Vietnam don't think so, but these boys, some of our brightest young men, represent the agony of our age."

THE DRAFT SHOULD BE ABOLISHED

Senator Mark O. Hatfield

. . . . I believe the draft is basically wrong; we should get rid of it.

With our nation at war in Vietnam, many will be horrified by this suggestion. But the facts are that, even with 3.4 million men under arms today, we do not need a draft; we can afford not to have a draft; we are long overdue in ending this invasion of the liberties of our young men.

The inequities of the draft are obvious. Critics have pointed to deferments that discriminate in favor of the wealthier and brighter young men who can go to college. Less privileged groups suffer—including even people from other countries. I was shocked to learn recently that several young Peruvians who were here as students or on work permits had been drafted, and that three of them had been killed in Vietnam.

The nature of Selective Service itself has produced inequities. There are more than 4,000 local draft boards, each with wide latitude in interpreting and administering draft regulations. Indeed, there are no clear, uniform standards as to which boy is to be called up and which is to be left free.

Several years ago, when I was dean of students at Willamette University in Oregon, I also served as military adviser. I could see how some draft boards differed. The members of one board, for example, felt that as long as a student was a warm body in a college classroom, he could keep his deferment. For the

Reprinted from Senator Mark O. Hatfield, The Draft Should Be Abolished, *Saturday Evening Post,* **240,** no. 13, pp. 12-14, July 1, 1967.

members of another board, it was a different story: The moment a student fell one one-hundredth of a grade point below the accepted line, away he went.

The most basic inequity of the current system is the fact that a smaller and smaller minority of our young men is carrying the burden of national defense. The principle of "universal sharing" of the national-defense effort—the principle on which the system was sold to the public years ago—is a transparent falsehood today. As President Johnson has admitted to Congress, "The unavoidable truth is that complete equity can never be achieved when only some must be selected and only some must serve."

Currently, only about 46 percent of the men reaching the age of 26 have seen military service. By 1974—at pre-Vietnam war levels—that figure will shrink to 34 percent. Even under today's crisis conditions, the military services draft only about 300,000 men a year out of a draft-eligible pool that totals nearly 12 million. I submit that we cannot tolerate a system that capriciously requisitions two years out of the lives of some young men while allowing others their liberty.

The draft has long been accepted on the theory that it is the only practical method of providing the military with the necessary quantity of men. This justification has served for too long to excuse national complacency. To be sure, the draft does provide the necessary *number* of young men. But the "success" of this system must be measured against its costs and inefficiencies.

According to the Pentagon's own figures, the current turnover rate among draftees ranges between 92 and 95 percent. Men who did not want in are naturally eager to get out. They are replaced by other men who do not want in. All these men go through the same cycle of training and assignment. Since it costs at least $6,000 just to train the average foot soldier, the total training cost for draftees now in uniform—men who will leave the service the moment their two-year hitches expire—approximates three billion dollars.

Even this sum cannot buy fighting men of the quality we now need. Since the peacetime draft was instituted in 1940, the nature of military strategy and technology has undergone radical change. No longer do we merely require large masses of GI's. Weapons have become more sophisticated, and so we need a higher percentage of specialized personnel who, in turn, require extensive training. The draft is not designed to satisfy this need. In fact, it frustrates it. The high turnover rate produced by the draft ties down many of the services' most experienced personnel, at least 10 percent of them, in training new recruits. Some 70 percent of the Army's enlisted men have less than two years' experience. At any given time, the equivalent of as many as 14 infantry divisions (210,000 men) may be categorized as students, trainees or transients. As Brig. Gen. Lynn D. Smith has noted: "As soon as we are able to operate as a unit, the trained men leave and we have to start all over again."

For more than 25 years we have accepted the draft as an immutable fact of life. Our keen sense of the value of liberty has been dulled by habit. Simply stated, conscription is involuntary servitude. It is complete usurpation by the Government of an individual's freedom of choice. As Daniel Webster put it—in speaking against a draft proposal in 1814—"The question is nothing less than whether the most essential rights of personal liberty shall be surrendered and despotism embraced in its worst form."

To my way of thinking, there should be one and only one circumstance when a free nation should condone the draft—and then reluctantly. That is when preserving the liberties of us all requires the sacrifice of liberty by some; when it is clear beyond any reasonable doubt that military manpower needs are so great that only coercion can produce the necessary numbers of men.

For personal liberty is not a privilege. It is not a concession granted by Government that must be paid for by military service. It is the guaranteed right of democracy. It must not be compromised.

The deprivation of individual liberty is not the only danger of conscription. There is also the danger that the Government may be unable to resist the temptation to indoctrinate hundreds of thousands of young men with ideas inimical to the workings of a free society. This attitude has been demonstrated by no less an authority than Lt. Gen. Lewis Hershey, director of the Selective Service System. Testifying before a House committee in June, 1966, he made this remarkable statement in defending the draft and opposing a volunteer army:

"I do not want to go along on a volunteer basis. I think a fellow should be compelled to become better and not let him use his discretion whether he wants to get smarter, more healthy or more honest. . . ." Now who is going to decide what is "better" for each recruit? The Federal Government? That is not the American way. That sounds like Russia.

For the past three years, the Johnson Administration has conducted a seemingly endless series of studies on the draft. Last March the President sent his recommendations to Congress. Under the President's plan, deferments for all graduate students (except those preparing to be doctors, dentists and ministers) would be abolished. The age priorities for induction would be reversed; 19-year-olds would be drafted before 26-year-olds. The manpower requirements of the services would be met through a lottery.

A lottery! The Administration calls this scheme FAIR (for Fair and Impartial Random) selection. A colleague of mine points out that FAIR is really an acronym for Futile and Irresponsible Roulette.

The lottery approach does not remedy the basic inequity of the draft—the injustice of forcing one man to serve while allowing another man his liberty. As Bruce Chapman asks in his book, *Wrong Man in Uniform:* Is injustice handed out by a machine any more tolerable than injustice handed out by other men? Nor does the lottery method reduce the inefficiency of the draft, increase the quality of military personnel, or alter the fact that forcing young men into uniform contradicts our belief in the right of the individual to freedom from governmental interference. The lottery just makes the denial of personal liberty a little more arbitrary.

Obviously, the U.S. requires a sizable military force. The question is which system of manpower recruitment best meets our needs. The ideal system should provide the maximum amount of individual liberty; it should be fair; it should supply the services with the necessary quantity—and quality—of men as economically as possible. In my opinion, an all-volunteer military would satisfy these requirements far better than the draft.

Many argue that a voluntary system could not provide enough men at reasonable cost. The evidence is to the contrary. Despite the war in Vietnam, the Marines needed few draftees in 1966, and the Air Force, Navy and Coast Guard none at all. The only service dependent upon conscription is the Army. And of its 1.45 million men, about 60 percent are volunteers.

Critics of a volunteer military like to cite a Pentagon study which shows that 38 percent of all volunteers entered service only because they felt the draft was breathing down their necks. Even if this is true, the fact remains that we still have more men in our manpower pool than the military can possibly handle. Each year more than 1.9 million men reach draft age. Of these, even under war conditions, only about 300,000 must be drafted. Surely, with reasonable pay scales, fringe benefits and a progressive recruitment program, the military could induce that many men to enlist.

Another step that might be taken to insure the success of a voluntary system would be to accept many men who now try to volunteer but who are rejected because of "deficiencies." As General Hershey has stated, "the volume of requests . . . indicates to me that significant numbers of young men not qualified for military service really want to serve."

Don't misunderstand me. I am not suggesting that we lower our standards for combat duty. I simply feel that by adjusting our present mental and physical standards and by providing special training, we could enable thousands of "unqualified" young men who want to become members of the armed services to have that chance.

It also seems to me that the number of volunteers actually required by the military could be reduced by substituting civilians for servicemen in many jobs. According to the Pentagon's own figures, only a small percentage of men are involved in combat. More than 50 percent are listed as "mechanics and repairmen, administrative and clerical, crafts and services." In June, 1966, Assistant Secretary of Defense Thomas D. Morris said that the Pentagon had already filled 74,000 such positions with civilians. We can do better. I'm convinced that we could hire a civilian as a bartender at an officers' club, or as a clerk-typist, for less than the estimated $18,000 a year that it costs to maintain the average foot soldier—the man who often performs these jobs.

Finally, under a voluntary system, the services would need to recruit fewer men simply because the turnover rate (which ranges between 92 and 95 percent among draftees) would be drastically reduced. Using Defense Department figures, Prof. Walter Oi of the University of Washington has computed that if all recruits were "true" volunteers, the turnover rate would plummet to 16.9 percent. An all-volunteer force would enjoy increased status, and this would encourage many to enlist without further inducements.

Some members of Congress are currently being influenced by a study submitted to the President last March. This report rejected the idea of a voluntary military force primarily because it supposedly lacked "flexibility." I submit that a voluntary, professional military force, coupled with a strengthened reserve system, could respond to a crisis more quickly, more effectively, indeed more "flexibly" than any force composed of draftees. As Brig. Gen. Lynn D. Smith has pointed out, 43 percent of the Army at any given time has less than one year's experience, meaning they are raw recruits. In the past, when confronted with crises that demanded an *immediate* buildup, the Pentagon has declined to rely upon draftees. During the Korean War, for example, more than 600,000 World War II veterans were called back into service while 1.6 million potential draftees were ignored. During the Berlin crisis, approximately 150,000 reservists were called back to duty.

Critics have also claimed that under a voluntary system, we would find ourselves with an all-Negro military. That argument has racist overtones. It implies that Negroes have different goals from whites. It denies all the progress that has been made in recent years to raise the standards of the Negro. Critics also say that a voluntary system would lead to the development of a military elite and would thus be a threat to civilian control. The danger of military elitism comes primarily from senior officers who are and always have been professionals. At the top we have and will continue to have civilian control.

The question is no longer whether a voluntary military is feasible or desirable but rather whether we can afford it. The Pentagon cannot say: Its cost estimates range from $4 billion to $17.5 billion. Dr. Oi has estimated that we would have to allocate roughly $8 billion for the salary increases to attract such a force. This sum must be measured against the economies that would inevitably result from a reduction in the turnover rate. The savings in training costs, material and maintenance, would be significant—perhaps billions of dollars. It seems to me that the economics of ending conscription may not be as terrible an obstacle as the draft's defenders insist.

We must have the foresight to accept logic over habit, reason over the retarding security of tradition. We must dispel the myth that the draft, besides being undesirable, is also inevitable. Again and again Congress will be asked to extend the draft. Our committees will provide one "study" after another. But the time for studies is over. In my opinion, Congress should enact legislation immediately to provide for an orderly transition to a volunteer military. It is never too late to start moving away from the draft—and toward the restoration of liberty, equity and military efficiency that a truly volunteer military would bring.

13

AMERICAN DEMOCRACY
AND MILITARY SERVICE

Morris Janowitz

.... Recommendations for change in the Selective Service System usually rest on an admixture of . . . arguments based on moral justification, plus economic costs, military efficiency, and broad conceptions of the national interest in both domestic and foreign policy. Three basic positions of criticism contain some similar features, but express different conceptions of who shall serve in the armed forces of a political democracy.

The armed forces should be a completely voluntary establishment based on a competitive pay scale, regardless of the costs. Immediate personnel shortages should be made up by some form of a temporary lottery system to meet particular emergencies.

The Selective Service System should be reformed. The current system is inefficient as well as morally unjust but to rely exclusively on a "mercenary" army is politically risky and disruptive and probably not economically feasible. Into the foreseeable future, some form of selective service is required to produce manpower for the military establishment. The current

Reprinted from Morris Janowitz, American Democracy and Military Service, *Trans-action*, 4, no. 4, pp. 8-11, 57-59, March, 1967.

system should be reformed mainly by a lottery to augment those who volunteer to serve.

There should be some form of national service in which most young men of draft age serve the country either in the armed forces or in other national programs. In this perspective effective education as well as the pressures of social and political change underscore the desirability of broad involvement of American young people for one or two years in various types of national service, both domestic and international. Selective service is required, but it must operate in a moral and political setting which makes it legitimate. To insure military needs, selective service would rely on a lottery plus differential incentives. Those who do not serve in the military either as volunteers or selectees would be expected (or alternatively, required) to perform national service in a variety of programs, including non-governmental ones. In my own view, the alternative service should be voluntary, and I believe if properly administered it would succeed in involving the bulk of the youth who don't serve in the armed forces.

All three positions give a role to a lottery system if only as a temporary or stand-by device. Civilians who urge this change must recognize that the idea of a lottery system strikes at a sensitive theme in the military self-image. The professional soldier often believes that civilians perceive him as a man who has somehow failed in the occupational competition of the larger society. Many officers hold the view that a lottery for the selection of enlisted men would strengthen and substantiate this stereotype that military service is a job for losers, as members of a luckless legion. Further, the military believe that the motivation of the soldier selected by a lottery might contaminate the attitudes of regular personnel and thus weaken efficiency.

I believe a national service system to be the most desirable format as a long term alternative to the Selective Service System, even though it clearly could not be launched overnight. In the summer of 1966, Secretary NcNamara delivered a speech on national service which served to focus attention on this topic. It produced widespread response, and the President's Commission on Selective Service is specifically charged with exploring the dimensions of national service. In considering the logic of a national service system two elements are of crucial importance:

In my opinion the national service system supplies a sound basis for coping with the deficiencies of any draft system, including one that must rely on a lottery system. In other words, I have no objection to arguing that some form of national service would make the lottery, if it had to be used, more acceptable to all involved. The national service program would emphasize voluntarism plus positive incentives.

More crucial is the argument that a national service program supplies a powerful weapon for preventing the creation of a predominantly or even all-Negro enlisted force in the army, an "internal foreign legion," which would be disastrous for American political democracy.

SUPPLY AND DEMAND

To anticipate military manpower requirements for even a year or two in advance has been hazardous in the past. However, to design an alternative to the current Selective Service System, it is necessary to make assumptions for a 10- to 20-year time period. While the military manpower aspects of a national service system could be introduced very rapidly, other elements of a national service system would have to be developed over a five-year period.

Chart I shows that the number of new personnel procured by the armed forces in 1965 was over 570,000. This includes the small number in the special federal programs of the Coast Guard, US Public Health Service, and the Merchant Marine Academy. In 1966 with the South Vietnam build-up this figure went well over 800,000.

As a point of departure for planning a national service program, it is assumed that the required level of manpower will be equal to that before the current build-up. This implies a reduction of international tensions and in particular some degree of stabilization in Southeast Asia, without which even larger amounts of military manpower will be required. For the purposes of this analysis

Chart I—New military manpower actually procured in 1965

National Military Establishment		
Enlisted: First Enlistments	318,209	
Inductions	102,555	
Reserves—Active Duty Training	94,374	
TOTAL		515,138
Officers: Commissioned	46,535	
Officer Candidates		
Academy Cadets (Entering Class)	2,449	
Aviation Cadets and OCS	2,856	
TOTAL		51,840
Coast Guard		
Officers	385	
Enlisted: Regular Terms	4,912	
Active Duty Training	3,038	
TOTAL		8,335
U.S. Public Health Service		665
Merchant Marine Academy		200
TOTAL NEW PERSONNEL		576,178

(Includes special federal programs—Coast Guard, US Public Health Service, and Merchant Marine Academy)

Chart II–Number of males attaining age 18 for selected years, July 1st

1966	1,791,000
1967	1,787,000
1968	1,775,000
1969	1,823,000
1970	1,871,000
1971	1,938,000
1972	1,974,000
1973	2,028,000

(Source: *Current Population Reports,* November 30, 1965)

it is projected that all the various procurement programs for officers and enlisted men will need 550,000 to 600,000 men for each of the next 10 years and a slowly decreasing number during the tenth to the twentieth year.

Each year in the United States approximately 1,800,000 young men reach the age of 18. This figure can be expected to increase slowly in the years ahead before it declines. To many manpower specialists this presents a real dilemma. (See Chart II.) We have too many young men to operate only with a selective service system, and on the other hand, military manpower requirements are too large to rely upon a voluntary system. Among other issues, a national service system is designed precisely to deal with this dilemma.

ALTERNATIVES TO ARMS

National service is based upon a dual concept. Military manpower needs must be met by a fair and flexible selective service system, recognizing that there will be hardships and imperfections in any system. At the same time all young men should engage in some type of national service. The notion of national service could apply to young women also, but for the purposes of this discussion it is given a second level of priority.

For those young men who do not enter military service, either as volunteers or under a reformed system of selective service, national service should be voluntary. There must be a maximum amount of free choice in the type of national service and a heavy emphasis on the role of private and voluntary groups in developing opportunities for national service. In short, the goal is to fuse a reasonable selective service system with a broad concept of national service. The basic features and principles are strikingly simple.

First, each new group of 18-year-old men would be required to participate in a national registration at which each young man would make known his personal service preference. He would have the opportunity to indicate his choice of three basic alternatives:

–*Declare intention to volunteer for military service* and indicate interest in the various specialized procurement programs including enlistment in a reserve program with active duty training.

—Declare himself subject to selective service and indicate what type of alternative volunteer national service he prefers in the event he is not selected by lottery for military service.

—Apply for exemption on the basis of being a conscientious objector by virtue of religious conviction or other criteria set forth in the decisions of the US Supreme Court. There would be no marital exemptions and while there would be some family hardship and financial hardship exemptions, a federal allotment system would be used wherever required to eliminate gross inequalities. Deferment on the basis of critical skill (as defined by the Department of Labor) would be kept to a minimum, handled as under present arrangements, and administered by local selective service boards.

Second, entrance into the military service takes place when the young man is 19, or in an orderly fashion on a basis of completing a given school year. Those who wish to volunteer for military service are directly incorporated on the basis of their preference and qualifications. Volunteers, of course, must be matched against the available openings. Military manpower requirements beyond those filled by voluntary choice would be met by the Selective Service System through a lottery. Normally, a young man would be subject to the selective service lottery only once in his life—at age 18. Such an approach would eliminate the great uncertainty which exists in the present system. It would be expected that young men who did not enter the armed forces would complete their alternative volunteer national service by the time they reach 26 years of age. Only in the event of a national emergency would young men between the ages of 19 and 26 be liable for subsequent exposure to selective service procurement.

Third, it is clearly recognized that there would be differential incentives and rewards. Those who served in the armed forces would receive a GI Bill of benefits, while alternative national service would not have such features, or very limited ones in the case of the Peace Corps. Alternative service might very well be longer than military service. The Peace Corps, for example, requires 27 months in contrast to 24 months of military service, reflecting an appropriate differential incentive and differential obligation. The type of alternative national service would depend on the skills and qualifications of the man involved as well as his preference. The time at which a person would complete his national service would be determined by his convenience and by the time he is best prepared to perform his national service.

This system does not imply that the armed forces will become the manager of large numbers of young men. To the contrary, the administration of selective service would rest in the present structure. Once military manpower needs are met, the armed forces would have no involvement with the rest of the age group. For example, young men might voluntarily enter the Peace Corps after they had been exposed to the lottery system. The same is true for all forms of alternative service described below.

The national service concept emphasizes maximum reliance on voluntary compliance along with the lottery which is designed to meet military manpower needs. But it is a system of voluntary service in a context of already changing social and political goal definitions. Expansion of the voluntary aspects would be based upon the creation of real and meaningful opportunities for fulfilling these goals, requiring both public and private funds of noteworthy magnitude.

THE LOGISTICS OF NATIONAL SERVICE

The initial step in examining the logistics of national service is to recognize that the existing standards of eligibility for selective service—both medical and educational—are not relevant. In the past, of those young men who were subject to examination by selective service, 15 percent were rejected on medical grounds. If one adds those rejected by educational standards and on administrative grounds (moral and criminal records), rejections in some years rose to over 45 percent with the bulk turned down for educational deficiencies. Men who volunteered for military service had, of course, a much lower rate of rejection, so a more realistic rejection rate on the basis of past military standards for 18-year-olds would be approximately 30 percent. Thus under present arrangements the 1,800,000 young men of a given 18-year-old cohort would be allocated as follows: 600,000 enter military service; 600,000 are rejected; and 600,000 become surplus by various forms of exemptions and deferments.

A basic objective of national service is to eliminate arbitrary educational standards either through remedial efforts by the armed forces, or by substitute service in a National Job Training Corps. Thereby, many young men would have a second chance to enter the mainstream of American life. However, those with severe medical problems, gross bodily deformities, incapacitating psychiatric maladjustments, mental retardation, or asocial personalities would be rejected under any circumstances. There are, in addition, those young men who suffer from limited defects, especially medical ones, who would be better off not participating in any of the group experiences of national service. In all, about 15 percent of the 18-year-old group, approximately 270,000 persons, would be rejected—leaving a total manpower pool of roughly 1,530,000. In Chart III allocations of manpower to the various programs of a national service system are set forth on the basis of this figure.

ARMED FORCES

If force levels can be reduced to their size before the South Vietnam build-up, the armed forces will require approximately 575,000 new men each year. For the normal intake of enlisted personnel, both volunteer and selected by a lottery system, 500,000 will be required. Because of the impact of a lottery, the Air Force, Navy, and Marine Corps will be able, as in the past, to meet their military manpower requirements on the basis of volunteer three-year enlistments. The Army will have to rely on a mixture of volunteers and those procured by the lottery system.

The majority of enlisted men, including volunteers, do not re-enlist. For

Chart III—Manpower allocations under projected national service program

Total age group (19 years old)		1,800,000
Not eligible for National Service (15 percent medical and administrative)		270,000
Eligible annual manpower		1,530,000

Projected Annual Allocations for National Service:		
National Military Establishment		
Enlisted Personnel	500,000	
Officer Personnel	75,000	575,000
Military Remedial Programs		40,000
Special Federal Programs (Substitute Service)		
U.S. Public Health Service, Coast Guard, Merchant Marine		10,000
Police Cadet Corps (Substitute Service)		100,000
National Teacher Corps		150,000
National Health Corps		50,000
Vista Workers and similar Public Programs		70,000
Private Domestic Programs		30,000
Peace Corps		50,000
Private Peace Corps Programs		20,000
National Job Training Corps		400,000
Conscientious Objectors		10,000
Not allocated		25,000
		1,530,000

(Does not include 90,000 enrolled in high school ROTC programs)

example, in 1964 only 25 percent of all armed services regulars re-enlisted. The armed services, because of the realities of the market place, still tend to lag behind civilian pay, especially for trained technicians. Some improvement in re-enlistment rates might be expected, especially in second and subsequent re-enlistments, by improving the conditions of work. But a high rate of personnel turnover at the enlisted level still is to be expected, and is in fact desirable.

If the situation were otherwise, it might be a dangerous indication that the armed forces did not have flexible policies and were being burdened with personnel who could not find comparable positions in civilian life. Moreover, it should be recognized that the men who do not re-enlist bring back into the civilian sector crucial skills required for economic growth and personal mobility. This training proceeds with a high degree of effectiveness because of the organizational environment. Perhaps one of the most important changes would be to reduce the first term of voluntary enlistment in the ground forces to two years so it would be comparable with those procured under the draft. Specialized training would come wherever possible after the first period of two years of service.

An additional 40,000 young men would be taken on a volunteer basis into the Army for the proposed specialized training program designed to supply remedial education and health services. This would amount to only 10 percent of those eligible for such training—the remainder would be allocated to the National Job Training Corps.

To meet officer manpower needs, 75,000 men would have to enter the various procurement programs. This would include new entrants into the military academies and into the various college ROTC programs. This does not include the 90,000 students in the high school ROTC since the bulk of these cadets would enter service as volunteers and become non-commissioned officers or, in a minority of cases, participate in an officer training program.

SPECIAL FEDERAL PROGRAMS

In the United States there are various national programs which operate as substitutes for service in the armed forces. These include the Coast Guard, the Merchant Marine, and the Public Health Service. In all, approximately 10,000 men each year are involved. Entrance into these has been and should be considered substitute service for involvement in selective service. A police cadet corps could be established as another type of substitute service.

Police Cadet Corps.
One hundred thousand young men could be given a substitute service in some form of police work. Increasing the number and quality of police officers is a pressing issue in the United States and bears a resemblance to the issues of military manpower procurement. Police departments require a broader base from which to recruit personnel, and professionalization would be enhanced by an increase in the flow of personnel in and out of the lower ranks. The opportunity for promotion of career police personnel would also be increased. Such service would exempt the person from selective service.

In addition, a number of federal programs could be established as part of the national service. Young men would have the opportunity to enlist after exposure to the lottery.

National Teachers Corps.
One hundred fifty thousand teachers could be recruited annually for work in the inner city. Present policies and resources make it impossible for the inner city to have an adequate supply of teachers and teaching personnel. The whole trend in teaching is to make use of more personnel with general liberal arts background and special summer training. The Teachers Corps concept would also make use of semi-professionals with two years of college, and Teachers Aides with a high school background. Service in the national teaching corps would be an alternative for national service and would not exempt an individual from being subject to the lottery system.

National Health Corps.
Similar to the National Teachers Corps, 50,000 young men could be utilized in the health service field.

Peace Corps.
The present Peace Corps could be expanded to include 50,000 young men each year. The organizational procedures are well worked out and involve 27 months of service. Because of the small number involved, Peace Corps service could be either substitute service that exempts individuals from the lottery or merely alternative volunteer service which the individual would perform if he was not selected by the lottery system. In addition, opportunities could be created for 20,000 men annually in private equivalents of Peace Corps operations abroad.

Domestic Vista Programs.
Domestic equivalents of the Peace Corps under government sponsorship could employ 70,000. Private voluntary national service, under the auspices of church groups, voluntary associations and the like, would involve another 30,000 young men in the United States.

Conscientious Objectors.
Conscientious objectors, in effect, constitute a very small proportion of the population, even if present Supreme Court definitions are used which include both political and religious opposition. At a maximum, 10,000 men per year would be involved under the broadest definitions.

National Job Training Corps.
Of special importance in a national service program is a National Job Training Corps along the lines of the Civilian Conservation Corps which would annually accommodate up to 400,000 young men. The United States is witnessing a crisis in the ability of its educational institutions to meet the needs of low income groups. During the last three years we have witnessed an increase in social tension in the inner city to the point of outright explosion. It is unlikely that the schools can handle these problems. A National Job Training Corps under civilian jurisdiction, with clear paramilitary elements, would supply an opportunity for fundamental education and satisfactory interpersonal experience for achievement during the difficult years between dropping out or being forced out of school and being available for employment. In the past, the armed forces performed some of this job. But this becomes impossible as war becomes more automated and as the weapons of the military become more destructive. Service in a National Job Training Corps would be a substitute for military service; upon successful completion, the young man would be in a position to volunteer for the armed services.

LONG-TERM IMPLICATIONS

For the next five to ten year period, the national service concept must be evaluated against a purely voluntary armed force based upon competitive economic compensation. From an economic point of view, an armed force based on "competitive" salaries is not a real possibility because of the imperfections of the market place. The military would always be disadvantaged relative to the private sector which could raise its prices and salaries at a more rapid rate. Each official inquiry into these topics produces higher and higher cost estimates.

The counter argument to a purely volunteer force is not merely economic. It is also political and professional. An armed force reflects the social structure and the basis of its recruitment. The effectiveness of the armed services is linked to its social composition and its ties to civilian society. In a communist society, professional standards and political control are maintained by a system of party control. It should not be overlooked that this system operates with a considerable degree of effectiveness, although it is incompatible with the standards of a democratic society. By contrast, the armed forces in a political democracy cannot operate without a variety of social links to civilian society. Executive and Congressional control at the top level is not sufficient. The military must find its place in the larger society through a variety of contacts and points of interaction and control. A wide degree of representativeness of its personnel contributes to a willingness to accept the controls of the outer society. A long-term and highly professionalized force, especially at the enlisted man's level, is likely to be less representative and have weaker civilian ties.

But the case for national service is not to be based on a refutation of the volunteer force concept. The arguments for national service involve positive ideas of institution building and facilitating social change, although they fundamentally must deal with the task of selecting men for the armed forces.

National service is an attempt of a democratic society to find an equitable approach to sharing the risks of military service without disrupting the management of its universities. The present system is unfair because of its reliance on educational deferments and inefficient because of the exclusion of those who do not meet contemporary standards. The present system is dangerous because of the disruptive impact on the administration of higher education. It has led students into post-graduate study as a basis of avoiding military service. Universities and colleges can best perform their educational functions if they are free from excessive involvement in the administration of selective service.

The present system cannot long endure regardless of the projected size of the military establishment. The United States is faced with the prospect of a segregated Negro enlisted men's ground force if the present trends are permitted to continue. In fact, the strongest argument against a volunteer force is that such a procedure would merely hasten this transformation. A lottery system is an initial step toward the control of this form of disequilibrium. A national service system would be another important step, for it would both make the lottery system more meaningful and help bring the Negro into the mainstream of American life. To the extent that Negroes become integrated into the larger society and have the same physical and educational qualifications as their white counterparts, concentration in particular sectors of the armed forces is likely to be reduced.

National service is an experiment in education. National service is more than an effort at rehabilitation and a second chance for those youngsters who come from the most deprived segments of our society. It is designed to deal with fundamental problems of personal maturation for all social levels of contemporary society. The present structure of American education is unable to supply those group experiences required for the socialization of successive generations. The search for personal development and individual identity in a social setting which has a narrow emphasis on individual classroom performance leads all too often to various forms of rebellion and withdrawal.

Also, there is every reason to believe that the recent increased academic effectiveness of the American educational system, especially at the high school level, has been purchased at the price of complicating the process of personal development. In a democratic society it is particularly dangerous to make school and academic performance the exclusive route to mobility in adult society. The results of this danger are already clearly manifested by the existing levels of hostility, negativism, and apathy toward school.

National service is designed to make contributions to the educational objectives of all social strata. National service is designed to interrupt classroom experience at appropriate points, so as to give the young man alternative educational experiences. These experiences are designed to develop intense and close group solidarity, based on collective rather than individualistic goals.

National service is an effort at "institutional building" to assist social change both at home and abroad. At home, it is an expression that traditional methods in educational and social welfare need drastic revision. We are dealing not only with the results of restrictive policies in the education and training of professionals, but with the inescapable fact that many operational tasks are better performed by persons who do not have trained incapacities. One way of organizing these work situations is to have persons perform them for short periods of time without having to confront the issue of a career in that particular vocation. Such experience is also vital preparation for more fully trained professional careers. The national service concept is designed particularly to meet this need, recognizing that there are limitations to the allocation of labor by economic incentives. Abroad, national service is part of the growing realization that United States foreign policy requires new approaches to produce economic, social, and political development. It is also a device for making service abroad part of the education and responsibility of each generation of highly trained professionals.

In the last analysis, national service is a form of enlightened self-interest on a world-wide basis.

14

NOTES TOWARD A DEFINITION OF THE UNIFORM CODE OF MILITARY JUSTICE, AS PARTICULARLY APPLIED TO THE PERSON OF CAPTAIN HOWARD LEVY

Don Duncan with J.A.C. Dunn

. . . . As with so many epic things in military life, the Levy court-martial took place because of a massive screw-up.

The mistake was that of Levy's superior officer and chief accuser, Colonel Henry Fancy, the Fort Jackson hospital commander and post surgeon, who had come to view the maverick dermatologist with the same affection Captain Queeg held for his crew. One can only speculate on the traumas suffered by Colonel Fancy while Levy worked for him, since the only certain thing these two men have in common is their medical degrees. The "lawful order of a superior" that Levy was convicted of disobeying was Fancy's command to teach Special Forces

Reprinted from Don Duncan with J.A.C. Dunn, Notes Toward a Definition of the Uniform Code of Military Justice, as Particularly Applied to the Person of Captain Howard Levy, *Ramparts,* 6, no. 1, pp. 52-55, July, 1967.

medics the fine art of dermatology. Levy refused, on the grounds that Special Forces medics were combat soldiers who specialized in killing people primarily and curing them only secondarily. Levy considered it a violation of medical ethics to train medics whose use of medicine would be for political and military, not humanitarian, ends.

Colonel Fancy admitted under questioning that he originally planned to punish Captain Levy under Article 15 (a procedure which would result in a reprimand for an officer) until he was shown the G-2 (Intelligence) file on Levy. One reading, and Levy became "pinko"–apparently one of Colonel Fancy's favorite pieces of argot. The intelligence report revealed that Levy had been under investigation as a possible security risk ever since he entered the Army, primarily because he attended some suspect political meetings in New York. At one such meeting he had heard Malcolm X speak, the Army report said.

After reading that, Colonel Fancy decided to court-martial Levy and throw in a few charges about undermining discipline and morale, since the captain was well known around the camp as an opponent of the war in Vietnam. Fancy could have granted Levy status as a conscientious objector, but he rejected the doctor's application even though it had been approved by a psychiatrist and a chaplain. So the Army got the court-martial it never really wanted. Lt. Colonel Roy Harms, the Fort Jackson public information officer, was clearly depressed about so many reporters streaming to Fort Jackson to observe so closely such a crucial military event as a general court-martial generated by such un-Army-like issues as medical ethics and free speech. "There is no way we can make the Army look good," Harms said with gloomy objectivity, and contented himself with making sure there was plenty of soap available in the latrine of the small yellow building at Fort Jackson which became working headquarters for the press.

Colonel Coppedge, who instituted the original Special Forces medic training program, testified that if he had been in command at Fort Jackson, Levy would never have come to trial. That was the private consensus among other officers, who said that such a freak court-martial could have never occurred at a regular Army post–only at such an authoritarian basic training camp as Fort Jackson.

Colonel Fancy is no Captain Queeg, but he is an extraordinarily simple-minded man whose apparent provincialism is due to an absorbing preoccupation with medicine and the Army. The son of a New Hampshire nurse and a New Hampshire lumberman, Henry Franklin Fancy went to medical school in Montreal, and, despite service in France, Japan and all over the United States, seems to have maintained a narrow mind. His reaction, once, to a conversational mention of Vietnam was to ask how it smelled.

Tall, gray-headed, gaunt, crisply uniformed, a distant look in his eyes, the mild-mannered colonel is apparently capable of vindictiveness towards those he dislikes. He admitted at the trial, for instance, that a patient's letter thanking Dr. Levy for successful treatment had not been included in Levy's military record. Henry Fancy conceded that such an exclusion was rare.

The colonel's testimony provided many insights into the reasoning behind the court-martial of Dr. Levy:

Q. What do you mean by the word "pinko"?

A. This is a slang term that refers to someone who tends to follow communist beliefs . . . .

Q. What have you read about communism?

A. I have read the usual things and the various news media and magazines and have read about communism in various military courses that I have taken and lectures that have been delivered to me on that subject. So, I have a general impression of communism without any detailed knowledge of it at this time.

Q. Have you read any books on Vietnam?

A. Certainly.

Q. Name one.

A. I will retract the statement. I have not read any books on Vietnam, but I have read the news media and articles in magazines and in many of the courses that I have taken in the Army.

If the perfect polar opposite of Colonel Fancy exists, it is Howard Brett Levy. Intelligent, talkative, sensitive, bespectacled, Levy—despite Colonel Fancy's impression of "pinko"—is more flower child than revolutionary. Levy once cried when the petals fell off a rose, and he became a dermatologist because "skin patients don't die." "I've never been to Russia," said Levy, "but if I went I'd be in jail there, too."

Some people at Fort Jackson say that Levy is hard to like because he is loud, abrupt and abrasive, but Captain Dreyfus' fellow officers said that about him, too. Levy appears to have a definite propensity to be disliked by his "equals," like the officers whose club he wouldn't join, but loved by those for whom he feels a humanitarian kinship or a doctor's concern. After a day in court Levy drove me back to town and stopped at his "pad" to pick up mail. Negro matrons along the street recognized his car, waved as we passed and shouted, "Hi!, Dr. Levy!" An orthodox rabbi (a captain) testified to his character and loyalty, as did fellow physicians. A much decorated infantry captain returned from Vietnam to testify for him. They disagreed on Vietnam and many other things, but they were friends. "If Howard goes to jail for what he has done and said, then I'm wasting my time in Vietnam. It's his right to say those things that I'm fighting for." A private stopped him outside the cafeteria to shake his hand and say, "Good luck, Captain—I hope everything works out for you." Negroes stepped forward and asked to testify on his behalf.

Faced with the alternative of being drafted as a private, Howard Levy, M.D. decided to accept his call-up as an officer-doctor. The doctor whom he replaced at Fort Jackson sent him a letter extolling the camp and its working conditions. This dispelled Levy's reservations. However, the doctor later called on him to explain he had been ordered to write the letter and that it had been censored by the camp command.

One day he was a practicing physician in New York, the next Dr. Levy was working in the Fort Jackson hospital in a captain's uniform. Unlike most doctor-draftees, he was never sent to Fort Sam Houston for military indoctrination. Besides teaching the doctors how to wear a uniform and salute, the course is primarily designed to teach a physician how to compromise his medical ethics and beliefs and still live with himself. Not being so easily indoctrinated, Howard Levy remained a doctor with a civilian conscience.

At Fort Jackson Dr. Levy tried saluting a few times, but felt foolish. He substituted a hand wave and words of greeting. To the consternation of his superiors, and probably of the enlisted men as well, he addressed all his patients—privates or officers—as "Sir."

Howard Levy gives the impression of a person who witnessed militarism close up, became horrified and consciously did everything possible to remain a civilian. His shoes appear never to have been contaminated by polish. His belt buckle seems in an advanced stage of gangrene. He invariably forgets to button at least one pocket. The day he had to stand before the ten field grade line of officers of his court-martial and hear himself pronounced guilty, he strolled forward with his right hand in his pocket.

At precisely 0900 hours, on a bright Wednesday (the Army called it 10 May 67), in T-9536, a small frame building painted military yellow propped atop one of Fort Jackson's slight knolls, the United States Army took Dr. Howard Levy to task for being a flower child.

The court-martial began on the anniversary of the birth of the Confederacy and ground on through Armed Forces week. With the sounds of bayonet and combat courses—new "pacification teams" readying themselves for Vietnam— drifting into the crowded 82-seat courtroom, Levy's defense rested its case on Memorial Day. On 3 June 67, Dr. Levy was sentenced to three years at hard labor. . . .

As the chrome handcuff snapped around the physician's wrist, a wail went up from spectators in the courtroom. Unable to direct the hands of the healer for its own ends, the military had shackled them.

That histrionic scene was the finale in the theatrical court-martial, but it wasn't the way the Army had meant to stage it. Colonel Brown, who had tried to make the Army out as the paragon of reason during the trial, looked duly amazed as a burly lieutenant colonel crashed through the swinging gate of the spectator's section seconds after the verdict had been announced and grabbed the doctor by the arm. Lt. Colonel Chester Davis, the hospital administrator, and a former patient of Dr. Levy's, his pink face turned deep red, the paunch over his belt buckle quivering, said that the doctor was under arrest. Levy looked distastefully at Davis' hand. "You don't have to hold my arm," he said.

"Where are you taking him?" Morgan demanded. Davis didn't answer; he was trembling. "May he be accompanied by counsel?" His voice choked, Davis said, "He will not be accompanied by counsel." "May he be accompanied by military counsel, then?" Davis said no, then reached for the handcuffs. Captain Shusterman, the prosecutor, blinked. "Sir, that's not necessary," protested Captain Sanders, Levy's military attorney. "But he's a doctor!" shouted a spectator in the courtroom, and Davis rushed the manacled Levy out the door and into a waiting military police car.

At that moment, the code of Uniform Military Justice showed its true colors. All the easy dignity and military propriety with which Brown and Shusterman had tried to imbue the court-martial's proceedings were shattered. The arbitrary manacling of Dr. Levy was an act of raw power, showing the hard layer of what seemed to be pure hatred for the troublesome doctor beneath the Army's hitherto gentlemanly facade.

It is ironic, reflecting on this scene, that Howard Levy was the one convicted of conduct unbecoming an officer and a gentleman.

PART THREE

Speaking Up Civilly:

A New Pluralism or a Death Rattle?

The preceding sections demonstrate that the new politics has two major characteristics. First, the political times are a-changin'. Involvement in politics has reached new levels of intensity, at the very least. Indeed, we may be moving toward some new definition of citizenship with unprecedented responsibilities. But whatever the outcome, the process is already clear. For good or ill, our political and social institutions will be tested in vigorous and direct ways. Second, significant numbers of people today reject important social institutions and values to the degree of dropping out of a society they perceive as unjust. The combination of high intensity with a spirit of rejection or alienation is highly combustible.

This section attempts to provide some perspective on the probability that the explosiveness of today's social and political situation can be dampened by relatively peaceful means, by what we call speaking up civilly. The specific focus is on teachers and the poor, who share certain characteristics despite their significant differences. For one thing, teachers and the poor alike constitute a test of the viability of our social and political institutions. That is, one of the basic precepts of our system of government holds that such minorities have an inherent right to speak up civilly. Peaceful protest has always been accepted in theory by the First Amendment to the Constitution. "Congress shall make no law," reads the First Amendment, "abridging the freedom of speech, or of the press; or the right of the people peaceably to assemble, and to petition the Government for a redress of grievances." The purpose is to discourage the use of violence to gain political objectives.

If the theoretical argument for civil speaking up is compelling, practice has been uneven. Two generalizations reflect this uneveness. First, definitions of the acceptable boundaries for free speech often have been fiercely disputed. The point applies equally well to the union activities of the 1930s and to the civil rights struggles of the early 1960s. Both movements raised the same basic question: At which point does a peaceful protest by a minority seeking redress of an injustice begin to deprive a majority of its rights of person or property? Our traditions and institutions historically have permitted the peaceful evolution of new balances of political forces. New interests have been able to gain an effective voice in their governance in essentially peaceful ways. Many "interests"—women, immigrants, labor, and so on—have resorted to a degree of violence in gaining an effective voice in their own governance; and they have experienced violent backlashes. Through it all, however, that degree of violence has not been so deep and pervasive as to create permanent social and political cleavages which continually induce violence. The point even holds for that monumental and tragic violence, the War between the States.

Second, despite a general reluctance to honor our forefathers' commitment to open dissent, the steam generated by social unrest has been traditionally allowed to escape before the cauldron of discontent brewed much civil violence. Although many interests have become new participants in the expanding pluralism that characterizes American politics, response to their demands usually has been slow and almost always grudging. Typically, the pace of response has meant that the social and economic costs involved—for example, in minimum hourly wage laws—have been well within our willingness and capability to pay. But this pattern of response is always open to the charge that so much more could be done for so many other interests.

These two generalizations suggest that our traditions and institutions for speaking up civilly will be put to a real test in the development of the new politics. For tests of the definition of free speech are being made in intense ways on all fronts. Demands for greater shares in the good things of life are being made by an unprecedently wider range of interests than ever before, interests whose needs and aspirations are bewilderingly complex and often conflicting. These two factors will sorely test the ability of our traditions and institutions.

Americans are once more challenged to provide timely responses to legitimate demands peacefully presented. We shall give special attention to two such sets of demands which to this time have been expressed in more or less peaceful ways:

Teacher Militancy: is hitting the bricks compatible with educating youth?
The War on Poverty: "maximum feasible participation" or maximum misunderstanding?

Our focus is illustrative rather than exhaustive. But even sparse illustrations support two broad generalizations. First, failure to peacefully include such interests in a new pluralist balance implies the threat of uncivil actions. And, as the following section establishes, America is already ravaged by an unusual amount of violent civil protest. Hence, success in peacefully expanding our pluralist balance of interests carries an especial premium today. Indeed, failure may signal the demise of our pattern of change through essentially peaceful methods.

Second, avoidance of uncivil acting out will require great skill, mutual tolerance, and considerable good luck. Satisfying the aspirations of the poor has meant threatening the interests of the teachers. There are no easy ways out of such binds, as in the recent New York City situation, where the desire of some poor (usually black or Puerto Rican) to influence the educational policies affecting their children ran headlong into the fact that a large proportion of the teachers are Jewish. It was not possible to avoid overtones of anti-Semitism on the one hand and white racism on the other, with the core issue being who was going to hold which jobs under what conditions.

A. A BASIC DILEMMA

Militant teachers and the poor share several characteristics, even though their interests may conflict. First, both were largely silent over the years even though ill-treated. The pain felt by both teachers and the poor has, in the past, been narcotized by popular myths of inadequacy. Teachers in elementary and high schools until the 1960s either believed, or were too insecure to challenge, their poor-but-honest stereotype. Although they played crucial and expanding roles in the education and socialization of the young, they learned to accept inferior rewards and support along with the honor. The poor were deprived even of the psychic income often lavished on teachers. The poor were kept docile by frequent doses of Protestant ethic prattle. They were told that their plight was caused by their own sloth, drunkenness, and immorality. If poverty were self-imposed, it followed, society had no obligation to alleviate it. The poor were twice shamed, by their immediate environment and by society at large. This atrophied spirit caused many to protest their condition in antisocial ways; by violent behavior that merely reinforced the stereotype of their unworthiness for greater sharing in the good things of life.

Second, for a host of reasons, both the teachers and the poor suddenly and simultaneously have come to a greater appreciation of their power. The phenomena of crowds of poor people demanding free food stamps, increased welfare payments, and other poverty-reducing programs is as recent as the growing militancy among American teachers in elementary and high schools.

Third, teachers and the poor have to this point used similar tactics. Having common antecedents in the civil rights demonstrations of the late fifties and early sixties, as well as in the labor union movement, the teachers and the poor have relied on picketing and strikes and marches on City Hall.

A basic dilemma inheres in these common characteristics. Even if the claims of both the teachers and poor are just, to sketch one horn of the dilemma, the economic costs may be seen as prohibitive. Specifically, if strikes by teachers succeed in improving their working conditions, what of work stoppages by even more meagerly rewarded, essential, and far more numerous public employees, such as policemen or firemen, and garbage collectors or hospital attendants? Opposition to teacher militancy is thus bound up with broader political questions of how any public employee can improve his working conditions. Rising employee demands may run into resistance from taxpayers who are increasingly reluctant to support tax levies. The point applies even more forcefully to fulfilling the expectations of America's many millions of destitute and deprived, for whom relief hinges on the willingness of taxpayers to part with a larger share of their spendable income.

The other aspect of the dilemma questions how cost considerations can discipline demands by teachers and the poor without creating other problems. For example, one way to curb the demands of militant teachers is to accuse them of putting personal gain ahead of the education of the young. Or laws can be passed to prohibit strikes by teachers. However, these strategies may weaken the position of the teachers in the classroom by disparaging their motives. The same bind inheres in putting off the poor by arguing that increases in anti-poverty tax dollars seem contingent upon the conclusion of the war in Vietnam, continued economic expansion, and the interim good manners of the poor. Thus, the poor, like public school teachers, are told to keep their cool for a few more years. They are warned that even peaceful protests can do no good under present conditions. Docility and continued sacrifice may be properly rewarded "when the time comes." The question, however, concerns how much time there is.

The dilemma is real, given the costs of our present international commitments in Vietnam and elsewhere. The degree to which policy makers can slip between the horns of the dilemma will be crucial in determining whether we further expand pluralist participation in American politics, or whether we will see greater violence among teachers and the poor, adding to our burdens of governance.

B. TEACHER MILITANCY: IS HITTING THE BRICKS COMPATIBLE WITH EDUCATING YOUTH?

The basic question for militant teachers is one of long standing, but it is being answered differently today by increasing numbers of educators in elementary and high schools. Can teachers strike, can they "hit the bricks" as labor union members have long done, and still maintain their position in the classroom? Sylvia Barrett, the teacher heroine in *Up the Down Staircase*,[1] gave one answer. She quietly endured administrative bungling and interference, insolent students, and inadequate facilities, all for the love of teaching. In the fall of 1968, however, Miss Barrett might have joined other New York City teachers who closed the school system for weeks. The same decade in which armed national guardsmen have shot black Americans in Detroit and students have guzzled the Chivas Regal of university presidents, has also seen the development of teacher-

[1] Bel Kaufman, "Up the Down Staircase," Prentice-Hall, Englewood Cliffs, N.J., 1964.

picketers who have learned to scream obscenities at scabs, or strike-breakers.

A number of factors have propelled the teacher out of the classroom and into the streets. Consider the general notion of environmental change.[2] Many teachers seem less committed to their schools or districts than in the past. This result has complex causes. Many teachers, especially those working in ghetto schools, do not reside in the districts in which they teach. Moreover, schools have grown to have thousands of students and hundreds of teachers. In learning factories of this size, school administrators have become increasingly divorced from classroom teachers and schools have become more impersonal. Among other factors, these helped undercut the pious notion that there could be no legitimate differences of opinion between teachers and administrators because they share the goal of educating the young. Once this premise was widely questioned, teachers could more easily see themselves as employees of administrators rather than as their partners. And if you are an employee, why not organize like other workers so as to gain greater influence over the conditions under which you work?

This feeling of teachers being isolated from decision making came at a time when they were being burdened in many other ways as well, encouraging them to speak out forcefully, if civilly.

The new demands on teachers in elementary and high schools may be cataloged briefly. First, teachers are performing a wider range of functions than ever before. Let us simplify. Teachers are expected to educate the college-bound, train the job-bound, patrol the jail-bound, and chaperone the mating ground. In capsule, teachers were doing relatively much more and making relatively much less. Unionized workers have long known how to put a stop to that. Teachers are learning the same lessons today.

Second, inadequate moral support, salaries, and facilities have increased frustration among educators. This frustration is heightened by the popular belief that teaching in elementary or high schools is a lesser-grade occupation than business or other professions, which has resulted in teacher salaries below those earned by others with college or graduate training. In the past, apparently, there have been enough dedicated souls to staff our primary and secondary schools despite poor pay and a generally poor image. Or perhaps there simply were fewer attractive opportunities for professional employment. In any case, the times are a-changin', especially in slum schools.

Third, as a result of the civil rights movement, the tactics of speaking up forcefully have gained a substantial respectability among the college-trained. These tactics worked for those blacks and middle-class and college-educated whites who wrote the civil rights history of the early 1960s. Moreover, teachers patently could not have missed the obvious lesson that their plight was in part due to their previous unwillingness or inability to forcefully make their demands.

---

[2] Much of the following discussion of the causes of teacher unrest is drawn from James Cass and Max Birnbaum, What Makes Teachers Militant?, *Saturday Review,* January 20, 1968.

Fourth, increasing numbers of militant teachers are more interested in earning good wages than in being "professional," defined as not using trade-union tactics defined as somehow sub-professional. Teachers of the now generation tend to be better trained, which encourages their insistence on better working conditions. Since teachers see themselves as full partners in the revolution of rising expectations, they wish to share economic prosperity in common with other classes of workers.

The 1960s were ripe for teacher militance, for they had unparalleled leverage after Sputnik. Education increasingly became involved in an issue of national pride and power, as opposed to a local concern to keep taxes low. Because a good education became increasingly perceived as the surest key to success, taxpayers became more amenable to the support of teacher demands. There was power for teachers in these changing attitudes.

The prime mover behind teacher demands for better working conditions in elementary and high schools has been the fast-growing American Federation of Teachers (AFT). Peter Janssen in "The Union Response to Academic Mass Production" describes the growth of the AFT and the ways in which it differs from the more sedate National Education Association (NEA). Janssen also describes some of the victories and failures of AFT locals, while presenting an overall view favorable to the new militancy among teachers. You can almost hear the chant in Janssen's prose: "Two, four, six, eight—pay us or we don't educate."

Not everyone, however, marches to the tune of the same drummer. James LeSure provides critical counterpoint in "And Gladly Strike?" LeSure's stinging criticisms of teacher strikes reflect the views of the educational administrators whom he represents. LeSure argues that strikes are unprofessional and unnecessary, since teachers have made great advances without them. Moreover, and he really socks it to them on this point, some teachers are not worth what they now earn. Get his message? "Two, four, six, eight—you're not paid to agitate."

The balance of power is still in the hands of the LeSures, but teachers show less and less tendency to roll over and play dead. Among other elements, militant teachers are developing counter-arguments to the traditional guidelines that they see as so inhibiting. For example, a wide variety of arguments have been used to exclude teachers from collective negotiations about the conditions under which they work. Henry Weinstock and Paul Van Horn detail six such arguments in "Impact of Negotiations Upon Public Education." The authors refute each of the six arguments commonly made by school boards to justify their refusals to negotiate with teachers.

What of the future? Educators in elementary and high schools probably will continue or escalate their demands for higher salaries, improved facilities, and a greater voice in shaping their work environment. The outcome is less predictable. If administrators are insufficiently willing to recognize such demands as legitimate, we might expect that teacher strikes will become as much a part of the autumn scene as football and colorful leaves. Conceivably, things could get more intense.

C. THE WAR ON POVERTY: "MAXIMUM FEASIBLE PARTICIPATION" OR MAXIMUM MISUNDERSTANDING?

Presently America is engaged in at least two major wars. One is in Vietnam. The other war is in our own ghettos, on played-out farms, and in jobless coal-mining areas. Although the wars are literally worlds apart and are being fought with very different weapons, there is a striking similarity in the strategy with which they are being waged. Neither war has seen us bring our full resources into play to gain victory. Relatedly, it might not be possible in either case to bring these full resources to bear without creating dissension and disunity between interests who are quite far from seeing eye-to-eye.

The war on poverty, declared in 1964, heralded the first major change in our welfare policies since the depression. That three decades of inaction were suddenly replaced by a spurt of activity requires some explanation. Awakening the conscience of the American public and its elected representatives can be largely attributed to the dynamic young President Kennedy. On his way to Camelot, Kennedy campaigned in the dark hollows and paralyzed coal-mining towns of West Virginia. There he saw poverty in the hopeless faces of men seeking jobs now gone, in the hungry eyes of the women perhaps fantasying what it could mean to be a Kennedy woman or one of the beautiful people in their circle. More depressing were the portents of the future—the unkempt children who dropped out of school because they lacked clothes, shoes, or (far worse still) incentive. Kennedy's sensibilities also were touched deeply by the tragic descriptions of the poor in Michael Harrington's *The Other America.*[3]

Ironically, Kennedy in death prompted Congress to give the poor an opportunity for a better life. President Johnson, seeking innovations which would earn him history's judgment as a great and empathic president, pushed through Congress the Economic Opportunity Act (EOA) of 1964. The fanfare was enthusiastic. Existing welfare programs dealt only with symptoms of poverty and were paternalistic. EOA, it was promised, would permanently cure the causes of poverty, in part by getting the maximum feasible participation of the poor in their own resurrection.

EOA sought to prepare the poor to compete in industrialized America. The attack moved simultaneously on three fronts. One focus was unemployment, especially the untrained young. The Job Corps, the Neighborhood Youth Corps, and a proposal to provide federal grants to private companies which would initiate job-training programs for hardcore unemployables all were designed to make youth jobworthy. A second aspect of the war on poverty was intended to improve the education of the poor. Programs were proposed to meet the needs of everyone—from the deprived pre-schooler eligible for Project Headstart, to the Upward Bound college preparatory program for ghetto kids, to the Work-Study

[3] Michael Harrington, "The Other America," Penguin Books, Baltimore, 1963.

Program which was to help students earn college expenses. Still a third goal of EOA was to help poor adults get a new start. Legislation provided for loans to small businessmen and farmers. Academic and vocational education were offered to adults.

Kennedy's Camelot was unrealized, in many respects and in many degrees. EOA was no exception. Some see as much maximum feasible misunderstanding in its brief history as they do "maximum feasible participation."[4] The focus is on the complex blend of participation/misunderstanding reflected by our poverty programs. An important sense of that complexity is reflected in James Anderson's "Poverty, Unemployment, and Economic Development." He discusses the dimensions of poverty in America, noting various ways of measuring substandard incomes. Anderson also outlines various techniques and programs for eliminating poverty. He includes a catalog of the provisions of the war on poverty and the Appalachian Regional Development Act.

Enthusiasm about the war on poverty has waned, it is easy to establish. In the early days, the commanding field general of the war vowed that poverty could be eliminated by 1976. This sincere judgment seems very naive today, just a few years later. In the intervening half decade, commitment to rebuilding slums and uplifting their residents has faded. These efforts have become secondary to the war in Vietnam, for one thing. And the coordinating Office of Economic Opportunity has been stripped of many of its functions, while critics of poverty proposals have magnified its failings. President Nixon gives every evidence of putting his own distinctive stamp on our welfare programs, moreover, which implies the death of an approach that has been hanging onto life.

Why the war on poverty lost momentum is no simple matter. But some contributing factors seem clear enough. Some poverty programs and administrators had a genius for inviting wrath from diverse sources. Especially susceptible to attack has been the Community Action Program, which (among many other projects) paid salaries to members of a Chicago youth gang and was plagued by delinquency at some of its Job Corps camps. Sometimes the purposes of the program were even more seriously perverted. For example, John Berry estimates that perhaps half of the Neighborhood Youth Corps projects in Rhode Island "were not being operated properly." Thus "poverty money" was used to provide summer jobs for middle-class teenagers instead of ghetto youths, in part because of apparent unclarity about criteria for participation but in part also due to questionable administrative practices.[5]

Some proponents of the war on poverty no doubt felt a diminished sense of support for community action as it evolved, and particularly after the outbreaks of civil disorder that are introduced in the next section. At an ideological level, supporters of community action programs were naive about the willingness of those having power to give it up without a struggle. Escalation on both

[4] Patrick Moynihan, "Maximum Feasible Misunderstanding," Free Press, New York, 1969.
[5] John M. Berry, Rhode Island's Misspent Youth, *Reporter,* 34 no. 2, pp. 29-33, January 27, 1966.

sides was the short-run consequence, then disillusionment. As Moynihan concludes:

> Seemingly it comes to this. Over and over again, the attempt . . . to organize poor communities led first to the radicalization of the middle-class persons who began the effort; next to a certain amount of stirring among the poor, but accompanied by heightened racial antagonism *on the part of the poor* if they happened to be black; next came retaliation from the larger white community; whereupon it would emerge that the community action agency, which had talked so much, been so much in the headlines, promised so much in the way of change in the fundamentals of things, was powerless. A creature of a Washington bureaucracy, subject to discontinuation without notice. Finally, much bitterness all around.[6]

At a practical level, community action programs often became "agitational" efforts whose basic strategy was based on win-lose competitions between interests, some of which had previously been mutual supporters. Consider the case of New York City Jews,[7] long supporters of liberal causes. By various twists and turns, one local community action program essentially pitted Negroes and Puerto Ricans against teachers who were largely white or Jewish. The in-fighting got rough on both sides. It may have been tactically useful for blacks to describe "the so-called liberal Jewish friend [with] his tricksy, deceitful maneuvers [as] really our enemy [who] is responsible for the serious educational retardation of our black children." But such tactics are also well designed to severely test the faithfulness of traditional urban Jewish support for liberal causes like the war on poverty.

Finally, there is suggestive evidence that the war on poverty was oversold by policy makers who got carried away in the euphoria of President Johnson's "politics of consensus" which marked his early days in office. That rosy bloom quickly faded, and hard second looks at the war on poverty convinced many that expectations had been set impossibly high.[8] The expectations of the poor had been increased, however, and failure to deliver even the impossible left a legacy of frustration and disillusionment that may have found outlets in civil disorder; in burning and looting, loss of life, and diminished respect for authority.

The war on poverty also draws fire from left-liberal-intellectuals who see as its basic defect that it attempted too little rather than sought so much. Social reformer Michael Harrington wrote "The Will to Abolish Poverty" soon after the end of the 1968 Poor People's Campaign, and his feelings were strong and clear. The war failed where it must succeed—in providing food, jobs, and a decent standard of living for the vast majority of the poor. Saul Alinsky is even more

---

[6]Moynihan, *op. cit.*, pp. 134-135.

[7]*Ibid.*, pp. 115-117.

[8]*Ibid.*, pp. 144-164.

ascerbic in "The War on Poverty—Political Pornography." Alinsky, a freelance
poverty fighter, has had more success in eliciting participation of ghetto residents, a stated goal of the war, than have any of the federally financed poverty
programs. Too much poverty money is spent on administrators' and consultants'
salaries, he charges. He is even more irate that its funds are sent to such dens of
political intrigue as city halls, as well as to social welfare agencies which have
already demonstrated their ineffectiveness.

A conclusion inheres in such criticisms. This venture of the Great Society was
undertaken with shining ideals and bold promises. It has made some major gains.
But it has left many of its intended beneficiaries with the bitterness which
accompanies shattered hopes. To say that they expected too much too soon is
correct, but it does not lessen the sting of disappointment and disillusionment.

Granted that the war on poverty has suffered at least a major tactical setback,
the search for viable programs still goes on. Since none of our multitude of
welfare programs has eliminated poverty, or even put much of a dent in it, many
demands have been heard for new ways to share our wealth. President Nixon
made such a proposal, which is sketched in "Family Assistance Supplements and
the New Federalism." This proposal would alter the existing welfare system in
numerous ways. It would establish a national minimum for welfare payments,
basically, and would encourage the poor to work by expanding job training
facilities and child day-care centers. Welfare payments would be provided without reducing the incentive to work, thereby helping the working poor to live and
encouraging the able poor to work.

It is far too early even to guess whether President Nixon's program will get
congressional approval and effective implementation; it is clear now that it is
only one approach among many. Consider the "guaranteed income" plan advocated by Robert Theobald. Theobald's plan, unlike Nixon's, lacks a work incentive. Indeed, Theobald assumes that automation will eliminate most jobs, so he
sees no particular merit in encouraging work. Hence he provides a subsidy for
every poor family to bring its annual income to $3,400 whether the family
earned nothing or $3,300 during the year.[9]

Conservatives like Henry Hazlitt have criticized both plans. He is scandalized by
the suggestion that tax money be doled out with no strings attached. The misplaced generosity of compensating many non-workers, Hazlitt argues, will make
it impossible to hire people to perform unpleasant tasks.[10] Every society needs
its hewers of wood and carriers of water, he implies. He prefers our existing
system with its case-by-case evaluation of welfare applicants patrolled by a
means test. The innovation Hazlitt recommends is to deny the suffrage to the
poor who will otherwise use their votes to raid the public treasury.

[9]Robert Theobald, The Guaranteed Income: What and Why, in John Bunzel, ed., "Issues
of American Policy," pp. 99-108, Prentice-Hall, Englewood Cliffs, N.J., 1968.

[10]The prolific writing of Henry Hazlitt can be found in many places. Most of his ideas set
forth here are found in The Coming Crisis in Welfare, *National Review,* 19, no. 15, pp.
416-418, April 18, 1967.

Providing an income may not be enough to wrest the poor out of the poverty cycle, in any case. Consider that the impoverished—old, young, and in the prime of life—are usually also ill-housed. They live in America's 12 million dilapidated or deteriorating houses and apartments. They have not benefited from our building industry. Private builders find profits scarce in the low-income market, and consequently have turned their attention to more lucrative fields. Hence federally financed public housing has been the only major source of new inexpensive dwelling units, and this source has been woefully inadequate.[11]

Thus, experience with inexpensive housing reflects more failure than success, just as with other programs ostensibly intended to benefit the poor. The objectives of the programs have been clearly stated and the government's commitment has been firm. But implementation has been blighted by hesitation, inconsistency, and diversion. Available data do not permit an unequivocal judgment about whether the disadvantaged—whether black or white—retain a faith in government action and programs.[12] Some signs indicate at least some decrease in such faith. For example, in the past blacks have seemed ever ready to turn the other cheek one more time. They seemed to retain a faith that the government intended to carry out the reforms it embraced and that conditions would improve. The recent growth of militant black groups may indicate that this trust is fast evaporating. Our future may depend on whether we can and will honor the IOUs of faith drawn against the Great Society's bank account.

D. THE "NEW FEDERALISM": TOWARD RECONCILING INTERESTS OR ISOLATING THEM?

Such efforts toward a new pluralism as those by teachers and the poor have prompted a good deal of rethinking about basic political questions, prominent among them being the issue of the relative balance between federal and local authorities. Aaron Wildavsky directs our attention to that balance and to its consequences in "Empty-Head Blues: Black Rebellion and White Reaction." He is not certain whether we are witnessing the development of a new pluralism, or the death rattles of the old. But Wildavsky does believe he knows how we can increase the probability of a more viable pluralism. And he concludes that the only real question is how much rebellion we will have in the process.

Broadly speaking, the period since 1930 has been one of more or less unbroken increases in the power of the federal level of government, and Wildavsky sees major advantages in reversing that trend. He writes of new financing of state and local governments and, beyond that, creating and financing a complex of

[11] For several approaches to encouraging private investment, see James Ridgeway, Rebuilding the Slums, *New Republic,* 156, pp. 22-25, January 7, 1967.

[12] Everett Cataldo, Richard Johnson, and Lyman Kellstedt, "Political Attitudes of the Urban Poor: Some Implications for Policy-Makers." Paper delivered at 1968 Annual Meeting, American Political Science Association, Washington, D.C., September 4-7, 1968.

neighborhood corporations with a significant voice in their own destinies. The rationale is straightforward and attractive, up to a considerable point. For example, such an approach might strengthen local governments, and encourage citizens to increasingly look toward these units for the satisfaction of their needs. The interrelated problems of poverty and education might be attacked in the context of specific local traditions and customs, and by local officials with authority to make necessary adaptations with less need for securing complex authorizations from higher levels of authority. Rich experimentation might be encouraged, as diverse communities did their own things. Overall, the basic thrust is toward reconciling interests where they live. Many new issues would become "political issues" (to use the Supreme Court's early phrasing) to be decided at the local ballot box or in various representative forums.

The rationale for the new federalism has its questionable features as well, especially in its more exuberant forms. "We are all decentralists now," Kristol concludes. But he is worried that "liberal intellectuals . . . have opted for decentralization with the same kind of enthusiastic abstractness they once brought to centralization."[13] Even given that decentralization is a value, approaching it could conflict with other values. Consider the issue of minority rights, for example. Suppose a local corporation has a membership which is 85 percent black (or white or whatever). What of the treatment of the 15 percent remnant? Without doubt, much historical involvement in local affairs by the federal government has been motivated by the need to provide protection for such minorities which the local community variously denied them. Such leverage is difficult to gain, and perhaps easy to lose. If political men were angels, in short, extreme decentralization would pose no problem. But neither would any pattern of organizing.

Broader issues also are bound up in the question of the new federalism. Kristol puts the matter in a nutshell. He worries about whether "we can decentralize our services without fractioning our heterogeneous political community."[14] This is a critical political question. Suppose you were a member of a minority which had to rely in large measure on support from the Federal government—let us say, a Negro from the Mississippi Delta. You might be very leery about transfers of authority and funds to local units from the Federal government. The new federalism, to you, might seem only a way of fragmenting your own national Negro interest groups and threatening the political power so laboriously gained. If decentralization is a subterfuge to limit black power nationally, its effect would be to leave Delta blacks more vulnerable to local pressures. Such feelings could also induce separateness, a fractioning of our heterogeneous political community just at the historical moment when it is beginning to confront the question of racial integration.

No one can yet definitively evaluate the new federalism. It may help reconcile interests which have a local stake in policy outcomes. Or it may be seen as a threat, as a way of isolating some interests into either local majority or minority

[13] Irving Kristol, Decentralization for What?, *The Public Interest*, no. 11, p. 19, Spring 1968.
[14] *Ibid.*, p. 23.

pockets. The majority pockets would be allowed to exist as local units, as in a black Harlem with substantial local control over schools and welfare and other services, but broader representation systems might be so rigged as to deny them just voice. The minority pockets would be easier to handle, as minor partners in some larger local unit.

Like much of life, how things will work out is a matter of balance. And that balance is not yet clear.

15

THE UNION RESPONSE
TO ACADEMIC MASS PRODUCTION

Peter Janssen

Ten years ago, the American Federation of Teachers (AFL-CIO) was so limp it employed—and could afford—only one organizer to recruit new members in the entire United States east of Lincoln, Nebraska. Today, the AFT is powerful enough to shut down many of America's largest school systems—and often does. In the idiom of the cities where it musters its strength, the AFT is "what's happening, baby." Now its very success begins to raise serious questions about the applicability of trade union techniques to the classroom—and, beyond that, about the possibility that the AFT itself will become as rigid and hierarchical as the school systems in which it operates.

The AFT is enjoying a period of almost frantic growth. Its membership has doubled in the last four years, reaching more than 146,000 today. In a series of chain-fire victories, it has beaten the established 1,000,000-member National Education Association in elections to represent teachers in collective bargaining with school boards in New York, Chicago, Detroit, Boston, Philadelphia, Cleveland, Providence, Gary, and Washington, D.C.

The federation's growth is a direct product of the malaise of big-city schools with their all-too-familiar litany of problems: crowded classes, deteriorating

Reprinted from Peter Janssen, The Union Response to Academic Mass Production, *Saturday Review*, L, no. 42, pp. 64-66, 86-88, October 21, 1967.

buildings, overwhelming bureaucracy, irrelevant curriculum. In these conditions, teachers have more often been wardens than instructors. Suffering under mounting clerical and disciplinary chores, they are rewarded with subsistence-level pay. Last year, the average pay for teachers was $6,821; for construction workers, $7,525. Only 6.5 per cent of all teachers made more than $10,000. To dissatisfied teachers, the AFT promised a change, playing the theme that the NEA was so tied in with the existing system that it somehow was responsible for the deterioration. Above all, the AFT stresses that it is a teachers' organization. "Teachers want to do things for themselves," says Charles Cogen, diminutive (5 feet, 2 inches) AFT president. "They want the freedom and the power to control their own professional destiny."

The AFT gave teachers a clear chance to break with the past by separating them from their administrators, urging them to band together to protect their interests from oppressive bosses. AFT leaders even stepped out of the gentlemanly schoolteacher mold to emphasize the point. "Martinets, authoritarians, petty tyrants—these are too often the characteristics of administrators," Cogen has said. In too many cases his charge rang true. The AFT constitution prohibits anyone with the rank of principal or higher (or any organization of such persons) to become members. Union organizers point out, meanwhile, that the American Association of School Administrators is a branch of the NEA.

The secret ballot has become a key to the AFT's success. Significantly, in almost all its elections with the NEA, the federation is the decided underdog. The fact that it often wins—receiving far more votes than it has members— supports Cogen's assertion that teachers feel coerced into joining the NEA by supervisors who for decades have moved through a series of NEA departments. In November 1964, for example, the Philadelphia federation did not even have a representative in 40 per cent of the city's schools. Three months later, in a secret ballot election, it handily defeated the NEA affiliate which had twice as many registered members.

The union, of course, doesn't win all its bargaining contests. The NEA has beaten it in Rochester, Buffalo, Denver, and twice in Milwaukee—where it is still weak—and Newark, where the AFT was licked at its own game. Both the New Jersey Education Association and its Newark affiliate are among the most militant in the NEA. The Newark teachers association has even walked out on strike, with the support of the NJEA—exercising a form of protest frowned on by the NEA. And the federation's chances in Newark weren't helped when labor leaders there lobbied publicly against the state's sales tax to help support education.

Usually the AFT manages its power more effectively. Catching the public sympathy with the early tactics of the civil rights movement, it has often broken state laws by taking to the streets to win a point. In the last school year alone, the AFT sponsored twenty-two strikes across the country, from New York and Baltimore to the Camp Parks Job Corps Center in California. "If teachers don't fight for better schools," Cogen asks, "who will?" The growing number of male teachers, and the declining enchantment with being merely a white-collar "professional"—regardless of pay and working conditions—have helped the AFT carry the battle. In general, its appeal is to younger teachers who have seen the dark realities of urban schools and are persuaded that a romantic attachment to "dedication" is not enough, either for them or their pupils.

The strikes have been helped substantially by $250,000 grants in each of the last three years from the Industrial Union Department of the AFL-CIO. Strikes further have given the AFT's growth a snowballing effect, advancing its image as a militant fighter for teachers' rights, destroying the picture of the teacher as a silent partner in the educational process. Nothing kills the Mr. Chipps fantasy faster than a picture of striking teachers being loaded into police vans in Baltimore.

Most of the AFT's strikes have paid off as teachers sit at negotiating tables as equals with their school boards. Such collective bargaining usually produces higher salaries and smaller class size in rapid order. The United Federation of Teachers, the AFT's New York local, achieved an average pay increase of $750 per teacher in 1962, when it negotiated the city's first contract. That document also contained thirty-four fringe benefits and guaranteed teachers a duty-free lunch period for the first time in memory. Contracts also often emphasize straight labor items. The contract which went into effect last January 1 in Chicago, for instance, stipulates that "the high school day may begin and end at different times from school to school but shall not exceed 406 minutes in length for a high school teacher"—establishing a nice round number. Philadelphia teachers were ecstatic when the federation won a contract guarantee of $7.50 an hour for extracurricular duties—particularly since the previous rate was $2.75.

Such victories, and the battles that precede them, have raised serious questions about the use of trade union techniques in the educational process. The questions have to do not only with the right of public employees to strike or with the philosophical problem arising from definitions of "professional conduct," but also with the issue of power itself. The traditional union aims— shorter hours, more pay, protection of members—are not necessarily consistent with the improvement of education, and a union contract which stipulates the maximum number of hours a teacher can work is not likely to reduce the dropout rate. Stamping out fenders in an automobile plant requires a different set of incentives and different organization from the process of teaching children to read, and the critics of the union have not been slow to point out the difference. Yet, not surprisingly, the AFT has been most successful in exactly those school systems which look and operate like factories. The big-city administrations and the public have created the factory school; the teachers' union is the employees' response.

If the AFT acts like an industrial union, its traditional loyalties—and its current public relations efforts—tend to place it with the liberal wing of the labor movement. The organization promotes its image of currency by aligning itself with the civil rights movement and by borrowing some of its techniques. In 1951, three years before *Brown v. Topeka,* it ordered its Southern locals to desegregate or get out. (This was not a costly decision. It had only seven.) The

AFT provided teachers and $50,000 to set up Freedom Schools in 1964 for more than 4,000 Southern Negro pupils. Last year it created a civil rights department and then sponsored a "Racism in Education" conference in Washington. More than 1,000 teachers there resolved to drop the "slave name" of "Negro" from the curriculum and use "Afro-American" instead. Finally, on the first day of the recent New York strike, Bayard Rustin, the movement's philosopher and leader of the 1963 March on Washington, was out walking the picket lines with UFT President Albert Shanker. Estimates are that as many as one-fifth of the AFT's members are Negroes.

In practice, however, the federation's commitment is less certain. The union and the movement have developed divergent interests. The UFT, for example, did not support the Reverend Milton Galamison's massive school boycott to promote integration in 1964. As a result, many disgusted New York teachers formed their own organization, the African American Teachers Association, which now claims half the city's 4,800 Negro teachers as members—and has its offices in Bedford-Stuyvesant. (The UFT's offices are on Park Avenue.) "The UFT," says the association's president, Albert Vann, "is concerned with teachers' rights and salaries, but not so much with community problems." At a time when ghetto parents are asking for year-round schools, the union demands shorter hours; while black parents ask for local control, as at Intermediate School 201 last year, the union adopts as protective a response as does the Board of Education hierarchy. AFT locals also often work against civil rights by vetoing plans to integrate faculties, insisting that teachers have the right to transfer to any school. This insistence places large numbers of inexperienced teachers in ghetto schools, but it doesn't disturb federation members who have seniority.

The AFT was founded by four teachers' groups in Chicago in 1916 and affiliated with the American Federation of Labor. Its first charters went to locals in Chicago, Gary, Oklahoma City (Oklahoma), Scranton (Pennsylvania), New York, and Washington, D. C. The new union's growth was slow. By 1934 it had fewer than 10,000 members (including professors from Harvard, Yale, Princeton, Chicago, and Wisconsin—a clientele the AFT would like to renew). Throughout the Thirties the federation was split bitterly by internal Communist problems. In 1941 its members voted to expel locals in New York and Philadelphia (which subsequently reorganized) after investigations found too much Communist influence.

But AFT leaders then made a policy decision to concentrate on New York, where teachers were split into scores of competing and overlapping organizations. Cogen, then president of the UFT, led a one-day strike (the first in the city's history) in November 1960, to force the New York school board to hold a teacher-representation election. When the election was granted the next year, the UFT beat a hastily organized Teachers Bargaining Organization supported by the NEA and kept its momentum by staging a one-day strike during its first contract negotiations the next spring. More than half the system's 40,000 teachers stayed home, and the AFT had arrived almost overnight as a power.

To a large degree, the federation's growth is due to Cogen and Selden. . . .

The headquarters services are minimal. The research department exists on $68,832, yielding dubious documents like the one on the need for an immediate $5,000 raise for every teacher in the United States. The research on this particular item was so poor that many reporters at a press conference where it was announced refused to write a word about it. Other departments are hardly more impressive. The AFT's federal relations staff consists of Carl Megel, past AFT president, and a secretary. "We always go along with labor," Megel told me. "That's our strength and prestige." The federation's twenty-two state organizations are similarly weak. The AFT just got around to hiring a coordinator of state federations last year.

A member of a teachers' local automatically belongs to the AFT, but dues vary from city to city. In Philadelphia, for example, a starting teacher pays $42 in annual dues. The AFT constitution says each local must pay $1 per month for each member into the national treasury. Two cents is set aside in a defense fund.

The support of labor is crucial to the AFT. "The labor affiliation is a great help to us," Cogen says. "There've been a number of situations—New York, Detroit—where unions have helped us out, organizing a strike, putting moral pressure on the board of education." In smaller communities the teachers' local often uses AFL-CIO staff and facilities.

The teachers also are important to organized labor. The UFT, with more than 50,000 members, is the largest local in the AFL-CIO. And Nick Zonarich, director of organization for the Industrial Union Department, says that "the teachers have been the greatest inspiration in instilling new life in the labor movement." The work force is changing—from blue-collar, private employment to white-collar, public employment—and the IUD hopes that teachers can set the pattern for other fields to follow. To keep pace with the shift, the AFL-CIO earlier this year formed a Council of Unions for Scientific, Professional, and Cultural Employees to help organize the new workers. Cogen is vice president.

The AFT's programs, meanwhile, are geared directly to the present of the urban schools, particularly the schools of the poor. The major program (Cogen calls it the "AFT's most important contribution to our profession") is the More Effective Schools campaign. The New York federation first proposed MES three years ago during contract negotiations after the school board offered $1,000 "combat pay" to lure experienced teachers to slum schools. The federation countered with MES to provide intensive educational, remedial, and counseling services to the ghetto. MES is now in twenty-one New York schools, costing $10,000,000 a year. A teacher's dream, it limits class size to twenty-two pupils in elementary grades and establishes a guidance team of a social worker, psychologist, and part-time psychiatrist in each school. To make sure all this attention filters down to the child, four teachers are assigned to every three classes.

Despite the increased manpower, MES is far from an unqualified success. For one thing, the Center for Urban Education, evaluating MES for the New York school board, found that many teachers didn't know how to work with all the program's special help. The Center cited "little evidence that materials or teaching techniques had been adapted to capitalize on the smaller classes," while there was a "general absence of creative or innovative teaching practices." Still, teachers, principals, and pupils were enthusiastic about the program. More startling, however, was the conclusion that MES produced disappointing gains in pupil achievement. MES pupils scored only slightly higher on reading achievement tests than did children in non-MES control schools, and MES was not strong enough to pull its pupils up to grade-level. Indeed, even MES pupils fell farther behind the longer they stayed in school, starting only a month below grade level in the second grade but dropping more than a year behind in the fifth grade. As a result of these findings, the board was reluctant to expand the program this fall as the federation desired, producing a major issue in the September strike. The AFT, however, hopes to export MES to Boston, Detroit, Los Angeles, and New Orleans.

Another major federation goal is to persuade the federal government to expand its categorical aid to city schools and to set national standards which systems must meet to qualify for federal aid. The AFT also supports a national assessment to measure pupil performance, a testing opposed by many elements of the NEA. Occasionally the federation's policies take a quixotic turn. At the recent convention, Cogen urged President Johnson to call a "national educational strategy conference" to be attended by many classroom teachers. The proposal drew no comment from the White House. And Cogen, with a straight face, also suggested at the convention that the federal government set $8,500 as the minimum pay for a teacher with a bachelor's degree.

The federation has brought an explosive impact to the cities where it represents teachers. It has awakened school boards, shaken bureaucracies. Its impact also can be quite tangible. The Philadelphia federation sent its own recruiters throughout the East last spring, helping to cut teacher vacancies in the city from more than 1,000 to a handful. So far, however, the AFT has demonstrated little influence on national policies. Recognizing the void, the union moved its national offices during the summer from Chicago to two floors in the Continental Building, about five blocks from the White House. . . .

What happens next? As the AFT grows larger, it faces the danger of institutionalization. There are indications it already is joining the Establishment. A recent study of change in big-city schools by two professors from the City University of New York and one from Teachers College said that in the few areas where the New York federation has taken a public position "it appears to have been motivated largely by a desire to maintain the status quo." The study added that "in interviews conducted with union leaders, there was some expressed concern that their own positions of power might be threatened if they violated the narrower interests of their membership. Thus, the New York teachers' union acts as an obstacle to change in the system rather than as an innovator."

The AFT, however, undoubtedly will continue to grow, although perhaps at not as rapid a rate. It has no large organizing drive planned this year, but hopes to move to the smaller cities and the suburbs. Union leaders are sanguine about the future. Cogen, riding the crest of the wave, predicts, "We'll continue our growth at the expense of the NEA—certainly among the million or so teachers who are unorganized." Unless school conditions change dramatically, the AFT probably will remain where the action is. Increasingly, though, the action will have to do not with wages or working conditions, but with power. The union thus becomes not merely a bargaining agent or an organization of professionals, but a political force that will represent a major element in the operation of city schools. It is thus a major new entry in the political equation that determines the future of public education in America.

16

AND GLADLY STRIKE?

James S. LeSure

"This is no time for strikes." So spoke U.S. Commissioner of Education Francis Keppel in an address this past summer to the American Federation of Teachers. I wish he had said, "There is never a time for teachers to strike." I wish this, not because strikes of public employees are unlawful (as they frequently are), not because teachers strike primarily against children (a view quite widely held), but because the strike, or the sanction, or blacklisting as a bargaining weapon is not, in the long run, in the best interest of teachers.

If the aim is simply more money now, or better working conditions now, or smaller classes now, perhaps we must admit that coercion and extortion (for that is what strikes and sanctions are, no matter how they are glossed over) are the answer. But I submit that the real objective of teachers is recognition of teaching as a profession. Such recognition, with all its prerequisites, cannot be acquired by force. The only kind of professional status that means anything is that which the public accords on the basis of professional behavior. And, right now, teachers' organizations are emphasizing teacher welfare. Strikes or sanctions and professional recognition are mutually exclusive—teachers cannot have it both ways.

Organization leaders who favor the more militant posture now being assumed by teachers agree that coercive measures are not desirable. They insist, however,

Reprinted from James S. LeSure, And Gladly Strike?, *Saturday Review*, **XLIX**, no. 8, p. 79, February 19, 1966.

that without effective use of force when society refuses to yield them what they regard as their due, teachers are powerless. "What are we supposed to do," one of them asked me not long ago, "sit back and wait for the kindly politicians to vote us more money?"

But those kindly politicians, if they are to remain in office, must, if our version of democracy means anything, reflect the opinion of their constituents— and the opinion of those constituents is based today on considerably less naiveté than used to be the case. Parents, for a variety of reasons, have become vitally concerned with the kind of education their kids are getting. Books like Koerner's *The Miseducation of American Teachers* and Conant's *The Education of American Teachers,* different though they are in approach and tone, have raised very serious questions, some of which educators have been hard put to answer effectively, about the education of the people responsible for our children's schooling.

It takes no supernatural insight to acquaint an intelligent parent with the fact that not all teachers are alike in ability. That same parent, who is also a taxpayer, has heard about the importance of "individual differences" of pupils in the classroom, and he wonders why these differences should not be recognized among teachers, especially in paying them. He wonders, too, why teachers expect to be paid as much for thirty-eight weeks' work as others are paid for fifty, yet be virtually guaranteed a lifetime job after three years of avoiding being fired. He has heard that teaching cannot attract topnotch young people; but he wonders in what other field so many women can do so well—and a good two-thirds of our teachers are women. Then he looks at Anna Doakes, who is repeating for the thirtieth time her first year of teaching, rarely reads a book, and scarcely lifts a finger outside the classroom. Why should she be making $9,500 a "year"?

In the past fifteen years, salaries in many states have doubled, whether one looks at bottom, top, or average, and the trend is still steadily upward. In the larger cities and "better" suburbs, teachers in their mid-thirties are reaching five-figure salaries—with complete job security through tenure laws, and with fourteen weeks' paid vacation. If so much has been accomplished virtually without recourse to strikes and sanctions, can much more be accomplished through coercion? So long as the unions threaten strike on the one hand, and the associations rattle the sanction saber on the other, the public, to be sure, knows where it stands. And it knows where the teachers stand: squarely with the rest of labor battling for their share of the consumer dollar, and as much more as they can get. They will never be classed with doctors, lawyers, and clergymen in prestige, nor with the engineers, accountants, and entrepreneurs in income. Their ceiling in status and in salary will be lower, much lower, if they continue on this road.

Some teachers seem to feel that they have been forced to their present position, that they have no choice. I believe there is at least one alternative. Many teachers, probably a majority, are, by anybody's definition, professional.

They are interested in doing the best job they can in the classroom. They care about the children for whose learning they are responsible. They would like better pay, of course, and better working conditions and more prestige. Who wouldn't? But they expect to earn it, not take it at the point of a gun.

Let *these* teachers organize, through existing organizations or through a new organization. Let them then bend their collective effort toward better performance of teachers in the classroom, toward weeding out deadwood from teaching, toward attracting better people into careers in education, and toward achieving higher standards for the preparation of professional personnel for the public schools, to mention a few of the more obvious needs. For the kind of public support education needs in this country will come only when the people recognize *by their deeds* that the primary, the overriding goal of teachers' organizations is the improvement of the quality of education offered in the public schools.

Then, and only then, will teaching have become a profession.

17

IMPACT OF NEGOTIATIONS UPON PUBLIC EDUCATION

Henry R. Weinstock and Paul L. Van Horn

The controversy surrounding professional negotiation has noticeably affected teachers, administrators, school board members, and the general public alike. The issue seems to be rooted in the means by which the public schools of a community have traditionally been governed by their school boards with regard to the determination of teachers' salaries, prescription of employment conditions, and formulation of educational policies.

Many boards have been reluctant to extend to teachers the privilege of negotiating with them on matters of mutual educational concern. This may be illustrated by the fact that only 36 out of 419 professional negotiation agreements undertaken through the auspices of the National Education Association were signed jointly by both teachers and board members.[1]

The current rivalry between the American Federation of Teachers and the National Education Association, therefore, appears to be largely the consequence of a growing number of teachers desiring to effectively improve their professional status through increased involvement in the formulation of local educational policy.[2]

Reprinted from Henry R. Weinstock and Paul L. Van Horn, Impact of Negotiations Upon Public Education, *The Clearing House*, pp. 358-363, February, 1969.

[1] Wesley A. Wilderman, What Prompts Greater Teacher Militancy?, *American School Board Journal*, **CLIV**, pp. 27-32, March, 1967.

[2] Myron Leiberman and Michael H. Moskow, "Collective Negotiations for Teachers," Rand McNally and Co., Chicago, 1966.

SIX CRITICAL IMPLICATIONS FOR EDUCATION

One commonly accepted definition for "professional negotiation" was provided by the National Education Association when it stated that it is

A set of procedures, written or adopted by the local association and the school board, which provides for an orderly method to negotiate, in good faith, through professional (educational) channels, on matters of mutual concern, to reach agreement on these matters, and to establish educational channels for mediation and appeal in case of impasse.[3]

Many authorities have maintained, however, that conflicts between school boards and teachers have evolved from basic disagreements with such a view mainly on the part of the members of the boards. These differences appear to be generally based upon the following common assumptions:

1. Professional negotiation is unnecessary, since the working relationship between school boards and teachers is already a satisfactory one.
2. Professional negotiation between teachers and school boards cannot take place because it is illegal.
3. Professional negotiation will enable teachers to undermine administrative authority and threaten school board autonomy.
4. Whenever professional negotiation procedures are exercised, teachers are not concerned with the public's interest.
5. Whenever professional negotiation procedures are exercised, teachers are not concerned with the students' interests.
6. If an impasse does arise between teachers and board members, the ensuing disruption of the educational process would result in great loss to the students.[4]

Need for professional negotiation

General concensus among school board members seems to exist in viewing professional negotiation as unnecessary, in light of their own view of a traditional good working relationship with teachers. The high degree of teacher militancy being presently demonstrated, however, has lent doubt to this outlook, perhaps due to a difference in meaning ascribed by board members and teachers to the term "good relations."

Although school boards have traditionally exercised sole prerogative in making decisions regarding the school environment, it has also been the profes-

---

[3]William R. Hazard, Semantic Gymnastics, *American School Board Journal*, **CL**, pp. 14-16, October 1967.

[4]Forbes Bottomly, Negotiating with Teachers, *School Management*, **IX**, pp. 81-91, May 1965.

sional privilege of teachers to render recommendations about salaries and working conditions. As such suggestions have in the past been accepted or rejected at the discretion of the boards, the only recourse for teachers has been either their tacit acceptance of the boards' decisions or resignation from their teaching posts.

Because of a growing desire by teachers to have greater choice in such matters, however, such a view of good relations has therefore been made the subject of questioning. This, in turn, has culminated in an increasing incidence of representatives of local teachers' associations and school boards engaging in discussions of policy matters of mutual concern and the resolution of potential impasse between the parties.[5]

Legality of professional negotiation

The legality of engaging in professional negotiation has also become a controversial subject. Many board members have tried to interpret local, state, or even federal laws as containing stipulations *against* their negotiating with teachers. This legal question, however, also appears to be dependent upon semantics, particularly where "professional negotiation" has been interpreted in terms of "collective bargaining."

The issue becomes even more confusing in light of the fact that collective bargaining has already taken place in at least 14 states.[6]

Generally speaking, the common usage of these terms has been left to the interpretation of whichever group, union, or association was utilizing them.[7] Thus "collective bargaining" has usually been related with the American Federation of Teachers and the AFL-CIO Union. Because it involved the use of labor channels in resolving conflict, it has also been subject to state and federal laws. On the other hand, "professional negotiation" has been associated with the National Education Association, as it has depended on educational rather than labor channels for the settlement of disputes.[8]

Certain federal legislation has also appeared to play an interdictory role in the issue. Both the Wagner Act of 1935 and President John F. Kennedy's Executive Order 10988 have permitted employees of both private and public institutions to organize and petition their employers for the privilege to sit in and react during decision-making sessions.

It may thus take the testing of a case at the Supreme Court level to ultimately decide the difference between engaging in "collective bargaining" or in "professional negotiation."

[5] National Education Association Field Staff, The Marvelous Potential of Professional Negotiation, *National Education Association Journal*, **LVI**, pp. 28-29, November 1967.

[6] Jack H. Kleinmann, Professional Sanctions: What, Why, When, Where, and How?, *National Education Association Journal*, **CL**, pp. 42-45, January 1968.

[7] Lieberman and Moskow, *op. cit.*

[8] Hazard, *op. cit.*

Undermining of administrative authority and board autonomy by teachers
Perhaps the assumption which has created the greatest conflict has been the fear that teachers, through professional negotiation, would eventually wrest control of the schools from the boards.[9]

From a professional standpoint teachers have long insisted on certain privileges for the purposes of effectively carrying on their teaching duties.[10] As school board members seem to have been reluctant to include teachers in their decision-making processes, however, there has resulted a disproportionate representation of teachers in the total school program.

The consequences of this situation may well have had a great deal to do with contemporary scenes of educational unrest unparalleled in the history of the United States.

Teachers, for the most part, have been insisting on increased financial remuneration, more effective learning environments, increased "professional" treatment, self-determination of educational policies, and greater public support for "quality" education. This "militancy" among teachers has been overtly demonstrated on a national basis in such states as Connecticut, Florida, Illinois, Texas, Washington, and New York.[11] As a consequence, school districts across the country have begun to consider professional negotiation agreements as one means of dealing with such problems.

Nevertheless, numerous school board members themselves have persisted in interpreting the professional negotiation process as illegal, as it purportedly removes the public's delegation of authority from the board. This opposition has been questioned by many authorities, however, since the courts have already denied that a party which must bargain collectively has consequently been forced to delegate away either its ultimate authority or its responsibility.[12]

Viewed from an ethical, rather than legal standpoint, it also seems that neither concession nor compromise has been demanded by the legal concept of bargaining in good faith. Within the context of power relationship which marks true professional negotiation, discussions of purposes for mutual decision-making have often been compromised when they became the subjects of dispute.[13]

Consequently, board members may soon be forced legally to involve teachers in decision-making processes about ideas or innovations, in light of the mutual concern of both parties for public education.

Professional negotiation and public interest
School boards and teachers have generally agreed that the "public interest"

[9]Wilderman, *op. cit.*

[10]Kleinmann, *op. cit.*

[11]*Ibid.*

[12]LeRoy Peterson, Legal Status of Teacher Personnel, *Review of Educational Research,* **XXXVII,** pp. 296-299, June 1967.

[13]Wilderman, *op. cit.*

should be a decisive criterion applied to any consideration of conditions for employment or innovation in education. There are, however, many who have had reservations about the meaning of the term, questioning whether its use has been synonymous with that of the "public will."

One authority has maintained that "public interest" became universally equivalent to "public will" when government officials first became accountable to the wills and values of the majority of their constituents.[14]

Another reservation about "public interest" has been its contextual usage, namely whether reference was being made to either the interest of the general society or to that of the specific community.

Because of the high mobility of the American people, the public interest of each community seems to have become isomorphic with the public interest of society at large. Yet some school districts purportedly have refused to pass the school bonds and tax liens deemed professionally necessary to support a local educational level acceptable as adequate on a national scale.[15] Thus when their students eventually move into society at large, many are faced with the rather unpleasant dilemma of competing against students of superior educational background.

It is of little wonder why the "public interest," when viewed in this educational perspective, has thus involved much speculation about its communality with the "public will."

Lastly, the use of the term "public interest" as a tool for individuals in control of a situation appears to be rather obvious. It has at various times been accused of serving as a scapegoat for local or even private purposes in the making of judgments about an issue's validity.[16]

On the other hand, many teachers, realizing the accountability of the school board members to the public's interest or will, have been more optimistic. They have tended to view the process of professional negotiation chiefly as a means of encouraging the board members and the public to cooperate with them in elevating educational standards.

Professional negotiation and students' interests

Most school board members and teachers would probably agree that a major purpose of educators should be the improvement of the educational process affecting the student. Both parties have in the past, however, levied charges at one another, many boards citing a militant selfishness on the part of teachers assumed at the expense of their concern for the student.[17]

In turn, perhaps, teachers have referred to the large-scale educational defi-

[14] Robert E. Doherty, Public Interest at Stake, *American School Board Journal,* **CL,** pp. 11-13, October 1967.

[15] *Ibid.*

[16] *Ibid.*

[17] Charles S. Benson and Lester A. Dunn, Employment Practices and Working Conditions, *Review of Educational Research,* **XXXVII,** pp. 272-279, June 1967.

ciencies which have resulted from the school boards failing to involve them in the formation of educational policy, construction of curriculum, development of courses, and assignment of audio-visual aids. Teachers have also resented their being appointed to nonteaching duties.

In the light of such charges, therefore, it may well be that teachers have been seeking to elevate their own status by means of professional negotiation. Most authorities and teachers, however, seem to feel that members of the education profession have a mutually legitimate interest in the decisions that affect their pupil clientele, the effectiveness of their own work, and the quality of the total educational program.[18]

When teachers would therefore bargain about their own welfare, the resulting improved working conditions should logically have a positive effect on recruiting and retaining the best teachers.[19] Thus the benefits derived from professional negotiation might signally overcome those public pressures and educational deficiencies which have worked against the development of an optimal educational level for all students.

Effect of impasse

Many school board members, and also laymen, have maintained that if an impasse with their teachers were reached, its magnitude would disrupt the educational process to the extent of seriously impairing the total educational process. Most officials of the National Education Association and similar organizations have suggested, however, that if the school board and teachers negotiate in good faith, then such need not be a forgone conclusion.[20]

In the eventuality that accord between teachers and school board policy was not forthcoming, the subsequent disruptive measures might still be averted through the successive initiation of five recommended steps:

(1) *Mediation.* Mediation would be the effort of a neutral third party appointed by both parties to help them reach a voluntary agreement.

(2) *Factfinding.* Factfinding would be the investigation by a neutral third party to discover the issues and to make recommendations that would not be binding but could be made public. Either party could initiate the factfinding.

(3) *Arbitration* (when legal and agreed upon by both parties). Arbitration by a neutral third party would hopefully result in a recommendation for settlement which *would be binding upon both the parties.* The parties would have to agree in advance that the matter at issue would be submitted to binding arbitration.

(4) *Political Action.* Political action would be comprised of a variety of activities to be pursued by the organized teaching profession to resolve impasses with, or influence decisions of, governmental bodies. These would include

[18] Harold J. McNally, Professional Negotiation and Collective Bargaining, *National Elementary Principal,* **XLVI,** pp. 33-37, April 1967.

[19] Benson and Dunn, *op. cit.*

[20] National Education Board of Directors, Resolution on Impasse in Negotiation Situations, *National Education Association Journal,* **LVI,** pp. 38-39, October 1967.

persuasion, recall elections, lobbying, and campaigns to convince citizens to support the public schools.

(5) *Sanctions.* Sanctions would be deterrents imposed against a public agency controlling the welfare of schools, or one or more steps in the withholding of services which would include (a) public censure through public notice, (b) notification to educational and placement agencies of unsatisfactory conditions for professional services, (c) notification to members of the profession of unsatisfactory conditions for professional services, (d) refraining from extracurricular activities, and (e) withholding of contracts and the seeking of employment elsewhere.[21]

In light of the last step in particular, it appears that the fear of many board members of the disruptive educational effect of impasse does have merit. According to one authority, however, such sanctions have not as yet been invoked where professional negotiation agreements have existed.[22]

POSITIVE EFFECTS OF PROFESSIONAL NEGOTIATION

In surmising the common assumptions found to prevail among their members, it seems that school boards view the traditional working relationship between teachers and themselves as largely satisfactory. This is supposedly illustrated by increased salaries for teachers, more use of audio-visual aids, better working conditions, and the privilege of *informal* negotiation with them.

On the other hand, there are strong indications that many teachers feel somewhat less than satisfied with this time-honored arrangement. Many teachers apparently agree that the school boards do listen to their petitions. They seem to believe, however, that the final authority of a board over a local educational structure has granted the teachers only that which the school board originally intended to give them anyway.

Many schoolboard members maintain that it is impossible to negotiate with teachers, since it is illegal to do so according to state statutes. Although approximately two-thirds of the states do, in fact, have statutes prohibiting collective bargaining, the remaining one-third have statutes either permitting or actually requiring such for teachers.[23]

Teachers, thus realizing that certain states permit collective bargaining, seem increasingly desirous to change their own state statutes with regard to this matter. This desire is reinforced by the fact that professional negotiations, which require neither arbitration, labor unions, nor union strategy, are legally permitted within many of the states which have prohibited collective bargaining for public employees.

School board members generally believe that professional negotiation tends

[21] *Ibid.*

[22] McNally, *op. cit.*

[23] National Education Association Field Staff, *op. cit.*

to undermine both their own authority and that of the professional administrator. They have categorically assumed in the past that professional negotiation
removes the solidarity which has been their right and that it gradually tends to
deteriorate the whole educational structure in the process of its being conducted.

Administrators have usually felt that the questioning of their traditionally
unchallenged authoritative position could produce a stamping ground for
teachers who have pet peeves and an ax to grind.

Many teachers, however, view their teaching responsibility as a requisite for
granting them the privilege to negotiate on such matters of mutual concern as
working conditions and improved educational procedures. Thus teachers may
well be demanding an integral position paralleling that of the school board and
administrative staff in many of the decision-making processes.

School boards and administrators, as well as teachers, seem to agree that the
"public interest" should be one of the decisive considerations in requiring,
permitting, or prohibiting the various procedures to be used in determining
conditions of employment in education. Since school board members are elected
to represent the public interest, they are therefore responsible to the public's
will in contriving educational policy.[24]

Contrary to this position, however, many teachers advocate that "public
interest" is a concept to be used only as a guiding principle in arguing the
validity of certain proposals according to arbitrary standards. What may thus be
of immediate interest to a particular community may not necessarily be of
general interest to society at large.

It is likely that most school board members, administrators, and teachers
would agree on a major purpose of education being the improvement of the
educational environment, regardless of philosophical considerations.[25] Some
school board members have in the past, however, levied charges that teachers
have become militant and selfish, thus permitting concern for the student to
assume a secondary position. Teachers, in responding to this charge, have
alternately suggested that the present teacher is better educated, is using newer
methods of instruction, and is raising general teaching efficiency by requiring
complacent teachers to take refresher courses.

Many concerned individuals maintain that if an impasse does arise between
school board members and teachers, the ensuing disruption of the educational
process could be highly detrimental to the affected students. Contrary to this
belief, however, teachers seem to feel that such would not be the consequence if
both parties agreed to negotiate in "good faith" (i.e., "The willingness of both
parties, teachers and school board members to consider proposals seriously, not
rejecting them without a cause or reason, and the avoidance of frivolous
proposals").[26]

[24] Bottomly, *op. cit.*

[25] *Ibid.*

[26] Leiberman and Moskow, *op. cit.*

Finally, it appears that professional negotiation has not been as unduly restrictive as some have predicted it would be. It has already displayed at least one largely desirable role, namely, its provision of mechanism for the effectuation of innovative activities. When used by teachers who have become highly enthusiastic about new educational programs, it has enabled many to introduce such concepts not only to school boards but also to administrators and other experienced teachers as well.

It is thus highly likely that "professional negotiation" may become a commendable means to the end of elevating the caliber of public education on a national scale, if the particular parties involved proceed with diligence, through proper channels, and in good faith.

18

POVERTY, UNEMPLOYMENT, AND ECONOMIC DEVELOPMENT

James E. Anderson

The focus of this paper is on the antipoverty campaign of the 1960's. After an examination of the nature of the poverty problem, consideration will be given to antipoverty strategies, the use of the curative strategy, and some of the political aspects of the war on poverty. In all, the discussion is intended to provide a broad perspective on the national government's war on poverty and the development of antipoverty policy in the United States.

One.

It is quite apparent that many people have not shared in the general economic growth and prosperity which have characterized the United States since World War II. If one third of the nation is no longer "ill-housed, ill-clad, and ill-nourished," as Franklin Roosevelt stated in 1937, it is nonetheless true that many

Reprinted from James E. Anderson, Poverty, Unemployment, and Economic Development: The Search for a National Antipoverty Policy, *The Journal of Politics,* 29, pp. 70-93, February 1967.

This is a revision of a paper originally presented at the 1965 Annual Meeting of the Southern Political Science Association. In addition to the printed sources cited, this paper draws on a number of interviews with Washington officials involved in the war on poverty.

millions of people are still afflicted by poverty. Much debate has occurred in the past few years over what constitutes poverty and how many people are poverty stricken.[1] Among the questions in this "debate" are: Is poverty definable as a family income of less than $2,000 annually, or $3,000, or $4,000, or what? Should the poverty-line be higher for urban dwellers than for rural residents, for those under 65 years of age than for those over 65? Do the poor number 30 million, or 35 million, or 40 to 50 million, or how many? Is poverty only a "state of mind," a situation in which some think they are poor because they have less income or material possessions than others? Or is poverty merely a statistical phenomenon with, say, the lowest fifth of the income pyramid being considered poverty-stricken?

There is much room for controversy and statistical manipulation in answering such questions. In some studies the conclusions reached appear to be skewed by ideological considerations, with the conservative defining poverty more narrowly and consequently finding both less poverty and less need for governmental action than the liberal. To wit: A study prepared for the conservative American Enterprise Institute used an income standard ranging from $1,259 to $3,155 for nonfarm households whose size ran from 2 to 7 or more.[2] On this basis, one tenth of the nation's household units (around 17 million people) were in the poverty category. In contrast, Leon Keyserling and the liberal Conference on Economic Progress,[3] using an annual income of less than $4,000 before taxes as the poverty standard for a household, held that in 1960 almost 10.5 million families were living in poverty (or 23 per cent of all families). Some 4 million unattached individuals with annual incomes below $2,000 were also designated as poverty-stricken.

A third study, which seems soundly conceived and ideologically "neutral" and which yields data similar to that used by many public officials, was prepared by the Department of Health, Education, and Welfare using the Census Bureau's sample statistics for 1963.[4] Annual incomes necessary to maintain nutritional

---

[1] Important statistical examinations of poverty include: Robert J. Lampman, "The Low Income Population and Economic Growth," Study Paper No. 12, prepared for the Joint Economic Committee, 86th Cong., 1st Sess., 1959; Conference on Economic Progress, "Poverty and Deprivation in the U.S.," Conference on Economic Progress, Washington, 1962; Michael Harrington, "The Other America," pp. 187-203, The Macmillan Company, New York, 1963; Herman P. Miller, "Rich Man, Poor Man," Thomas Y. Crowell Company, New York, 1964; Council of Economic Advisors, "Annual Report, 1964," pp. 55-84, Government Printing Office, Washington, 1964; Mollie Orshansky, Counting the Poor: Another Look at the Poverty Profile, *Social Security Bulletin*, XXVIII, pp. 3-29, January 1965; and James N. Morgan, *et al.*, "Income and Welfare in the United States," McGraw-Hill Book Company, New York, 1962.

[2] Rose D. Friedman, "Poverty: Definition and Perspective," American Enterprise Institute, Washington, 1965.

[3] Conference on Economic Progress, *op.cit.*, pp. 19-23.

[4] Orshansky, *op.cit.* See also the discussion by Herman P. Miller, Changes in the Number and Composition of the Poor, in Margaret S. Gordon (ed.), "Poverty in America," pp. 81-101, Chandler Publishing Company, San Francisco, 1965.

adequacy were calculated for different types of families classified by farm and nonfarm residence, age and sex of head, and number of children. Using these criteria, a flexible poverty standard was developed, which ranged from $880 annually for a single female aged 65 or over living on a farm to $5,100 for an urban family of 7 or more headed by a male under 65 years of age. On the basis of the flexible standard it was calculated that, in 1963, 34.5 million persons (or 18 per cent of the population) were in families with incomes insufficient to purchase a minimally nutritional budget. This supports the frequently heard statement that one-fifth of the nation still lives in poverty. It might be noted that the much criticized Council of Economic Advisers study, which used a fixed $3,000 standard, yielded similar results: 35 million people living in poverty.[5]

To end this phase of the discussion, the disagreement over the nature and precise amount of poverty should not be permitted to obscure the "problem of poverty." As one close student of poverty has stated:

it would be a mistake to conclude from this [lack of agreement] that there is no evidence to demonstrate that tens of millions of people have incomes that are insufficient to provide minimum levels of living for this society. Most Americans would agree that a family is poor if its income is below the amount needed to qualify for public assistance. Many would also count as poor some families with incomes well above this level. The 1960 Census data show that *at least 23.5 million people—one person out of eight in the United States—lives in a family with an annual income that is less than the amount needed to qualify for aid under the public assistance laws of each state.*[6]

In addition to aggregate statistics, an understanding of the poverty problem also requires discussion of the causes of poverty and the various groups included among the poor. This will focus attention on the problems facing policy-makers. In his *The Affluent Society*, Galbraith makes a useful distinction between case poverty and insular poverty.[7] Case poverty related to the personal qualities or characteristics of the affected persons. Given our present socio-economic system, some persons and families have been unable to participate satisfactorily in the nation's general prosperity because of such limiting factors as old age, inadequate education or illiteracy, lack of needed job skills, poor health, inadequate motivation, and racial discrimination, regardless of where they live—rural and small town areas, urban areas, or metropolitan areas.

Insular poverty appears in what are called "pockets of poverty" or depressed areas, as in West Virginia, much of the rest of Appalachia, and many parts of

[5] Council of Economic Advisers, *op.cit.*

[6] Herman P. Miller, Statistics and Reality, *The New Leader,* **XLVII**, p. 18, March 30, 1964. (His emphasis.)

[7] John Kenneth Galbraith, "The Affluent Society," chap. 23, Houghton Mifflin Company, Boston, 1958.

rural America.[8] Such areas are characterized by higher and more persistent rates of unemployment and underemployment and larger proportions of low income persons than in the country as a whole. The *proximate* cause of this condition is the lack of adequate employment opportunities for the current population. Some of the people in these areas will also suffer from lack of education, poor health, inadequate job skills, etc., because the two types of poverty are not mutually exclusive. The lack of job opportunities, in turn, may be the product of a number of factors, including technological change, depletion of national resources, shifts in consumer demand, and the movement of industries to other areas.[9]

Both insular and case poverty are usually viewed as "structural" in nature, resulting from individual shortcomings and from temporary or limited imperfections in the economic system. They differ from the "mass poverty" of the 1930's, which was a product of general economic decline and which was markedly reduced by the revival of the economy in the early 1940's. Poverty of the structural sort does not automatically disappear as the economy expands and general affluence increases.

A close relationship exists between unemployment, low wages, and poverty. Many of the poor are unemployed or are completely outside of the labor force. But poverty is also the result of underemployment and employment at low wages, as in the cases of migratory workers and unskilled domestic workers. Thus a Department of Labor study on the employment status of families with incomes below $3,000 in 1963 reported that 30 per cent of the poor families were headed by persons who held jobs throughout the year. Another 14 per cent were headed by persons who worked at fulltime jobs for part of the year but who were never counted as unemployed because they moved into or out of the labor force. The heads of 16 per cent of the families experienced unemployment. Finally, 39 per cent of the families were headed by persons who were completely outside the labor force in 1963. Included in this last category are many aged or retired workers, the disabled, the dispirited, and women with child-rearing responsibilities. While most of the persons in the three categories listed would benefit from economic growth and increased job opportunities, most of those in the last category would not because they are largely outside of the productive economy.

Although poverty exists in all regions of the country, in both rural and urban areas, and among all elements of the population, its incidence is heaviest among the following: nonwhites (Negroes, Puerto Ricans, and Mexican-Americans); the

[8]For examples of the latter, see "Incomes of Rural Families in Northeast Texas," Bulletin 940, Texas Agricultural Experiment Station, College Station, Texas, 1959; and "Incomes, Resources, and Adjustment Potential of Rural Families in the Clay-Hills Area of Mississippi," AEc. M. R. No. 29, Mississippi Agricultural Experiment Station, State College, Mississippi, 1960.

[9]Sidney C. Sufrin and Marion A. Buck, "What Price Progress?: A Study in Chronic Unemployment," esp. chaps. 1, 2, Rand McNally and Co., Chicago, 1965.

aged; families headed by females; families without a breadwinner; the unemployed; families headed by farmers and unskilled laborers; families headed by very young persons or persons with less than an eighth-grade education; very large families; and unrelated individuals living alone.[10] As this listing and the previous discussion should indicate, the problems of poverty and unemployment are multiple rather than monolithic in nature. Consequently there must be a variety of policy responses, geared to particular forms of causation and need, if these problems are to be dealt with effectively.

Two.

There are a number of general strategies which the government may use in dealing with the problems of poverty and unemployment. The major ones are discussed in this section.

Aggregationist Strategy

Involving the use of broad fiscal and monetary policies to maintain a high level of economic growth and employment, this strategy is based on the assumption that much unemployment and poverty are the product of inadequate demand for labor and insufficient employment opportunities. According to the Council of Economic Advisers:

> The maintenance of high employment—a labor market in which the demand for workers is strong relative to the supply—is a powerful force for the reduction of poverty. In a strong labor market there are new and better opportunities for the unemployed, the partially employed, and the low paid. Employers have greater incentive to seek and to train workers when their own markets are large and growing. . . . To fight poverty in a slack economy with excess employment is to tie one hand behind our backs.[11]

The national government is generally committed to the aggregationist strategy by the Employment Act of 1946, which pledges the government to use its various programs and policies to maintain "maximum employment, production, and purchasing power." The 1964 cut in the income tax rates and the 1965 excise tax reduction both were in line with the aggregationist strategy.

Alleviative Strategy

This is the oldest strategy for aiding the poor and the unemployed. Emphasis here is on relieving or easing the hardships and misery associated with poverty

[10]See Oscar Ornati, "Poverty Amid Affluence," passim, The Twentieth Century Fund, New York, 1966.

[11]Council of Economic Advisers, op. cit., pp. 73-74. Cf. Hyman P. Minsky, "The Role of Employment Policy," in Gordon, op. cit., pp. 175-200.

and unemployment by providing financial or material aid to the distressed on either a short-term or long-term basis. Alleviative programs have become more numerous and more generous in recent decades as the views that poverty and unemployment are often neither individually caused nor controllable and that public aid is necessary to protect the dignity of the individual have gained increased acceptance. Programs which are primarily alleviative include unemployment compensation, public assistance, medicare, general relief, and work relief. All involve some sort of "transfer payment."

Curative Strategy

In contrast to the alleviative strategy, the curative strategy stresses efforts to help the poor and unemployed become self-supporting and more capable of earning adequate incomes by bringing about changes in either the individuals themselves or in their environment. This strategy is expressed in the slogan "Rehabilitation not relief" and, to use President Johnson's somewhat inelegant terminology, the desire "to make taxpayers out of taxeaters." Programs in accord with the curative approach include area and regional development, work training, vocational education, job experience and literacy training, and much of the community action program under the Economic Opportunity Act. Curative programs are largely a development of the past decade.

Equal Opportunity Strategy

The focus here is on eliminating discrimination against Negroes, Indians, Mexican-Americans, and Puerto Ricans and providing them with equal educational and employment opportunities. Almost half of all nonwhite Americans are poor, and discrimination—in employment, wages, education, housing—is an important cause of poverty here.[12] Negroes, for example, are often hired last, paid less, and fired first. Illustrative of this strategy is the Civil Rights Act of 1964, which bans discrimination on the basis of race, color, religion, national origin or sex by many employers and labor unions. The Act also prohibits discrimination under any program or activity—in education, welfare, manpower training, etc.—receiving federal financial assistance. The civil rights movement, by broadening its concern to economic as well political discrimination, has stimulated increased use of this strategy.

It is now generally agreed that the aggregationist strategy alone is inadequate to eliminate poverty and unemployment. It is, however, a necessary condition for their elimination; and the other antipoverty strategies, to be most effective, presuppose a high level of employment. But even if increased job opportunities are available many will not be able to take advantage of them because of inadequate job skills, low education, old age, discrimination, geographic location, and the like. Curative and equal opportunity programs should help many of these to become self-supporting or to enlarge their incomes. But others will still be un-

[12] See *e.g.*, Alan Batchelder, Poverty: The Special Case of the Negro, *American Economic Review*, **LV**, pp. 530-540, May 1965.

able to provide for themselves—such as many of the aged and females with large families—and here alleviative programs come in. In short, the various strategies set forth are interdependent; and the national government is currently utilizing all of them in the war on poverty.

The strategies under consideration here can obviously be implemented by a variety of means or tactics, which can usefully be divided into economic and welfare categories.[13] Economic programs are tied into the regular economic system and either make previous employment a requirement for eligibility for benefits or they relate benefits to the economic value of the work done by the recipients. Illustrative of economic programs are unemployment compensation, public works, area and regional development, and most job training programs. Welfare programs provide benefits not directly related to previous employment or value of work done. When a means test is used to determine eligibility for benefits they are often designated as relief programs. The Job Corps is somewhere in between welfare and relief—no means test is used (in a strict sense) but the cost of providing jobs considerably exceeds the value of the work done. Examples of welfare programs include old age assistance, aid to families with dependent children, literacy training and work experience programs, and general relief.

The selection and use of antipoverty instruments are affected by existing policy objectives and traditional national values and beliefs. Our society has customarily preferred the use of economic programs over welfare programs as the former are generally in accord with beliefs and values relating to individualism, self-reliance, and personal dignity. Conversely, welfare-type programs, especially those of the relief sort, are often stigmatized as "doles," "handouts," and, less harshly, charity. Programs of cash subsidies to the poor, such as the negative income tax[14] and the Guaranteed Annual Income,[15] run counter to our ideas about the relation of work and income and thus far have had little support. Only recently has there been a great deal of pressure for major increases in benefits under such programs as old age assistance and Old Age, Survivors and Disability Insurance, which would do much to eliminate poverty.

To the extent that antipoverty programs appear to strengthen or expand the economy, the likelihood of favorable attitudes toward them is increased. Educa-

[13] Joseph M. Becker, William Haber, and Sar A. Levitan, "Programs to Aid the Unemployed in the 1960's," pp. 4-8, The W.E. Upjohn Institute for Employment Research, Kalamazoo, Mich., 1965.

[14] Under the negative income tax proposal, grants would be paid to poor families whose incomes were too low to permit them to take full advantage of the exemptions and deductions to which they are entitled under existing tax laws. See Robert J. Lampman, Approaches To the Reduction of Poverty, *American Economic Review,* LV, pp. 526-527, May 1965.

[15] Michael D. Reagan, For a Guaranteed Income, *The New York Times Magazine,* pp. 20 ff., June 7, 1964. A group of publicists, economists, and educators, calling itself the Ad Hoc Committee on the Triple Revolution, has proposed that every family be guaranteed an income of $3,000 a year.

tion and training programs gain considerable support as "investments in human capital" designed to increase opportunity for the poor and help assimilate them into the "mainstream" of American economic life. Programs which appear to encourage economic growth are also apt to gain favor while those that seem to reduce the incentive to work can be expected to encounter substantial resistance.

Three.

In this section some of the curative legislation enacted in the war on poverty will be surveyed in roughly chronological order to convey a notion of its evolution. The discussion will illustrate the multifaceted nature of the war on poverty and the essentially pragmatic approach following in waging the war. Some particular political problems and controversies will be noted, although discussion of the "macro-politics" of poverty is reserved for the next section.[16]

AID TO DEPRESSED AREAS

. . . As adopted, the Area Redevelopment Act of 1961 established a four-year program of assistance for depressed areas—those in which the unemployment rate was above average and persistent—under the supervision of an Area Redevelopment Administration located in the Department of Commerce. The broad objective of the Act was to reduce unemployment by encouraging the formation of new businesses or the expansion of existing businesses in depressed areas, thereby increasing the available number of jobs (i.e., by bringing jobs to the workers). To this end, the Area Redevelopment Administration was empowered to provide: long-term loans at low interest to attract or expand businesses in depressed areas; loans and grants to local governments for public facilities needed to attract businesses; technical assistance to help communities formulate economic development programs; and worker retraining programs. A total expenditure of $394 million over a four year period was authorized. The Act essentially followed a "trickle-down" approach to poverty and unemployment, with most of the direct benefits going to businesses and not to unemployed workers. . . .

MANPOWER AND DEVELOPMENT

Another curative approach to the problem of poverty and unemployment is illustrated by the Manpower Training and Development Act of 1962. This legis-

[16]On the concept of macropolitics, see Emmette S. Redford, "American Government and the Economy," pp. 58-60, The Macmillan Company, New York, 1965.

lation attempts to attack poverty and unemployment wherever they may exist, in depressed areas or elsewhere, by helping workers who are unemployed or under-employed to acquire new job skills or to improve and update their existing skills. The 1962 statute, as amended, authorized a program of loans and grants for worker training programs operated by state agencies and private institutions and for on-the-job training programs conducted by employers, state agencies, labor unions, and other groups. Subsistence payments are made to many workers while they are undergoing training. Basic literacy training may be provided for workers who need it in order to benefit from vocational training.

Although the MTDA program originally was scheduled to expire in 1965, it has proven to be quite popular with both parties in Congress. Legislation expanding and extending the programs was enacted in 1963 and again in 1965, with the 1965 legislation passing by votes of 76-9 in the Senate and 392-0 in the House.[17] The manpower training program has enjoyed general support from both business and labor groups although the Chamber of Commerce has suggested, but less than vigorously, that the matter should be left to the states. Liberals and conservatives alike prefer for people to support themselves and not be dependent on public funds. Both have shown considerable interest in retraining programs. . . .

THE ECONOMIC OPPORTUNITY ACT OF 1964

This is an omnibus piece of legislation which seeks to deal directly with poverty, with both the causes and symptoms of poverty. Its various sections provide for programs geared to the needs and situations of different groups in the population. Much stress is placed on local initiative and leadership and voluntary participation, on giving "new opportunities to those who want to help themselves or their communities."[18]

A primary focus of the Economic Opportunity Act is on youth and breaking the "cycle of poverty," whereby poverty in one generation of a family often begets poverty in the next generation and so on. To realize this goal a number of programs are created, especially for youth between the ages of 16 and 21. First, the Job Corps is designed to provide education, vocational training, and work experience in rural conservation camps and residential training centers to increase the employability of youth and prepare them for "responsible citizenship." Second, under the Neighborhood Youth Corps program vocational training and work experience (and income) are provided for youth while living at home. Third, the work-study program helps students from low-income families remain in college by giving them financial assistance in the form of part-time employment. Only the first of these programs is handled solely by the national

[17] Congressional Quarterly Almanac, **XXI** pp. 810-815, 1965.

[18] House Committee on Education and Labor, "Hearings on the Economic Opportunity Act of 1964," 88th Cong., 2nd Sess., **I**, pp. 20-22, 1964.

government. The latter two involve state or local initiative with the Office of Economic Opportunity, which administers the statute, paying up to 90 per cent of the cost.

Another major section of the Economic Opportunity Act authorizes federal financial assistance for "grass roots" community action programs carried on by public or private nonprofit agencies. This program is intended to encourage the development of comprehensive and coordinated community efforts to help the poor become self-sufficient. Projects in these local antipoverty programs may include literacy training, health services, homemaker services, legal aid for the poor, or early childhood development activities. In the last category is Project Head Start, designed to provide "cultural enrichment" for pre-school poor children. (It is now a permanent feature of the war on poverty because, President Johnson has stated, it has been "battle-tested" and "proven worthy.") Up to 90 per cent of the cost of community action programs is paid by the national government.

Other antipoverty activities authorized by the 1964 law include: grants and loans to low income rural families to help them enlarge their income-earning capacity; loans to small businessmen, especially as these may contribute to work-training and job opportunities for low income persons; financial assistance to the states for special adult literacy programs; grants, loans, and loan guarantees to assist state and local governments in aiding migratory farm workers, grants to encourage the states to set up programs to help unemployed fathers and other members of needy families with children gain work experience and job training. The statute also established a domestic service corps—Volunteers in Service to America, or VISTA—to recruit and train workers for service in state and local antipoverty projects, slum areas, Indian reservations, hospitals, and the like.

The Economic Opportunity Act thus provides a quite varied, and highly experimental, set of techniques for combating poverty. Whether they represent the best set of means, or even an adequate set, for eliminating poverty is an open question. The Act, however, does represent a distinct departure from previous legislation, which can be regarded as both more conservative and less direct in its thrust (*e.g.*, ARA and the "trickle-down" approach, MTDA and the focus on training and unemployment). This, plus the vigor with which it has been implemented, explains why the 1964 law has generated considerably more political controversy than its predecessors. Conflict has developed over such matters as the location of Job Corps camps; the rate of pay for Neighborhood Youth Corps workers; the role of the poor in community action programs; the question of who should control local antipoverty programs; and the use of the governors' power to veto community action and Job Corps projects in their states.[19] A

[19]Shriver and the War on Poverty, *Newsweek,* **LXVI**, pp. 22-30, September 13, 1965; and William F. Haddad, Mr. Shriver and the Savage Politics of Poverty, *Harper's,* **CCXXXI**, pp. 43-50, December 1965, are especially useful. A running account of the political conflicts generated by the Economic Opportunity Act programs can be found in *The New York Times.*

program as comprehensive as that of EOA is bound to challenge a variety of particular interests.

THE REGIONAL APPROACH: APPALACHIA AND BEYOND

The Appalachian Regional Development Act of 1965 manifests yet another curative approach to the poverty problem—the use of federal funds to promote the social and economic uplift of an entire geographical region and its inhabitants. The name Appalachia denotes an eleven state region centered around the Appalachian Mountains, extending from northern Pennsylvania to mid-Alabama, and including all of West Virginia and part of Pennsylvania, Ohio, Maryland, Kentucky, Tennessee, North Carolina, South Carolina, Georgia, and Alabama. The region has been described as a "victim of both geography and automation, [lagging] . . . behind the nation as a whole in employment, education, health facilities, housing, and virtually every other yardstick used to measure a healthy economy."[20] It is generally conceded to be the largest economically depressed area in the nation, although it does contain such "pockets of prosperity" as Charleston, West Virginia.

The Appalachian Act authorizes the expenditure of $1.1 billion in federal funds to encourage the economic development of the region. Around four-fifths of these funds will be used over a five year period for the construction of major regional development highways and local access roads. The national government will pay up to 70 per cent of a project's cost with the remainder coming from the states involved. The emphasis on roadbuilding resulted from the facts that adequate highways are lacking in many parts of the region and that the governors, senators, and congressmen in the Appalachian states wanted roads to be given priority. Better road systems were believed necessary to open up the region and to stimulate new traffic.

The remainder of the funds provided by the Act are, it should be noted, for a two year period. They will go for such purposes as health facilities, vocational schools, land improvement programs, reclamation of mining areas, and the development of timber and water resources. . . .

The Appalachia program is geared to the economic needs of the region, not to particular localities, and is intended to increase economic growth and employment opportunities in the region as a whole. The funds expended will not go directly to needy people nor, necessarily, to the most depressed towns and counties. There is no "means test," such as a level of unemployment, to determine eligibility for aid as in the Area Redevelopment Act and the Economic Development Act. The focus is on those areas and communities within the region which have the most potential for economic growth, thus substituting a region-wide approach for the "scattershot" approach manifested in other programs, such as the ARA. As John L. Sweeney, federal co-chairman of the Appalachian Regional Commission, has stated: "Most programs of economic help in

[20]Marjorie Hunter in *The New York Times*, p. E5, February 7, 1965.

the past have been based on the theory that a man has a right to a job where he lives and that government should bring him that job. The Appalachia approach is that a man has a right to a job, but it is reasonable to expect him to be willing to commute to it or move to it if necessary."[21] This new theory is made manifest by the emphasis on roadbuilding and assistance to "economic growth centers."

The Appalachia program, in short, stresses economic development and is a long range program whose impact on poverty will be largely indirect. It is not "people centered," as one ARC official put it, in contrast to the Office of Economic Opportunity which "concentrates on helping people, through training education, and the like, to live a middle-class existence."[22] It will probably be a decade or more before the "real results" of the Appalachia program are apparent. . . .

Why has poverty become a major political issue? Several factors can be mentioned. First, both Presidents Kennedy and Johnson have used the presidency to inform the population of the existence of poverty in prosperity, the evils of poverty, and the need for governmental action to eliminate it. Motivated at least partly by the desire to be recognized as great presidents, which requires important accomplishments, they identified poverty as a major subject for national action. Second, the writings of various scholars and publicists have helped focus attention on poverty and inform people about its causes and consequences. The books by Galbraith, Harrington, Caudill, and Myrdal come readily to mind.[23] Third, the "race problem" and the civil rights movement have also been contributory. The incidence of poverty is much higher among nonwhite than white groups and, in many large cities, a majority of those seeking public assistance are Negro. The Negro leadership is focusing attention on the poor and the civil rights movement is demonstrating much concern for jobs as well as legal rights. Herman P. Miller makes the point:

> The rural poor, the aged poor, and even the poor hillbillies in Appalachia and the Ozarks could not arouse the nation to their urgent needs. They continued to suffer indignities of body, mind, and spirit year after year in quiet desperation while they lived in hovels and their children were poorly educated. Action came only recently. It followed a prolonged period of marches, sit-ins, and other forms of protest by the Negro community. There is no reason to believe that the war on poverty and these protest activities are unrelated.[24]

[21] Quoted in Jerald Ter Horst, No More Pork Barrel: The Appalachia Approach, *The Reporter,* **XXXII**, pp. 28-29, March 11, 1965.

[22] Interview with the writer, September 1965.

[23] Galbraith, *op. cit.;* Harrington, *op. cit.;* Harry Caudill, "Night Comes to the Cumberlands," Little, Brown and Company, Boston, 1963; and Gunnar Myrdal, "Challenge to Affluence," Pantheon Books, Inc., New York, 1963.

[24] Poverty and the Negro, in Leo Fishman (ed.), "Poverty Amid Affluence," p. 104, Yale University Press, New Haven, 1966. Cf. Nathan Glazer, A Sociologist's View of Poverty, in Gordon, *op. cit.,* p. 20. Many of the Washington officials interviewed by me spontaneously mentioned the civil rights movement as a major cause of antipoverty action.

Fourth, the belief that poverty is a significant cause of crime and delinquency and growing concern about mounting welfare expenditures are also worth mention. In his opening statement on the Economic Opportunity Act, Representative Landrum (Dem., Ga.), who served as its floor manager in the House, advocated its enactment partly as a means of lowering welfare costs and of reducing crime and delinquency.[25] Fifth, the paradox of poverty in the midst of affluence is both ugly and disturbing to many who are not poor, while many of the poor are less than quiescent in their poorness. An attitudinal change has occurred. As one commentator states:

> A revolution of expectations has taken place in this country as well as abroad. There is now a conviction that everyone has the right to share in the good things of life. . . . The legacy of poverty awaiting many of our children is the same as that handed down to their parents, but in a time when the boon of prosperity is more general than the taste of poverty is more bitter.[26]

Finally, many people have become convinced that the problem of poverty requires political action for its solution, the play of automatic economic processes being viewed as insufficient. Moreover, success in the war on poverty is perceived as quite probable by many persons. Success, or the good prospect thereof, in dealing with a problem is often highly productive of both concern and action on the part of reformers. Also contributory may be the apparent fact that many Americans are presently more "cause-minded" than the were a decade ago.

To turn now to our second question, in contrast to most important economic legislation, the various antipoverty acts discussed in the preceding section did not originate in the demands of strong, organized interest groups. Rather, these programs have been developed largely within the executive branch and Congress. (The principal exception is the Appalachia Act, which grew out of efforts by the region's governors to solve common problems.) Thus, the Area Redevelopment Act was started on its way by Senator Paul Douglas and was a product of the interest in depressed areas which he developed while campaigning for re-election in Southern Illinois. Again, it is said that the idea for the Economic Opportunity Act originated with Robert Lampman, then associated with the Council of Economic Advisers. The idea was taken up and promoted by Walter Heller, Chairman of the CEA, partly as a way of stimulating the economy through spending. Given tentative approval by President Kennedy just prior to his assassination, the proposal was quickly and strongly accepted by President Johnson within a few days after his accession to the presidency.[27]

Organized group support and opposition to proposals for antipoverty legisla-

[25] Congressional Record, **CX**, pp. 18208-18209, August 5, 1964.

[26] Orshansky, *op. cit.,* p. 3.

[27] The comments on the Economic Opportunity Act are based on a report in *Newsweek, op. cit.,* and an interview with Sar A. Levitan.

tion have formed after their development. A wide variety of labor, liberal, welfare, civil rights, civic, and professional organizations have supported the various antipoverty laws. Among the groups supporting the Economic Opportunity Act were the AFL-CIO, National Grange, National Farmers Union, National Urban League, National Council of Churches, National Education Association, General Federation of Women's Club, American Friends Service Committee, and the National Association of Counties. The group support for antipoverty legislation is somewhat generalized in nature, lacking the intensity which characterizes, say, the AFL-CIO's support of legislation to repeal the right-to-work laws and the National Right To Work Committee's opposition to repeal. Although the broad group support would seem to make legislative and executive support of such legislation "good politics," it does not appear to be a really compelling force.

Opposition to the antipoverty programs has come primarily from the Chamber of Commerce, the National Association of Manufaturers, and the American Farm Bureau Federation. (Some right-wing ideological groups are also in opposition.) These three groups have not been vigorously opposed to such legislation as it does not significantly impinge on their interests. It does run counter to the conservative ideology they espouse and they oppose it as unnecessary, or as improperly and hastily prepared, or as not really a proper activity for the national government. Then, too, the position of the opponents has been weakened by the fact that one appears to be in favor of poverty when he opposes legislation put forward as necessary to eliminate it.

The contention here is that, given a climate of opinion favorable to antipoverty action and generalized favorable group support, a political situation emerged in which Presidential action has been a (if not *the*) crucial factor in securing antipoverty legislation. Presidents Kennedy and Johnson have been strong supporters of antipoverty legislation and this, within the context of a "permissive" political environment, appears to have been the determining factor. It seems quite doubtful, for example, that either the Economic Opportunity Act or the Appalachian Regional Development Act would have been passed without President's Johnson's strong endorsement and support. Conversely, area redevelopment legislation was not enacted during President Eisenhower's administration because of his opposition in the form of vetoes.

Most of the major antipoverty legislation has come during the Johnson administration. While Johnson has been a vigorous and skillful legislative leader, he appears to have benefited initially from the favorable climate of opinion and congressional cooperation resulting from the Kennedy assassination. Following his sweeping victory in the 1964 presidential election, he regarded himself as having a clear mandate to implement his proposals for the "Great Society," which include the elimination of poverty. Moreover, the 1964 Goldwater debacle served to emasculate the opposition to Johnson's program within Congress and apparently to demoralize it elsewhere. These broad developments have obviously favored the antipoverty campaign.

Within Congress the various antipoverty bills have been passed by substantial majorities, especially in the Senate. The one exception is the House defeat for the ARA in 1963. This appears to have been caused by such factors as poor leadership and the loss of some southern votes because of the reaction to President Kennedy's 1963 civil rights proposals. Northern Democrats have been almost unanimous in their support of the various statutes, with somewhere between half and two-thirds of the Southern Democrats also in favor. A scattering of Republicans from Eastern and urban states have been among the supporters. In opposition have been two-thirds or more of the Republicans, a third to a half of the Southern Democrats, and an occasional Northern Democrat. However, large majorities of both parties have supported manpower training and vocational education legislation. The vote on the Vocational Education Act was 378 to 21 in the House and 80 to 4 in the Senate.

What has caused the broad pressure group and Congressional support for antipoverty legislation? Material or economic interests are certainly one factor affecting group and Congressional action here, but they are clearly not the only factor. Most of the members of Congress voting for the Appalachia Act did not come from states and districts directly benefiting from it and, it can be added, some who came from such states and districts voted against the Act. While some were perhaps swayed into support by the promise of regional programs of their own, these were few in number.[28]

Party affiliation and ideological orientation have undoubtedly been vital in shaping the positions of many persons. The large proportion of Congressional Democrats voting for the legislation is what one would expect because of the party's general orientation in favor of liberal-labor legislation. Further the supporters of antipoverty legislation articulate, and presumably are influenced by, a liberal ideology of action which combines humanitarianism and practical economic considerations with a belief in the need for national action. Antipoverty legislation is generally advocated as necessary to alleviate and prevent misery and to improve the economic opportunities and quality of life of the poor. At the same time, it is frequently advanced as a way of aiding economic growth and reducing welfare costs. This thought-pattern is illustrated by the following statement: "We pay twice for poverty; once in the production lost in wasted human potential, and again in the resources devoted to coping with poverty's social by-products. Humanity compels our action, but it is sound economics as well."[29]

The opposition to antipoverty legislation also can be explained in a variety of ways: material interests; southern concern about segregation; partisan politics; and ideology. Much of the opposition has been within the framework of a conservative political-economic philosophy which includes hostility toward big government and national action (which are often treated as synonyms), a preference for localized solutions to economic problems, and considerable faith in the operation of the market place.

[28]Don Oberdorfer, The Proliferating Appalachias, *The Reporter,* **XXXIII**, p. 26, September 9, 1965.

[29]Council of Economic Advisers, *op. cit.,* p. 56.

In short, the argument here is that the enactment of antipoverty legislation can not be satisfactorily explained in terms of pressure group politics and material interests. These have had greater impact on the details of legislation than on its broad outline and final adoption. A favorable climate of opinion, strong executive support, party affiliation, and ideology are more useful variables in accounting for the war on poverty programs.

19

THE WILL TO ABOLISH POVERTY

Michael Harrington

The United States is beginning to understand how to abolish poverty. The question is whether we have the will to do it.

In 1964, Lyndon Johnson ordered a skirmish against impoverishment and called it an "unconditional war." But the problem then was not simply that the Administration was unwilling to commit resources commensurate with its rhetoric. For even if the necessary billions had been available, no one would have been quite sure how to spend them effectively. In those first days of the antipoverty reconnaisance, the Department of Health, Education, and Welfare and the Council of Economic Advisors thought almost exclusively in terms of community action, the Department of Labor urged emphasis on manpower and full employment, and the argument was resolved by giving each side approximately half of the original law.

Now there is a vague, but recognizable, consensus developing among those who seriously want to end the scandal of unnecessary misery in the other America of the poor. Although there are, to be sure, popular illusions as well—with support ranging from Richard Nixon to the black militants, and thus a considerable confusion—the broad outlines of an effective program are becoming visible. But this Congress—and, most probably, the next one as well—is not the least bit

Reprinted from Michael Harrington, The Will to Abolish Poverty, *Saturday Review,* LI 30, pp. 10-12, 40-41, July 27, 1968.

interested in redeeming the solemn legal pledge which this nation took in 1964 to end "poverty in the midst of plenty."

To accomplish this goal requires that the nation adopt the program which Martin Luther King, Jr., formulated just before his death: to provide a decent job, or a decent income, for every citizen (this demand applies equally to the one-third of the poor who are black and the two-thirds who are not). After the Reverend King's assassination, the Southern Christian Leadership Conference sought to struggle for his economic bill of rights through the Poor People's Campaign. This Washington phase of the effort faced a flinty Congressional majority and sorely missed King's tactical genius. Yet it dramatized a crucial outrage, that of hunger, and laid bare an important mechanism for the maintenance of impoverishment in America.

That there are hungry people in this fat land is horrible enough. But the Poor People's Campaign also raised the broader, and incredible, point that agribusiness has imposed a sort of vested interest in malnutrition upon a large section of the federal bureaucracy. And that is not an isolated instance but a typical case of the relation which so often obtains between private economic power and public policy in this country.

During the winter, the Citizens Board of Inquiry into Hunger and Malnutrition defined the shocking dietary inadequacies which afflict millions of the poor. Since then, there have been attempts to discredit the report—one Congressional committee haggled over the precise meaning of starvation—but its main conclusions remain very much intact. The Citizens Board pointed out, among other things, that Government food programs had reduced their coverage by 1,400,000 people in the last six years and that "malnutrition among the poor has risen sharply over the past decade." It showed that only 5,400,000 of the 29,900,000 citizens officially defined as poor (the Government figures are, in my opinion, low) participated in surplus-commodity or food-stamp programs, and that two-thirds of the school-age children in poverty do not receive help under the School Lunch Act. Some just watch their classmates eat.

These statistics do not, however, simply define the pangs of empty stomachs. For the lack of adequate nutrition in the very first years can literally maim a person for life, in the mind as well as the body. There is, the report noted, a "permanent brain damage which, it appears, results from severe and prolonged protein deficiency."

It is monstrous that such a reality should persist in a nation with the most productive agriculture in the world. But it is even more intolerable when one realizes that the Government, sometimes with the best intentions in the world, actively helps to promote this suffering. "We are fairly confident," Benjamin Mays and Leslie Dunbar wrote in the Introduction to the Citizens Board report, "that most Americans must believe—if they think at all—that the Federal food programs (including the school lunch program) are designed to serve the interests and needs of beneficiaries. That is not true. They are designed and administered within the context of the national agricultural policy ... [which] is dominated by a concern for maximizing agricultural income, especially within the big production categories."

What this currently means was revealed in some data on Government subsidies to big farmers released in May when the Poor People's Campaign was already in Washington. Agricultural subsidies totalled $4 billion in 1967—roughly double the poverty program in the same year. Giant farm corporations were the most spectacular gainers: the Hawaiian Commercial and Sugar Corporation received $1,300,000, U.S. Sugar $1,200,000, and three California operators took in a total of $8,100,000. Another payment was somewhat more modest, but had a political interest. Senator James O. Eastland, a member of the Senate Agriculture Committee and a strong proponent of self-reliance and individualism, got $157,000 for keeping one-third of his 5,000-acre cotton plantation out of production.

When a food program fits into this scheme for maximizing the income of the rich and corporate farmers, the poor receive a grudging calorie or two. But if their hunger does not happen to parallel the surpluses which the Government underwrites, that is usually just too bad. And in all of this the most effective reactionary organization in the United States, the Farm Bureau, has a major private say in what the federal authorities will do. In this sector of the economy dominated by laissez-faire conservatives the malnutrition of the poor is therefore not a very important consideration.

This fantastic situation, documented by the Citizens Board and dramatized by the Poor People's Campaign, is typical. The McCone Commission reported several years ago that public highway programs had helped to isolate the people of Watts—and incite disorder—by putting almost all of the subsidies into private cars and ignoring mass transit. Last winter the riot commission noted that, in thirty-one years, the United States had built 650,000 units of low-cost housing while in thirty-four years it had underwritten the construction of more than 10,000,000 upper- and middle-income units.

The Poor People's Campaign marched to call attention to hunger, perhaps the most callous single example of this society's charity for the rich and indifference for the poor. But scholars and experts have also become aware of the issue. Senator Walter F. Mondale of Minnesota has been pushing for an annual "social report" parallel to the Economic Report of the Council of Economic Advisers; in Washington, Baltimore, and New Orleans, the Department of Transportation has resisted road schemes which would destroy communities or deface the beauty of public places; and academics such as Herbert Gans and Daniel Bell are at work trying to develop indices of social growth and change which will be as useful as Keynesian economic categories.

This is not to suggest that the battle for social control of social spending is won. Far from it. Powerful forces, such as agribusiness and the auto and petroleum industries, which have made the tax dollar maximize the private interest, are still extremely strong. They yield, as the automobile safety controversy showed, to political *force majeure* and not to friendly persuasion. Moreover, at least some of the official and academic involvement in the demand for social cost accounting is clearly of a technocratic nature, i.e., determined to change the miserable objective circumstances of the poor while leaving the subjective sense—and the reality—of powerlessness intact.

Still, this radical insistence that Government policy actually serve human needs is the first element in an effective program to end poverty in America. To fulfill its real promise, this approach would have to be urged by a mass movement capable of challenging both the corporate interests and the technocrats.

The emergent antipoverty consensus agrees on the two aspects of Martin Luther King's economic bill of rights: that the citizen must have either a decent job or a decent income. Before his tragic death, Robert Kennedy had placed a great emphasis upon socially useful employment as a means to ending poverty. In effect, Kennedy had gone back to the demand first articulated by Franklin Roosevelt in 1944 that every citizen have a federally guaranteed right to work. (FDR's proposal was amended into impotence when a timid Congress passed the Employment Act of 1946, and the pious hopes of that Act have been violated by chronic joblessness during most of the years since its passage.) Something like this idea was put forward by the Automation Commission when it said that the Government should become a "last resort" employer for the hard-core unemployed. And it is quite possible that Hubert Humphrey will pick up this theme in his campaign.

Yet there is a catch to this progressive version of the right to work (which has nothing to do with the dishonestly labeled "right to work" advocated by foes of trade unionism). Recent evidence makes it clear that it is not enough simply to provide *a* job; there must be a decent job. The UCLA study of the Watts disorders, and the Kerner Commission report, point out that the typical participant in urban riots does not come from the poorest stratum of the ghetto. Those at the very bottom of misery are so demoralized that they normally lack the initiative to protest or even to loot. The rioters had better than average (in slum terms) educations and most were employed. But it is clear from the Kerner study, and subsequent police reports on the Washington disorders after King's assassination, that it is precisely the menial, dead-end job which so often drives an individual into despairing, nihilistic action.

At this point, the right-to-work demand must be joined with one of the most important single innovations of the "war" on poverty: the creation of new careers for the poor. Slum dwellers have proved that they are capable of acting as teachers' aides, social-work assistants, peace-keepers, and even research assistants. The Automation Commission said two years ago that there are 5,200,000 such jobs in areas such as health, education, beautification, and others. And scholars like Frank Riessman have rightly insisted that the aim of filling such posts should be, quite literally, to create new "careers," i.e., jobs with training and hope built into them.

In short, the Government cannot pay private industry to "provide training for such menial positions as dishwasher, porter, maid, and stock clerk," as the *Wall*

Street Journal reported it was doing in some places at the beginning of July. Neither can it support the hiring of hard-core unemployed for jobs in the auto industry which, as *The New York Times* said earlier in the year, will be abolished as soon as there is the least downturn in the car market. That simply puts a stamp of Government approval on the classic pattern of the black poor, "last hired, first fired."

There are literally millions of new career possibilities which can improve the level of the entire society. Realizing these possibilities is much more to the point than pursuing the "black capitalist" utopias of Richard Nixon and some Negro militants. In attacking that panacea, I do not in the least oppose the idea that ghetto residents should own ghetto businesses or that the Government should subsidize such efforts. The small number of slum citizens who can become entrepreneurs should do so; but it is impossible and dangerous to think that such a program can transform the lives of twenty or thirty million people. The vast majority of the underemployed among the poor require decent jobs, for they simply cannot become entrepreneurs. (Underemployment is a much better measure of their misery than unemployment: typical ghetto rates range between 30-50 per cent of the labor force.)

It is significant that one of the most thoughtful critiques of the black capitalist notion recently came from Andrew Brimmer, the first Negro member of the Federal Reserve Board and, as an Assistant Secretary of Commerce, a man who has had firsthand experience with the attempt to create small business among the poor. The corporations, Mr. Brimmer pointed out, avoid the ghettos for economic reasons. The conditions there are simply not conducive to a high profit or even capable of providing the proper environment for a modern, sophisticated technology. The idea of bringing big companies into slums will not work (though an occasional firm will make the nonprofitable investment because of conscience or public relations). And, I would add, there is no point in thinking that salvation will be found by making black men the small shopkeepers of poverty.

But jobs—and even new careers—attack only one part of the problem. For roughly half of the poor are not in the labor market at all (most of them are either too young or too old). So their fate depends on the most pinch-penny, spiteful, and inadequate welfare system to be found in any advanced nation of the world. The riot commission discovered that in Detroit, Newark, and New Haven the median number of ghetto dwellers reached by any federal program was one-third. This finding dovetails with the report of the Council of Economic Advisers two years ago, which said that two-thirds of the American poor are not covered by public assistance.

It is in response to this scandal that compassionate leaders, such as Senator Eugene McCarthy, have come out in favor of a guaranteed annual income. There is, however, a catch. The conservative advocates of the guaranteed income, such as Milton Friedman, essentially see it as a substitute for the welfare state. They propose that the nation fulfill its total responsibility to the poor by giving them a cash payment (and usually a cheap payment at that). Yet even if every American were brought above the poverty line tomorrow morning—which would cost only about one-third of what is spent in Vietnam in a year—they would still be destitute in terms of social consumption. A $3,335 annual income does not put an urban family of four in the private-housing market, give them access to a decent school, or even provide them with clean air. Such goods will either be provided socially or not at all.

The guaranteed income can therefore be a desperately needed response to the present and unconscionable stinginess of the American welfare state—or it could be a reactionary device for institutionalizing poverty by pensioning off the poor with a few dollars and leaving their basic problems unchanged. Martin Luther King and Senator McCarthy have obviously talked of the first option, but the public must be wary of the second.

Poverty can be abolished if tax monies are actually spent on social purposes and, above all, on the fulfillment of the promise made in 1949 by the conservative Republican, Robert Taft, that every citizen would have a decent dwelling. Undertaking such a renewal of American housing would provide many jobs in addition to the potential of more than 5,000,000 new careers. And for those who are not in the labor market, a guaranteed annual income could, for the first time in our history, offer adequate social benefits to those who need them.

The country will not, of course, fight the right, life-giving war in the slums and backwoods so long as it is committed to a tragic, destructive war in Vietnam. But even if that conflict comes to an end, and even with the $18 billion in spending power which the Economic Advisers this year said would become available to Washington within eighteen months after the peace, it is not at all certain that America will honor its commitments to the poor. There are powerful interests that will attempt to divert a large portion of that sum into tax cuts—that is, into disproportionate aid to the rich and a maximizing of individual, rather than social, consumption. And it will take a most determined political struggle to get this money spent on human needs.

It is this last point which underlies the theme of this article: that America knows how to abolish poverty but doesn't want to do it. For what is lacking is organized political power which will insist that the country use the social knowledge it already possesses. Some of the problems of the Poor People's Campaign provide a case in point.

The crisis which became so painfully visible at Resurrection City did not begin there—and it did not even start with Martin Luther King's death. King had not succeeded in organizing a coalition to deal with the central problems he himself had defined: jobs, education, and housing. His brilliant victories in the struggle against Southern segregation achieved open accommodations, the right to vote, and other historic gains. But they did not show how to organize the masses in the ghettos of the North or how to unite the black poor with a majoritarian movement capable of winning national social and economic legislation.

King's moving speech that night before his death, when he said that he had seen the Promised Land but, like Moses, would not be permitted to enter it, has widely been interpreted as a premonition of his assassination. That is quite possible. But I think he was also voicing his own weary, agonized frustration with the problems of the movement he led. He knew that the attack now had to be directed against the hidden economic and social structures of discrimination and therefore against some of the cherished premises of the nation as a whole and not just against sectional prejudices. But he had failed in Chicago in 1966 and, with the war, the liberal-labor-Negro coalition had been split and the Administration had turned its energies and monies toward Asia.

America knows how to abolish poverty. It could be done in less than a generation. But so long as the war in Vietnam continues, there is not a chance that it will do so. Even when peace comes, it will be extremely difficult to bring together a new coalition, particularly because of some of the bitterness which now exists among those who must become brothers in the struggle if the cause is to prevail.

We now know how to provide every American with a house, a job, an income. But right now, we don't want to do it.

20

THE WAR ON POVERTY
—POLITICAL PORNOGRAPHY

Saul D. Alinsky

I heard a loud voice proclaiming from the White House. 'Now at last the Great Society has come to men. They shall dwell decently and with dignity. The Great Society will wipe away poverty; there shall be an end to war, and to discrimination and lack of medical care and unemployment; for the old order has passed away.'

> The New Democratic Testament,
> Book of Johnson
> Revelation 21:4

And so it came to pass the War on Poverty was declared; it began as a revelation as the first war ever launched in history on a balanced budget. It began as a popular program for who could be on the side of poverty. To criticize an anti-poverty program would be like being against Mother. It began as a plausible program for surely a great society as wealthy and powerful as ours could wage war and win over poverty. It began as a political program for history would

Reprinted from Saul D. Alinsky, The War on Poverty—Political Pornography, *Journal of Social Issues,* pp. 41-47, January 1965.
Prepared for the Institute for Policy Studies, Washington, D.C., May 26, 1965. Parts of this paper were presented before the American Orthopsychiatric Association, Inc., 42nd Annual Meeting, Section on Poverty, New York City, March 18, 1965.

not be able to record this era as that of The Great Society as long as its expensive clothing had ragged linings of poverty. And so we begin with the political program.

The anti-poverty program was publicly launched in wrappings of nobility of purpose and yet with a certain dedication which smacked of sanctimoniousness. Unless there are drastic changes in direction, rationale and administration, the anti-poverty program may well become the worst political blunder and boomer-ang of the present administration. If ever a program demanded an aggressive, partisan, unafraid-of-controversy administration it is the anti-poverty program. It must be a program which contends that poverty involves poverty of power as well as poverty of economy. We have seen this in the struggle for civil rights as well as for jobs. Our slums are not foreign nations to be worked with in such manner as never to constitute a challenge to the status quo. The Peace Corps mentality does not apply to America's dispossessed. Our poor are Americans and this is America where challenge and change are the élan vitae of the democratic way. This is not the program for a silky smooth Madison Avenue approach with a major talent for the avoidance of controversy; which fails to understand that dissonance is the music of democracy.

Today the anti-poverty program is emerging as a huge political pork barrel, a wielding of anti-poverty funds as a form of political patronage. Its disguises as a war on poverty are thin and clumsy. The use of this kind of money for that purpose is particularly repulsive. The American people will accept to a certain degree the variance of programs from professed purpose and a certain amount of wasteful administration. Even some plain graft is not shockingly unexpected; however, when this occurs in a program which bursts forth like a modern Sir Galahad then the American public will react in a rage. Americans, in common with most of mankind, have a contempt and revulsion for a phony, hypocritical piety. We don't particularly object to the sermon denouncing sexual promiscuity but we hold our noses when at the same time we know that the sermonizer is having an affair with the organist.

In city after city we find City Hall sitting on top of the pile of poverty funds. They have their Committees on Economic Opportunity stacked at least two to one with payrollers or the party faithful. They pursue a policy of identifying what they define as positive and negative programs and positive and negative community leaders. The distinction is simple. Positive means that you do what City Hall says, that you can be counted upon to stay in line, that you are "responsible" (to City Hall of course). Negative means that you are a maverick; that you are so subversive that you think for yourself, that your primary loyalty is to the people of your community, that you are so stubborn that the words, "Go fight City Hall" are not a cliche of resignation but a battle cry. You are therefore negative and "irresponsible." The same qualities are used to differ-entiate between programs.

These poverty funds are then used to suffocate militant independent leader-ship and action organizations which have been arising to arm the poor with their share of power. Organization of the poor themselves whereby they can take their rightful and legitimate place in the American scene. They can take it the only way any people can take or achieve a position of dignity and strength of citizenship, not through a sophisticated charity but through their own efforts. Good potential (negative) leadership is seduced by payoffs, rentals of premises, jobs and specialized pressure such as money grants or projects to "company union" rivals.

They will attempt to throttle a major independent militant organization of the poor by using the current con game gimmick of "consensus." Consensus is a word which is bandied about by those who are either political illiterates, and in this group we find primarily sociologists—or by representatives of the status quo who want to prevent any change and who are fearful of militant action. Their definition of consensus is not the compromise which ensues from negotiation between power organizations; the inevitable compromise which is the cost of human coexistence. Nor do they recognize that it is always conflict which leads to the negotiations table and to agreement or consensus. They attempt to introduce an artificial non-existent dichotomy between conflict and consensus. To them consensus and conflict are simply defined; it is the definition always held by the status quo; that if you agree with the status quo you represent consensus and that if you disagree with them you represent conflict.

They begin by creating a so-called consensus group (of course consensus with City Hall) whereby they pick up every two-bit little store front, every little agency which has been struggling along in the community, which not only has a complete lack of any impact on the life of the people, but are largely unknown to the local people. And all of these tiny groups are brought together on an overall committee on which the major representative organization is relegated and reduced to being one of 25 groups. Furthermore, all of these tiny outfits, many of them defined as stooges controlled and supported by outside hostile interests, are then fortified with poverty grants and suddenly acquire influence in the community purely by the power of being able to dispense a big chunk of money. In the field of organized labor this is what is known as union-busting and is a common pattern. The usual response of a union in that kind of a situation is a strike to the death. The alternative is death. It is also analogous to a ploughed and planted community field where a crop of independent power and hope is coming up and is suddenly threatened with a deliberate dollar flood of destruction instead of helpful irrigation through "maximum feasible representation of the poor themselves." A Chicago newspaper brazenly editorialized that the key word was "feasible" and that feasible could mean any number including one or none as far as the planning and administration of the anti-poverty program. "Feasibility" then becomes a fraud. Today all bona fide community movements are flying storm warnings. Let the buyer of the poor beware.

Subsequently the Washington Office of Economic Opportunity announced that one-third of those to be appointed to the planning and administration of the anti-poverty program would be the poor themselves. "Maximum feasible representation . . ." has therefore become numerically defined as one-third. Like so many things in life which look good, the real issue is beneath the surface. The question is 'Who is going to select the third? The poor themselves?' Or will they be poverty specimens hand picked by the prevailing political powers? The issue of selection is the all important one as otherwise one can have a committee of 100% "representatives of the poor" which could be nothing more than a puppet of City Hall.

Similarly another reported recent adjustment would permit various independent community action groups to by-pass the local City Hall establishment and make their application directly to Washington. While this, too, sounds good, it will have to await the test. Will Washington call Chicago City Hall for the final decision? If so, then this move would be not only meaningless but bad as it would take City Hall off the hook.

Another aspect of the anti-poverty war which should be scrutinized is a vast network of sergeants drawing general's pay. The startling contrast of their pre anti-poverty salaries and that which they are now paid is a strong argument that nowhere in this great land of ours is the opportunity more promising than in the Office of Economic Opportunity. In Chicago the head of the Office of Economic Opportunity is paid $22,500 as compared to a previous salary of about $14,000. One of his top associates went from $11,880 to $16,000. The Directors of the "Urban Progress Centers" or the Baby City Halls are getting about $12,490 (an interesting figure so they can say they have few salaries at $12,500 or above) where before they were averaging between $8,000 and $9,000. A police detective who was making $7,000 is now a Credit Education Consultant (whatever that means) at $10,000. Public relations personnel get $18,000 a year where $10,000 was the average previous income. However, public relations is a major function of economic opportunity. All of these are the ones who really appreciate the Great Society right down to the guts of their billfolds.

In many towns there are outcries from the civic leaders of New York's swank Fifth Avenue or Chicago's Lake Shore Drive for represenation on the poverty program. City Hall takes care of them by setting up a nice blue-ribbon "Planning and Coordinating Committee" where they can go have all their conferences and prepare reports for the wastebaskets of the Mayor's Committee on Economic Opportunity. I think that's where they ought to go. What business does Fifth Avenue or Lake Shore Drive have talking abour representing the poor? And what do they know about poverty?

This is accompanied by the injured self-righteous protests from the social agencies and their complaint that the program has become political patronage administered by untrained personnel. These charges will continue until the welfare industry can get their snouts into the trough and then all will suddenly become "a cooperative venture between private agencies and public authorities."

A leading Chicago newspaper in a series on the war on poverty reported that after the elected leader of an independent militant mass Chicago organization based in a poor Chicago Negro ghetto had criticized the welfare program that an official of a private welfare agency, leaving a meeting said, "I don't know what's wrong with him. He must have given up hope for a poverty grant or why would he be taking a chance, talking like that?"

What many of the poor in Chicago regard as Black Wednesday followed the attack of this Chicago organization on the politics of the anti-poverty program when 50 so-called social workers immediately flew to Washington to defend the honor of City Hall. If ever the social workers showed themselves to be nothing more than pimps of the poor, it was on that day; of using the problems of the poor to secure anti-poverty grants for their own agencies. One of the executives of a major private social agency in Chicago confided to a newspaper reporter, "All right, so a lot of stuff like the Urban Progress Centers will be straight City Hall politics, but after all, we got ours (it was a good one) and you've got to take the bad to get some of the good."

The anti-poverty program may well be recorded as history's greatest relief program for the benefit of the welfare industry. Graft wears many faces and one of the most sickening is the dedicated one. The use of poverty funds to absorb staff salaries and operating costs by changing titles of programs and putting a new poverty label here and there is an old device. They will be as effective in their new hats as they were in the old.

Apart from all this the war on poverty has become big business. We now have poverty planning professional outfits which draw poverty proposals and provide technical advice on poverty programs for substantial fees. Some are prepared to follow up the specifics of their proposals with packaged programs of remedial reading and all kinds of other sorts of instant poverty programs. Washington even recommends to the local authorities that they hire these outfits because they know the right gobbledy-gook language for phrasing poverty proposals and they'll even locate the poor.

A number of these firms have gone public and they represent the best growth stocks on the market. Poverty is a blue chip investment.

Around and through all of this crawls that new specie of professional parasites known as consultants and coordinators. Their voracious appetite insures that only the discarded droppings will drip down to the poor.

What can be done about getting a poverty program to function? First, I would have serious doubts about any really meaningful program to help and work with the poor until such time as the poor through their own organized power would be able to provide bona fide legitimate representatives of their interests who would sit at the programming table and have a strong voice in both the formulation and the carrying on of the program. This means an organized poor possessed of sufficient power to threaten the status quo with disturbing alternatives so that it would induce the status quo to come through with a genuine decent meaningful poverty program. After all, change usually comes about because of threat, because if you don't change, something worse is going to happen. Rarely in history do we find that the right things are done for the right reasons such as an anti-poverty program launched on a moral dynamism. It has always been done for other political reasons. One of the many examples would be our current worldwide anti-poverty program known as Foreign Aid. If prior to World War II anyone had suggested the use of American tax dollars for Foreign Aid for the starving Hindese or famines or plagues in Africa, Asia or anyplace, he would have been regarded as a case for Bellevue Hospital. "What! Spend American tax.dollars for non-Americans?" It is true that whenever there was an epidemic or catastrophe in Africa or Asia or South America or anyplace else outside of the United States we would send a Red Cross ship filled with medicine and food but not a sustained extended aid program.

The only reason we embarked upon the worldwide anti-poverty program or the Foreign Aid program was that after World War II we were threatened by the Russians in the world political arena. We, like the Russians, were desperately trying to get all the other countries allied on our side and so the Foreign Aid program came into being. *But its genesis did not spring from any moral principle but from a threatening political urgency.* However, if today through some miracle we got a sudden illumination between the tensions of Moscow, Peking and Washington, I believe that we would still go on with our Foreign Aid policy, probably in a reduced form, for *now* it has become part of our moral code. However, we should not forget that it did not begin for that reason.

Therefore, under present circumstances a poverty program based on a moral dynamism is not going to carry the thrust which comes from the threat. Until then what can be done? There is only one way in which federal funds can be siphoned into the hands of the poor, into the kind of bona fide community action programs of the city which are so glibly described in the official programs. This would require that local authorities or local City Halls be by-passed. That specially trained federal representatives who are in sympathy with the spirit of independence, have a faith in the democratic credo, in opposition to the welfare colonialism of the social welfare industry or that of the City Halls, be sent into local communities with the following objectives: When they enter a community of the poor which is organized by a militant independent organization such as T.W.O. in Woodlawn, that they would recognize and respect them and work out programs with and through this kind of an organization. That when these federal agents come into a community which is not organized that they will then begin to search out for those leaders of vital interest, those leaders defined by substantial parts of the community as leaders and spokesmen. That they will then encourage the gathering together of community sources of power through community block meetings and mass meetings whereby temporary representatives can be elected to help develop a poverty program such as they would believe would meet their needs. That in the ferreting out of leaders and of power centers that these federal agents would not be looking through the eyes of City Hall.

Poverty means not only lacking money but also lacking power. An economically stable Negro in Mississippi is poor. When one lives in a society where poverty and power bars you from equal protection, equal equity in the courts and equal participation in the economic and social life of your society, then you are poor. The meaning of money is in what it can purchase and how it can be used. Therefore an anti-poverty program must recognize that its program has to do something about not only economic poverty but also political poverty.

Basically our problem is still the central issue of the debate in the Federalist Papers as to whether or not the people can be trusted. If the Madison and Monroe position is accepted then the entire orientation of the anti-poverty program will be based upon a concept of working with the poor in such a way as to politically incorporate them into the democratic body; in such a way wherein a consequence of the anti-poverty program would be the development of power among our poor; and that the development of power among our poor will be welcomed instead of feared. Like so many other government programs, this becomes the central issue.

In a previous statement I pointed out that pronouncements of policy or program by authority in a free society are always prefaced and closed with an acknowledgement of the primacy of the people. This political statement of grace before and after each pronouncement is cast in variations of the proposition of, by and for the people. While to many of the custodians of policy and authority this bow in the direction of the people constitutes a civic ritual, the pragmatics of practice do not long permit it to remain an empty gesture. No policy or program lacking popular agreement, support, or participation, can long survive. It may be unveiled as a high-powered locomotive rolling at full speed, but suddenly it runs out of track. Our national history has been replete with such.

The poverty program as it stands today is a macabre masquerade and the mask is growing to fit the face and the face is one of political pornography.

21

FAMILY ASSISTANCE SUPPLEMENTS AND THE NEW FEDERALISM

Richard M. Nixon

... It is no accident ... that we find increasing skepticism and not only among the young, but among citizens everywhere—about the continuing capacity of government to master the challenges we face.

Nowhere has the failure of government been more tragically apparent than in its efforts to help the poor, and especially in its system of public welfare....

My purpose tonight, however, is not to review the past record, but to present a new set of reforms—a new set of proposals—a new and drastically different approach to the way in which government cares for those in need, and to the way the responsibilities are shared between the state and Federal Governments.

I have chosen to do so in a direct report to the people because these proposals call for public decisions of the first importance; because they represent a fundamental change in the nation's approach to one of its most pressing social problems; and because, quite deliberately, they also represent the first major reversal of the trend toward ever more centralization of government in Washington....

This new approach aims at helping the American people do more for them. It aims at getting everyone able to work off welfare rolls and onto pay-rolls....

From a Presidential speech delivered August 8, 1969.

WELFARE

Whether measured by the anguish of the poor themselves, or by the drastically mounting burden on the taxpayer, the present welfare system has to be judged a colossal failure.

Our states and cities find themselves sinking in a welfare quagmire, as case-loads increase, as costs escalate, and as the welfare system stagnates enterprise and perpetuates dependency. What began on a small scale in the depression thirties has become a monster in the prosperous sixties. The tragedy is not only that it is bringing states and cities to the brink of financial disaster, but also that it is failing to meet the elementary human, social and financial needs of the poor.

It breaks up homes. It often penalizes work. It robs recipients of dignity. And it grows.

Benefit levels are grossly unequal—for a mother with three children, they range from an average of $263 a month in one state, down to an average of $39 in another state. So great an inequality is wrong; no child is "worth" more in one state than in another. One result of this inequality is to lure thousands more into already overcrowded inner cities, as unprepared for city life as they are for city jobs.

The present system creates an incentive for desertion. In most states, a family is denied welfare payments if a father is present—even though he is unable to support his family. In practice, this is what often happens: A father is unable to find a job at all, or one that will support his children. To make the children eligible for welfare, he leaves home—and the children are denied the authority, the discipline and the love that come with having a father in the house. This is wrong.

The present system often makes it possible to receive more money on welfare than on a low-paying job. This creates an incentive not to work; it also is unfair to the working poor. . . .

To put it bluntly and simply—any system which makes it more profitable for a man not to work than to work, and which encourages a man to desert his family rather than stay with his family, is wrong and indefensible.

We cannot simply ignore the failures of welfare, or expect them to go away. In the past eight years, three million more people have been added to the welfare rolls—all in a period of low unemployment. If the present trend continues, another four million will have joined the welfare rolls by 1975. The financial cost will be crushing; the human cost will be suffocating.

I propose that we abolish the present welfare system and adopt in its place a new family assistance system. Initially, this new system would cost more than welfare. Not unlike welfare, it is designed to correct the condition it deals with and thus to lessen the long-range burden.

Under this plan, the so-called "adult categories" of aid—aid to the aged, the blind and disabled— would be set, with the Federal Government contributing to its cost and also sharing the cost of additional state payments above that amount.

But the program now called "Aid to Families with Dependent Children"—the program we normally think of when we think of "welfare"—would be done away with completely. The new family assistance system I propose in its place rests essentially on three principles: equality of treatment, a work requirement and a work incentive.

Its benefits would go to the working poor, as well as the nonworking; to families with dependent children headed by a father, as well as to those headed by a mother; and a basic Federal minimum would be provided, the same in every state.

I propose that the Federal Government build a foundation under the income of every American family with dependent children that cannot care for itself—wherever in America that family may live.

For a family of four now on welfare, with no outside income, the basic Federal payment would be $1,600 a year. States could add to that amount and most would do so. In no case would anyone's present level of benefits be lowered. At the same time, this foundation would be one on which the family itself could build. Outside earnings would be encouraged, not discouraged. The new worker could keep the first $60 a month of outside earnings with no reduction in his benefits, and beyond that the benefits would be reduced by only 50 cents for each dollar earned.

By the same token, a family head already employed at low wages could get a family assistance supplement: those who work would no longer be discriminated against. A family of five in which the father earns $2,000 a year—which is the hard fact of life for many families—would get family assistance payment of $1,260 for a total income of $3,260. A family of seven earning $3,000 a year would have its income raised to $4,360.

Thus, for the first time, the Government would recognize that it has no less of an obligation to the working poor than to the nonworking poor; and for the first time, benefits would be scaled in such a way that it would always pay to work.

With such incentives, most recipients who can work will want to work. This is part of the American character.

But what of the others—those who can work but choose not to.

The answer is very simple.

Under this proposal, everyone who accepts benefits must also accept work or training provided suitable jobs are available either locally or at some distance if transportation is provided. The only exceptions would be those unable to work, and mothers of preschool children. Even mothers of preschool children, however, would have the opportunity to work—because I am also proposing along with this a major expansion of day-care centers to make it possible for mothers to take jobs by which they can support themselves and their children.

This national floor under incomes for working or dependent families is not a "guaranteed income." Under the guaranteed income proposal, everyone would be assured a minimum income, regardless of how much he was capable of earning, regardless of what his need was, regardless of whether or not he was willing to work.

During the Presidential campaign last year I opposed such a plan. I oppose it now, and will continue to oppose it. A guaranteed income would undermine the incentive to work: the family assistance plan increased the incentive to work. A guaranteed income establishes a right without responsibilities: family assistance recognizes a need and establishes a responsibility. It provides help to those in need, and in turn requires that those who receive help work to the extent of their capabilities. There is no reason why one person should be taxed so that another can choose to live idly.

In states that now have benefit levels above the Federal floor, family assistance would help ease the states' financial burdens. But in 20 states—those in which poverty is most widespread—the new Federal floor would be above present average benefit levels, and would mean a leap upward for many thousands of families that cannot care for themselves. . . .

REVENUE SHARING

We come now to a proposal which I consider profoundly important to the future of our Federal system of shared responsibilities. As we look ahead to the nineteen-seventies and the nineteen-eighties, it also is vital in terms of ensuring that states and localities can continue to do their part in dealing with the kinds of social problems I have been discussing tonight.

When we speak of poverty or jobs or opportunity, or making government more effective or getting it closer to the people, it brings us directly to the financial plight of our states and cities.

We can no longer have effective government on any level unless we have it on all levels. There is too much to be done for the cities to do it alone, or for the states to do it alone—or for Washington to do it alone.

For a third of a century, power and responsibility have flowed toward Washington—and Washington has taken for its own the best sources of revenue.

We intend to reverse this tide, and to turn back to the states a greater measure of responsibility—not as a better way of solving problems. Along with this should go a share of Federal revenues. I shall propose to the Congress next week that a set portion of the revenues from Federal income taxes be remitted directly to the states—with a minimum of Federal restrictions on how those dollars are to be used, and with a requirement that a percentage of them be channeled through for the use of local governments. . . .

As we look ahead to the complex tasks of the seventies, as we contemplate the diversity of this vast and varied country, it is clear beyond question that effective, responsive government will require not one center of power, but many.

This start of revenue sharing is a step toward the new federalsim. It is a gesture of faith in America's states and localities, and in the principles of democratic self-government.

22

THE EMPTY-HEAD BLUES: BLACK REBELLION AND WHITE REACTION

Aaron Wildavsky

Liberals have been moaning those empty-head blues. They feel bad. They know the sky is about to fall in. But they can't think of anything to do. Having been too sanguine and too self-righteous about their part in the civil rights movement, they are too easily prey to despair when their contribution is rejected by those they presumed to help. Torn between a nagging guilt and a secret desire to turn on their black tormentors, white liberals have become spectators watching with frozen horror as their integrationist ideals and favorite public programs disintegrate amidst violent black rebellion. How did this maddening situation come about? What can be done about it?

HOW TO ENRAGE WHITES WITHOUT HELPING BLACKS

A recipe for violence: Promise a lot; deliver a little. Lead people to believe they will be much better off, but let there be no dramatic improvement. Try a variety of small programs, each interesting but marginal in impact and severely under-

Reprinted from *The Public Interest*, no. 11, pp. 3-6, 10-16, Spring 1968.

financed. Avoid any attempted solution remotely comparable in size to the dimensions of the problem you are trying to solve. Have middle-class civil servants hire upper-class student radicals to use lower class Negroes as a battering ram against the existing local political systems; then complain that people are going around disrupting things and chastize local politicians for not cooperating with those out to do them in. Get some poor people involved in local decision-making, only to discover that there is not enough at stake to be worth bothering about. Feel guilty about what has happened to black people; tell them you are surprised they have not revolted before; express shock and dismay when they follow your advice. Go in for a little force, just enough to anger, not enough to discourage. Feel guilty again; say you are surprised that worse has not happened. Alternate with a little suppression. Mix well, apply a match, and run. . . .

The dilemma of liberal politicans is exquisite. Now they play only "minus-sum" games in which every player leaves the contest worse off than when he entered. The first rule is to get yourself hooked on purely symbolic issues. This guarantees that if you fail to get your policy adopted you are revealed as impotent and useless to the deprived. If you win your policy objective, you are even worse off because it is soon clear that nothing has changed. A typical game played under this rule is called "Civilian Police Review Board." The objective is to force a racist response from the voters who are fearful of their safety on subways and in the streets. The game begins with a publicity campaign focusing on fascist police, various atrocities, and other lurid events. The police and their friends counter with an equally illuminating defense: nothing is wrong that a little get-tough campaign would not cure. The game ends with a ballot in which white voters are asked to choose between their friendly neighborhood policeman and the specter of black violence. The usual result is that the whites vote for the police and defeat the review board. If a review board is created, however, it soon becomes apparent that a few judgments against policemen have no effect on the critical problem of securing adequate protection for Negroes. But the game is a perfect loser: everyone's feelings are exacerbated and the conflict continues at a new height of hostility.

There are many similar games. In Milwaukee, for example, wave after wave of Negro demonstrators cry out for a fair housing ordinance. The certain result is that whites are made furious. The sad thing is that, if the punitive marches succeed in their immediate goal, only a handful of Negroes at most will be helped. Or consider the drive to achieve school integration by bussing children to different parts of the city. If such integration is accompanied by huge efforts to create equality of educational achievement among black and white, all praise is due. But if black children continue to read poorly, race hatred may well increase. Black radicals will then be certain to condemn the liberal integrationists who have again left them and their children holding an empty bag.

The liberal politician is damned if he does and damned if he doesn't. He breaks his back to get two historic civil rights acts passed only to find himself accused of coming in too little and too late. The rat control bill is a perfect example of the classic bind. When Congress originally failed to pass the bill, it was made into a bitter example of inhumanity. Yet it can safely be said that had the bill sailed through Congress it would also have joined the list of those liberal measures that are not good enough to do the job. Too little and too late. How much all this is like Groucho Marx's famous crack that any country club willing to have him as a member wasn't exclusive enough for him to join.

We have learned some hard lessons. Every time we try to deal with problems of race we end up with symbolic gestures that infuriate everyone and please no one. Why? The American dilemma is a compound of racism suffused with class differences. Since America appears to be richer in economic resources than in brotherly love, it would be natural to tackle economic problems first. Few of us expect a quick solution to the lesser problems posed by large class differences among white people. None is surprised that upper-class whites do not integrate with their lower-class racial cohorts. Yet we persist in following policies that attack racism before economic equality has begun to be established. The result is that neither poverty nor racism is diminished.

Disheartened by the magnitude of the change required in racial behavior, unwilling to recognize the full extent of the resources required to improve economic conditions, we are tempted to try a lot of small programs that create an illusion of activity, ferment, and change. But nothing much happens. Confusion is rampant because it looks to some (mostly white) like so much is being done, and to others (mostly black) that nothing is happening. Hence the rival accusations of black ingratitude and white indifference. It is apparent that we should abandon symbolic policies that anger whites and do not help blacks and should concentrate instead on programs that will materially increase the well-being of poor people in the United States. Programs should be large rather than small, and provide tangible benefits to many citizens, not symbolic rewards for a few.

INCOME AND EDUCATION

The most compelling need is for a fast and vast job program designed to virtually end unemployment among Negroes. The best alternative would be a superheated economy in which jobs searched for people and employers served their own interests by training any available man. Inflation would be a problem, but one of much lesser magnitude than present dilemmas. The next best alternative would be large government subsidies to finance decent jobs with futures, again leaving training to employers and motivation to indigenous groups and the near-universal desire for legitimate gain. Nothing else is possible until we end high rates of unemployment.

But any program designed to improve the longer-range prospects of the disadvantaged would also have to involve a fundamental change in elementary education. There are many things we do not know about improving education.

But we do know that the child who reads well can do most anything, and the child who cannot is lost. If you are fourteen and cannot read, you know there is no future for you in ordinary American life. Following the principle of "bottle-neck" planning (i.e., concentrating every effort on the most critical resources), one might abolish all subjects in the curriculum except reading and a little mathematics. Every six months there would be examinations in reading, and teachers whose classes fell behind would be held to account. Principals would be promoted on the basis of the accomplishment of their students in reading. Although family conditions may overwhelm all other factors in ability to learn, as the Coleman report suggests, this is a conclusion to which we should be driven only after making the absolute maximum effort to get every child to read.

Would these employment, income, and education policies stop black rebellions?[1] . . .

The great question raised by black rebellion is: Who will call himself an American? That has been the modal drama of life in America. Loyalist and patriot, patrician and plebian, slave and freeman, Southern man and Northern man, employer and worker, ethnic and Wasp, all have shattered the quiet of our vast continent with their wars. Today's rebellion is part of this struggle to forge a worthy American identity for black men. Black rebellion presents a crisis of legitimacy—a questioning of "white" authority. Hence the incessant demands for new power relationships. The immediate problems posed by black rebellion are, therefore, political, and require a political response.

POLITICAL SOLUTIONS

The most obvious political need is for mechanisms to reduce the blatant conflicts between Negroes and police with the police being the most visible and oppressive manifestation of governmental authority. Increasing the number of Negro policemen (and firemen) might help by blurring the purely racial nature of the encounters. The measures necessary to accomplish this end—allowing entry to people with minor police records, changing various requirements for health and examinations—are within our grasp. There are also various proposals for altering the role of policemen by putting them more in the role of helpers, and by sensitizing them to the problems of life among the severely deprived. It is difficult to quarrel with such humane measures. Yet they do not quite go to the heart of the matter. For policemen do have certain evident law-enforcement

[1]One has to be careful not to commit semantic aggression. The word "riot" is too aimless to apply to a phenomenon that is national in scope and that is clearly directed at expressing rage against the conditions of life of black people. To use "revolt," however, would suggest far more leadership, organization, and concerted action than appears to have been the case. So we are left with "rebellion," an appropriate word to designate violence by people who wish to express their hostility toward prevailing conditions but who are not yet organized to attack the larger society.

functions that may be blurred but not hidden. The rest of us manage to get along with police, not through mutual good will, but by avoiding contact with them unless we make a specific request for help. Not love but distance is the answer. A substantial increase in employment and rise in income will reduce the opportunity and need for crime. (Even the dope addict with a higher income is likely to be able to make arrangements that will keep him clear of the police.) Relationships with police could also be markedly improved by following Jacobus ten Broek's proposal to abolish the law of the poor. One reason that we have "two nations" in America is that there is literally a separate law for poor people. The difficulty is not merely that poor people receive less justice, but also that laws about sexual conduct, home finance, drug addiction, and dozens of other matters apply severely to them but laxly to other Americans. Hiring more Negro policemen will not be successful unless the frequency of unhappy contacts between them and the citizenry is sharply reduced.

Even were all this accomplished, however, it would not meet the profound Negro demand for autonomy, for control of some portion of their lives, for the self-esteem that comes from being powerful. If we cast aside the cynicism that tells us no man is truly master of his fate, we can recognize insistent political demands that may be accommodated or crushed but cannot be ignored. For present purposes we can dispense with a lot of research and simply assume that the best way to feel in control is to exercise control. Can this be done at all? Can it be done without generating the violence that will bring about the retribution that ends our hopes?

The usual American response to difficult political problems has been to disperse and fragment them into smaller conflicts that take place in different localities and times. Problems of church and state and education have been handled in just this way. Applying this procedure to racial problems in the past, however, has meant victory for racism or at least the status quo. Deprived of opportunities to exert influence at state and local levels because of official racism or lack of effective political resources, Negroes had no alternative except to look to the national government. This choice of a favored site for conflict was always opportunistic. Calhoun's doctrine of the concurrent majority meant control for regional racists. States rights and local autonomy were doctrines for keeping the Negro and the poor in their places. Now the old men are justified who say that if you live long enough everything comes full circle. Black nationalists, having little hope of a large voice in national and state politics, are talking about local autonomy. They demand a voice and a veto over policies affecting neighborhoods in which black people are in the majority. Bringing government closer to the people is a slogan that is no longer the exclusive property of conservatives. The pursuit of group interest by racial blacks thus creates opportunities for unusual political coalitions.

The Heller proposals for block grants to states, much of which would be distributed to cities, provide a strong basis for agreement. Local government would be strengthened. Negroes would find it more worthwhile to make demands on city governments. Cities would have the resources to grant some of these demands. The formation of neighborhood corporations or governments would be the next step. Run by elected councils within specified geographical boundaries, the corporations would provide a forum for airing grievances and working out common demands. In order to avoid complete focus on demands, and to provide experience in self-government, the neighborhood corporations would also negotiate with the city government to take over certain limited functions. Education has long been considered a neighborhood function and there are already moves toward further decentralization. If health and housing inspections are serious sources of grievances, cities may be willing to let neighborhood corporations hire and guide local people to do the job. Part of the energies within the neighborhood would thus be devoted to resolving disagreements among the local people about how they should run their own affairs.

We should be clear about what we are doing. The neighborhood corporation involves a return to earlier patterns of local rule that were regarded as offensive to principles of good government. The movement from the spoils system to neutral competence through civil service will, for a time, be reversed. What were previously despised as the worst attributes of boss rule and ethnic depravity—favoritism, trading of jobs for favors, winking at abuses when perpetrated by one's own kind, tolerance of local mores regarded by some as corrupt—will be reinstituted. Political practices worked out to accommodate the needs of lower-class immigrants, arrangements abandoned when they conflicted with rising professionalism and economic status, may understandably be preferred by underprivileged black people. The uneven development of all our people makes it difficult to pursue national practices. And Negroes, too, will have to reconcile themselves to the fact that programs which permit greater autonomy for urban Negroes may leave rural Negroes at the mercy of hostile state and local governments.

Today the black ghettoes resemble nothing so much as newly emerging nations faced with extraordinary demands and few resources. There is the same ambivalence toward "foreign" aid: you must have it and yet you hate the giver because of your dependence on him. Highly educated and skilled people (black as well as white) are deeply resented because of the well-founded fear that they will "take over." The greater the disparity between aims and accomplishments, the greater the demagoguery and destructive fantasy life. Yet underneath the pounding rhetoric there are men and women who are learning the skills of leadership. They must be given a chance to learn—that is, to make mistakes. They must have an opportunity to generate growth in human resources in their own communities. Otherwise, they will lack the pride and security to re-enter American life on conditions of mutual interest, respect, and allegiance.

We need to be reminded, however, that without a drastic decrease in unemployment no other programs will be meaningful. It will prove extraordinarily difficult to abolish the law of the poor because so many people will be dependent on governmental assistance that the tax burden will generate additional demands for obnoxious restrictions. When so many men cannot make a living now, educational improvement will seem hopelessly long-range. Community action programs suffer the most because of the utter futility of finding local measures to create vast employment. Expectations are raised that no local or state political system can meet. Ordinary politics are discredited. Each generation of community leaders is rejected as soon as it becomes part of an "Establishment" that cannot deliver.

Income, education, and power are mutually supportive. They are the bastions of legitimacy in our political system. Better education will enable Negroes to receive higher income and to gain the communications skills necessary to carry on political activity. The exercise of governmental power will strengthen the sense of mastery that makes the long road of education seem worthwhile. Political power also creates jobs. Good jobs at decent pay provide additional resources for education and political activity.

POLITICAL SUPPORT

What about the political feasibility of the economic and political programs advocated here? Will the President and Congress agree to spend the $5 or $10 billion a year that a job program will cost? Will mayors and city councils agree to share limited powers with neighborhood corporations? Will a policy of suppression appear more attractive as well as less expensive? There is an old story that goes, "Harry, how's your wife?" "Compared to what?" he replies. The political desirability of these programs depends in part on how they compare with what we have been doing. Take the sad plight of our mayors.

Mayors in the United States are in an incredible position. The only things they can do, such as providing better recreation facilities, improving housing inspection, and the like are strictly marginal improvements. They lack the money and the power to do more. Yet they are held responsible for every evil. Rebellions appear to occur at random, afflicting cities whose mayors try hard to do the right thing and cities whose mayors are indifferent or hostile. What incentives will mayors have to do what good they can do? Since they cannot possibly do enough, the do-nothing mayor appears no worse off than the better mayors. (A major possibility is that mayors will learn to concentrate on the one area in which they might do well and reap credit from some segments of the population—suppression of rebellions.) Therefore, working with neighborhood corporations, invigorated by fresh infusions of federal funds, should prove attractive to mayors who despair of their present situation.

Politicians in the Democratic party are frantically pursuing ways of handling racial problems that will not end in disaster for everyone concerned. Buffeted between the hostility of blue-collar workers to civil rights legislation and the inability to satisfy radical Negroes no matter what, the politicians fear their party will be split on racial grounds. They foresee waves of repression and a permanent estrangement between black and white in America. But consider what a new orientation would have to offer to Democratic party politicians. They would not try to bid for the support of racial radicals, white or black. The Democrats would turn down both mass suppression and mass violence, avoiding especially symbolic issues that embitter whites and do not help blacks. The politicians would espouse primarily policies promising immediate and substantial improvement of the economic condition of poor people. Decent jobs at good pay come first. Next, there should be the most powerful education program that can be devised to enable the presently disadvantaged to participate as equals in the market place and the political arena. These policies should be presented at face value as measures for making good the promise of American life. These policies are consonant with the traditions of the Democratic party, and they need not divide the races. The poor need help. We are a rich nation. We can and should give that help.

No doubt a party promoting these income policies might lose an election or two. But when it did get into power it would have goals worth achieving. The difficulty with existing policies is that even when properly pursued they do not help enough people immediately in direct ways. The usual mode of alleviating difficult problems by incremental attack along diverse fronts does not work because there is no solid base on which to rest these efforts. We will never know what long-run contributions anti-poverty programs can make if we continue to insist that secondary programs substitute for primary ones, that supporting programs be adopted in place of the basic efforts they are intended to assist.

Democratic divisions over these issues also provide extraordinary opportunities for Republicans to recover from decades of declining support. The danger is that an anti-Negro stance will appear to offer hope of detaching white voters from the Democratic party. The resistance of these voters to conservative economic policies would be submerged under a tide of racial anger. There is another stance, however, that would be productive at the polls and fit comfortably with Republican principles. A massive employment program could be expected to win over some Negroes and poor whites while not alienating existing Republican support. Such a program would hold out greater long-run hope of alleviating rebellious conditions than would suppression. Republicans would presumably not support federal subsidies for radical community action. But a program that stressed local autonomy through neighborhood governments should prove attractive to conservatives. Indeed, Republicans are much less weighed down than are Democrats with commitments to existing welfare and education policies that Negroes find so disagreeable.

A RESPONSE TO REBELLION

There will be rebellions; that much we can take for granted. The question is not whether these things will happen but how Americans will choose to react. It is easy to win tactical victories—disperse mobs brutally—and lose strategic battles. In the midst of consummate gall and endless effrontery, there is considerable danger of committing strategic suicide. What we do should depend on what we want. The prevailing confusion makes it advisable to take the risk of restating the obvious.

Just as Lincoln put preservation of the Union above all else in his times, so should we put construction of a multi-racial nation as our major objective. Our goal is that we all consider ourselves Americans who pay allegiance to the same political symbols and participate as citizens in the same national life. In pursuit of this goal, we must reaffirm our dedication to integration of the races for all who wish it. Wholly white or black communities can be one mode of participation in a common life. But integration is the preferred way of life for those who believe that there must be a single nation in America. A surface integration, however, must not be pursued at the expense of equality of achievement among black and white, for then integration will become a barrier to the creation of a joint American identity.

If we do not wish white and black men to live as citizens in the same country, we will have no difficulty in finding policies appropriate to that end. We can continue what we are doing. Better still, we can let violence feed on violence. The early riots have largely been aimless affairs in which destruction has been visited by Negroes on their own neighborhoods. Mass repressions visited indiscriminately upon black people can give them new reasons for race hatred and further violence. White people can be turned into proto-blacks—people who fear destruction because of their color. The difference between the races is that whites possess more abundant means of committing mayhem.

Americans who wish to hold open the possibility of emerging as a single people should not engage in mass repression. The surest way for black bigots to get a following is for white racists to create it. We want to open and not to foreclose the possibilities of being American together. There will be riots, and they will have to be put down. But our aim should be to separate the actively violent from the rest of the black community. Force should be limited, specific, and controlled.

Capitulation to lawless behavior would be bad. The hunger for humiliation shown by the New Left can only succeed in demeaning everyone. The black man's dignity cannot be won by the white man's degradation; the bread of humiliation will feed few people. The most destructive elements will simply be encouraged to raise the level of abuse. White anger will rise. Acting out the ritual frenzy of hatred will close all doors.

Our program should be neither suppression nor capitulation, but affirmation of common possibilities in a civil society. Without promising what no man can deliver—an end to the rebellions that are the consequences of our past failures—we can try to do what we now see to be right and just: A massive employment program, a concerted effort to improve educational achievement, and then support for a process of self-generating growth in the urban ghettos.

PART FOUR

Acting Out Uncivilly:

New Forms of Representation or Old Forms of Tyranny?

Our theme in this section is direct; that the development of the new politics will see much uncivil acting out no matter how effective our traditions and institutions for speaking up civilly are, and the test will be severe. By definition, nonauthoritarian institutions are more geared to handle discussion than insurrection, talk than truculence. Uncivil acting out presents American society with major challenges. Civil talking out is the strength of our nonauthoritarian institutions, to put the point in yet a third way.

Our approach to American institutions rests on two basic notions. First, American institutions are relatively nonauthoritarian. Enormous exceptions may be cited, such as the historic debasement of Negroes, the "pacification" of the American Indians, or the harsh treatment of Japanese-Americans during World War II. But worldwide perspective permits only one conclusion. This country has fostered uniquely widespread and growing participation in the good things of life, both spiritual and material, both here and abroad.

Second, America is poised on a knife's edge. We can develop more effective ways of representing and meeting the needs of more and more of our people, or we can lapse into old forms of tyranny employing modern technologies to stifle and to subjugate. The major headings of this section bluntly express a dangerous balance:

Student Demonstrations: representation or rape?
Black Is Beautiful: dialog or division?
Urban Disorder: will America learn or continue to burn?

A. A BASIC DILEMMA

A basic dilemma inheres in the bias of nonauthoritarian institutions, as Lincoln observed. Representative political institutions must be strong enough to survive and to guarantee the rights of their members. But these institutions cannot be so strong as to restrict the liberties of their people. At best, the balance is a delicate one. It implies viable feedback linkages between members, who can and will report when their rights and needs are not being met, and central authorities, who will listen effectively and make appropriate adjustments. The whole edifice is a multichannel communication network that is kept open by mutual trust. Members must trust that central authorities will listen, that they can be influenced or removed. The central authority also must have trust in the competence and validity of what they hear. Nonauthoritarian systems, then, require both two-way channels for sharing information and two-way trust.

A "shoe-pinching" model underlies all nonauthoritarian institutions. The theory assumes that members of the institution best know if they chafe under some policy or procedure. In these reactions, Everyman is the only expert. If people can and do report their reactions early, and if remedial action is taken soon enough in enough cases, civic tranquility can be gained or preserved. The underlying philosophy is to keep as many problems as possible as small as possible. Small problems are easier to solve.

That is the shoe-pinching theory, but the practice is something else again. Restrictions may limit who can provide political feedback, or whose voice will be heard. Take away a person's vote, and you have limited his ability to express his needs. Keep a person in inferior schools, and you make him inarticulate and perhaps ashamed. Keep a person underemployed or underfed, and he is so frantic eking out a subsistence that he has little will or energy to "fight City Hall." Self-deception is likely to develop even among those whose reactions are being heard. Being out of touch with many whose "shoes" are causing agony, those whose needs are heard are likely to feel that theirs is the best of all possible worlds. Indeed, *for them*, it may be.

But what of the others, the unheard and unresponded to? Some release is necessary, if they have any hope at all. The real rub comes when even as little as a fraction of one percent of an institution's members decide to act out uncivilly. Acting out uncivilly comes when people reject talking to reach reasoned compromise. They may really feel they have not been heard or responded to for an unbearable period, and they act out their disaffection in diverse forms in all institutions. Children in a family may throw a tantrum, employees in a plant may strike, students in a university may "liberate" a campus building, concerned whites and blacks in a region may unite for sit ins or Freedom Rides, and citizens of a nation may attack a public official or set the torch to a public building. All these examples imply two similar points: they show that the actor really means what he has been saying; and they show that the actor wants to attract attention to what he has been saying, forcefully.

Uncivil acting out, properly responded to, can serve as a kind of pressure gauge in a nonauthoritarian institution. Or so the theory has it. Uncivil acting out implies that the representative system has failed. That failure can inspire anxiety or guilt on the part of those members of an institution who want their system to work. Acting out signals a significant malfunctioning in the feedback system, which can motivate early efforts to prevent even more serious misadventures. Preserving the character of the institution requires careful attention to cases in which even a small minority feels *that* strongly. Authoritarian institutions can use less subtle strategies, such as destroying the minority. That will preserve the character of authoritarian institutions, of course, quite simply and directly.

Practice, again, may tell a different story. The theory applies least well in extreme cases. Acting out, especially in more violent forms, can frighten people into a spasm of reaction rather than motivate a search for the causes that led to the behavior. The typical early civil rights project of the Southern Christian Leadership Conference, for example, tried to walk that narrow line. The assumption was that a critical mass of support had to be attained if the project was to succeed. Gaining this support is complicated. It depends, in part, on enough people acknowledging the grievance as just and amenable to realistic resolution, and also on agreement, by enough people, that the means used to highlight the problem are more or less acceptable.

There is a hooker in all this. The charge of tokenism may be a common one in nonauthoritarian institutions. Indeed representative systems are geared to token adaptations, but ones that ideally come early enough to prevent problems from mushrooming. If the feedback network is too slow or ineffective, however, tokenism can only incite disgust and despair about the system's ability to change. For one thing, tokenism in a supposedly representative institution with poor feedback implies one clear message: Getting a big enough and committed enough and, perhaps, violent enough, group is the only way to influence public policy. This comes close to implying that might is right, the wide acceptance of which would be the death of nonauthoritarian institutions.

Nonauthoritarian institutions face additional problems. How do you react to those who act out? And, when do you do so?

Choosing an appropriate reaction is a difficult matter, for many reasons. For example, acting out may signal that a minority's needs or rights have gone unheeded, due to inadvertence or inability to do everything at once. Or the acting out minority may intend to deprive the vast majority of their needs and rights. The two cases require different reactions. Reality usually presents even more difficult cases. Thus, most of the acting out minority may have a just cause which deserves expression. But that minority may also contain some "crazies," individuals who are more or less pathologically vicious. Or a committed elite may use the just cause of their temporary fellows as a cover for purposes of their own. Witness complaints by blacks that they were used as "shock troops" by the Students for a Democratic Society (SDS), who employed Negro discontent in attempting to destroy an unjust society while jeopardizing the narrower objectives of the blacks. Separating the acting out sheep from the goats is no easy matter, then.

When the reaction to acting out occurs is also important. Moving too late to isolate the "crazies" or a revolutionary elite, may leave the authorities with a situation that has been blown out of proportion. If authorities move too early, or seem arbitrarily bent on knocking the heads of everyone in the immediate vicinity, this also may give the "crazies" or revolutionary elites support they would not otherwise enjoy. Perhaps worse still, premature and vicious action by authorities undercuts the delicate balance necessary in a nonauthoritarian state. The authorities may become strong enough to deprive rights, which in turn encourages despair about using nonviolent processes to raise and resolve issues.

This chapter focuses on three related varieties of acting out uncivilly that are so much with us; by students, blacks, and urban dwellers. We cannot predict their long run consequences. Matters are still up for grabs. Specifically, all three varieties of acting out seek to find new forms of representation. That tendency must be nurtured. For viable nonauthoritarian institutions must carefully respond to member needs, or change their character. They must also set and enforce limits on acting out, however, lest the search for new representative forms become an exercise in the use of old forms of tyranny, whether by the establishment or by the dissenter. A narrow line must be walked: permissible varieties of acting out must be defined, while basic disaffections are responded to. Much of the future of our nonauthoritarian institutions depends on how well that balance will be kept. Things still could go either way.

B. STUDENT DEMONSTRATIONS: REPRESENTATION OR RAPE?

The two selections reprinted below provide diverse perspectives on how student demonstrations reflect aspects of seeking representation in the formulation of educational policy as well as of raping the goddess of learning. They focus exclusively on colleges and universities. Many elementary and high schools have also experienced much the same kind of trauma. This permeation throughout the educational structure, grade by grade, implies the special seriousness of the issues involved.

Untidily, the student mass movements in question typically involve the full spectrum of motivations. This is at once the strength of such demonstrations, and their basic dilemma. The strength patently lies in welding into a coherent mass large numbers of individuals whose motivations overlap only in part. The dilemma is in controlling that suddenly coherent force, or even responding to it. Trying to control a mass movement, or a mob, is something like trying to feed a Hydra, each of whose heads has different tastes and more or less animosity for the others.

These general comments come to life in the selections that follow. Bonnie Barrett Stretch provides an in-depth anatomy of a student demonstration in

"The Ordeal of Academic Revolt," a case study of the furor at Columbia University in 1968. Mrs. Stretch catalogs the life of that demonstration from its tentative beginnings, through administrative intransigence in the early stages, unto the explosion of "The Bust" and beyond.

Revolutionaries may take detailed notes, for all the stages are there. As always, Columbia had its committed elites and the inchoate masses going this way, then that. There was *the* overriding issue: the threat of the draft felt by the most nonpolitical student, and the Vietnam War which made that threat so real to many. And powerful psychological forces may have been operative in the minds of many students. For example, how many Columbia students felt so guilty about having student deferments that they may have been precipitated into violence to prove their personal courage? In addition, there were specific issues, such as callous treatment of blacks living near Columbia. As in many revolutions, moreover, the themes of protection and destruction somehow became ineluctably related at Columbia. For most participants, apparently, the underlying theme was protection: of self, of ideals, of a minority, and of the opportunity to make a difference when it counted. Variously, this theme became as one with the goal of destroying Columbia as an institution.

The establishment can read Stretch's selection and be regretful, for all its attributed incapacities are shown there. There was the remoteness of those in authority from what was going on below, coupled with their uncommon concern for preserving smooth relations with those above. There was the early resort to pseudo-participation, with little remedial action. Finally, the resort to that two-edge sword of the establishment, too much police intervention too late. In short, the establishment galvanized massive resistance where only tiny pockets of opposition and inchoate anxiety had existed. And this with all of America watching.

As the Columbia story makes plain, a student demonstrator is not a student demonstrator. Albert W. Levi provides useful detail on the participants in student rebellions in his "Violence and the Universities." Levi isolates three categories of participants:

1. the small "hard core of radical students whose aim is nothing less than the destruction of the university as a prelude to the destruction of an unequal and unjust society"
2. a larger but unorganized group of students who have a burning concern about, or who have suffered from, a variety of international or social problems, including Vietnam and the draft, injustice to Negroes, and so on
3. the enormous bulk of undergraduate and graduate students, who will participate under such conditions as uncompromising unconcern by university administrators or brutality by police

Faculties and administrators should respond differently to demands from students in the three categories, Levi advises. When administrators alienate the third group, the vast bulk of their students, the situation is critical indeed. These are "the sheep," but they are not easily led into action. Levi sees the second group as having solid moral credentials, and as providing feedback to administrators that would come less easily from the bulk of the students. Nurturing by administrators of this second group is critical, for two reasons. They can help gauge the adequacy of administrative responses to needs felt by students. Moreover, their dissatisfaction is necessary to energize the mass of students. The radicals must be recognized as such, Levi advised. They cannot be satisfied, except on their own terms. Clear guidelines and firm enforcement are necessary to define permissible behavior. Granting amnesty merely permits them to seek their ends another day, and probably emboldens them to do so without considering the legal consequences for their actions.

The faculty and administration play critical roles in student demonstrations, and many observers do not like what they have seen. For example, Sidney Hook stresses, in an article not included here, the "ritualistic liberalism" he sees as dominant among faculty and administrative officials who in the main have not aggressively suppressed behavior he views as hooliganism.[1] For example, one faculty facing the prospect of student violence almost passed a resolution "not to call upon the police *under any circumstances.*" This strategy would be reasonable, Hook notes, only if all demonstrators were of the second and third types isolated by Levi. Given that radical revolutionaries were involved, the resolution was a license for mayhem. The root-belief of ritualistic liberalism, Hook notes, is the hamstringing proposition that "true tolerance requires that we tolerate the actively intolerant." Hence, although faculties and administrators at universities may strive to be nonauthoritarian, they can hardly avoid it. In a wide variety of areas, the students obviously know less than the faculty about the business of running the university. Hook rejects attempts by university officials to avoid a reasonably authoritative role, as in judging which professors are qualified or which students are doing acceptable work. Hook does not thereby urge neglect of the special competence that students have. The students know if the shoe pinches, better than anyone else. Some student demands are just, and they must be met by men of goodwill among faculty and students. Indeed, universities can serve as a model in this regard for other institutions. The alternative is successive escalations and backlashes, which could mean the death of universities as teaching institutions.

What has been the result of the uncivil acting out by students, and of the underlying apathy of educators and administrators that explain so many educational opportunities missed long before the pot of discontent bubbled over? Student Maoists see the past as preliminary to a real revolution; and others see the past as having gone too far already. Much informed opinion still sees the outcome as in deep doubt. One can grant that dissent is a good thing but draw the line at the supposition that more dissent is a better thing. So, while the moral sensitivities of youth are refreshing in a land which worships material success achieved at virtually any cost, the attitude that some faction of the youth

[1]Sidney Hook, Who Is Responsible for Campus Violence?, *Saturday Review,* **LII,** no. 16, pp. 22-25 and 54-55, April 19, 1969.

movement has the single key to the eternal verities is repugnant to most people and probably incorrect.[2] Thus, many people today find attractive Edmund Burke's proposition that:

> Men are qualified for civil liberties in exact proportion to their disposition to put moral chains on their appetites. . . . It is ordained in the eternal constitution of things that men of intemperate minds cannot be free. Their passions forge their fetters.

Radical youth would reject this as a cop out or as further evidence that you "can't trust anyone over thirty." Such sentiments prevent moderation, and shift the balance of student activism beyond dissent and on toward destruction.

C. BLACK IS BEAUTIFUL: DIALOGUE OR DIVISION?

Negroes have been acting out uncivilly, in schools and elsewhere, and it is still unclear whether their efforts will lead to fruitful dialogue or to bitter reaction and divisiveness. On the one hand, developments among blacks can be read as signaling an enhanced self-respect and consciousness of mutual needs among blacks. Such a change could serve as a basis for meaningful dialogue in social, political, and economic encounters. No longer need blacks enter these transactions in a one-down state, or have thrown up to them that "they don't stick together." This is the profound hope of the new gospel: black is beautiful.

Developments among blacks can also be interpreted as tending toward a new kind of segregation. Here black self-respect and collective consciousness find extreme expression in the calculated use of threats or violence.[3]

The balance of late has shifted significantly toward bitter reaction and divisiveness. Witness the change since the days of the sit ins and Freedom Rides of the early 1960s. The themes in those days were "black and white together," and lovingly so. Dr. Martin Luther King was the apostle of nonviolence, and he sought white support. Those themes are crystal clear in Harold E. Fey's "Revolution Without Hatred," a moving testament of one man's participation in the 1963 March on Washington that was the high-water mark of the early civil rights movement. Since 1963, the situation has changed radically. The civil rights movement of the 1960s, one observer notes, was characterized by "a devotion to the fulfillment of the American Dream, to nonviolence, and to integration." That movement, however, "seems now to be over."[4] Today's major theme is a more exclusive one—black power—and some expressions of it take delight in rattling racial sabres and promising Armageddon of convulsive violence. "I'd

[2] Eric Sevareid, Dissent or Destruction?, *Look*, **31**, pp. 21-23, September 5, 1967.

[3] David Brudnay, from a conservative's vantage point, develops this conclusion in, Black Power and the Campus, *National Review,* **20**, pp. 1001-1004, October 8, 1968.

[4] Martin Oppenheimer, "The Urban Guerrila," p. 13, Quadrangle Books, Chicago, 1969.

rather do it myself" is more the motto of the blacks, in any case, when they do not vilify the civil rights movement as tokenism, or Tomism, or imposition on them of the values of white liberals.

Given forces toward both dialogue and division the outcome remains in doubt. To some observers it appears that rejection of the futile attempt to become whites with dark skins has led to a coalescence among blacks. For example, a soul brother has written, "Baby, if the soul folks of America ain't together now, and becoming more so every day, togetherness ain't been born yet. Yes, at long last, it seems we've found ourselves."[5] The successful protests such as sit ins and freedom rides resulted in a new sense of self-esteem among blacks. The motto "black is beautiful" has replaced the old caste system based upon pigmentation in which light-skinned blacks disdained darker blacks. The confidence produced by unity and racial pride has led many blacks to go it alone demanding control of institutions serving their community.

More detailed inspection of variations of "black is beautiful" reinforces the view that either a new dialogue or a new divisiveness is still a possible outcome of the ferment among Negroes. The more detailed inspection here has three foci:

1. the Black Muslims
2. advocates of "black power," including the Black Panthers and black extremists
3. the Negro reaction to black extremism

The Black Muslims were one of the early and powerful stimulants to "black is beautiful," as well as to divisiveness. We review their history here briefly.[6] They seem to attract members for two basic reasons: the aggressive black nationalism of the movement; and its emphasis on hard work and rigid personal morality, a kind of black Protestant Ethic. The combination has in it the seeds of both dialogue and division. Adherence to the WASP virtues of hard work and moral straightness would be acceptable to many middle-class whites, but such adherence differentiated the Muslims from many Negroes. Moreover, the Muslims emphasized their separateness from whites in many ways. Many whites feared the Muslims, or perhaps they feared any organization among blacks that would permit them to try to rectify the injustices of the past. Indeed, Black Muslims more or less openly declared they were preparing to take over from the whites. This sent shivers up many white spines.

Major elements of the official Muslim ideology also emphasize division. Black Muslims believe that they are destined to take over by divine plan rather than violent revolution. The white race had been created as a tragic mutation by a Muslim scientist named Yakub, it seems. Allah punished Yakub and his fellow blacks by permitting a period of rule by whites despite their inferiority on all

[5] T. George Harris, Is the Race Problem Insoluble, *Look,* **31,** pp. 28-36, June 27, 1967.

[6] This review is based on John R. Howard, The Making of A Black Muslim, *Trans-action,* **4,** pp. 15-21, December, 1966.

counts. "Their very whiteness," Howard explains, indicated "their physical degeneracy and moral depravity." Black *is* beautiful baby. See? The Muslims live ascetic lives in preparation for reassuming their rightful supremacy, after a suitable period of suffering for Yakub's willful tampering with the divine order of things. Other related tenets of the Muslim ideology include:

1. The American black man, despite his lofty heritage, is ignorant of his own past history and future role.
2. The major task is to alert the American black man to his past and especially his future, for the period of enforced dominance by whites is ending.
3. American blacks "must do it themselves": give up habits encouraged in him by whites to keep him weak and dependent; gain economic control; and avoid integration with whites, which is only a white man's plot to forestall his own doom.

The new black self-respect and collective consciousness have been expressed in other ways that also encourage much more division than dialogue. Consider the variation on a theme in a publication of the Black Students Union at the University of Georgia, "White Colored Folk." That selection implies a rejection of "the man", as well as of those Negroes who worked with or for him. The latter are all Uncle Toms, or worse. Black power is the only alternative to white oppression, the selection continues, but the object is less violent separateness than "to beat the man at his own game." As the BSU publication at Georgia explained:[7]

The whites once again ask "What is the goal of the Black movement?" This can be answered in one word—POWER! To the new nigger, integration is irrelevant. The emphasis is on "how to beat the man at his own game." The whole direction of the integration movement was built upon alleviating the tension between the races and bringing about physical proximity of Blacks and whites; however, very little, if any emphasis at all was put on the problem of the powerlessness of Black people. It is to this problem that the present Black movement is addressing itself.

Perhaps the most extreme expression of "black is beautiful" is found in the Black Panther movement. The "October 1966 Black Panther Party Platform and Program" apparently calls for a radical separation of blacks and whites in America, a nation within a nation. And the extent of black power is wide indeed. The program calls for freedom for all blacks presently in jail, with all subsequent trials for blacks to be held before all-black juries. "American Black Guerillas" leaves even less to the imagination. The civil rights movement of the 1960s is dismissed as an effort by Uncle Tom Negroes and their white masters to emasculate the blacks. "That whole nonviolence thing," Rap Brown explains, "was nothing but a preparation for genocide." Getting Negroes to be nonviolent in the

[7]*Weusi Wapadeza,* I, No. 1, p. 2.

early civil rights demonstrations was only a devious prelude to herding them all off to the gas chambers, Brown implies. That mistake would not be made again, if the Black Panthers had their way. They would be armed, and they would alert all black people about their right to carry guns. "We are already at war," a leader of the Black Panthers explained. "The racist dog police must withdraw from the black community. . . ."

Whatever its variations, black power as a political concept serves a useful function for Negroes, as Stokely Carmichael and Charles Hamilton explain in a well-known book.[8] Basically, the concept is a part of the process of the Negro reassessing his "long-standing values, beliefs, and institutions." Carmichael and Hamilton note that black power "is a call for black people in this country to unite, to recognize their heritage, to build a sense of community." The consequences are a matter of degree, of what is meant by rejecting "racist institutions and values of this society." If blacks can somehow distinguish racist from non-racists aspects, concepts like black power in the long run may help Negroes participate more fully than before in dialogue with whites. If such differentiation is not achieved, polarization of blacks and whites will occur.

Given that blacks require new values, beliefs, and institutions, it is not clear that black power will enhance black self-esteem and solidarity. Only educated guesses are possible now. But the concept seems likely to serve some blacks at the expense of alienating many whites, and apparently also by leaving a substantial number of Negroes cold. Joel D. Aberbach and Jack L. Walker provide support for the point in "The Meanings of Black Power," a report of an opinion study among both blacks and whites. The findings are arresting. Nearly a quarter of the Negroes see black power as meaning racial unity, but just as many say that the concept means nothing to them. Of white respondents, over 28 percent see the concept as meaning that blacks will rule whites. Neither finding promises much in the way of supporting meaningful dialogue between the races. The findings also imply that the concept may divide blacks and thus undercut their recently enhanced solidarity. At the very least, more precise definition of the concept is needed to aid both blacks and whites.

Not all of the new black solidarity and self-esteem have been expressed in support of the black power concept, in any case. For example, Samuel DuBois Cook—himself a black—has written of "The Tragic Myth of Black Power." For Cook, the concept fails four tests:

1. the concept is "pragmatic nonsense," for "political suicide" is the Negro minority's only alternative in most electoral jurisdictions to forming "alliances and coalitions with liberal, progressive, and moderate whites"
2. the concept can gut the civil rights movement, and is thus strategically and tactically ill-advised
3. power exercised by blacks need not necessarily better serve the needs of

[8]Stokely Carmichael and Charles Hamilton, "Black Power," pp. 34-35, Random House, New York, 1967.

the mass of Negroes than "white power"

4. ethically, black supremacy is equally as repugnant as white supremacy

More generally, evidence also exists that most American Negroes reject at least some of the major elements of extreme black power interpretations.[9]

D. URBAN DISORDER: WILL AMERICA LEARN OR CONTINUE TO BURN?

"Black is beautiful" is not an issue that stands by itself; it is the woof of the warp of America's urban social fabric. Demands by blacks for acknowledgment of their new solidarity and self-esteem come at a time when a broad range of urban problems is reaching a crescendo. These include: pollution, traffic strangulation, business and residential blight, a diminishing tax base, and a numbing array of lesser and greater issues that demand attention. These problems have festered, in large part, because of the out-migration of whites to the suburbs and the in-migration of minority groups with no real access to political processes. Urban disorder has been one of the bitter fruits of this unhappy coincidence of pyramiding expectations and mushrooming problems.

Urban disorder is not a black problem. It is inextricably an interactive problem of black revolt and white repression, of the unavailability to blacks of ways to make their needs effectively felt as well as of white intransigence or looking the other way. Although blacks are now a major ingredient in the present mixture of urban combustibles, other disadvantaged groups may come to play an even greater role in urban disorders, so that these days may appear, in retrospect, to have been peaceful days. There are significant enough urban concentrations of the Mexican-Americans and poor whites, for example, to create truly incendiary conditions. In general, these potential groupings have not been organized, as has the black minority over the years. This implies a tragic irony in today's attempts to extend the good material and spiritual life to more and more Americans. Today's black militancy was at least aided by the determined efforts of the 1960s to remedy historical injustices. These efforts provided a kind of launching platform of enhanced self-respect and solidarity that encouraged expectations to increase faster than they were being met. Somewhat the same consequence may be one of the intermediate effects of all efforts to help disadvantaged or repressed groups. In short, we had better learn from the experience with urban blacks.

Our urban problems both contribute to, and are exacerbated by, various aspects of the "black is beautiful" theme. Since Negroes tend to be concentrated in urban areas, their position is both tragic and strategic. Their position is more tragic because the raw wounds of historic deprivation have the salt of the multiple dilemmas of urban governance rubbed into them; more strategic because of

---

[9]Some data supporting the point are reported in Raymond W. Mack, The Negro Opposition to Black Extremism, *Saturday Review,* pp. 52-55, May 1964.

their concentration, whether the game is exerting political influence or creating civil insurrection.

The horrendous challenge seems clear enough. America will have to learn to cope with its urban Pandora's box, or America will continue to burn. The burning may be of the kind a number of our urban areas have felt in some long, hot summers of the past; or it may be a raging frustration that finds more subtle ways to pollute the quality of contemporary life. But learn or burn it will be.

Substantial energies are being devoted to learning about the "why" of urban unrest, as well as about the "how" of coping with it. The "Summary of Report" of the 1967 President's Commission on Civil Disorders does a noteworthy job of spelling out the complex "why" of urban disorders and it also suggests the formidable "how" of avoiding them. There is no better way of summarizing the thrust of that summary than by quoting its last words:

> We have provided an honest beginning. We have learned much. But we have uncovered no startling truths, no unique insights, no simple solutions. The destruction and the bitterness of racial disorder, the harsh polemics of black revolt and white repression have been seen and heard before in this country.
>
> It is time now to end the destruction and the violence, not only in the streets of the ghetto but in the lives of the people.

At least one thing America must learn seems clear enough in all the complexities of burgeoning urban problems. We cannot expect blacks to follow the patterns of successive waves of immigrants to America, that of assimilation to the prevailing white culture over a period of generations. Several reasons for this are cited by John H. Strange:[10]

1. because of their color, Negroes cannot assimilate as easily as previous immigrant groups
2. because "black is beautiful," Negroes who assimilate are especially liable to being called "race-traitors"
3. because opportunities for social mobility such as small businesses, political machines, and even crime, are less available today than they were to earlier immigrants, fewer avenues of economic mobility exist for Negroes
4. because earlier immigrants arrived during a period of great demand for unskilled labor, while Negroes today must have substantial skills or suffer recurring underemployment
5. because earlier immigrants tended to have more stable family units, with a male in a dominant role, while Negro families tend to be matriarchal and unstable.

[10] John H. Strange, Race, Conflict, and Urban Politics, pp. 7-8. Paper prepared for the Third Conference on Democratic Theory, November 14-16, 1968. Airlie House, Warrenton, Va.

Learning how to cope with urban unrest requires innovating ways to enhance the possibility that urbanites can influence their immediate environments. This poses a real problem, for the bias among urban reformers has been to remove as many issue areas as possible from politics, by creating "professional" school systems or developing a protected career civil service. With so many issues of direct concern to blacks and the urban poor being defined out of politics, John H. Strange argues in "Race, Conflict, and Urban Politics," despair could induce them to raise such issues in more violent ways. Strange briefly isolates a substantial catalog of the ways in which the range of urban issues defined as within politics could be enlarged.

Whatever the evaluation of the individual suggestions made by Strange, evidence implies that he is on the correct trail. Strange argues that ways be found to

1. facilitate *social contact* between the races, by encouraging the training of Negroes for various professions in which they are underrepresented
2. reduce the sense of *powerlessness* felt by blacks, by encouraging maximum feasible participation in projects involving the poor and underpriviledged
3. reduce racial *dissatisfaction*, the feeling among blacks that their treatment depends only on their race, by opening various institutions to them more than has been the case.

H. Edward Ransford reports an attempt to test just such variables in "Isolation, Powerlessness, and Violence." The results of that study are not definitive, but two suggestive findings deserve emphasis. First, Negroes report attitudes favoring *greater* willingness to use violence as they report less social contact with whites; greater feelings of powerlessness; and greater dissatisfaction with their treatment due to their blackness. Although Ransford's focus is on attitudes about violence, as opposed to violent behavior, his findings suggest the soundness of the theory underlying Strange's recommendations. Second, although Ransford has only a few cases to work with, Negroes who reported attitudes favoring the use of violence were also likely to have participated in the major urban disorders in the Watts area of Los Angeles.

Whether it will be learning or burning only history will reveal, but some feelings of deep pessimism already exist. Daniel H. Watts, the black editor of a magazine of radical thought, expresses his feelings directly in "America Will Burn."[11] In an article not reprinted here, Watts described progress in civil rights as a cruel fraud perpetrated by self-righteous white liberals and by Negroes like Roy Wilkins and Whitney Young who Watts sees as out of touch with the black community. "The promises made to Negroes are cruel hoaxes for a people," he notes, "who must still be concerned about mere survival." Watts sees little or no evidence that whites are willing to significantly share the pie of affluence with

[11] Daniel Watts, America Will Burn, *Saturday Evening Post,* **241**, no. 1, pp. 6-10, January 13, 1968.

their black brothers. Since "white America has no reason to share the pie willing-ly," Watts observes, "inevitably the Negro will have to take a torch and gun to get his slice." America *will* burn, that is, short of an unanticipated willingness on the part of whites to allow blacks to really share in the good things of life.

It is not pleasant to hear prophecies of a smouldering America, especially since rhetoric may be the mother of revolution. But it is vital to get at the basic needs that commentators like Watts reflect. For example, he puts down the civil rights movement as "white liberal paternalism" that imposed its needs on the Afro-American community. "Not once have we been allowed to decide what *we* want," he writes with a clear passion. If there seems overstatement in the rhet-oric, the core message is unmistakable. One thing America must learn is how to create institutions and attitudes that will permit more of its people to express what they do want. Only thus can a real amalgam of needs result. This can never mean getting all of what one desires, and right now. It must mean, however, a growing confidence that a broader and broader range of needs is really (but really) being taken into account, given the reality that it is not yet possible for all or even most of us to have all that we wish.

23

THE ORDEAL OF ACADEMIC REVOLT

Bonnie Barrett Stretch

No one will ever be certain of all that happened at Columbia University in the weeks following April 23, why it happened, or what it meant. At times, events on the campus constituted a theater of the absurd which defied all comprehension; at others, Columbia appeared to be in the grip of a violent revolution, an academic civil war, in which scholars manned barricades to protect student from student and to hold off charging police. At still others—and perhaps ultimately— the revolt at Columbia was nothing less than the denouement of a tragedy that still awaits its catharsis.

What made it a tragedy was not only the brutality and violence, the intransigence of the parties in conflict, nor the resulting paralysis of a great center of learning, but the fact that the university, despite its admitted disregard of the interests of students and faculty, was caught by external events and conditions that converted local discontent to uncontrollable rage. Columbia *had* ignored student and faculty pleas for reform, and for greater participation in university decisions; and it *had* treated the neighboring Harlem community as an inferior colony. Yet the university had little—if any—control over the Vietnam war, the draft, and the hostilities they produced; it had assurances—perhaps naively accepted—that the police who were called in to clear student-occupied buildings would refrain from violent acts even if provoked; it did believe that ultimately

Reprinted from Bonnie Barrett Stretch, The Ordeal of Academic Revolt, *Saturday Review,* LI, no. 24, pp. 61-63, 81-83, June 15, 1968.

students would act like students, not like the agents of a revolt whose ultimate cause and targets were far beyond the campus.

The immediate issues of the revolt were more symbolic than real. The original protest, led by Students for a Democratic Society (SDS), a radical group of the New Left, and by the Student Afro-American Society (SAS), an organization of black undergraduates, was aimed at stopping the construction of a gymnasium in Morningside Park, which separates Columbia from Harlem, and at severing Columbia's affiliation with the Institute for Defense Analysis, a private research organization that engages in military research for the Pentagon. Each represented far broader issues: the gymnasium, increasingly unpopular in Harlem, was another in a series of university real estate maneuvers which had been angering Harlem and other neighboring areas for years; in the IDA, the university indicated—at least to the militant students—an institutional complicity with all acts of war.

Even as symbols, the gymnasium and IDA could not have produced the revolt that followed without a history of mistrust that has marked student relations with President Grayson Kirk in recent years. In the university's past reluctance to heed more moderate demands for reform, and in a series of tactical blunders at the beginning of the strike, it gave the initiative to the most radical students and helped fan what otherwise might have been minority protest into a mass movement.

As in all such movements, the resulting acts—and the responses to them— produced divisions and conflicts that will take years to heal. "The university," said Vice President David B. Truman, who had been a popular dean and became a target of vilification, "has been deeply wounded." As he spoke—a few days after a police raid had resulted in 700 arrests and uncounted beatings—he could not yet gauge how much deeper those wounds would go in the ensuing weeks. Students destroyed the notes of a history professor who had opposed the strike; others threatened to break up the university's commencement; still others, frustrated by the disruption of the university, threatened to bomb or burn university buildings if the strikers were not punished. Within the student body and among the faculty, faction vied with faction, committees were formed and reformed, political debates took place in various parts of the campus, rallies and picket lines were organized, and "liberation classes" conducted. Meanwhile the university—with the exception of certain schools and divisions—came to a halt. . . .

The spark that converted the Columbia strike from a minority action into a university-wide crisis was what everyone on campus now calls The Bust. Shortly after 2 a.m. a week after the student revolt began, 1,000 policemen stormed the campus to drive student demonstrators out of five buildings. Faculty members, who "interposed" themselves to prevent violence, were beaten and bloodied, and a crowd of bystanders was inexplicably charged by club-swinging police.

"Let me make perfectly clear for anyone who does not yet understand," declared Mike Nichols, vice president of the Columbia University Student Council (CUSC) and unofficial spokesman for the great majority of moderate students, the next day, "The students who are striking this week are not necessarily the students who were striking last week."

During the week before The Bust, when undergraduates and graduate students were occupying five "liberated" buildings on campus, the administration devoted itself primarily to attempting to negotiate with the black students who had established sole possession of Hamilton Hall, main classroom building of Columbia College. Ever in the background was the fear of a major racial uprising from neighboring Harlem. After consultation with the Mayor, the president and trustees announced a temporary suspension of construction on the controversial gymnasium, and agreed to meet with community leaders before a decision was made on whether to proceed with the building at all.

Meanwhile faculty members, stunned and confused by the unprecedented events, tried to mediate between the administration and the white students. Their chief concern was the threat of violence—between right-wing and left-wing students, as well as between police and students. The professors' vehement opposition to police action was a major factor in restraining the administration for a full week.

Eventually some of the faculty set up a cordon around the occupied buildings to keep right-wing students out and to keep strike sympathizers from joining the crowd within. Then, two nights after the crisis began, the administration made an abortive attempt to bring in the police for the first time. Vice President

---

THE SIX DEMANDS FROM STRIKE CENTRAL

"In order to form the desired unity of all concerned members of the University community, the strike committee moves that this body accept as precondition for negotiations the following:

That the administration recognize our right to participate in the restructuring of the University and also recognize the legitimacy of our demands by agreeing that there shall be no legal or disciplinary reprisals against those who participated in the demonstrations on campus or on the gym site, and that the five demands listed below and the details of University restructuring be the substance of the negotiations to end the strike. These five demands are as follows:

1) Construction of the gym must be terminated.

2) The University must break all ties with I.D.A.

3) The ban on indoor demonstrations must be revoked.

4) A permanent student-faculty commission, democratically elected, must be established to hear and pass binding judgment on all future disciplinary action.

5) The University must use its good offices to have the City of New York drop all charges made against those having demonstrated on the gym site or on the campus."

Truman, who announced the decision to a faculty gathering, was greeted with cries of "Shame!" Many professors ran to join those on the cordon. The faculty line stood up against the attack—some were clubbed, one was left bleeding—and forced the administration, aware for the first time of an aroused faculty, to call off the police.

It was at this point that many faculty members became aware that this was no passing demonstration, that more than mediation was required. A round of informal faculty meetings produced a resolution to form a commission of students, faculty, and administrators to help negotiate the question of disciplining the strikers. (Unlike many institutions, Columbia has no judiciary body; all disciplinary matters are handled by the administration.) But negotiations got nowhere. At last, the senior members prevailed on President Kirk to call a joint meeting of the university faculties—an action unprecedented in recent university history. The question was raised of "restructuring" the university to give greater role to faculty and students, but no concrete action was taken. Approximately thirty-six hours later, the police took over the campus.

If in those early-morning hours after The Bust the administration thought "normalcy" had returned to Columbia, it soon became clear that "normalcy" would never return again. Faculty and students alike were horrified at the violence of the police and outraged that the administration had resorted to force. Rebellion took the form of a general strike. A headquarters (Strike Central) was established in Ferris Booth Hall, and the inevitable mimeograph machines began grinding out the literature of revolution. The groups that had held the buildings labeled themselves communes (Math Commune, Fayerweather Commune, etc.) and, with other students, formed a Strike Coordinating Committee. Departments, schools, and student organizations circulated petitions supporting the strike; every seventy signatures put one representative on the committee, which grew from ten (representing the original demonstrators), to fifty, then to seventy. Offices were set up to deal with the press, to handle charges of police brutality, to set up "Liberation Classes," to organize picket lines, and to paint posters. Signs plastered the walls with slogans of STRIKE!; UP AGAINST THE WALL!; CREATE TWO, THREE, MANY COLUMBIAS! Near the rear of the hallway one lone sign read: IF YOU ARE LOST, YOU'VE COME TO THE RIGHT PLACE. The third floor of Ferris Booth became a political happening.

Many junior instructors and some senior professors supported the strike. But most felt the students' tactics were identical to the administration's resort to the police and were wholly antithetical to the nature of a great center of learning. As thirty-five law professors put it in a later statement:

> The force of reason rather than the force of massed bodies must be the reliance of those who wish to influence a community guided by intelligence as is Columbia. Disrupting institutional proceedings is an impermissible substitute for rational persuasion. Using muscles instead of minds to express dissent has no place in the academic setting.

A round of meetings began, mostly on the departmental level. The tripartite commission (renamed the Joint Committee on Disciplinary Affairs) was formed ("I don't know where they got the students on it, but it has some good men," conceded a "moderate" striker) and began to function in earnest. The Joint Faculties met again and set up a twelve-man executive committee comprised of such academic stars as Eli Ginzberg, Daniel Bell, Polykarp Kusch, and Lionel Trilling. Headed by Alan Westin and Michael Sovern, it was empowered "to call the faculty together and to take other needed steps to return the university to its educational task at the earliest possible moment."

The faculty had declared itself an autonomous body. Kirk, meanwhile, had disappeared into the bowels of Low Library behind an armed guard. Groundsmen went about their normal business, setting out neat rows of pansies and tulips. The electric and heating systems continued to function. But the president, never very accessible, now appeared more remote than ever.

The trustees, no less than anyone else, had difficulty grasping the true dimensions of the revolt. Shaken by the crisis in the midst of a $200-million fundraising campaign, they were at pains to assure themselves and the public that it was a minor incident caused by a small group of agitators, that nothing was seriously wrong. But when the police action resulted in a general strike, it was obvious that what was happening was neither minor nor incidental.

It has never been the business of trustees to deal with the daily operations of a university or to concern themselves with the subtleties of student affairs and frustrations. At Columbia, as elsewhere, trustee concern has been with the university as a corporate institution—funding its endowment, maintaining and expanding its facilities, and protecting its public image. The trustees viewed themselves as "the modern representatives of 'orthodoxy and authority' " (to quote from *The Role of the Trustees of Columbia University,* a special report issued in 1957), replacing the clergy of old, and most saw their duty as preserving a place of scholarship and learning free from political and socioeconomic pressures of the more mundane world. The academic affairs within this ivory tower they left to the academics, and expected that the president would inform them if all were not well.

When The Bust failed to end the strike, however, the initiative passed from the administration to the faculty and trustees. For the first time in memory, representatives of the two bodies met directly and formally. After that the trustees too began to talk publicly of "restructuring." A special committee was appointed "to study and recommend changes in the basic structure of the university" in consultation with a similar committee appointed by the faculty executive committee, and with students, administrators, and alumni.

Unimpressed, the students denounced the executive committee as unrepresentative of the university community and powerless to effect change. They remembered many committees at Columbia in recent years that had failed to affect university policy. In the atmosphere following The Bust, this latent mistrust and hostility toward the administration came to dominate the decisions of even formerly moderate students. The new Strike Coordinating Committee represented a broad spectrum of the student body; graduates and undergraduates from almost every department, members of clubs and extracurricular groups, moderates, liberals, and some formerly non-political students now outnumbered the original radicals. Thus, it came as a shock to the faculty and administration when this strike committee endorsed the "six demands" of the original strikers. Particularly surprising was the insistence on "no legal or disciplinary reprisals" as a "precondition" to any talk between strikers and administration.

On this point above all others, the administration held fast. "We were acutely conscious, throughout the time that we were making our decisions," said Vice President Truman, "that Columbia was a battleground that was representative of every university in the country and that what we were doing was being done, not just for Columbia, but for every university in the United States." Beyond holding the line for the country's universities (other institutions—Stanford most recently—have granted amnesty to demonstrators to prevent further divisiveness, to calm emotions, and to bring the situation under control), Columbia officials had to deal with the criminal acts of rifling the president's files and publicizing copies of his private letters, as well as with charges of destruction of property by students. Although only a minority of students was given to such acts, and although most students condemned them, the strike committee members regarded amnesty as a political position, holding it to be the only acceptable evidence that the administration intended to give them the new role they sought.

Meanwhile, the hard work of planning for reorganization was proceeding within the departments. Students, faculty members, and administrators met formally and informally, and the "group therapy," as one professor called it, began to work. "People have been thinking around here for a long time," he said, "but now things seem more possible. The older faculty are more open to suggestion and the power structure no longer seems impervious to change."

As the strike entered its second week, the administration gave individual professors the option of continuing classes, and recommended that students work out with their teachers whether to take a "pass," an "incomplete," or a letter grade. Faculty and students honored picket lines and refused to hold classes in the buildings. Groups met on the lawns or in apartments, and "liberation" classes, in which students and teachers—mainly junior faculty members—decided together the subject matter and approach, became popular.

The faculty Executive Committee hailed the first steps toward cooperation and urged more students to "join us." Then the Joint Committee on Disciplinary Affairs announced its recommendations—one-year probation for the rebels who had held the buildings, suspension or expulsion for those guilty of vandalism or theft, and the dropping of criminal charges. These terms were by no means agreeable to the strikers, but President Kirk, in perhaps the outstanding tactical error of this affair, reasserted his authority and insisted on his right to overrule the Joint Committee and increase penalties if he saw fit.

The faculty reaction was quick and strong. Within forty-eight hours, Kirk changed his mind. But his abortive assertion of authority indicated to faculty and students that despite all the committees and negotiations, the fundamental issues had not been solved. Frustrated by intransigence on all sides, a group of seven moderate students, after nearly three weeks, broke with the strike committee and set up their own committee, Students for a Restructured University. While still supporting the strike, the new group declared that its chief concern was with the university and not, like that of SDS members, with the reform of society in general. They sought wide student support, and offered their cooperation to the faculty executive committee, which rebuffed them. Determined, nevertheless, to play a role in reforming the university, they sought and found support at Teachers College, which had opened its doors to students from all parts of the university.

Then, just as the strike committee seemed to be losing its drive and relevance to campus events, the administration started disciplinary action against the original student demonstrators shortly before their cases were scheduled to appear in court. The move resulted in renewed violence and another police raid. It was almost as if the protagonists had accepted their predetermined roles and were fated to play them out without reference to each other or to the demands of the situation.

The crisis had developed a dynamic of its own. The grievous wounds the university had suffered refused to heal, and the community seemed to lose its cohesion. An atmosphere of unreality spawned irrational action. Some students threw up barricades and provoked the police in childish, if dangerous, imitation of the Paris students they had seen on television. Rock-throwing, arson, bomb threats, and similar wantonly destructive acts of leftists and rightists were lunatic spin-offs of the weeks of spreading anarchy. Instead of losing its original momentum, the crisis, feeding on itself as well as on outside tensions, slipped inexorably into a new phase.

The struggle is far from over, and the question remains: In what form will Columbia emerge from her ordeal? The situation is still open, seemingly without direction and control. Mistrust and hostility among faculty, students, and administrators have been greatly exacerbated in recent weeks. During the second week after The Bust, senior professors spoke confidently of a positive outcome, of a rejuvenated institution. Now, no one knows. The university has never developed the institutional gyroscopes that make for stability in rough weather. There is no faculty senate, and virtually no student government. Even the president of CUSC declares it is not representative of the student body: "It is what the administration recognizes as representing student opinion on campus, but it is totally powerless. Students have to find other channels if they want their voice heard."

At the same time, Columbia recruits a first-rate student body, many of whom are attracted by the urban environment and the opportunity to encounter the major social issues of the day. The university encourages this kind of involvement in city government, welfare, and civil rights programs, but it has refused the students' requests to participate in the affairs of their own institution.

A faculty-student advisory committee submitted a report on student life to Kirk last August. Although the changes it recommended were so mild that all four student members filed a "minority report," the report was ignored. One recommendation—to continue to permit indoor demonstrations—was directly defied by the president in September when he placed a ban on such demonstrations. The report remained on Kirk's desk until April, when CUSC threatened to release it itself. Kirk then released it without comment.

The question of the gymnasium and of university involvement with IDA, CIA recruiters, and the armed forces in general, had come up many times throughout the year. Demonstrations led to a ban on CIA recruiting on campus, and a faculty committee to study the IDA affiliation. But when Kirk overruled a student-faculty committee's recommendations on disciplining the CIA demonstrators, the students again felt betrayed.

Aggravating all other frustrations is the question of the Vietnam war. "Vietnam had already unhinged them from their classes," one professor told *The New York Times*. Vice President Truman was even more pessimistic. "If the war continues" he said, "it is debatable if the university would continue. The stress on the faculty and students is too great." The threat of the draft affects even the most nonpolitical student. The sense of huge impersonal forces closing in on his life is acute. For many, an apparently insensitive university administration is simply the nearest available target.

The faculty, too, is dissatisfied. Many speak of a sense of drift in the administration and the need for more vigorous leadership. After the strong reign of Nicholas Murray Butler, which lasted forty-two years, the university government was largely decentralized. Each division set its own standards, recruited its own faculty, and even raised its own money.

In recent years the administration and faculty have come to recognize the need for more central guidance. A year ago Columbia "reshuffled" its administrative staff, appointing Truman (then Columbia College dean) provost and academic vice president—the first time in ten years those posts had been joined. But the primary purpose of the reshuffle was to facilitate the university's $200-million fund drive, the first in years to be centrally run. As one administrator pointed out, this reorganization led to better business administration, but has not affected the process of governing the university community. The nature of the university remains the same. Students and faculty still have little voice in university affairs.

Now as the parties seek to restructure the university, they must begin to ask what kind of an institution they want. Is a university, as President Kirk and many others believe, a private corporation managed by the trustees and administration, whose academic services are available to qualified students who want them? Are students there simply to learn whatever the scholars have to teach? Or is it a community of scholars whose members are mutually engaged in pursuit of knowledge and truth? And if the latter is true, how does this jibe with another popular idea—that the ivory tower has fallen? When professors are consultants to governments and industries around the world, can a community within the university be maintained?

The radical students who seek the "politicalization" of the university must ask themselves how a community of scholars—or the pursuit of learning in any form—can survive amid the constant political struggles some of them envision. Many seem to have engaged in a battle for power without asking what the power is for. If students are not merely transients, they nonetheless attend the university for only a few years. In what role can they contribute the most in that limited time?

The issues go beyond the campus. One of the central questions the students raise concerns the power and responsibility of the university in its changing relation with society at large. They argue that an institution whose mission is to increase man's knowledge should not engage in secret research. They contend that the power of the university should not be used to shut out the surrounding community of Harlem, but to find new ways to invite it in. An institution that develops expertise in technology, urban planning, and social change, they claim, should use that expertise in its own undertakings.

The ordeal of April and May has opened Columbia to fundamental reorganization. It seems clear that responsibility for the university government must now be shared by faculty, students, and administration. But the precise role of each is still to be worked out. The faculty, through its executive committee, has already laid the groundwork for a new partnership with the trustees. The question remains whether trustees and faculty will now admit the students in a new role as well.

There may also be areas—such as Columbia's Urban Affairs Program—where community representatives should influence decision-making. And one might even ask if a self-perpetuating board of lifetime trustees is the best kind of body to look after the university's welfare in a time of rapid change.

In working out answers to these and related questions, Columbia will mark the road for American higher education seeking the combination of flexibility and stability it needs to survive. If Columbia fails to deal with these issues, it will suffer a heavy indictment as a place of higher learning. If it faces them squarely, it may emerge from the ordeal not unscathed but renewed.

24

VIOLENCE AND THE UNIVERSITIES

Albert W. Levi

Who are the students who participate in violent protest in American universities, and what are their moral credentials—the ideas and the grievances which motivate their violence? Tentatively I have come to the conclusion that there are at least three very different groups with profoundly different aims, and that although they frequently combine to stage sit-down strikes, confront administrators, and battle with police unwisely called to the campus, our assessment and our moral valuation must be vastly different as we pass from group to group.

There is, first, the hard core of radical students whose aim is nothing less than the destruction of the university as prelude to the destruction of an unequal and an unjust society. Represented largely in this country by the SDS—the Students for a Democratic Society—(and in France by Daniel Cohn-Bendit and his followers), they are firmly convinced that real democratic education is impossible in what they describe as bourgeois, capitalistic society, and they view the university not as something to be reformed, but as something to be destroyed—as perhaps the soft underbelly of a corrupt society, infinitely vulnerable to the concerted attack of their violent intentions.

At Columbia, Mark Rudd, president of the local chapter of SDS, in an open letter to Columbia President Grayson Kirk wrote: "If we win, we will take control of your world, your corporation, your university and attempt to mold a

Reprinted from Albert W. Levi, Violence and the Universities, *Washington University Magazine,* **39,** no. 1, pp. 10-14, Fall 1968.

world in which we and other people can live as human beings. Your power is directly threatened, since we will have to destroy that power before we take over." Further, in an interview published in a recent issue of *Partisan Review*, when asked about his goals, Rudd said frankly: "Our original goals took into consideration the Harlem gymnasium, the Institute for Defense Analysis, and so forth, but they also had the purpose of raising consciousness concerning the structure of American capitalism. That, really is the primary goal of radicals engaged in this kind of issue-oriented struggle. . . . And the harvest of this planting will not be seen this year . . . not in ten years . . . but sometime in the future when this understanding of capitalist society bears fruit in a much higher level struggle. In revolution."

That this kind of activity is premeditated and conspiratorial there can be little doubt. The *New Republic* of May 11, 1968, reported: "Months before, at an SDS conference in Maryland, the decision had been reached to take physical control of a major American university this spring. Columbia was chosen because of its liberal reputation, its situation in New York, and the fact that it was an Ivy League school. SDS felt it was important at this time to disrupt a private, prestige, tactically vulnerable university." And, as Mark Rudd admits, the manifest aims of the Columbia rebellion were largely pretexts.

The *New Republic* continues: "The point of the game was power. And in the broadest sense, to the most radical members of the SDS Steering Committee Columbia itself was not the issue. It was revolution, and if it could be shown that a great university could literally be taken over in a matter of days by a well-organized group of students then no university was secure. Everywhere the purpose was to destroy institutions of the American Establishment in the hope that out of the chaos a better America would emerge."

What ought to be our reaction to violent acts of student dissenters of this type? The late Winston Churchill once said: "I have not become Her Majesty's Prime Minister in order to preside over the liquidation of the British Empire." Similarly, I do not believe that teachers and administrators who have devoted their lives to the cultivation of the mind, the transmission of the tradition of humane learning, and the education of the next generation propose to sit quietly while the entire edifice of higher education is pulled down by the forces of a sometimes conscientious, but dangerously misguided and fanatical youth.

As we have come to recognize through the unhappy events at Columbia, nothing is easier than for a group of determined students to take over a university which is, after all, no fortress, but an unguarded pasture for the life of mind, has no army, no police force of its own, and is ill-suited by the very nature of its institutional life for the rigors of violent combat and defense. The university has, of course, its own legitimate internal sanctions of discipline against lawlessness and impermissible acts: probation, temporary suspension, even permanent expulsion from the academic community, but these it has often seemed unaccountably reluctant to use. I think it will use them more frequently, more determinedly, and more responsibly in the days to come.

One of the most irrational and inconsistent demands of the leaders of the

Columbia revolt was that after the shouting had died down no punishment or discipline should be exercised against them—"amnesty" was, I think, the word they used. And it indicated how egocentric and morally immature they essentially were, since even proponents of civil disobedience like Ghandi and Martin Luther King were prepared to accept the legal consequences of a profound moral protest. No university seriously interested in its own survival and mindful of its educational responsibility for the disciplining of lawlessness dare refuse its obligation to punish those who engage in the tactics of disruption, especially those whose very political philosophies commit them to acts of violence rather than the legitimate protest which seeks for adjudication through responsible democratic processes.

The escalation of outrage received in silence is a danger too enormous to risk, as we of the last generation have experienced it in the days of Nazi insolence before the invasion of Poland, when the provocations were continuous and no resistance was forthcoming. David Low, the great British cartoonist, caricatured this infamous patience in a cartoon of Neville Chamberlain, the British Prime Minister, saying to the German Chancellor: "Sir, you have starved my ancient mother, kidnapped my wife, raped my daughter, burned down the Houses of Parliament and sunk the British Navy, but beware, Herr Hitler, someday you will go too far."

I can see before me now the image of the tender-minded and perhaps conscience-stricken section of the Columbia faculty saying to Mark Rudd and his associates, and this time not hyperbolically, but in literal truth: "You have seized five university buildings, barring students and professors from holding classes without their vote or consent, you have broken into the offices of the President of the University, opening, ransacking, photographing, and making public his confidential files, you have held a college dean prisoner in his own office for over 26 hours, calling him to his face names unprintable in the public press, you have burned the offices of three professors who have been unsympathetic to your strike, including the research notes of one of them which were the fruit of ten years of patient research, but beware, SDS, one day you will go too far!"

The second class of students who participate in violent protests is considerably larger, relatively unorganized, more heterogeneous and amorphous in its composition. It is made up of those who have a burning concern for such aspects of American foreign policy as the Vietnam War and our defense commitments around the world, as well as our ongoing internal social problems; justice for the black community, poverty as a specifically anchored disgrace, the pageant of American brutality and neglect in its many ugly guises. It is also composed of those who have concretely suffered from these evils—students anxiously awaiting a draft for a war to which they are profoundly opposed, black students feeling the burning injustices to their kind, representatives of disinherited and disadvantaged minorities of every stripe.

It is characteristic that at the Columbia uprising it was black students who alone occupied Hamilton Hall, re-christened it "Malcolm X Hall," and declared with quite unconscious humor that it was now finally a part of Harlem. When the leaders of this group of black commandoes were later interviewed, they said frankly that in their view the chief issue of the Columbia rebellion was neither student power nor world revolution, but simply the threatened building by Columbia of a Jim Crow gymnasium on public park land in the heart of Harlem. They opposed chiefly the flagrant use of Columbia's position of political strength to take advantage of the political powerlessness of the black community.

It is equally significant that when one of these leaders was asked: "In your view is the role of black students at a university different from that of white students?" he answered at once: "I would say that black students at this university have demonstrated that they view themselves essentially as an extension of the black community and that their primary identity is with the black community and not with the university community." There is a sense, then, in which the bias of this second class of protesters against the university, as well as that of the first class is *a protest from outside.*

How are we to view the protesting acts of student dissenters of this second class? With considerable sympathy, I think, for in most cases their moral credentials are high. The Vietnam war *is* a dirty and immoral war and it is heartbreaking to any true American patriot, jealous of the reputation of his country and of its good name in his affections and in the sight of the world. The condition of our negro population and the way it has been deprived of economic opportunity and civil rights *is* a disgrace. The level of political morality and of simple honesty in speech and intention of those who govern our nation and who aspire to its governance *is* dangerously low.

Students of the present generation, as distinguished from those of a decade or two ago, have markedly political interests, and a reservoir of resentment against social injustice which, like a permanent floating libido is ready to be mobilized at any moment, on any issue, against any opponent who presents himself. Yet one cannot escape the conviction that these students of the second class are too ready on the trigger, too mindlessly committed to violent methods, too irrelevantly directed in most cases in expressing their anger within the university environment. They are like those foolish ones who have lost a dollar at night, and who look for it not where they have lost it, but under the street lamp where the light is better. Their grievances are real, but they are expressed at the wrong places—where the vulnerability is high and the defenses weakest, but not where the true blame and the true responsibility lies.

The last class of student protestors is enormous in number and is composed of almost all the undergraduate and graduate students in the school of arts and sciences. These are the 8,000 who sat down outside Sproul Hall at the University of California in 1964, the 4,000 who milled about in front of Low Library at Columbia last spring. These are the ones who initially are politically uninvolved, who stand curiously around the small group of militant protesters watching to see what will happen. Only in the face of truly monumental administrative unconcern or outside police brutality do they join the ranks of the violent minority. Why are they prepared to do so? Why is their loyalty almost never to the university as such? This class of third-act walk-ons (without a particle of disrespect), I shall call "the sheep."

Men live less by firm sensory reality than by images, by the pictures in their heads, and by the abstract concepts through which they interpret experience. In attending to the literature of violent student protest and to its rhetoric, I have been struck over and over again by the imagery which pervades this discourse. On last April 28 a large sign was to be seen over the balcony of Columbia's Mathematics Hall which read "Rudd Hall, Liberated Zone #5." Interviewed later, Rudd and his associates spoke of the university as an institution for the transmission of bourgeois and racist ideology.

Four years before at Berkeley, the leaders of the Free-Speech movement spoke of their university as a factory—a knowledge factory and a manpower factory, utilizing all the techniques of a computerized and a coldly impersonal science to separate, classify and process their human materials to serve the interests of the larger technological society. To be sure, in this latter case, they were but taking their cue from their own Chancellor Clark Kerr who, in his famous Godkin Lectures at Harvard on "The Uses of the University" the previous spring, had noted the change of the older colleges into universities which were now but enormous corporations for marketing knowledge and skills, and had, he intimated, in the process lost considerable of their intellectual and moral identity.

It is obvious the behavior of students will be patterned upon the conception of the university which they hold, the conceptual model which they accept as genuine and valid. Naturally, if to you the university is the battleground of class war, you will find the manuals of guerrilla warfare of Ho Chi Minh and Ché Guevara supremely relevant, and you will convert Mathematics Hall into "Liberated Zone #5" as soon as you have the opportunity. Naturally, if you see the university as the skill factory of the technological society, you will resent the impersonality and unconcern of the professorial speed-up system, and you will resist with a slow burning resentment the attempt to turn you from a person into a thing—a mere educational commodity. Naturally, if you consider the university as the creature of the business establishment, as the selfish and unloving great modern corporation, you will see your chancellor as the tool of his conservative board of directors, and you will strike for better hours, better working conditions, and more privileges as if you were the 19th-century victims of a system of brutal child labor.

The rhetoric of student protest is pervaded by the imagery of the battlefield, the corporation, and the factory, but what is singularly absent is the imagery upon which I was raised, and which has never ceased from influencing my own conception of what education, both higher and lower, is all about. This is the imagery not of the *gesellschaft* but of the *gemeinschaft*, not the cold contractual association, but the intimate community of the teachers and the taught, the *family* of learning, where the school, like the real family, is the great social invention for the making of persons, the intellectual and moral community where the sexes and the generations live together in the harmonious atmosphere of a common intention and a common aim.

If this is crass sentimentalism, it is a kind for which there is real historic precedent and justification. For it represents the consensus of the longest segment of the tradition of humane learning. The affectionate analogizing of the university to the family has a venerable history. She is the "alma mater"—the *nourishing mother*—and her offspring is the "alumnus," in the original meaning of the Latin "one who is, or has been, nourished." From philology we may therefore learn that the essence of the university is the concept of "nourishment," and we may infer that most of its contemporary evils and misfortunes spring from the impoverishment or corruption of this pristine idea.

Thirty-five years ago Robert Maynard Hutchins, then President of the University of Chicago, delivered a lecture whose message was to be prophetic. His text and his title was taken from a line of John Milton: "The sheep look up and are not fed," and he used this text to illustrate the plight of students whose real needs for liberal and humane education were thwarted by crude vocationalism in the universities, the absence of properly equipped and dedicated teachers of the liberal arts, and the many impediments which a noisy and unenlightened business civilization had put in the way of the only kind of education worthy of a liberal democracy—one which should produce not technological trainees or narrow specialists, but intelligent citizens, broadly educated and with minds prepared to deliberate the course of intelligent social action.

Hutchins' message was, as I say, prophetic, and it is entirely in the meaning of his Miltonic text that I refer to the third class of student protesters as sheep. For it may precisely be that when the sheep look up and are not fed, not given that type of nourishment which they have every right to expect from an "alma mater," then it is not so infinitely puzzling that they should from time to time become wolves in sheep's clothing, roving the campuses of the 20th century and joining the violent minority at the last moment out of the suppressed sense of outrage that their legitimate educational demands have not been met.

The concepts of the "community" of scholars and of the "family" of learning require some manageability of size, some smallness, some intimacy of concern and social interaction. At Berkeley at the time of the riots there were 18,000 undergraduates, 10,000 graduate students, and 1,500 faculty members, or, in our language, 18,000 lambs, 10,000 full-grown sheep, and 1,500 shepherds, most of them not particularly interested in minding their flock. Here there is no question but that the sheep looked up and felt that they were not being fed. Students complained that the atmosphere and condition of the University of California were conducive neither to free expression nor to good education. They asked for an improvement of undergraduate instruction, the adequate recognition by administration and department heads alike of superior teaching skills, a curriculum that should serve the liberal goals of the student as well as the research interests of the teacher, and an end to the manipulative attitudes which seem to have replaced the idea of comradeship among scholars and students.

The spring before, Clark Kerr had said: "Federal grants for research have brought a major revolution and the resultant student sense of neglect may bring a minor counter-revolt." He was right. Sooner than he thought. And closer to home than he ever dreamed. Ironically the counter-revolt commenced in his own back yard and brought about his own downfall.

There is an obvious correlation between violent student protest and a monstrous size, impersonality in human relations, student neglect, faculty self-centeredness, and administrative remoteness and Olympian grandeur. At Columbia too, the student body is enormous, classes are much too large, the faculty lives in Scarsdale or Queens and hardly knows the university as a place, a locale, a living environment, and Grayson Kirk, its president spoke only to the Chairman of Consolidated Edison on whose board he sat, the President of IBM whose educational nest he feathered, and the Secretaries of State and Defense.

Who can deny today that the university plays a somewhat different role in the family constellation? Somehow in this age of ambiguity and organ transplants, the university has changed its sex. It is no longer the "alma mater"—the nourishing mother—but the "nefarius pater"—the wicked father—and I am afraid largely for reasons which make the rhetoric of "factory" and "corporation" not so irrelevant after all.

In an article entitled "Universities as Big Business" in *Harper's*, James Ridgeway says: "The universities have been so successful in safeguarding their privacy —particularly with respect to their finances—that few people are aware of the extent to which the worlds of higher education, big business, and banking are linked through interlocking relationships among professors, college presidents, and trustees, industry and government, relationships whose chief victims are the more than six million students the universities are supposed to teach."

It is no new thing that a university must be related to its surrounding community, as a power station or an art museum are so related—as a center of light or a source of culture and aesthetic taste radiating outward. And it is natural that it should be supported by local wealth as an object of pride and respect, and not for reasons which are selfish and profit-seeking.

However, all of the economic relations of a university are not so innocent. Much of the income of Columbia comes from exploited slum property in the ghettoes of New York and some of Harvard's from large holdings in Middle South Utilities Inc. whose constituent companies in Mississippi and Louisiana are allegedly managed by white racists and members of the Ku Klux Klan. Harvard undergraduates have in recent years repeatedly challenged the legitimacy of this income source.

To command respect, particularly from the young, the university must be like Caesar's wife—morally beyond reproach. What church worthy of the veneration of its members is built out of the profits from dope peddling and prostitution? Nor can a university claim to propose the principles of the just society if it is fed by rent from ghettoes and slums. The issue here is one of a strict and stern moral consistency, and it is one of which students today are militantly and violently aware.

It has been said that ours is an age of rising expectations for economic well-being and consumer opportunity. Perhaps it is also for the young an age of rising expectations for social justice and public morality. And I think that to those political demagogues and cliché-ridden college administrators who find either that every student protest originates in Moscow or is the work of Satan's hands, we must say: Make the nation honorable, the society decent, equal, and just, and return the university to its pristine task of great teaching, personal concern, and relevant and humane academic research, and the violent student protests will be gone with the wind.

I have attempted here to distinguish three types of violent student protest and to furnish, at least implicitly, a differential evaluation for each. For the first class, the hard core of radical students whose aim is nothing less than the destruction of the university—their violence should be dealt with justly but determinedly. Their aim is not improvement but disruption, and their offenses, if continuous, should be met with permanent expulsion from the academic community. For the second class, those who have a burning concern for social justice in general, or are members of militant minorities, we must say: We have sympathy for your motivation, but your acts are misdirected. For the university is not a political institution nor the underwriter of social policy at large. Your business here is learning in one of the few environments left in the modern world where some objectivity is possible, where freedom of expression and inquiry are actively encouraged, where rational debate is permitted to follow wherever the argument leads. Be thankful for your opportunity and take your violence else-where. Do not use it to destroy one of the few remaining centers of liberal democracy in the modern world.

For the third class, the vast majority, who feel rightfully that somehow the modern university has gone astray in its neglect of undergraduate teaching and student concern, we must be most attentive of all. For this is criticism from within, directed to the one thing which we within the university have the power to affect and to improve. Here we all have something at stake and a rededicated faculty and wisely leading administration will do everything in their power to reduce the educational environment to manageable size, to promote fruitful interaction, and to make the campus, indeed, a family of learning.

How will the present violence terminate? Who can foretell? As Tocqueville said of the Revolution of 1848: "In a rebellion as in a novel, the most difficult part to invent is the end." In taking as my title "Violence and the Universities" I have been conscious of a certain quaint incongruity of two concepts which do not really belong together, of something like the paradox of the round square in mediaeval theological disputation. But that is because underneath I am convinced that the imagery of the battlefield, of the factory, of the establishment corporation have really nothing to do with the domain of liberal education. I look forward to a rebirth and a restoration—to the time when the university shall be once again in fact the community of scholars, the family of learning, the "alma mater"—nourishing mother of us all.

25

REVOLUTION WITHOUT HATRED

Harold E. Fey

Washington, August 28.

Sore of foot but inspired in spirit, I was one of more than 200,000 people who marched and sang for freedom here today. The march was disciplined; throughout a long and wearisome day I saw not a single act of discourtesy, nor did I hear even one expression of irritation. But no one should be deceived by the serenity and orderliness of this mighty flow of men, women and children to the Lincoln Memorial. This march was an expression of deep purpose, and it resulted in still deeper resolution in support of civil rights "NOW!" People dressed in their Sunday best and others in work clothing, women carrying babies and fathers with young sons astride their shoulders, senior citizens and cripples with canes—and at least one man swinging along on crutches—all these marching souls were sustained by the conviction that their cause is just, that its time has come, that the Lord of history is behind that insistent, uncompromising "NOW."

On the day preceding the march I talked with a number of people on Capitol Hill, among them several congressmen. It is no exaggeration to say that their views on the march ranged from worry to fear and anger. Senator Thurmond's postmarch TV interview indicated that the obvious success of the enterprise had served to intensify his rejection of equal civil rights for Negroes, and it is prob-

Reprinted from Harold E. Fey, Revolution Without Hatred, *Christian Century*, **80**, no. 37, pp. 1094-1095, September 11, 1963.

able that his reaction will be echoed by the Wallaces and Barnetts throughout the south. Such fear is understandable; the movement which marched today is designed to strip them of their power. The cheer which greeted the N.A.A.C.P.'s Roy Wilkins when he assured southern whites who support civil rights but fear to speak out that one goal of the Washington march was to emancipate *them* witnessed accurately to the breadth of the movement's purpose. The message from Congress of Racial Equality leader James Farmer, relayed from a Louisiana jail by an associate, broadened the horizon of the march to include the world. He declared that freedom is indivisible, that success in the nonviolent struggle for full civil rights for Negroes in the United States is necessary if this nation is to survive and do its share in extending freedom to all mankind.

Participation by the churches, Catholic, Jewish and Protestant, was everywhere evident and widely welcome. But like the participation by labor unions (most notable of which was that of the United Automobile Workers and the International Ladies Garment Workers), church participation was supportive rather than dominant. Though the sponsoring organizations included the National Council of Churches, the National Conference of Catholics for Interracial Justice, the American Jewish Congress, the industrial union department of the A.F.L.–C.I.O. and the Negro American Labor Council, the march was staged primarily by the five major civil rights organizations—the National Association for the Advancement of Colored People, the Southern Christian Leadership Conference, the National Urban League, the Congress of Racial Equality and the Student Non-Violent Coordinating Committee—which joined together for the first time in a major effort to speak to the Congress and the country. Chairman of the march was veteran A. Philip Randolph, head of the Brotherhood of Sleeping Car Porters and major spokesman for Negroes in the ranks of organized labor.

Attending the churchmen's breakfast held prior to the march were Catholic Archbishop Patrick A. O'Boyle and Methodist Bishop John Wesley Lord of Washington; Presbyterian Eugene Carson Blake, acting chairman of the National Council of Churches' civil rights program; the United Church's Robert Spike, executive and coordinator of that program; Galen Weaver, director of the Catholic, Protestant and Jewish continuing program which grew out of the Chicago conference on religion and race; Rabbi Marc Tannenbaum of the American Jewish Committee; and many others.

The Washington march was a religious event of first importance, and its effect will be felt far beyond the political arena. Its religious impact came through in every speech, ending with the stirring prophetic appeal by Martin Luther King, Jr., whom Chairman Randolph introduced as the "moral leader of the nation." It was evident in the addresses of Mathew Ahmann, who spoke for Catholics ("The wind of the racial revolution has finally bent the reeds of the conscience of our people"); Joachim Prinz, president of the American Jewish Congress and formerly a rabbi in Hitler's Berlin ("We have a complete sense of solidarity with the Negro people born of our painful historic experience. . . . America must not become a nation of onlookers, as Germany was under Hitler"); and Eugene

Carson Blake ("Our churches have for long stood publicly for a nonsegregated church in a nonsegregated society, but they have failed to put their own houses in order. We come, and late we come, to offer our bodies as a sacrifice unto God, which is our reasonable service. We come in faith that God will overrule hatreds and bring justice and liberty for all").

There were few marching delegations which did not include one or more clergymen. As the delegations moved in a broad stream flowing for hours down Independence and Constitution avenues, they chanted the freedom chant, sang "We Shall Overcome," often joined in spirituals or in Julia Ward Howe's "Battle Hymn of the Republic." But these were outward signs of religion on the march. The inner quality expressed in subtle ways one had to experience to appreciate. Such courtesy, quiet conviction, patience—yes, even joy—in the face of suffering, deprivation, and struggle against great odds would be impossible without deep faith. Together they attest to the immense power which can be generated by a revolution which explicitly and resolutely refuses to weaken itself by hatred.

Such a revolution is something new in the Western world. It is not surprising that its opponents find it difficult to understand and to measure. Even its friends and practitioners are surprised, as were the leaders of the Washington march, by the response it is capable of arousing among great masses of people, white as well as colored, educated as well as uneducated or poorly educated. The unprecedented TV coverage of the march was matched by the press generally; over 2,800 press passes were issued—indicating a greater coverage than for any previous Washington event, even presidential inaugurals.

It remains to be seen how soon and in what way Congress will respond. The presence of 150 congressmen on the steps of the Lincoln Memorial was a good sign, particularly in view of the fact that both houses were acting with unusual speed to avert an impending railroad strike. The Washington march will, I believe, advance and stiffen the resolve of the administration and the supporters of civil rights of both parties even more than it will rouse the determination of their opponents—thus improving the chances that a good measure will be voted.

Both sides are aware that the march on Washington can be repeated. If the present enlightened and principled leadership of the civil rights movement fails, if the democratic program of this revolution without hatred is defeated, another 200,000—or it might be 500,000—could march on Washington, led by leaders of a different sort who know how to manipulate hatred and violence for their own ends. That would really be a mob, as this assemblage was not, and it would bring about change. Nobody who saw this march can doubt that change is coming. It had better come in the way this demonstration has indicated it should come. I believe it will come—is coming—that way.

26

WHITE COLORED FOLK

Black Students Union, University of Georgia

Throughout the Black liberation movement, there have been Blacks who have been in leadership positions not for the purpose of accomplishing goals for Black people but to hold back the tide of Black discontent. This type of leader has come to be known as "the white man's nigger." Every night before going to bed this lackey says the following prayer:

"Our father who is in heaven,
white man owe eleven and pay me seven.
Thy kingdom come, thy will be done;
And if I hadn't took that I wouldn't had none.

Whenever "the white man's nigger" was forced to confront "the man" he resorted to the tactics of turning the other cheek. As a result of this, the white man became bolder and stepped up his commission of atrocities upon Black people. As long as the foot shuffling, head scratching, yessir, no sir, thank you boss nigger was at the helm of the ship of Black liberation, the lowest form of honky-fied trash imaginable constantly wreaked havoc upon the Black community because he knew he would not be opposed.

Now the true ship of Black liberation has set asail, and there is no place at the

Reprinted from *Weusi Wapedeza,* **1**, no. 1, p. 2. Published sporadically by the Black Students Union, University of Georgia.

helm for the white man's nigger. In fact, he will be lucky if he can find a place in the galley. The Black movement is now in the hands of the Black masses and the white man's nigger is as much in place as tits on a boar hog. However we have not given up on our misguided brothers and sisters but in order for them to be fully accepted into the movement, they must heed the words of Marcus Garvey who said: "a race without authority and power is a race without respect." And the only way to gain that respect is to throw off the shackles of white oppression and take up the banner of BLACK POWER!

27

WHAT WE WANT; WHAT WE BELIEVE

The Black Panther

1. *We want freedom. We want power to determine the destiny of our Black Community.* We believe that black people will not be free until we are able to determine our destiny.

2. *We want full employment for our people.* We believe that the federal government is responsible and obligated to give every man employment or a guaranteed income. We believe that if the white American businessmen will not give full employment, then the means of production should be taken from the businessmen and placed in the community so that the people of the community can organize and employ all of its people and give a high standard of living.

3. *We want an end to the robbery by the white man of our Black Community.* We believe that this racist government has robbed us and now we are demanding the overdue debt of forty acres and two mules. Forty acres and two mules was promised 100 years ago as restitution for slave labor and mass murder of black people. We will accept the payment in currency which will be distributed to our many communities. The Germans are now aiding the Jews in Israel for the genocide of the Jewish people. The Germans murdered six million

Reprinted from What We Want; What We Believe, *The Black Panther,* **II**, no. 26, p. 18, March 16, 1969.

Jews. The American racist has taken part in the slaughter of over fifty million black people; therefore, we feel that this is a modest demand that we make.

4. *We want decent housing, fit for shelter of human beings.* We believe that if the white landlords will not give decent housing to our black community, then the housing and the land should be made into cooperatives so that our community, with government aid, can build and make decent housing for its people.

5. *We want education for our people that exposes the true nature of a deca-dent American society. We want education that teaches us our true history and our role in the present-day society.* We believe in an education system that will give to our people a knowledge of self. If a man does not have knowledge of himself and his position in society and the world, then he has little chance to relate to anything else.

6. *We want all black men to be exempt from military service.* We believe that Black people should not be forced to fight in the military service to defend a racist government that does not protect us. We will not fight and kill other people of color in the world who, like black people, are being victimized by the white racist government of America. We will protect ourselves from the force and violence of the racist police and the racist military, by whatever means necessary.

7. *We want an immediate end to POLICE BRUTALITY and MURDER of black people.* We believe we can end police brutality in our black community by organizing black self-defense groups that are dedicated to defending our black community from racist police oppression and brutality. The Second Amendment to the Constitution of the United States gives a right to bear arms. We therefore believe that all black people should arm themselves for self-defense.

8. *We want freedom for all black men held in federal, state, county, and city prisons and jails.* We believe that all black people should be released from the many jails and prisons because they have not received a fair and impartial trial.

9. *We want all black people when brought to trial to be tried in court by a jury of their peer group or people from their black communities, as defined by the Constitution of the United States.* We believe that the courts should follow the United States Constitution so that black people will receive fair trials. The 14th Amendment of the U.S. Constitution gives a man a right to be tried by his peer group. A peer is a person from a similar economic, social, religious, geo-graphical, environmental, historical and racial background. To do this the court will be forced to select a jury from the black community from which the black defendant came. We have been, and are being tried by all-white juries that have no understanding of the "average reasoning man" of the black community.

10. *We want land, bread, housing, education, clothing, justice and peace. And as our major political objective, a United Nations-supervised plebiscite to be held throughout the black colony in which only black colonial subjects will be allowed to participate, for the purpose of determining the will of black people as to their national destiny.* When, in the course of human events, it becomes necessary for one people to dissolve the political bands which have connected them with another, and to assume, among the powers of the earth, the separate and equal station to which the laws of nature and nature's God entitle them, a decent respect to the opinions of mankind requires that they should declare the causes which impel them to the separation.

We hold these truths to be self-evident, that all men are created equal; that they are endowed by their Creator with certain unalienable rights; that among these are life, liberty, and the pursuit of happiness. That, to secure these rights, governments are instituted among men, deriving their just powers from the consent of the governed; that, whenever any form of government becomes destructive of these ends, it is the right of the people to alter or to abolish it, and to institute a new government, laying its foundation on such principles, and organizing its powers in such form, as to them shall seem most likely to effect their safety and happiness. Prudence, indeed, will dictate that governments long established should not be changed for light and transient causes; and, accordingly, all experience hath shown, that mankind are more disposed to suffer, while evils are sufferable, than to right themselves by abolishing the forms to which they are accustomed. But, when a long train of abuses and usurpations, pursuing invariably the same object, evinces a design to reduce them under absolute despotism, it is their right, it is their duty, to throw off such government, and to provide new guards for their future security.

28

AMERICAN BLACK GUERRILLAS

Ramparts

"We are already at war. . . . The racist dog police must withdraw from the black community. . . ."

The speaker was Huey P. Newton, the 25-year-old leader of the Black Panthers of California. It was . . . before Newark and Detroit, before the Black Revolution in this country had taken its latest and most fateful turn into urban guerrilla warfare.

I thought about those words two months later as I watched the Battle of Detroit on television. All the talk about guerrilla warfare which had seemed so unreal became vivid as I watched tanks and armored cars move through the streets of Detroit, rattling their machine-guns against tenement buildings. It was like some phantasmagorical historical dream in which an American city was reenacting the Warsaw Ghetto 1943, Budapest 1956, Santo Domingo 1965. If such an analogy is objectively inappropriate, if the National Guard and paratroopers were not the Wehrmacht or the Red Army, the important fact, the fact that most whites fail to perceive, is that the cops were considered a foreign occupying army by the black men who were willing to pit their rifles against tanks. The snipers thus turned themselves in the eyes of many of their black comrades into "freedom fighters."

If Newark and Detroit did nothing else, they at least forced a more accurate vocabulary upon the press and public officials. What had merely been "riots" in

Reprinted from American Black Guerrillas, *Ramparts,* 6, no. 2, pp. 25-27, September 1967.

Harlem and Watts, what had been traditionally analyzed as primitive reactions to heat and frustration, was now in Detroit clearly recognizable as an uprising with revolutionary overtones. (Governor Hughes of New Jersey set the precedent by referring to Newark as an "insurrection." A newspaperman in Newark told me that the real explanation for the governor's enlightenment lies in the fact that the Prudential Insurance Company is Newark's biggest industry, and the insurance companies are off the hook for liabilities if the damage is caused by an insurrection.) . . .

The secret and anonymous interview with some of the Newark snipers published in Life magazine shows that they are middle class young men who organized themselves after doing civil rights work in Mississippi in 1965. One of them was reported to be a law student in an eastern university. Perhaps there was a bit of Life hyperbole hidden in the interview, but it had the ring of authenticity. For it is not the poorest, least-educated blacks, but a better-educated, indeed almost middle class, radical black intelligentsia that forms the vanguard of America's black guerrillas.

The Life interview was couched in familiar language. I had first heard this vernacular from the Black Panthers in the relaxed atmosphere of a San Francisco living room. The Panthers, a group of armed Negroes who make their home in the San Franciso Bay Area, consider themselves a political party, and their official name is the Black Panther Party for Self Defence. They first made local headlines when they appeared in public, in groups of about 20, armed with loaded shotguns and pistols, escorting the widow of Malcolm X around the city. Local cops were dumbfounded to discover that there was no law which prohibited the Panthers from carrying loaded weapons so long as they were unconcealed, a legal fact which the Panthers had carefully researched and briefed themselves on. That situation produced some dramatic confrontations between the cops and the Panthers, like one scene I witnessed: A cop approached a Panther and asked him to hand over his gun. The Panther asked, "Am I under arrest?" The cop answered, "No." The Panther replied, "Then get your . . . hands off my gun."

It was a dangerous act of bravado, but it typified the embattled mentality of the new black guerrillas. Behind it was a deadly serious purpose. The Panthers' public display of guns had both a real and a symbolic meaning—real because they believe that they will have to use the guns eventually against the power structure, yet symbolic because of the political effect on the black community of a few blacks openly carrying guns.

"Ninety per cent of the reason we carried guns in the first place," says Panther leader Huey P. Newton, "was educational. We set the example. We made black people aware that they have the right to carry guns."

Newton and his co-leader, 30-year-old Bobby Seale, quietly tried to explain to me why the black people have to have guns and what they must do with them. They see the United States as the center of an imperialist system which suppresses the world-wide revolution of colored people, of which American Negroes are only one part. But, says Huey Newton, "We can stop the machinery.

We can stop the imperialists from using it against black people all over the world. We are in a strategic position in this country, and we won't be the only group rebelling against the oppressor here."

The Panthers are only a small cadre in the Negro community. Their membership figures are hard to come by. When you ask them, they answer by quoting Malcolm X: "Those who know don't say and those who say don't know." Nevertheless, it has not affected their revolutionary fervor or their confidence. Theirs is a vision of an American apocalypse in which all of the blacks are forced to unite for survival against the white oppressors. Huey Newton puts it this way: "At the height of the resistance they are going to be slaughtering black people indiscriminately. We are sure that at that time Martin Luther King will be a member of the Black Panthers through necessity. He and others like him will have to band together with us just to save themselves."

There has always been something of the rhetoric of Armageddon among Negro militants, but it has never had such a serious ring. Once it was more a matter of literary allusion and wish-fulfillment of revenge, as in the plays of LeRoi Jones or the essays of James Baldwin. But Detroit has made it suddenly a very real business.

In Detroit on the Tuesday night of the outbreak, the most modern symbol of the counter-insurgency, the helicopter, went into action. The Pentagon sent in 25 Army choppers to assist the soldiers in ferreting out the guerrillas from the tangled jungle of tenement buildings. One resident of the ghetto said, "They came flying in low just over the rooftops, shining their big searchlights up and down the building. Once I saw one of them open fire. A soldier riding in front used an automatic weapon—he was firing at one of the rooftops."

But the guerrillas, according to reporters on the scene, struck back like Viet Cong by "laying siege to four separate police and fire stations." The only thing missing in the script were the satchel charges.

Detroit was a revolutionary battlefront. It was treated by the authorities not like a mere outbreak of criminal lawlessness, answerable by measured justice, but like a revolution that had to be suppressed by anti-population measures. Days after the fighting had ceased, 5000 men, women and children languished in Michigan's overcrowded jails. The injured never had their wounds treated. No one had been released on his own recognizance. Bail was set at an average of $5000. Even when it was possible for families and friends to raise the money to release a prisoner, they usually could not find him, for there was no central record of where each prisoner was being kept.

There is something of Detroit in the street corner rallies held by the Black Panthers in the black communities of the Bay Area. At these rallies small groups of young bloods gather to hear Bobby Seale and Newton tell them how, when the time comes, they can "take care of business" in groups of threes and fours. The "business" they are talking about is "executing white racist cops" or dropping molotov cocktails into strategic industrial installations. It is all suddenly very real and serious when you ask Huey Newton, who looks younger than his

25 years, why they talk of killing a couple of cops, and he tells you confidently that when the time comes, it won't be just the killing of a couple of cops but part of a whole nationally coordinated effort aimed at the entire "white occupying army." And it is, finally, very serious when you ask him what he thinks will happen to him and he answers, "I am going to be killed."

Where do they come from, these articulate and well-educated young men who have become black Kamikazes? And why have they become revolutionaries in the most unlikely place for revolution in the world? Huey Newton graduated from the excellent and integrated Berkeley High School, went to a two-year college, eventually spent a year in law school. Stokely Carmichael went to Bronx Science High School, probably the best prep-school for success in the U.S. Somewhere in the recent history of the country they, along with countless other young black men, decided that it was no use trying to liberate their people by appealing to the good sense and conscience of their white neighbors; instead, they became convinced that their freedom could only be wrested through force and turmoil.

It is somehow summed up by the answer Stokely Carmichael gave at a conference in London to the young hippies who asked him how they could help the Black Revolution. His sardonic answer was, "Well, I'll tell you what, when the police come into the ghettos to shoot us down in the streets, you can help us fight the police by throwing flowers at them."

Perhaps back in the early days of the movement Carmichael did believe in the power of flowers. If he now stands in Havana, surrounded by the veterans of the international revolution, publicly welcoming the emergence of guerrilla warfare in the United States, it is neither because he has been subverted by Peking propaganda or because he has flipped his lid. He has simply come to believe that America can only be regenerated as part of a world revolutionary process.

It is easy to bemoan the change in Carmichael and SNCC, as many liberals have been doing lately, and nostalgically recall the days when SNCC and the civil rights movement seemed to be a community of love. But one must remember that SNCC moved in its current direction as a result of careful, often anguished, deliberation by intelligent and dedicated young men and women who had tested their ideas in the crucibles of Southern and Northern jails.

In an exclusive interview with a Ramparts reporter recently, Rap Brown mused about the changing mood in SNCC. "That whole nonviolence thing was nothing but a preparation for genocide," he said. "At one point, not so long ago, the man could have sent a message to black people, saying meet me at such and such a concentration camp, and black people would have been there—on time!"

Asked about SNCC's attitude toward the rebellions, Brown answered that he was satisfied that they "were becoming more sophisticated on their own." He mentioned with pleasure the fact that in Tampa, for example, the police could not contain the actions in the ghetto area and that sniper fire against police was on the increase. He said this trend would continue, putting it, simply, that "people in the black community are coming to accept that tactic [guerrilla warfare], and as counter-revolutionary violence escalates against black people, revolutionary violence will rise to meet it."

On second thought, Brown said, "The trouble with black folks is that they wanna loot—but they don't want to shoot! [But that was before Detroit.] But black folks are not looting—they have a right to everying they take . . . this country has looted everything it has, beginning with black people."

Asked what exactly SNCC did when a rebellion broke out, Brown replied, "We do then what we always do—help the people get organized, tell them how to get the most out of it. We tell them they got the man by the balls, now the thing is to get the most out of it. You see how they got the hunkies promising them jobs now."

The turning point for Brown, as with so many others of his generation in SNCC, the point at which they began to understand that the system wasn't worth integrating into, came at the 1964 Democratic National Convention—when the Convention refused to seat the delegation from the Mississippi Freedom Democratic Party. Brown recalled this bitterly and was particularly vituperous about the hatchet job performed on the MFDP by Hubert Humphrey.

And so SNCC and Rap Brown have left the comfortable traditions of loyal opposition and gone their own way. They have moved toward an exclusive concern with black people. They are not racists, only pro-black, and very pessimistic about what they see coming out of the white community. "The only encouraging thing that has happened with white people," said Brown, "is when those white people in Los Angeles got beat up by the cops and started hollering about police brutality—hell, we told them that years ago, but they had to get their heads whipped before they could see it." The only other encouraging thing in the white community, he said chuckling, is that Lurleen Wallace has cancer.

It is not their own aberration but society's that this generation of young Negroes, who came to maturity in an organization founded on the principles of Ghandi, have come out sounding like Robert Williams. Williams is the American Negro who has lived as a political exile for the last half dozen years—first in Cuba, then in China—where he directed messages via a newsletter to American Negroes urging them to take up armed guerrilla warfare in the cities. In the late 1950's, Williams had been president of the Monroe, North Carolina, branch of the NAACP. He set off a furor in the national civil rights movement and turned himself into a pariah by suggesting that Negroes shoot back when armed bands of white rednecks start shooting up the Negro section of town. That was just a short time ago; black America has lived through much since the simple proposal of armed self-defense could provoke so much tumult.

Today bands of young Negroes around the country are preparing themselves for guerrilla warfare in the cities. The theory is chillingly simple. The ghetto is a vast sea in which the guerrilla can swim. He can venture forth to sabotage the installations of the government, or, hidden in the ghetto, he can hold down a whole company of infantry and then disappear into the crowded city. The guerrilla knows that he can never hope to overturn the government by such tactics, but his perspective is a world-wide one. America, the suppressor of world revolution, becomes over-extended. Every soldier that must be garrisoned at home to keep the lid on the ghetto is one less that can be sent overseas to suppress another colored revolution. As the pressure on America mounts, it must either come to terms with the revolution both overseas and at home or turn itself into a fascist garrison state and thus at least show the world its true color.

Whether or not the guerrilla warfare in Detroit was actively planned before-hand, the results of that warfare must have confirmed many a black revolu-tionary's belief in the potential of such tactics. He could not fail to have noticed the symbolic fact that two brigades of the 101st Airborne had to be dispatched to Detroit. The 101st third brigade was off in Vietnam fighting the Viet Cong. All together over 10,000 troops, plus 2000 police officers, were tied up by the four-day incident. At one point, over 140 square blocks of the city were under the complete control of the rioters and snipers. The police and the National Guardsmen had been completely routed, and only when they came back with tanks and .50 caliber machine-guns blazing were they able to reestablish control. And yet there were probably never more than a handful of snipers.

The spirit of Detroit is the spirit of the Black Panthers, of Rap Brown, of Stokely Carmichael—not because they participated in the Detroit revolution or planned it, or even knew about it, but because there is a new revolutionary consensus among militant blacks that is producing guerrilla fighters. It is wild and suicidal and romantic and very irrational. It is the spirit of revolution, and since America has shown very little capacity for understanding or coping with the forces of revolution abroad, it is unlikely that it will show much understand-ing of the new revolutionary spirit at home. When Ronald Reagan called the guerrillas of Detroit "mad dogs" he was at least reacting honestly—expressing a sentiment that was shared by the average white American. One deals with "mad dogs" by shooting them down quickly and peremptorily and America will be tempted to do just that with the blacks, thus sparing itself the necessity of trying to find out *why* young men become guerrillas in the most "successful" country in the world. When a few more jobs are created, and a few swimming pools built in the ghettos and the rebellion does not cease, Americans will be even more furious at the "mad dogs."

America will also be tempted to find scapegoats. Last year it was Stokely Carmichael. This year it is Rap Brown. Next year it may well be Mao Tse-tung. Some enterprising newspaperman or congressman with help from J. Edgar Hoover will probably discover that some of the captured guerrillas have been reading Mao or once belonged to a political group that defended the Chinese Revolution.

But then America will be deceiving itself further. If Rap Brown is jailed, SNCC will find another leader who will sound the same tones, not because he will have taken his cue from some foreign ideology, but because he has gone through an American experience and come out of it a revolutionary. The black guerrillas have become convinced that it is impossible to achieve decent human values within this system and that it must therefore be overthrown. If America in its arrogance refuses to confront this elemental fact, then the revolutionaries will have had the last laugh. For if it merely tries to purge itself of what it considers a foreign element in its midst, America will have lost its last chance to understand the horrors of ghetto life that produce black revolutionaries. And it is that failure of understanding which produces the Detroits in the first place.

29

THE MEANINGS OF BLACK POWER: A COMPARISON OF WHITE AND BLACK INTERPRETATIONS OF A POLITICAL SLOGAN

Joel D. Aberbach and Jack L. Walker

INTRODUCTION

Angry protests against racial discrimination have been a prominent part of American public life during the 1960's. The decade opened with the sit-ins and freedom rides, continued through Birmingham, Selma, and the March on Washington, and is now closing with the protests becoming even more passionate, often punctuated by rioting and violence. During the last few years the rhetoric of protest has become increasingly demanding, blanket charges of pervasive white racism and hostility are more common, and some Negroes have begun to actively discourage whites from participating either in protest demonstrations or civil rights organizations. Nothing better symbolizes the changing mood and style of Negro protest in America than recent changes in the movement's dominant symbols. Demonstrators who once shouted "freedom" as their rallying

Reprinted from a paper by Joel D. Aberbach and Jack L. Walker of the University of Michigan, The Meanings of Black Power: A Comparison of White and Black Interpretations of a Political Slogan, pp. 1-13.

cry now are shouting "black power"—a much more provocative, challenging slogan.

The larger and more diverse a political movement's constituency, the more vague and imprecise its unifying symbols and rallying cries are likely to be. A slogan like black power has no sharply defined meaning; it may excite many different emotions and may motivate individuals to express their loyalty or take action for almost contradictory reasons. As soon as Adam Clayton Powell and Stokely Carmichael began to use the phrase in 1966 it set off an acrimonious debate among Negro leaders over its true meaning. When Carmichael introduced the term during an angry speech in Mississippi it seemed blunt and threatening:

> The only way we gonna stop the white men from whippin' us is to take over. We've been saying freedom for six years and we ain't got nothin'. What we gonna start saying now is black power.... Ain't nothin' wrong with anything all black, because I'm all black and I'm all good. ... from now on when they ask you what you want, you know what to tell them: black power, black power, black power![1]

Speeches of this kind brought a swift, negative response from Roy Wilkins:

> No matter how endlessly they try to explain it, the term black power means anti-white power.... It has to mean going it alone. It has to mean separatism. Now separatism ... offers a disadvantaged minority little except a chance to shrivel and die.... It is a reverse Mississippi, a reverse Hitler, a reverse Ku Klux Klan.... We of the NAACP will have none of this. We have fought it too long.[2]

But advocates of the idea, like Floyd McKissick, defended the use of the slogan:

> Black power is no mere slogan. It is a movement dedicated to the exercise of American democracy in its highest tradition; it is a drive to mobilize the black communities of this country in a monumental effort to remove the basic causes of alienation, frustration, despair, low self-esteem, and hopelessness.[3]

Carmichael himself, in a book written with Charles Hamilton, later gave a more elaborate and sophisticated definition of the term:

> Black power is a call for black people in this country to unite, to recognize their heritage, to build a sense of community. It is a call for

[1] Louis Harris and William J. Brink, "Black and White," p. 50, New York, 1966.

[2] *The New York Times,* July 6, 1966, p. 14.

[3] *Ibid,* July 8, 1966, p. 16.

black people to begin to lead their own black organizations and to support these organizations. It is a call to reject the racist institutions and values of this society. . . .[4]

Regardless of these definitions and explanations, however, suspicions remained. Martin Luther King expressed the doubts of many when he said:

> It's absolutely necessary for the Negro to gain power, but the term "black power" is unfortunate because it tends to give the impression of black nationalism. . . . We must never seek power exclusively for the Negro, but the sharing of power with the white people. Any other course is exchanging one form of tyranny for another. Black supremacy would be equally evil as white supremacy. My problem with SNCC is not their militancy. I think you can be militantly nonviolent. It's what I see as a pattern of violence emerging and their use of the cry "black power," which whether they mean it or not, falls on the ear as racism in reverse.[5]

This noisy disagreement over the meaning of black power was caused partly by a clash of personalities and ambitions, but it was also the result of fundamental differences over the proper role of a black minority in a society dominated by white men. Should the ultimate goal be complete assimilation and the development of an essentially "color blind" society, or should Negroes strive to build a cohesive, autonomous community, unified along racial lines, which would be in a stronger position to demand concessions and basic social changes from the whites? For American Negroes, who bear the brutal legacy of slavery and are cut off from their African heritage, this is a terribly difficult choice. As James Baldwin said when he compared himself with the lonely, poverty stricken African students he met in Paris: "The African . . . has endured privation, injustice, medieval cruelty; but the African has not yet endured the utter alienation of himself from his people and his past. His mother did not sing 'Sometimes I Feel Like a Motherless Child,' and he has not, all his life long, ached for acceptance in a culture which pronounced straight hair and white skin the only acceptable beauty."[6] The slogan black power raises all the agonizing dilemmas of personal and national identity which have plagued black Americans since the end of slavery; the current dispute over its meaning is echoed in the speeches of Frederick Douglas, Booker T. Washington, W.E.B. DuBois, and Marcus Garvey.

Our purpose in this paper, however, is not to present an exhaustive analysis of the statements of contemporary Negro leaders about the meaning of black power. Instead, we will focus on the reactions to this slogan by the common citizens, both black and white, whose responses will ultimately settle all argu-

---

[4]Stokely Carmichael and Charles V. Hamilton, "Black Power: The Politics of Liberation in America," p. 44, New York, 1967.

[5]*The New York Times,* July 6, 1966, p. 15, and July 9, 1966, p. 8.

[6]James Baldwin, "Notes of a Native Son," p. 122, Boston, 1955.

ments about the slogan's usefulness as a tool for political organization. The analysis is based on data gathered in a survey of Detroit, Michigan completed in the fall of 1967. 855 respondents were interviewed (394 whites and 461 blacks); in all cases whites were interviewed by whites, blacks by blacks. Approximately half of the respondents were chosen in a random sample of the households in the entire city; the other half were chosen in a random sample of the zone within the city in which Detroit's 1967 riot took place. Each of our respondents was asked: "What do the words 'black power' mean to you?" The responses to this question are the subject of this paper.

Since there is such confusion and uncertainty over the meaning of black power among the writers, spokesmen and political leaders of both races, we might wonder if the slogan has had any impact at all on the citizens of Detroit. The first questions we must ask are simply: do our respondents recognize the term, have they formed an elaborate reaction to it, and if so, what meaning do they give it? Once we know what meanings are assigned to the term we will investigate the relationships between opinions about black power and other important social and political attitudes. Our central purpose is to discover the principal demographic and attitudinal factors which determine an individual's reaction to black power and to speculate, in light of our findings, about the future of race relations in Detroit.

A PROFILE OF COMMUNITY OPINION

Since there is little or no consensus among community leaders about the precise meaning of black power or even agreement on a common framework for discussing the slogan, we were reluctant to use a close-ended question to capture our respondents' interpretations of the term. In order to avoid the danger of biasing responses or eliciting a random choice we used a simple, open-ended question: "What do the words 'black power' mean to you?" This has the advantage of permitting people to speak with a minimum of clues, but it also has disadvantages which we recognized. Respondents may not have given the term a great deal of thought and their answers may be unreliable indicators of their opinion (or lack of opinion). Use of the vernacular at times inhibited interpretation of the answers. It was sometimes difficult to judge whether a respondent was sympathetic or unsympathetic to black power as he interpreted it. For example, a small number of Negro respondents (N = 3) could only define black power as "rebellion." We can guess their feelings about this word from the context of the interview, but this carries us a step away from their answers.[7] We have attempted to deal with problems of this kind by a conservative treatment of the data.

Table I presents a simple profile of community responses to our question on black power. Since there were no appreciable differences in the interpretations

[7]See our discussion below of "nothing" as a response.

TABLE I— Black power interpretations, by race

Responses to *What do the words "black power" mean to you?*

Interpretation	Blacks	Whites
Blacks rule whites	8.5%	38.6%
Racism	3.9	7.3
Trouble, rioting, civil disorder	4.1	11.9
"Nothing"	22.3	5.3
Negative imprecise Comments (ridicule, obscenity, abhorrence)	6.5	11.7
Fair share for black people	19.6	5.1
Racial (black) unity	22.6	5.6
Other*	4.3	5.9
Don't know, can't say	8.2	8.6
	100% (N=461)	100% (N=394)

*Other responses were scattered and inconsistent. They include references to black power as communism, radicalism, a return to segregation and a sophisticated failure to define the concept because of a perception that it has contradictory meanings. The latter answer was given by one black and five white respondents.

given by respondents in the riot and non-riot areas for either race, we have included all our respondents in our analysis.[8] As the table demonstrates, there are great differences in the reactions of whites and blacks to this slogan.

Almost 40 per cent of the whites believe black power means black rule over whites, while only 9 per cent of the Negro respondents hold this view. This attitude of the whites is clearly *not* a function of a rational projection that the increasing black population in the city of Detroit (now about 40 per cent) will soon elect a black mayor, but is an almost hysterical response to the symbolism of the slogan. White people in this category usually refer to Negroes taking over the entire country or even the world[9]:

(white, male, 47, 12 grades)   Nasty word! That the blacks won't be satisfied until they get complete control of our country by force if necessary.

(white, male, 24, 12 grades plus)   Black takeover—Take over the world because that is what they want to do and they will. There's no doubt

[8] For the blacks, the riot area respondents gave a greater emphasis to black unity as opposed to fair share interpretations of black power, but the differences are not great. Non-riot area respondents actually were slightly more favorable to black power if we consider unity and fair share responses as indicators of positive feelings.

[9] The quotes presented here are typical examples of black power definitions coded in each category. Respondents are identified by race, sex, age and educational attainment for the benefit of the reader. In cases where the respondent has some specialized training, he is coded with a "plus" after his grade level.

about it. Why should they care? I'm working and supporting their kids. In time they'll take over—look how many there are in Congress. It's there—when they get to voting age, we'll be discriminated upon.

(white, female, 28, 12 grades plus)   The colored are going to take over and be our leaders and we're to be their servants. Yes, that's exactly what it means.

(white, female, 28, 12 grades)   They want the situation reversed. They want to rule everything.

(white, male, 32, 11 grades)   The Negro wants to enslave the white man like he was enslaved 100 years ago. They want to take everything away from us. There will be no middle class, no advancement. He is saying, "If I can't have it neither can you." Everything will be taken away from us. We'll all be poor.

(white, female, 40, 12 grades)   I don't like the sound of it. Sounds like something coming to take you over.

Most of our black respondents *do not* interpret black power in this way. In fact, blacks who were coded in this category were usually also hostile to black power. For example:

(black, male, 28, 12 grades plus)   It means dominating black rule—to dominate, to rule over like Hitlerism.

(black, female, 38, 11 grades plus)   It means something I don't like. It means like white power is now—taking over completely.

(black, male, 29, no answer on education)   It means to me that Negroes are trying to take over and don't know how.

A few others gave this answer because they have very vague ideas about the concept:

(black, female, 50, 9 grades)   Sounds like they want to take over control.

(black, female, 34, 12 grades plus)   Nothing, really. I guess it means Negroes taking over and being the leaders.

There were only seven people in this group of 37 who saw black domination over whites as the definition of black power and whose answers could possibly be interpreted as approval of this goal.

A small number of whites and Negroes simply defined black power as racism or race hatred. The comments of Negroes holding this view were especially scathing:

(black, female, 57, 11 grades)   It's like the Ku Klux Klan and I don't like it.

(black, female, 38, 12 grades)   It means something very detrimental to the race as a whole. This is the same tactic the whites use in discriminating.

The black power definitions of about 12 per cent of the white population and 4 per cent of the Negroes sampled were directly influenced by the violence of the 1967 Detroit disorders. Terms like "trouble" and "rioting" were commonly used by these individuals, especially blacks in the riot areas and whites outside of it. Clearly, however, the vast majority of black people sampled do not see black power as a synonym for violence and destruction, racism, or even black rule over whites, while 57.2 per cent of the whites do.

Two views of black power predominate among our Negro respondents. One represents a poorly articulated negativism or opposition to the term and the other a positive or approving interpretation of the concept and its meaning. Roughly 23 per cent of the black respondents indicated that the term meant "nothing" to them. This category was coded separately from the "Don't know," "Can't say," and "No answer" responses because the word "nothing" is generally used as a term of derision in the black community. Some examples of extended responses give the proper flavor:

(black, female, 39, 10 grades)   Nothing! (Interviewer probe) Not a damn thing. (further probe) Well, it's just a word used by people from the hate school so it really don't mean nothing to me.

(black, male, 52, 12 grades plus)   It means nothing! (probe) A word coined by some nut. (further probe) There is only one power and that is God.

(black, female, 60, 5 grades)   It doesn't mean nothing. (probe) Biggest joke in the 20th century.

It is, of course, possible that some people use "nothing" as a synonym for "I don't know." We have two major pieces of evidence which indicate that this is not so for the major proportion of blacks giving the response: (1) while direct expressions of ignorance ("don't know," "can't say," etc.) are a function of educational level, "nothing" is used in the same proportion by blacks no matter what their academic accomplishments; and (2) blacks use the expression more than four times as often as whites (22% to 5%) in trying to express what black power means to them.

There are other individuals who give less ambiguous, clearly negative interpretations of the term. A small proportion of our respondents (1.3 per cent of the blacks and 0.7 per cent of the whites) found profanity indispensible as the sole expression of their definition. Others (5.2 per cent of the blacks and 11.0 per cent of the whites) were slightly more articulate in their condemnation, although their definitions were still imprecise. Often, especially for the whites, they reflect a general abhorrence of power in any form:

(white, female, 52, 12 grades)   I hate the expression because I don't like power. It's very domineering and possessive and (they) have only themselves in mind.

(white, male, 54, 4 grades)   No more than the words white power mean. They should cut that word out.

(black, female, 37, 9 grades)   Black power and white power means the same to me which is no good. Man should be treated as a man.

(white, female, 55, 12 grades)   Disaster! You know what you can do with your black power.

(white, female, 53, 12 grades)   Scare! Why should there be black power any more than white power? Don't the blacks agree that all races are equal?

The last remaining major category of answers clearly distinguishes the black from the white community in its views of black power. 42.2 per cent of our Negro respondents as compared to 10.7 per cent of the whites emphasized a "fair share for Negroes" or "black unity" in their statements. We coded all those answers which stressed the Negro getting his share of the honors and fruits of production in society, exercising equal rights, bettering his living conditions or gaining greater political power into our "fair share" categories. Definitions stressing black unity or racial pride were coded separately.[10] Since only 7 blacks and 2 whites mentioned racial pride specifically, we will refer in the text to "black unity" or "racial unity" only. We felt that a definition of black power in terms of black people gaining political power in areas where blacks are in the majority fell under our fair share concept, but there were only two statements of this type. This definition may be implicit in the statements made (or in some of our black unity interpretations) but virtually all references are to justice and equity rather than exclusive control of a geographical area.

Fair share answers were given by almost twenty per cent of our black respondents. People whose responses fall into this category see the black power

[10] In a few cases (N = 20) respondents stressed black unity in order to achieve a fair share. We are considering first mentions here and in our analysis, but will prove this in detail when we have more time.

slogan as another statement of traditional Negro goals of freedom, equality and opportunity. Respondents often take pains to reject notions of blacks taking advantage of others.

(black, female, 47, 12 grades plus)   That we should have blacks represent us in government—not take over, but represent us.

(black, male, 40, 9 grades plus)   Negroes getting the same opportunities as whites when qualified.

(black, male, 24, 12 grades)   Negroes should get more power to do the same things which whites do.

(black, female, 52, 12 grades plus)   Give us an equal chance.

(black, male, 41, 0 grades)   To me it means a open door into integration.

(black, male, 39, 12 grades)   Equal rights to any human being.

(black, female, 54, 7 grades)   That America is going to have a new power structure so black people can have a share.

(black, male, 23, 10 grades)   Getting in possession of something—like jobs and security.

(black, male, 55, 12 grades)   It means equal opportunities for both races. What's good for one is good for the other.

About 23 per cent of our Negro respondents gave "black unity" responses.[11] These were more militant in tone than the fair share definitions, sometimes extremely nationalistic, but always (as in the fair share answers) concerned with bettering the situation of the black man and not putting down the white man. In fact, blacks who are most favorably disposed towards black power simply do not see the political world as one where blacks can gain something only at the expense of whites and vice versa. As we have seen, however, large numbers of whites do see things this way. For them one group or the other must tend to "take over."

The major difference between the "fair share" and "black unity" group is that the former places heavy stress on the Negro as an equal participant in the total society, while the latter emphasizes black togetherness and achievement without the same attention to the traditional symbols of Negro advancement. We know from extended answers to our black question and others that individ-

[11]We will combine black unity definitions with the few racial pride references for purposes of analysis.

uals giving black unity responses want equality and a just share of America's goods, but "thinking black" and speaking militantly and with pride are given primacy when talking about black power.[12] It is not that they are against white people; they are simply *for* black people and deeply committed to the idea of black people working together:

> (black, male, 35, 9 grades)   People getting together to accomplish things for the group.

> (black, male, 36, 12 grades plus)   Negroes have never been together on anything. Now with the new movement we gain strength.

> (black, male, 24, 12 grades)   We people getting together, agreeing on issues and attempting to reach a common goal.

> (black, male, 28, 12 grades)   Sounds frightening, but really is what whites, Jews, Arabs, and people the world over do—divided we fall, united we stand.

> (black, female, 41, 12 grades plus)   Togetherness among Negroes; but it means you can get along with others.

> (black, female, 37, 10 grades)   It means being true to yourself and recognize yourself as a black American who can accomplish good things in life.

> (black, female, 57, 10 grades)   White man separate us when he brought us here and we been that way ever since. We are just trying to do what everybody else has—stick together.

As we have noted, the number of whites giving either the fair share or black unity response is small—just over 10 per cent of the white sample. To most whites—even those who think of themselves as liberals—the concept of black power is forbidding. The 1967 riot is certainly one factor that might account for this, but we found little evidence of it. Only 5 whites in the entire sample (one per cent) gave answers like the following:

> (white, female, 23, college)   It's gotten (away) from the original meaning. Means violence to me now.

[12] See footnote 10. About 20 per cent of the black respondents mentioning racial unity saw it as a means of achieving equality. For example:

> (black, male, 42, 12 grades) Negroes getting together and forcing whites to realize our importance—our worth to the United States. Gaining respect and equality.

The more articulate members of the black unity group are concerned with ends as well as means. See Carmichael and Hamilton, *op. cit.,* pp. 46-47.

In addition, as we shall see, even whites who have very sympathetic views about the causes of the disturbances can hardly be described as favorable to black power. The negative presentation of black power in the mass media may be responsible, but Detroit Negroes are also attentive to the same media and their views are quite different. The evidence points strongly towards a simple conclusion—the overwhelming majority of whites are frightened and bewildered by the words black power. Some of this seems rooted in abhorrence of stark words like power, but the term *black* power is obviously intolerable. The words conjure up racial stereotypes and suspicions deeply ingrained in the minds of white Americans. The slogan presents an unmistakable challenge to the country's prevailing racial customs and social norms; for precisely this reason it seems exciting and attractive to many blacks.

In summary, the vast majority of white people are hostile to the notion of black power. The most common interpretation is that it symbolizes a black desire to take over the country, deprive the white man, etc. Blacks, on the other hand, are most often clearly favorable to black power (seeing it as another call for a fair share for Negroes and/or as a rallying cry for black unity) or negative about it in a general way (our "nothing" category). They clearly do not interpret the term the way whites do. They do not see it as meaning racism, a general black takeover, or violence and those few blacks who do define the term in this way are negative about such meaning. It is evident that "black power" is a potent slogan which arouses contradictory feelings in large numbers of people. Interpretations of the term may differ, but the slogan clearly stimulates intense feelings and may be exciting enough to move men to purposeful action.

30

THE TRAGIC MYTH OF BLACK POWER

Samuel DuBois Cook

Man is, among other things, a myth-making creature. Indeed, the almost infinite capacity to create and perpetuate illusions is one of man's most generous and massive endowments. Myths, of course, serve a variety of functions in the human economy, and may be harmless, creative or destructive. Profoundly destructive and self-defeating is the myth of "Black Power." It is a dangerous romantic illusion. It is an illusion of power, but we should not underestimate the power of the illusion.

Social movements have a peculiar way of breeding internal rebels and of generating purposes and qualities quite different from, and at variance with, their initial character, direction, and moral tone. So, ironically, an important sector of the civil rights movement is beginning to wave the ominous flag of black nationalism and, in voices and style reminiscent of the demonic racism which has informed and inspired so much of the southern political process, shout incantations of "Black Power." Quite a reversal of meaning, value and aspiration.

What is the meaning of the slogan "Black Power"? The answer depends not only on who is defining the term but also the place, time, and atmosphere. Its chief proponents display a remarkable absence of consistency and specificity of meaning. One of the great hazards of the slogan is its ambiguity, complexity, and

Reprinted from Samuel DuBois Cook, The Tragic Myth of Black Power, *New South,* **21,** no. 3, pp. 58-64, Summer 1966.

mystical quality. It not only means many things to many people but also, judging from the record, many things to the same people.

Shorn of pretensions, hypocrisy, and intellectual dishonesty, the slogan "Black Power" does have, when words, context, and program are combined, a generic or core meaning, and that meaning is racist. It is anti-white. It is separatist and isolationist. Make no mistake about it: Vigorous denials under pressure notwithstanding, the unique dimension of the Black Power myth is racism. "If there is anything new in the slogan," Les Dunbar properly noted, "it is racism."

The racist character of the myth of Black Power is expressed in many ways: counsel to exclude whites from positions of leadership and influence in the civil rights movement, advocacy of independent all-Negro third parties, the symbol of the Black Panther, the call for a "black takeover of political and economic power," the declaration of the irrelevance of integration and the issue of violence, self-righteous and glib assertions of the moral decadence of white America, and the general ventilation of anti-white frustrations, emotions and bitterness. "Black Power" is meaningful only in the context of "white power." Thus an appeal to Black Power is necessarily an appeal against white power: hence, an anti-white mentality and strategy. Why is the slogan so dear to the hearts of its exponents? It is calculated not only to "develop" pride and self-confidence in "black people," but also to serve as a catharsis and to exploit anti-white resentment, frustration, bitterness, and sentiments.

Imitating the dishonesty and corporate hypocrisy of the substance of southern history (and much of northern history as well) on the score of race relations, the proponents of Black Power, for the most part, piously renounce any claim to racism. But no one should be deceived. . . .

FOUR FALLACIES OF BLACK POWER

The myth of Black Power is pragmatic nonsense, strategically self-defeating, anthropologically illusionary, and ethically destructive. It is impossible to divorce racism politics from other institutions and processes of culture. Bipolarity in politics means the polarization of the total culture on racial lines. Forms of power are integrally related. Racism in politics, as southern history clearly demonstrates, means racism in the socio-economic and other institutions of life. Splendid isolation and separatism in the political process mean splendid isolation and separatism in the whole web of culture.

A. Pragmatic Nonsense
Like so much of the political history of the white South divorced from reality, the myth of Black Power is a tragic exercise in futility. It is political mysticism, superstition, alchemy or astrology. The Negro must form alliances and coalitions with liberal, progressive, and moderate whites. Since he is a clear minority, constituting only about 10.5 per cent of the total population, sheer arithmetic is against the success of any isolated program of action. There is no possibility of

any black takeover of power. The Negro, therefore, must have allies and friends. In pragmatic terms, Black Power, or domination, is a dangerous myth and self-defeating illusion. It can only produce frustration, disappointment, heartache, bitterness, and disaster for the Negro. Because of both quantitative and qualitative considerations, polarization of politics on a white-versus-black basis would be, for Negroes, the height of folly and would mean political suicide.

Demographic factors will not be nullified by emotional outbursts and the incantations of political witchdoctors and magicians. In no state do Negroes constitute a majority (Mississippi, which is 42.0% Negro, has the highest ratio) and hence cannot hope to control such a primary center of power. . . .

Besides, the Black Power philosophy, in the very nature of the case, can have no strategy or program in counties where Negroes are a distinct minority. This doctrinaire concept would place Negro power in a strait jacket and political ghetto of the worst kind. If it were successful in the counties with Negro majorities, it would be, for that very reason, a supreme failure in that vast region in which Negroes are in the minority. Because of political retaliation, it would do havoc with the movement for racial justice and paralyze the civil rights movement. It would gain an inch but lose miles and miles.

It also should be noted that counties are simply creatures of state governments and hence at their mercy. They can be shifted, altered, merged or liquidated at will. White majorities, therefore, through control of state machinery, could manipulate, control, and starve counties with Negro majorities—assuming, of course, that white-dominated federal courts and national political institutions go along. It is worth remembering that the counties with Negro majorities are the poorest economically, educationally, and otherwise in the poorest section of the country. Getting control of them, in view of the poverty and continuous migration, would be governing ghost towns or cemeteries.

Negro voting power, even when maximized, will generally only be able to hold the balance of power in close elections. Ten thousand votes will not be effective against 100,000. History reminds us that, at the end of Reconstruction, the Negro was eliminated from participation in the southern political process precisely because he held the balance of power in interparty contests. To achieve his objective, the Negro has to work with others in the totality of American institutions.

It is, of course, true that alliances presuppose allies and in some local situations such as Lowndes County where Negroes have no present allies, Negroes will have to "go it alone" until some emerge. Negroes, however, must encourage, not discourage, the emergence of allies, and always extend the hand of political friendship and cooperation. The Black Power slogan is no more a way to encourage the cooperation of whites than the white supremacy slogan is to solicit the support of Negroes. The Black Panther symbol militates against collaboration and the democratization of the political process.

B. Strategy and Tactic
If the Negro had a cosmic enemy who had seized control of the department of strategy and tactics of the civil rights movement, he could not invent a more

disastrous political methodology. The mind shudders in disbelief. The slogan of "Black Power" is a terrible political tactic for a number of reasons. First, it facilitates division and warfare within the civil rights movement when so much needs to be done and solidarity is so much needed. Consider the time and energy lost in trying to define, clarify, and defend the slogan. Consider how it promotes misunderstanding and ill-will within the Movement. It pits leader against leader and organization against organization.

Second, the myth of Black Power gives moderate and even liberal whites a ready-made excuse to discontinue support of the Negro's struggle. It gives them an easy out. Third, it unnecessarily plays on the historic fears of many whites who think in terms of "black domination." It revives their myths of Reconstruction and assists their rationalization of the historic exclusion and alienation of the Negro from full partnership in the structure and process of power. It reinforces the irrational and fanatical fears of those whites who think that Negroes are interested in cheap retribution and bitter revenge. Fourth, the tactic of Black Power fosters racial polarization of the political process and thereby aggravates the brutally racist politics of so much of white America. Whites will organize more intensely against Negroes, and in cases of minority versus majority in this country the outcome is a foregone conclusion.

Above all, the myth of Black Power is politically self-defeating. Getting control of a few rural, poverty-stricken counties in the South will not solve any of the Negro's problems. In order to solve the great issues of housing, education, employment, political alienation, poverty, slumism, etc., the Negro desperately needs much more, rather than much less, support from the white community. He has to have wider and deeper public support if his miseries and frustrations are not to increase. To get new civil rights and other needed legislation, to win more elective and appointive positions, and to overcome his historic alienation from the public institutions of the country, the Negro must have allies. Once more, Black Power, when arrayed against white power, is a dangerous and self-defeating illusion.

C. Man and Black Power

Powerless individuals, and groups, while not necessarily dangerous, can be as self-righteous as powerful ones. The weak can be as vain and self-deceptive as the strong. Negroes have witnessed and suffered long and much from the way in which whites have used power. Some Negroes are on the brink of making the fateful assumptions of moral superiority, of thinking that Negroes with power are better than whites with power, of asserting that the uses of power are a function of race.

But race has nothing whatever to do with the exercise of power. Negroes are equal members of the human estate. They share all the defects as well as the virtues, all the misery as well as the dignity, all the tragedy as well as the glory, all the strengths as well as the weaknesses, and all the curses as well as the blessings of a common humanity. Negroes with power are as destructive and creative, as egoistic and altruistic, and as dangerous and self-serving as whites with power. Like whites, they are subject to all the temptations, perversions, tyrannies, pretensions, and abuses of power. Like whites, their possession of power is likely to make them indifferent, insensitive, arrogant, vain, self-seeking, morally complacent, and deaf to the cries of the suffering and disabled. Negro politicians are as bad and as good as white politicians. Their organizations are as corrupt and as noble, comparatively speaking, as their white counterparts.

Public life, therefore, might not be more blessed and creative under "Black Power." History and current experience demonstrate that Negro politicians are politicians first and Negroes second and, like white politicians, they are generally more concerned with getting elected and re-elected than with the promotion of racial justice. Reflect upon Congressmen Dawson and Powell as well as a host of lesser figures. Indeed, some of the worst enemies of racial progress are Negro public officials, some of whom were elected by Negro constituencies. If it is argued that they are that way because they are members of the "establishment" or "power structure," we might agree, but we would also add that men of power, whatever their breed or creed, have a way of creating their own "establishments" and power structures. It will be so of "Black Power."

In addition to Negro politicians, consider the rivalries and jealousies of certain civil rights leaders and organizations. Men will use the very slogan Black Power for selfish purposes—both personal and organizational. At the recent ceremony in Jackson, Mississippi, culminating the famous "Meredith March," one civil rights leader called for racial solidarity when, the previous night, he had voted to deny the NAACP the opportunity to participate in the program. Consider, too, the petty empires of tyranny and authoritarianism as well as the prominence of self-serving "leaders" of the Negro community—churches, schools, social and fraternal groups, and other organizations and institutions. They are a grim reminder that the psychology and evils of power are the common property of all humanity.

There should be no illusions about men of power—whatever their race. The myth of Black Power raises tragically false hopes and expectations. It promotes excessive optimism which, if not checked and sobered by a realistic appreciation of human nature, will reap a bitter harvest of disappointment, disillusionment, pessimism, frustration, cynicism, and despair.

D. Philosophical and Ethical Dimension

The ultimate argument against the myth of "Black Power" is ethical, the vision of the good, and the higher possibilities of human history, the quality of public life that ought to be created and conserved. It is the same simple and ancient argument against "white supremacy," "Nordic superiority," and every other form of racism and tribalism making a particular group the center of meaning and value: our common humanity and the need to create the Good Life, the beloved community. Black Power for what? How will it be used? To what end? Will it be used for the tragically self-defeating purpose of revenge and retribution, to substitute one system of injustice for another? Mankind has suffered enough from the irrationalism and incubus of racism. Somehow, somewhere, the vicious circle must be broken.

The kind of political and social order needed is one in which race is value-free: neither a curse nor a blessing, nor defect nor virtue, nor special privilege nor handicap. The goal must be the creation of the beloved community—a free, open, and pluralistic society whose very structure of being, whose very processes of existence, reflect the solidarity of the human family. Essential is a philosophy which unites rather than separates men, which makes men humble, not arrogant; free, not in new chains. The vision must be inclusive, not exclusive; universal, not particularistic; healing, not devouring.

The method must always be one that promotes the reconciliation of Negroes and whites, binds wounds, repairs torn social tissues, and makes the society morally healthy and whole in its fullest dimensions and highest possibilities.

Love, said Paul Tillich, means re-union of the separated. That, too, is the ultimate character of justice. Justice is the restoration of the harmony and ultimate glory of the social order—the coming together again, after a long night of tragic estrangement, of races and classes that have been fragmented and stunted by false doctrines, corrupt systems and ideologies, corporate evils, and perverted visions and institutions.

Negroes ought to use their expanding political power, therefore, to enlarge and deepen the good of history, to destroy wretched wrongs, to eliminate the cancer of racism, to usher in the Good Life, to create the beloved community, to re-unite the separated.

31

SUMMARY OF REPORT

President's Commission on Civil Disorders

INTRODUCTION

The summer of 1967 again brought racial disorders to American cities, and with them shock, fear and bewilderment to the nation.

The worst came during a two-week period in July, first in Newark and then in Detroit. Each set off a chain reaction in neighboring communities.

On July 28, 1967, the President of the United States established this Commission and directed us to answer three basic questions:

What happened?
Why did it happen?
What can be done to prevent it from happening again?

To respond to these questions, we have undertaken a broad range of studies and investigations. We have visited the riot cities; we have heard many witnesses; we have sought the counsel of experts across the country.

This is our basic conclusion: Our nation is moving toward two societies, one black, one white—separate and unequal.

Reaction to last summer's disorders has quickened the movement and deep-

Reprinted from the Report of the National Advisory Commission on Civil Disorders, 1968.

ened the division. Discrimination and segregation have long permeated much of American life; they now threaten the future of every American.

This deepening racial division is not inevitable. The movement apart can be reversed. Choice is still possible. Our principal task is to define that choice and to press for a national resolution. . . .

PART I   WHAT HAPPENED?

. . .

Chapter 2—Patterns of Disorder

The "typical" riot did not take place. The disorders of 1967 were unusual, irregular, complex and unpredictable social processes. Like most human events, they did not unfold in an orderly sequence. However, an analysis of our survey information leads to some conclusions about the riot process. In general:

The civil disorders of 1967 involved Negroes acting against local symbols of white American society, authority and property in Negro neighborhoods—rather than against white persons.

Of 164 disorders reported during the first nine months of 1967, eight (5 percent) were major in terms of violence and damage; 33 (20 percent) were serious but not major; 123 (75 percent) were minor and undoubtedly would not have received national attention as "riots" had the nation not been sensitized by the more serious outbreaks.

In the 75 disorders studied by a Senate subcommittee, 83 deaths were reported. Eighty-two percent of the deaths and more than half the injuries occurred in Newark and Detroit. About 10 percent of the dead and 38 percent of the injured were public employees, primarily law officers and firemen. The overwhelming majority of the persons killed or injured in all the disorders were Negro civilians.

Initial damage estimates were greatly exaggerated. In Detroit, newspaper damage estimates at first ranged from $200 million to $500 million; the highest recent estimate is $45 million. In Newark, early estimates ranged from $15 to $25 million. A month later damage was estimated at $10.2 million, over 80 percent in inventory losses.

In the 24 disorders in 23 cities which we surveyed: . . .

Disorder did not erupt as a result of a single "triggering" or "precipitating" incident. Instead, it was generated out of an increasingly disturbed social atmosphere, in which typically a series of tension-heightening incidents over a period of weeks or months became linked in the minds of many in the Negro community with a reservoir of underlying grievances. At some point in the mounting tension, a further incident—in itself often routine or trivial—became the breaking point and the tension spilled over into violence.

"Prior" incidents, which increased tensions and ultimately led to violence, were police actions in almost half the cases; police actions were "final" incidents before the outbreak of violence in 12 of the 24 surveyed disorders. . . .

Negotiations between Negroes—including young militants as well as older Negro leaders—and white officials concerning "terms of peace" occurred during virtually all the disorders surveyed. In many cases, these negotiations involved discussion of underlying grievances as well as the handling of the disorder by control authorities.

The *typical rioter* was a teenager or young adult, a life-long resident of the city in which he rioted, a high school dropout; he was, nevertheless, somewhat better educated than his nonrioting Negro neighbor, and was usually *under-employed or employed* in a *menial job*. He was proud of his race, extremely hostile to both whites and middle-class Negroes and, although informed about politics, highly distrustful of the political system.

A Detroit survey revealed that approximately 11 percent of the total residents of two riot areas admitted participation in the rioting, 20 to 25 percent identified themselves as "counter-rioters" who urged rioters to "cool it," and the remaining 48 to 53 percent said they were at home or elsewhere and did not participate. In a survey of Negro males between the ages of 15 and 35 residing in the disturbance area in Newark, about 45 percent identified themselves as rioters, and about 55 percent as "noninvolved."

Most rioters were young Negro males. Nearly 53 percent of arrestees were between 15 and 24 years of age; nearly 81 percent between 15 and 35. . . .

What the rioters appeared to be seeking was fuller participation in the social order and the material benefits enjoyed by the majority of American citizens. Rather than rejecting the American system, they were anxious to obtain a place for themselves in it.

Numerous Negro counter-rioters walked the streets urging rioters to "cool it." The *typical counter-rioter* was *better educated* and had *higher income* than either the rioter or the noninvolved.

The proportion of Negroes in local government was substantially smaller than the Negro proportion of population. Only three of the 20 cities studied had more than one Negro legislator; none had ever had a Negro mayor or city manager. In only four cities did Negroes hold other important policy-making positions or serve as heads of municipal departments.

Although almost all cities had some sort of formal grievance mechanism for handling citizen complaints, this typically was regarded by Negroes as ineffective and was generally ignored.

Although specific grievances varied from city to city, at least 12 deeply held grievances can be identified and ranked into three levels of relative intensity:

First Level of Intensity
1. Police practices

   2. Unemployment and underemployment
   3. Inadequate housing

Second Level of Intensity
   4. Inadequate education
   5. Poor recreation facilities and programs
   6. Ineffectiveness of the political structure and grievance mechanisms

Third Level of Intensity
   7. Disrespectful white attitudes
   8. Discriminatory administration of justice
   9. Inadequacy of federal programs
   10. Inadequacy of municipal services
   11. Discriminatory consumer and credit practices
   12. Inadequate welfare programs

. . .

A study of the aftermath of disorders leads to disturbing conclusions. We find that, despite the institution of some post-riot programs:

Little basic change in the conditions underlying the outbreak of disorder has taken place. Actions to ameliorate Negro grievances have been limited and sporadic; with but few exceptions, they have not significantly reduced tensions.

In several cities, the principal official response has been to train and equip the police with more sophisticated weapons.

In several cities, increasing polarization is evident, with continuing breakdown of inter-racial communication, and growth of white segregationist or black separatist groups.

Chapter 3—Organized Activity
The President directed the Commission to investigate "to what extent, if any, there has been planning or organization in any of the riots." . . .

On the basis of all the information collected, the Commission concludes that the urban disorders of the summer of 1967 were not caused by, nor were they the consequence of, any organized plan or "conspiracy."

. . .

PART II   WHY DID IT HAPPEN?

Chapter 4—The Basic Causes
. . . Despite [the] complexities, certain fundamental matters are clear. Of these, the most fundamental is the racial attitude and behavior of white Americans toward black Americans.

Race prejudice has shaped our history decisively; it now threatens to affect our future.

White racism is essentially responsible for the explosive mixture which has been accumulating in our cities since the end of World War II. Among the ingredients of this mixture are:

Pervasive discrimination and segregation in employment, education and housing, which have resulted in the continuing exclusion of great numbers of Negroes from the benefits of economic progress.

Black in-migration and white exodus, which have produced the massive and growing concentrations of impoverished Negroes in our major cities, creating a growing crisis of deteriorating facilities and services and unmet human needs.

The black ghettos where segregation and poverty converge on the young to destroy opportunity and enforce failure. Crime, drug addiction, dependency on welfare, and bitterness and resentment against society in general and white society in particular are the result.

At the same time, most whites and some Negroes outside the ghetto have prospered to a degree unparalleled in the history of civilization. Through television and other media, this affluence has been flaunted before the eyes of the Negro poor and the jobless ghetto youth.

Yet these facts alone cannot be said to have caused the disorders. Recently, other powerful ingredients have begun to catalyze the mixture:

Frustrated hopes are the residue of the unfulfilled expectations aroused by the great judicial and legislative victories of the Civil Rights Movement and the dramatic struggle for equal rights in the South.

A climate that tends toward approval and encouragement of violence as a form of protest has been created by white terrorism directed against nonviolent protest; by the open defiance of law and federal authority by state and local officials resisting desegregation; and by some protest groups engaging in civil disobedience who turn their backs on non-violence, go beyond the constitutionally protected rights of petition and free assembly, and resort to violence to attempt to compel alteration of laws and policies with which they disagree.

The frustrations of powerlessness have led some Negroes to the conviction that there is no effective alternative to violence as a means of achieving redress of grievances, and of "moving the system." These frustrations are reflected in alienation and hostility toward the institutions of law and government and the white society which controls them, and in the reach toward racial consciousness and solidarity reflected in the slogan "Black Power."

A new mood has sprung up among Negroes, particularly among the young, in which self-esteem and enhanced racial pride are replacing apathy and submission to "the system."

The police are not merely a "spark" factor. To some Negroes police have come to symbolize white power, white racism and white repression. And the fact is that many police do reflect and express these white attitudes. The atmosphere of hostility and cynicism is reinforced by a widespread belief among Negroes in the existence of police brutality and in a "double standard" of justice and protection—one for Negroes and one for whites.

Chapter 6—The Formation of the Racial Ghettos[1]

. . . Basic data concerning Negro urbanization trends indicate that:

Almost all Negro population growth (98 percent from 1950 to 1966) is occurring within metropolitan areas, primarily within central cities.[2]

The vast majority of white population growth (78 percent from 1960 to 1966) is occurring in suburban portions of metropolitan areas. Since 1960, white central-city population has declined by 1.3 million.

As a result, central cities are becoming more heavily Negro while the suburban fringes around them remain almost entirely white.

The twelve largest central cities now contain over two-thirds of the Negro population outside the South, and one-third of the Negro total in the United States.

Chapter 7—Unemployment, Family Structure, and Social Disorganization

Although there have been gains in Negro income nationally, and a decline in the number of Negroes below the "poverty level," the condition of Negroes in the central city remains in a state of crisis. Between 2 and 2.5 million Negroes—16 to 20 percent of the total Negro population of all central cities—live in squalor and deprivation in ghetto neighborhoods. . . .

In one study of low-income neighborhoods, the "subemployment rate," including both *unemployment and underemployment*, was about *33 percent*, or 8.8 times greater than the overall unemployment rate for all United States workers.

Employment problems, aggravated by the constant arrival of new unemployed migrants, many of them from depressed rural areas, create persistent poverty in the ghetto. In 1966, about 11.9 percent of the nation's whites and 40.6 percent of its nonwhites were below the "poverty level" defined by the Social Security Administration (currently $3,335 per year for an urban family of four). Over 40 percent of the nonwhites below the poverty level live in the central cities.

Employment problems have drastic social impact in the ghetto. Men who are chronically unemployed or employed in the lowest status jobs are often unable or unwilling to remain with their families. The handicap imposed on children

---

[1] The term "ghetto" as used in this report refers to an area within a city characterized by poverty and acute social disorganization, and inhabited by members of a racial or ethnic group under conditions of involuntary segregation.

[2] A "central city" is the largest city of a standard metropolitan statistical area, that is, a metropolitan area containing at least one city of 50,000 or more inhabitants.

growing up without fathers in an atmosphere of poverty and deprivation is increased as mothers are forced to work to provide support.

The culture of poverty that results from unemployment and family breakup generates a system of ruthless, exploitative relationships within the ghetto. Prostitution, dope addiction, and crime create an environmental "jungle" characterized by personal insecurity and tension. Children growing up under such conditions are likely participants in civil disorder.

Chapter 8—Conditions of Life In the Racial Ghetto

A striking difference in environment from that of white, middle-class Americans profoundly influences the lives of residents of the ghetto.

Crime rates, consistently higher than in other areas, create a pronounced sense of insecurity. For example, in one city one low-income Negro district had 35 times as many serious crimes against persons as a high-income white district. Unless drastic steps are taken, the crime problems in poverty areas are likely to continue to multiply as the growing youth and rapid urbanization of the population outstrip police resources.

Poor health and sanitation conditions in the ghetto result in higher mortality rates, a higher incidence of major diseases, and lower availability and utilization of medical services. The infant mortality rate for nonwhite babies under the age of one month is 58 percent higher than for whites; for one to 12 months it is almost three times as high. The level of sanitation in the ghetto is far below that in high income areas. Garbage collection is often inadequate. Of an estimated 14,000 cases of rat bite in the United States in 1965, most were in ghetto neighborhoods.

Ghetto residents believe they are "exploited" by local merchants; and evidence substantiates some of these beliefs. A study conducted in one city by the Federal Trade Commission showed that distinctly higher prices were charged for goods sold in ghetto stores than in other areas.

Lack of knowledge regarding credit purchasing creates special pitfalls for the disadvantaged. In many states garnishment practices compound these difficulties by allowing creditors to deprive individuals of their wages without hearing or trial.

Chapter 9—Comparing the Immigrant and Negro Experience

In this chapter, we address ourselves to a fundamental question that many white Americans are asking: why have so many Negroes, unlike the European immigrants, been unable to escape from the ghetto and from poverty? We believe the following factors play a part:

The maturing economy: When the European immigrants arrived, they gained an economic foothold by providing the unskilled labor needed by industry. Unlike the immigrant, the Negro migrant found little opportunity in the city. The economy, by then matured, had little use for the unskilled labor he had to offer.

The disability of race: The structure of discrimination has stringently narrowed opportunities for the Negro and restricted his prospects. European immigrants suffered from discrimination, but never so pervasively.

Entry into the political system: The immigrants usually settled in rapidly growing cities with powerful and expanding political machines, which traded economic advantages for political support. Ward-level grievance machinery, as well as personal representation, enabled the immigrant to make his voice heard and his power felt.

By the time the Negro arrived, these political machines were no longer so powerful or so well equipped to provide jobs or other favors, and in many cases were unwilling to share their influence with Negroes.

Cultural factors: Coming from societies with a low standard of living and at a time when job aspirations were low, the immigrants sensed little deprivation in being forced to take the less desirable and poorer-paying jobs. Their large and cohesive families contributed to total income. Their vision of the future—one that led to a life outside of the ghetto—provided the incentive necessary to endure the present.

Although Negro men worked as hard as the immigrants, they were unable to support their families. The entrepreneurial opportunities had vanished. As a result of slavery and long periods of unemployment, the Negro family structure had become matriarchal; the males played a secondary and marginal family role—one which offered little compensation for their hard and unrewarding labor. Above all, segregation denied the Negroes access to good jobs and the opportunity to leave the ghetto. For them, the future seemed to lead only to a dead end.

Today, whites tend to exaggerate how well and quickly they escaped from poverty. The fact is that immigrants who came from rural backgrounds, as many Negroes do, are only now, after three generations, finally beginning to move into the middle class. . . .

PART III   WHAT CAN BE DONE?

Chapter 10—The Community Response

Our investigation of the 1967 riot cities establishes that virtually every major episode of violence was foreshadowed by an accumulation of unresolved grievances and by widespread dissatisfaction among Negroes with the unwillingness or inability of local government to respond. . . .

The Commission recommends that local governments:

Develop Neighborhood Action Task Forces as joint community-government efforts through which more effective communication can be achieved, and the delivery of city services to ghetto residents improved.

Establish comprehensive grievance-response mechanisms in order to bring all public agencies under public scrutiny.

Bring the institutions of local government closer to the people they serve by establishing neighborhood outlets for local, state and federal administrative and public service agencies.

Expand opportunities for ghetto residents to participate in the formulation of public policy and the implementation of programs affecting them through improved political representation, creation of institutional channels for community action, expansion of legal services, and legislative hearings on ghetto problems.

. . .

Chapter 11—Police and the Community
The abrasive relationship between the police and the minority communities has been a major—and explosive—source of grievance, tension and disorder. The blame must be shared by the total society. . . .

The Commission recommends that city government and police authorities:

Review police operations in the ghetto to ensure proper conduct by police officers, and eliminate abrasive practices.

Provide more adequate police protection to ghetto residents to eliminate their high sense of insecurity, and the belief of many Negro citizens in the existence of a dual standard of law enforcement.

Establish fair and effective mechanisms for the redress of grievances against the police, and other municipal employees.

Develop and adopt policy guidelines to assist officers in making critical decisions in areas where police conduct can create tension.

Develop and use innovative programs to ensure widespread community support for law enforcement.

Recruit more Negroes into the regular police force, and review promotion policies to ensure fair promotion for Negro officers.

Establish a "Community Service Officer" program to attract ghetto youths between the ages of 17 and 21 to police work. These junior officers would perform duties to ghetto neighborhoods, but would not have full police authority. The federal government should provide support equal to 90 percent of the cost of employing CSOs on the basis of one for every ten regular officers.

Chapter 12—Control of Disorder
Preserving civil peace is the first responsibility of government. Unless the rule of law prevails, our society will lack not only order but also the environment essential to social and economic progress.

The maintenance of civil order cannot be left to the police alone. The police need guidance, as well as support, from mayors and other public officials. It is the responsibility of public officials to determine proper police policies, support adequate police standards for personnel and performance, and participate in planning for the control of disorders. . . .

The Commission believes there is a grave danger that some communities may resort to the indiscriminate and excessive use of force. The harmful effects of overreaction are incalculable. . . .

The Commission recognizes the sound principle of local authority and responsibility in law enforcement, but recommends that the federal government share in the financing of programs for improvement of police forces, both in their normal law enforcement activities as well as in their response to civil disorders. . . .

Chapter 13—The Administration of Justice Under Emergency Conditions

In many of the cities which experienced disorders last summer, there were recurring breakdowns in the mechanisms for processing, prosecuting and protecting arrested persons. These resulted mainly from long-standing structural deficiencies in criminal court systems, and from the failure of communities to anticipate and plan for the emergency demands of civil disorders.

In part, because of this, there were few successful prosecutions for serious crimes committed during the riots. In those cities where mass arrests occurred many arrestees were deprived of basic legal rights.

The Commission recommends that the cities and states:

Undertake reform of the lower courts so as to improve the quality of justice rendered under normal conditions.

Plan comprehensive measures by which the criminal justice system may be supplemented during civil disorders so that its deliberative functions are protected, and the quality of justice is maintained.

Such emergency plans require broad community participation and dedicated leadership by the bench and bar. They should include:

Laws sufficient to deter and punish riot conduct.

Additional judges, bail and probation officers, and clerical staff.

Arrangements for volunteer lawyers to help prosecutors and to represent riot defendants at every stage of proceedings.

Policies to ensure proper and individual bail, arraignment, pretrial, trial and sentencing proceedings.

Procedures for processing arrested persons, such as summons and release, and release on personal recognizance, which permit separation of minor offenders from those dangerous to the community, in order that serious offenders may be detained and prosecuted effectively.

Adequate emergency processing and detention facilities.

. . .

Chapter 15—The News Media and the Disorders

In his charge to the Commission, the President asked: "What effect do the mass media have on the riots?"

The Commission determined that the answer to the President's question did not lie solely in the performance of the press and broadcasters in reporting the riots. Our analysis had to consider also the overall treatment by the media of the Negro ghettos, community relations, racial attitudes, and poverty—day by day and month by month, year in and year out.

A wide range of interviews with government officials, law enforcement authorities, media personnel and other citizens, including ghetto residents, as well as a quantitative analysis of riot coverage and a special conference with industry representatives, leads us to conclude that:

Despite instances of sensationalism, inaccuracy and distortion, newspapers, radio and television tried on the whole to give a balanced, factual account of the 1967 disorders.

Elements of the news media failed to portray accurately the scale and character of the violence that occurred last summer. The overall effect was, we believe, an exaggeration of both mood and event.

Important segments of the media failed to report adequately on the causes and consequences of civil disorders and on the underlying problems of race relations. They have not communicated to the majority of their audience—which is white—a sense of the degradation, misery and hopelessness of life in the ghetto.

These failings must be corrected, and the improvement must come from within the industry. Freedom of the press is not the issue. Any effort to impose governmental restrictions would be inconsistent with fundamental constitutional precepts.

We have seen evidence that the news media are becoming aware of and concerned about their performance in this field. As that concern grows, coverage will improve. But much more must be done, and it must be done soon. . . .

Chapter 16—The Future of the Cities

By 1985, the Negro population in central cities is expected to increase by 72 percent to approximately 20.8 million. Coupled with the continued exodus of white families to the suburbs, this growth will produce majority Negro populations in many of the nation's largest cities.

The future of these cities, and of their burgeoning Negro populations, is grim. Most new employment opportunities are being created in suburbs and outlying areas. This trend will continue unless important changes in public policy are made.

In prospect, therefore, is further deterioration of already inadequate municipal tax bases in the face of increasing demands for public services, and continuing unemployment and poverty among the urban Negro population. Three choices are open to the nation:

We can maintain present policies, continuing both the proportion of the nation's resources now allocated to programs for the unemployed and the disadvantaged, and the inadequate and failing effort to achieve an integrated society.

We can adopt a policy of "enrichment" aimed at improving dramatically the quality of ghetto life while abandoning integration as a goal.

We can pursue integration by combining ghetto "enrichment" with policies which will encourage Negro movement out of central city areas.

. . . To continue present policies is to make permanent the division of our country into two societies; one, largely Negro and poor, located in the central cities; the other, predominantly white and affluent, located in the suburbs and in outlying areas.

The second choice, ghetto enrichment coupled with abandonment of integration, is also unacceptable. It is another way of choosing a permanently divided country. Moreover, equality cannot be achieved under conditions of nearly complete separation. In a country where the economy, and particularly the resources of employment, are predominantly white, a policy of separation can only relegate Negroes to a permanently inferior economic status.

We believe that the only possible choice for America is the third—a policy which combines ghetto enrichment with programs designed to encourage integration of substantial numbers of Negroes into the society outside the ghetto. . . .

Chapter 17—Recommendations For National Action

Introduction. No American—white or black—can escape the consequences of the continuing social and economic decay of our major cities.

Only a commitment to national action on an unprecedented scale can shape a future compatible with the historic ideals of American society.

The great productivity of our economy, and a federal revenue system which is highly responsive to economic growth, can provide the resources.

The major need is to generate new will—the will to tax ourselves to the extent necessary to meet the vital needs of the nation.

We have set forth goals and proposed strategies to reach those goals. We discuss and recommend programs not to commit each of us to specific parts of such programs but to illustrate the type and dimension of action needed.

The major goal is the creation of a true union—a single society and a single American identity. Toward that goal, we propose the following objectives for national action:

Opening up opportunities to those who are restricted by racial segregation and discrimination, and eliminating all barriers to their choice of jobs, education and housing.

Removing the frustration of powerlessness among the disadvantaged that affect their own lives and by increasing the capacity of our public and private institutions to respond to these problems.

Increasing communication across racial lines to destroy stereotypes, to halt polarization, end distrust and hostility, and create common ground for efforts toward public order and social justice.

We propose these aims to fulfill our pledge of equality and to meet the fundamental needs of a democratic and civilized society—domestic peace and social justice.

Employment. Pervasive unemployment and underemployment are the most persistent and serious grievances in minority areas. They are inextricably linked to the problem of civil disorder.

Despite growing federal expenditures for manpower development and training programs, and sustained general economic prosperity and increasing demands for skilled workers, about two million—white and nonwhite—are permanently unemployed. About ten million are underemployed, of whom 6.5 million work full time for wages below the poverty line.

The 500,000 "hard-core" unemployed in the central cities who lack a basic education and are unable to hold a steady job are made up in large part of Negro males between the ages of 18 and 25. In the riot cities which we surveyed, Negroes were three times as likely as whites to hold unskilled jobs, which are often part time, seasonal, low-paying and "dead end." . . .

Education. Education in a democratic society must equip children to develop their potential and to participate fully in American life. For the community at large, the schools have discharged this responsibility well. But for many minorities, and particularly for the children of the ghetto, the schools have failed to provide the educational experience which could overcome the effects of discrimination and deprivation.

This failure is one of the persistent sources of grievance and resentment within the Negro community. The hostility of Negro parents and students toward the school system is generating increasing conflict and causing disruption within many city school districts. But the most dramatic evidence of the relationship between educational practices and civil disorders lies in the high incidence of riot participation by ghetto youth who have not completed high school.

The bleak record of public education for ghetto children is growing worse. In the critical skills—verbal and reading ability—Negro students are falling further behind whites with each year of school completed. The high unemployment and underemployment rate for Negro youth is evidence, in part, of the growing educational crisis. . . .

The welfare system. Our present system of public welfare is designed to save money instead of people, and tragically ends up doing neither. This system has two critical deficiencies:

First, it excludes large numbers of persons who are in great need, and who, if provided a decent level of support, might be able to become more productive and self-sufficient. No federal funds are available for millions of men and women who are needy but neither aged, handicapped nor the parents of minor children.

Second, for those included, the system provides assistance well below the minimum necessary for a decent level of existence, and imposes restrictions that encourage continued dependency on welfare and undermine self-respect.

A welter of statutory requirements and administrative practices and regulations operate to remind recipients that they are considered untrustworthy, promiscuous and lazy. Residence requirements prevent assistance to people in need who are newly arrived in the state. Regular searches of recipients' homes violate privacy. Inadequate social services compound the problems. . . .

As a long-range goal, the Commission recommends that the federal government seek to develop a national system of income supplementation based strictly on need with two broad and basic purposes:

To provide, for those who can work or who do work, any necessary supplements in such a way as to develop incentives for fuller employment;

To provide, for those who cannot work and for mothers who decide to remain with their children, a minimum standard of decent living, and to aid in the saving of children from the prison of poverty that has held their parents.

. . .

Housing. After more than three decades of fragmented and grossly underfunded federal housing programs, nearly six million substandard housing units remain occupied in the United States.

The housing problem is particularly acute in the minority ghettos. Nearly two-thirds of all non-white families living in the central cities today live in neighborhoods marked with substandard housing and general urban blight. Two major factors are responsible.

First: Many ghetto residents simply cannot pay the rent necessary to support decent housing. In Detroit, for example, over 40 percent of the non-white occupied units in 1960 required rent of over 35 percent of the tenants' income.

Second: Discrimination prevents access to many non-slum areas, particularly the suburbs, where good housing exists. In addition, by creating a "back pressure" in the racial ghettos, it makes it possible for landlords to break up apartments for denser occupancy, and keeps prices and rents of deteriorated ghetto housing higher than they would be in a truly free market.

To date, federal programs have been able to do comparatively little to provide housing for the disadvantaged. In the 31-year history of subsidized federal housing, only about 800,000 units have been constructed, with recent production averaging about 50,000 units a year. By comparison, over a period of only three years longer, FHA insurance guarantees have made possible the construction of over ten million middle and upper-income units.

Two points are fundamental to the Commission's recommendations:

First: Federal housing programs must be given a new thrust aimed at overcoming the prevailing patterns of racial segregation. . . .

Second: The private sector must be brought into the production and financing of low and moderate rental housing to supply the capabilities and capital necessary to meet the housing needs of the nation. . . .

Conclusion. . . . We have provided an honest beginning. We have learned much. But we have uncovered no startling truths, no unique insights, no simple solutions. The destruction and the bitterness of racial disorder, the harsh polemics of black revolt and white repression have been seen and heard before in this country.

It is time now to end the destruction and the violence, not only in the streets of the ghetto but in the lives of people.

32

RACE, CONFLICT,
AND URBAN POLITICS

John H. Strange

The proposals that I make are based upon the argument that conflicts cannot be resolved by being avoided. It is this belief, I feel, that has been central to the theories and recommendations of the urban "reformers." They sought to solve the problem of conflict by limiting the issues settled through conflict, by attempting to remove politics from local government. I call for just the opposite: the establishment of conditions which will increase the number of issues around which there is conflict and which are decided, from moment to moment, through politics. I also advocate the development of new and better weapons with which Negroes can engage in political conflict in order that the outputs of the system will thereby be more egalitarian and also to insure that weapons of a more violent sort will not be necessary.

First, I suggest reform of voting and registration practices to insure the maximum registration of Negroes. I also advocate the financing of voter registration drives by private groups and the federal government. Prior to 1967 a number of community action programs engaged in "voter education activities" and registration drives. In that year a Congress unhappy with OEO prohibited such activities.

Reprinted from John H. Strange, "Race, Conflict, and Urban Politics," pp. 17-21, a paper prepared for the third Conference on Democratic Theory, November 14-16, 1968, Airlie House, Warrenton, Virginia.

The Congressmen who led the fight to prohibit voter education and registration activities by OEO employees were concerned that efforts by "poverty workers" in Durham and other North Carolina communities were succeeding in getting large numbers of Negroes registered to vote. I argue that it is *absolutely necessary* to insure that this basic method of political participation by Negroes be maximized, by whatever means possible.

Second, I urge the abandonment of many of the earlier reforms advocated by urban specialists. The re-establishment of wards as electoral districts could enhance the political power of Negroes. Relaxation of civil service regulations, modification of professional criteria now used in filling jobs and offices, and an appreciation of the contribution made by patronage in assimilating earlier ethnic groups could also give Negroes greater advantages in the political system. OEO programs and expanded mail deliveries are only two possibilities for increased patronage positions.

Third, I advocate the expansion of the application of current OEO provisions calling for the "maximum feasible participation" of the poor. Despite the fact that the inclusion of this phase in the Economic Opportunity Act of 1964 was an accident, and despite recent attacks upon the concept by politicians and bureaucrats alike, there is some evidence to indicate that it has affected the programs and policies of the Office of Economic Opportunity and its local agencies.[1] Housing authorities, school boards, city councils, urban renewal authorities, barber, electrical and heating contractor licensing boards, and all the other agencies of local government would, most likely, govern in a different manner if Negroes and the poor had, *by right*, access to positions of influence within these councils.

Fourth, I suggest the widespread adoption of the concept of advocacy planning for the poor which has been put forth by Professor Davidoff of Hunter College. Such arrangements would provide an opportunity for the desires of Negroes and the poor to be taken into account.[2]

Fifth, we need to devise some procedures which will enable Negroes and poor people to enter politics more rapidly. The number of Negro lawyers needs to be increased dramatically. (In 1966 there were only 84 Negro lawyers in North Carolina or 7.2 Negro lawyers per 100,000 Negroes. Comparable figures for whites were 5,000 lawyers or 147.2 per 100,000 whites.) And we must devise some way to allow Negroes and poor people to run for office without permanently risking their livelihood. V. O. Key, Jr. has noted the importance of participation in politics by members of *all* economic strata. Key says:

[1] See The North Carolina Fund, "Community Action in North Carolina;" Peter Marris and Martin Rein, "Dilemmas of Social Reform: Poverty and Community Action in the United States," Atherton Press, 1967; Sar A. Levitan, "The Design of Federal Anti-Poverty Strategy," Institute of Labor and Industrial Relations, the University of Michigan and Wayne State University, 1967; and Daniel P. Moynihan, What is Community Action?, *The Public Interest*, **2**, p. 5, Fall 1966.

[2] See Paul Davidoff, Advocacy and Pluralism in Planning, *Journal of the American Institute of Planners*, **31**, pp. 331-338, November 1965.

Another characteristic may be mentioned as one that, if not a prerequisite to government by public opinion, may profoundly affect the nature of a democratic order. This is the distribution through the social structure of those persons highly active in politics. . . . Conceivably the winning of consent and the creation of a sense of political participation and of sharing in public affairs may be far simpler when political activists of some degree are spread through all social strata. The alternative circumstance may induce an insensitivity to mass opinion, a special reliance on mass communications, and a sharpened sense of cleavage and separation within the political order. . . . In a modern industrial society with universal suffrage the chances are that a considerable sprinkling of political activists needs to exist in groups below the "middle class," however that term of vague referent may be defined.[3]

To facilitate this, governmental and/or private foundation support of programs to train young blacks for politics, including the provision of experience in politics, should be encouraged. One such program at Morgan State College, currently funded by the Ford Foundation, will soon be ended because of the reluctance of the Maryland state legislature to continue the program.

Sixth, I would encourage the granting of control to local neighborhoods (in effect, Negroes) for the operation of schools and other public services.

Seventh, support for efforts at the organization of the poor into effective, trained, and determined political groups should be encouraged either through government or private financing. OEO has, in the past, supported community organization efforts, but such efforts have recently been under considerable attack. Indeed, OEO itself is severely threatened.

Although no complete study on the impact of community organization has been completed, my research indicates that poor who are organized are more likely to participate in politics through non-violent means (that is if the organizations are allowed to play the game of politics and to share in the distribution of rewards). My studies also indicate that demands are made more precise as a result of community organization. This facilitates the response of the political system, if it can be forced into a response. It also makes it possible for the political participants to know when they are victorious and thus increases a respect for and interest in the continued operation of the existing system. By the same token, of course, a system which does not respond is more readily observed, and, most likely, more prone to attack.[4]

Eighth, and finally, efforts must be made to document the ways in which

[3]V.O. Key, Jr., "Public Opinion and American Democracy," pp. 541-542, Knopf, 1961.

[4]See Strange, The Politics of Protest. . . , and The North Carolina Fund, "Community Action in North Carolina." For a more complete examination of the impact of the poverty program see Howard W. Hallman, The Community Action Program—An Interpretative Analysis of 35 Communities, in U.S. Senate Committee on Labor and Public Welfare, "Examination of the War on Poverty," Volume IV, pp. 897-923, Government Printing Office, 1967.

attempts to remove issues from politics are disadvantageous to the poor and the Negro. In this way modifications of reforms previously implemented may be accomplished, advocates of anti-political reforms may be silenced or decreased in number, and future bureaucrats may come to have a healthy appreciation of the role of conflict and of politics.

In conclusion, my argument is that we must understand that conflict is central to the political process, that the outcome or results of conflict are as important as the methods employed in the conflict, that Negroes must be given increased tools of a non-violent type with which to enter into political conflict (or we can expect the use of violence), and finally, that we have a responsibility as citizens, as well as political scientists, to use whatever understanding of the political process we have for practical ends.

33

ISOLATION, POWERLESSNESS, AND VIOLENCE: A STUDY OF ATTITUDES AND PARTICIPATION IN THE WATTS RIOT

H. Edward Ransford

ABSTRACT

The hypothesis that isolated individuals are more prone to extremism is tested, using a sample of Los Angeles Negroes interviewed shortly after the Watts riot. It is found that racial isolation (low degrees of intimate white contact) is strongly associated with a willingness to use violence under two subjective conditions: (*a*) when isolated individuals feel a sense of powerlessness in the society and (*b*) when such isolated individuals are highly dissatisfied with their treatment as Negroes. Ideal types of the most and least violence-prone are developed from the cumulative effects of the three independent variables (isolation, powerlessness, and dissatisfaction).

Since the summer of 1965, it is no longer possible to describe the Negroes' drive for new rights as a completely non-violent protest.[1] Urban ghettos have

Reprinted from H. Edward Ransford, Isolation, Powerlessness, and Violence, *The American Journal of Sociology*, **73**, pp. 581-591.

[1] I am greatly indebted to Melvin Seeman and Robert Hagedorn for helpful comments and advice on earlier drafts of this paper. This is a revised version of a paper presented at the annual meetings of the Pacific Sociological Association, Long Beach, Calif., April, 1967.

burst at the seams. Angry shouts from the most frustrated and deprived segments of the Negro community now demand that we recognize violence as an important facet of the Negro revolution.

In attempts to understand the increase in violence, much has been said about unemployment, police brutality, poor schools, and inadequate housing as contributing factors.[2] However, there are few sociological studies concerning the characteristics of the participants or potential participants in racial violence.[3] Little can be said about which minority individuals are likely to view violence as a justifiable means of correcting racial injustices. It is the purpose of this paper to identify such individuals—specifically, to identify those Negroes who were willing to use violence as a method during a period shortly after the Watts riot.

A THEORETICAL PERSPECTIVE

Studies dealing with political extremism and radical protest have often described the participants in such action as being isolated or weakly tied to the institutions of the community.[4] Kerr and Siegel demonstrated this relationship with their finding that wildcat strikes are more common among isolated occupational groups, such as mining, maritime, and lumbering.[5] These isolated groups are believed to have a weak commitment to public pressures and the democratic norms of the community. Thus, when grievances are felt intensely and the bonds to the instututions of the community are weak, there is likely to be an explosion of discontent (the strike) rather than use of negotiation or other normative channels of expression.

More recently, mass society theory has articulated this relationship between isolation and extremism.[6] The mass society approach sees current structural

[2] See, e.g., "Violence in the City—an End or a Beginning?" (report of the Governor's Commission on the Los Angeles Riots, December 2, 1965 [commonly known as the "McCone Commission Report"]).

[3] One of the very few studies of the potential participants in race violence was conducted by Kenneth B. Clark, shortly after the Harlem riot of 1943. (See Clark, Group Violence: A Preliminary Study of the Attitudinal Pattern of Its Acceptance and Rejection: A Study of the 1943 Harlem Riot, *Journal of Social Psychology*, **XIX**, pp. 319-337, 1944; see also Alfred McClung Lee and Norman D. Humphrey, "Race Riot," pp. 80-87, Dryden Press, New York, 1943.)

[4] See, e.g., William Kornhauser, "The Politics of Mass Society," pp. 183-223, Free Press, Glencoe, Ill., 1959; Seymour Martin Lipset, "Political Man: The Social Bases of Politics," pp. 94-130, Doubleday & Co., New York, 1960; and Clark Kerr and Abraham Siegel, The Interindustry Propensity to Strike—An International Comparison, "Industrial Conflict," eds. Arthur Kornhauser, Robert Dubin, Arthur M. Ross, pp. 189-212, McGraw-Hill Book Co., New York, 1954.

[5] Kerr and Siegel, *op. cit.*

[6] W. Kornhauser, *op. cit.*; and Leon Bramson, "The Political Context of Sociology," p. 72, Princeton University Press, Princeton, N.J., 1961.

processes—such as the decline in kinship, the increase in mobility, and the rise of huge bureaucracies—as detaching many individuals from sources of control, meaning, and personal satisfaction. Those who are most isolated from centers of power are believed to be more vulnerable to authoritarian outlooks and more available for volatile mass movements. Indeed, Kornhauser instructs us that the whole political stability of a society is somewhat dependent upon its citizens being tied meaningfully to the institutions of the community.[7] He suggests that participation in secondary organizations—such as unions and business groups—serves to mediate between the individual and the nation, tying the individual to the democratic norms of the society.

The relationship between structural isolation and extremism is further accentuated by the personal alienation of the individual. Isolated people are far more likely than non-isolated people to feel cut off from the larger society and to feel an inability to control events in the society.[8] This subjective alienation may heighten the individual's readiness to engage in extreme behavior. For example, Horton and Thompson find that perceived powerlessness is related to protest voting.[9] Those with feelings of political powerlessness were more likely to be dissatisfied with their position in society and to hold resentful attitudes toward community leaders. The study suggests that the discontent of the powerless group was converted to action through the vote—a vote of "no" on a local bond issue being a form of negativism in which the individual strikes out at community powers. This interpretation of alienation as a force for protest is consistent with the original Marxian view of the concept in which alienation leads to a radical attack upon the existing social structure.[10]

In summary, there are two related approaches commonly used to explain participation in extreme political behavior. The first deals with the degree to which the individual is structurally isolated or tied to community institutions. The second approach deals with the individual's awareness and evaluation of his isolated condition—for example, his feeling of a lack of control over critical matters or his feeling of discontent due to a marginal position in society. Following this orientation, this research employs the concepts of racial isolation, perceived powerlessness, and racial dissatisfaction as theoretical tools for explaining the participation of Negroes in violence.

[7] W. Kornhauser, *op. cit.*

[8] E.g., Neal and Seeman found that isolated workers (non-participants in unions) were more likely to feel powerless to effect outcomes in the society than the participants in unions (Arthur G. Neal and Melvin Seeman, Organizations and Powerlessness: A Test of the Mediation Hypothesis, *American Sociological Review,* **XXIX**, pp. 216-226, 1964).

[9] John E. Horton and Wayne E. Thompson, Powerlessness and Political Negativism: A Study of Defeated Local Referendums, *American Journal of Sociology,* **LXVII**, pp. 485-493, 1962. For another report on the same study, see Wayne E. Thompson and John E. Horton, Political Alienation as a Force in Political Action, *Social Forces,* **XXXVIII**, pp. 190-195, 1960.

[10] Erich Fromm, Alienation under Capitalism, "Man Alone," eds. Eric and Mary Josephson, pp. 56-73, Dell Publishing Co., New York, 1962.

STUDY DESIGN AND HYPOTHESIS

In the following discussion, the three independent variables of this study (isolation, powerlessness, and dissatisfaction) are discussed separately and jointly, as predictors of violence participation.

RACIAL ISOLATION

Ralph Ellison has referred to the Negro in this country as the "invisible man."[11] Although this is a descriptive characterization, sociological studies have attempted to conceptualize more precisely the isolation of the American Negro. For example, those studying attitudes of prejudice often view racial isolation as a lack of free and easy contact on an intimate and equal status basis.[12] Though the interracial contact may be frequent, it often involves such wide status differentials that it does not facilitate candid communication, nor is it likely to give the minority person a feeling that he has some stake in the system. In this paper, intimate white contact is viewed as a mediating set of relationships that binds the ethnic individual to majority-group values—essentially conservative values that favor working through democratic channels rather than violently attacking the social system. Accordingly, it is reasoned that Negroes who are more racially isolated (by low degrees of intimate contact with whites) will have fewer channels of communication to air their grievances and will feel little commitment to the leaders and institutions of the community. This group, which is blocked from meaningful white communication, should be more willing to use violent protest than the groups with greater involvement in white society.

POWERLESSNESS AND RACIAL DISSATISFACTION

In contrast to structural isolation, powerlessness and racial dissatisfaction are the subjective components of our theoretical scheme. A feeling of powerlessness is one form of alienation. It is defined in this research as a low expectancy of control over events.[13] This attitude is seen as an appropriate variable for

[11] Ralph Ellison, "Invisible Man," Random House, New York, 1952.

[12] Many studies have brought forth the finding that equal status contact between majority and minority members is associated with tolerance and favorable attitudes. For the most recent evidence of the equal status proposition, see Robin Williams, "Strangers Next Door," Prentice-Hall, Inc., Englewood Cliffs, N.J., 1964. For an earlier study, see Morton Deutsch and Mary E. Collins, "Interracial Housing," University of Minnesota Press, Minneapolis, 1951.

[13] This definition of subjective powerlessness is taken from the conceptualization proposed by Melvin Seeman, On the Meaning of Alienation, *American Sociological Review*, **XXIV**, pp. 783-791, 1959.

Negroes living in segregated ghettos; that is, groups which are blocked from full participation in the society are more likely to feel powerless in that society. Powerlessness is also a variable that seems to have a logical relationship to violent protest. Briefly, it is reasoned that Negroes who feel powerless to change their position or to control crucial decisions that affect them will be more willing to use violent means to get their rights than those who feel some control or efficacy within the social system. For the Negro facing extreme discrimination barriers, an attitude of powerlessness is simply a comment on the society, namely, a belief that all channels for social redress are closed.

Our second attitude measure, racial dissatisfaction, is defined as the degree to which the individual feels that he is being treated badly because of his race. It is a kind of racial alienation in the sense that the individual perceives his position in society to be illegitimate, due to racial discrimination. The Watts violence represented an extreme expression of frustration and discontent. We would expect those highly dissatisfied with their treatment as Negroes to be the participants in such violence. Thus, the "highs" in racial dissatisfaction should be more willing to use violence than the "lows" in this attitude. In comparing our two forms of subjective alienation (powerlessness and racial dissatisfaction), it is important to note that, although we expect some correlation between the two attitudes (a certain amount of resentment and dissatisfaction should accompany the feeling of powerlessness), we propose to show that they make an independent contribution to violence.

UNIFICATION OF PREDICTIVE VARIABLES

We believe that the fullest understanding of violence can be brought to bear by use of a social-psychological design in which the structural variable (racial isolation) is joined with the subjective attitudes of the individual (powerlessness and dissatisfaction).

In this design, we attempt to specify the conditions under which isolation has its strongest effect upon violence. It is reasoned that racial isolation should be most important for determining participation in violence (a) when individuals feel powerless to shape their destiny under existing conditions or (b) when individuals are highly dissatisfied with their racial treatment. Each of the attitudes is seen as a connecting bridge of logic between racial isolation and violence.

For the first case (that of powerlessness), we are stating that a weak attachment to the majority group and its norms should lead to a radical break from law and order when individuals perceive they cannot effect events important to them; that is, they cannot change their racial position through activity within institutional channels. Violence, in this instance, becomes an alternative pathway of expression and gain. Conversely, racial isolation should have much less effect upon violence when persons feel some control in the system.

For the second case (racial dissatisfaction), we believe isolation should have a far greater effect upon violence when dissatisfaction over racial treatment is intense. Isolation from the society then becomes critical to violence in the sense that the dissatisfied person feels little commitment to the legal order and is more likely to use extreme methods as an outlet for his grievances. Statistically speaking, we expect an interaction effect between isolation and powerlessness, and between isolation and dissatisfaction, in the prediction of violence.[14]

METHODS

Our hypotheses call for measures of intimate white contact, perceived powerlessness, and perceived racial dissatisfaction as independent variables, and willingness to use violence as a dependent variable. The measurement of these variables, and also the sampling techniques, are discussed at this time.

SOCIAL CONTACT

The type of social contact to be measured had to be of an intimate and equal status nature, a kind of contact that would facilitate easy communication between the races. First, each Negro respondent was asked if he had current contact with white people in a series of situations: on the job, in his neighborhood, in organizations to which he belongs, and in other situations (such as shopping). After this general survey of white contacts, the respondent was asked, "Have you ever done anything social with these white people, like going to the movies together or visiting in each other's homes?"[15] The responses formed a simple dichotomous variable: "high" contact scores for those who had done something social (61 per cent of the sample) and "low" contact scores for those who had little or no social contact (39 per cent).[16]

[14] In contrast to the mass society perspective, in which structural isolation is viewed as a cause of subjective alienation, we are viewing the two as imperfectly correlated. For example, many Negroes with contact (non-isolates) may still feel powerless due to racial discrimination barriers. We are thus stressing the partial independence of objective and subjective alienation and feel it necessary to consider both variables for the best prediction of violence.

[15] This question was taken from Robin Williams, *op. cit.*, p. 185.

[16] As a further indication that this measure was tapping a more intimate form of interracial contact, it can be noted that 88 per cent of those reporting social contact with whites claimed at least one "good friend" ("to whom you can say what you really think") or "close friend" ("to whom you can talk over confidential matters"). Only 10 per cent of those lacking social contact claimed such friendships with white people.

POWERLESSNESS

Following the conceptualization of Melvin Seeman, powerlessness is defined as a low expectancy of control over events.[17] Twelve forced-choice items were used to tap this attitude.[18] The majority of items dealt with expectations of control over the political system. The following is an example:

The world is run by the few people in power, and there is not much the little guy can do about it.

The average citizen can have an influence on government decisions.

After testing the scale items for reliability,[19] the distribution of scores was dichotomized at the median.

RACIAL DISSATISFACTION

The attitude of racial dissatisfaction is defined as the degree to which the individual feels he is being treated badly because of his race. A five-item scale was developed to measure this attitude. The questions ask the Negro respondent to compare his treatment (in such areas as housing, work, and general treatment in the community) with various reference groups, such as the southern Negro or the white. Each of the five questions allows a reply on one of three levels: no dissatisfaction, mild dissatisfaction, and intense dissatisfaction. Typical of the items is the following: "If you compare your opportunities and the treatment you get from whites in Los Angeles with Negroes living in the South, would you say you are much better off——a little better off——or treated about the same as the southern Negro——?" After a reliability check of the items, replies to the dissatisfaction measure were dichotomized into high and low groups.[20] The cut was made conceptually, rather than at the median, yielding 99 "highs" and 213 "lows" in dissatisfaction.[21]

[17]Seeman, *op. cit.*

[18]The powerlessness scale was developed by Shephard Liverant, Jullian B. Rotter, and Melvin Seeman—see Jullian B. Rotter, Generalized Expectancies for Internal vs. External Control of Reinforcements, *Psychological Monographs,* **LXXX**, no. 1, pp. 1-28, (Whole No. 609, 1966).

[19]Using the Kuder-Richardson test for reliability, a coefficient of .77 was obtained for the twelve items.

[20]Kuder-Richardson coefficient of .84.

[21]With a cut at the median, a good many people ($N = 59$) who were mildly dissatisfied on all five items would have been placed in the "high" category. It was decided that a more accurate description of the "high" category would require the person to express maximum dissatisfaction on at least one of the five items and mild dissatisfaction on the other four.

VIOLENCE WILLINGNESS

The dependent variable of the study is willingness to use violence. Violence is defined in the context of the Watts riot as the willingness to use direct aggression against the groups that are believed to be discriminating, such as the police and white merchants. The question used to capture this outlook is, "Would you be willing to use violence to get Negro rights?" With data gathered so shortly after the Watts violence, it was felt that the question would be clearly understood by respondents.[22] At the time of data collection, buildings were still smoldering; violence in the form of looting, burning, and destruction was not a remote possibility, but a tangible reality. The violence-prone group numbered eighty-three.

A second measure of violence asked the person if he had ever used violent methods to get Negro rights.[23] Only sixteen respondents of the 312 reported (or admitted) that they had participated in actual violence. As a result of this very small number the item is used as an indicator of trends but is not employed as a basic dependent variable of the study.

SAMPLE

The sample was composed of three-hundred-twelve Negro males who were heads of the household and between the ages of eighteen and sixty-five. The subjects responded to an interview schedule administered by Negro interviewers. They were chosen by random methods and were interviewed in their own homes or apartments. Both employed and unemployed respondents were included in the sample, although the former were emphasized in the sampling procedure (269 employed in contrast to 43 unemployed). The sample was drawn from three major areas of Los Angeles: a relatively middle-class and integrated area (known as the "Crenshaw" district) and the predominantly lower-class and highly segregated communities of "South Central" and "Watts." The sample could be classified as "disproportional stratified" because the proportion of subjects drawn from each of the three areas does not correspond to the actual distribution of Negroes in Los Angeles. For example, it was decided that an approximate fifty-fifty split between middle- and lower-class respondents would be desirable for later analysis. This meant, however, that Crenshaw (middle-class) Negroes

---

[22] As an indication that the question was interpreted in the context of participation in violence of the Watts variety, it can be noted that our question was correlated with approval of the Watts riot ($\phi = .62$).

[23] The question, "Have you ever participated in violent action for Negro rights?" was purposely worded in general terms to avoid accusing the respondent of illegal behavior during the Watts violence. However, racial violence in the United States was somewhat rare at that time, so it is likely that most of the sixteen respondents were referring to participation in the Watts violence.

were considerably overrepresented, since their characteristics are not typical of the Los Angeles Negro community as a whole, and the majority of Los Angeles Negroes do not reside in this, or any similar, area.

Table 1—Percentage willing to use violence, by social contact, powerlessness, and racial dissatisfaction

Variables	Not Willing (%)	Willing (%)	Total (%)
Social contact:*			
High	83	17	100 (N = 192)
Low	56	44	100 (N = 110)
Powerlessness:†			
High	59	41	100 (N = 145)
Low	84	16	100 (N = 160)
Racial dissatisfaction: ‡			
High	52	48	100 (N = 98)
Low	83	17	100 (N = 212)

*$\chi^2 = 24.93, P < .001.$
†$\chi^2 = 22.59, P < .001.$
‡$\chi^2 = 30.88, P < .001.$

NOTE.—In this table and the tables that follow, there are often less than 312 cases due to missing data for one or more variables.

RESULTS

We have predicted a greater willingness to use violent methods for three groups: the isolated, the powerless, and the dissatisfied. The data presented in Table 1 confirm these expectations. For all three cases, the percentage differences are statistically significant at better than the .001 level.

The empirical evidence supports our contention that Negroes who are more disengaged from the society, in the structural (isolation) and subjective (power-lessness and racial dissatisfaction) senses, are more likely to view violence as necessary for racial justice than those more firmly tied to the society.

It is one thing to establish a relationship based on action willingness and quite another thing to study actual behavior. Unfortunately, only sixteen of the 312 respondents (5 per cent) admitted participation in violent action for Negro rights. This small number did, however, provide some basis for testing our hypotheses. Of the sixteen who participated in violent action, eleven were isolates while only five had social contact. More impressive is the fact that fifteen of the sixteen "violents" scored high in powerlessness, and thirteen of the sixteen felt high degrees of dissatisfaction. Even with a small number, these are definite relationships, encouraging an interpretation that those who are willing to use violence and those who reported actual violent behavior display the same tendency toward powerlessness, racial dissatisfaction, and isolation.

The next task is to explore the interrelationships among our predictive variables. For example, we have argued that powerlessness has a specific meaning to violence (a low expectancy of changing conditions within the institutional framework) that should be more than a generalized disaffection; that is, we expected our measures of powerlessness and racial dissatisfaction to have somewhat unique effects upon violence.

The data indicated an interaction effect (interaction $\chi^2 = 7.85$; $P < .01$)[24] between the two attitudes. The feeling of powerlessness is a more relevant determiner of violence for the highly dissatisfied or angry Negro. Similarly, racial dissatisfaction is far more important to violence for those who feel powerless. In sum, the data suggest that the powerless Negro is likely to use violence when his feelings of powerlessness are accompanied by intense dissatisfaction with his position. It can be noted, however, that, even among those who were relatively satisfied with racial conditions, powerlessness had some effect upon violence (a 13 per cent difference, $\chi^2 = 5.41$; $P = .02$). Presumably, a low expectancy of exerting control has a somewhat unique effect upon violence.

As a second way of noting an interrelationship between our predictive variables, we turn to the more crucial test of the isolation-extremism perspective in which the effect of racial isolation upon violence is controlled by powerlessness and dissatisfaction.[25] It will be recalled that we expected the isolated people (with a lower commitment to democratic norms and organized channels) to be more violence-prone when these isolated individuals perceive they cannot shape their destiny within the institutional framework (high powerlessness) or when they perceive differential treatment as Negroes and, as a result, are dissatisfied. It is under these subjective states of mind that a weak attachment to the majority group would seem to be most important to extremism. Table 2, addressed to these predictions, shows our hypotheses to be strongly supported in both cases.

Among the powerless and the dissatisfied, racial isolation has a strong effect upon violence commitment. Conversely, the data show that isolation is much less relevant to violence for those with feelings of control in the system and for the more satisfied (in both cases, significant only at the .20 level).[26]

---

[24] The χ^2 interaction test is somewhat analogous to the interaction test in the analysis of variance. A total χ^2 is first computed from the two partial tables in which all three variables are operating. Second, χ^2 values are obtained by cross-tabulating each possible pair of variables (e.g., $\chi^2 AB$, $\chi^2 AC$, and $\chi^2 BC$). These three separate χ^2 values are then summed and subtracted from the total χ^2. The residual, or what is left after subtraction, is the interaction χ^2. It can be viewed as the joint or special effect that comes when predictive variables are operating simultaneously. For a further description of this measure, see Phillip H. DuBois and David Gold, Some Requirements and Suggestions for Quantitative Methods in Behavioral Science Research, "Decisions, Values and Groups," ed. Norman F. Washburne, II, pp. 42-65, Pergamon Press, New York, 1962.

[25] The independent variables are moderately intercorrelated. For isolation and powerlessness, the ϕ correlation is .36, $P < .001$; for isolation and dissatisfaction, the ϕ is .40, $P < .001$; for powerlessness and dissatisfaction, the ϕ is .33, $P < .001$.

[26] The .05 level is considered significant in this analysis.

Table 2–Percentage willing to use violence, by social contact controlling for powerlessness and racial dissatisfaction

	Percentage Willing To Use Violence			
	Low Power-lessness (%)	*High Power-lessness (%)*	*Low Dis-satisfaction (%)*	*High Dis-satisfaction (%)*
Low contact	23 (N = 31)	53 (N = 78)	23 (N = 47)	59 (N = 63)
High contact	13 (N = 123)	26 (N = 66)	15 (N = 158)	26 (N = 34)
x^2	P < .20	P < .01	P < .20	P < .01

NOTE.–The interaction x^2 between powerlessness and contact: $P < .05$. The interaction x^2 between dissatisfaction and contact: $P < .01$.

The fact that isolation (as a cause of violence) produces such a small percentage difference for the less alienated subjects calls for a further word of discussion. Apparently, isolation is not only a stronger predictor of violence for the people who feel powerless and dissatisfied, but is *only* a clear and significant determiner of violence for these subjectively alienated persons. For the relatively satisfied and control-oriented groups, the fact of being isolated is not very important in determining violence. This would suggest that a weak normative bond to the majority group (isolation) is not in itself sufficient to explain the participation of the oppressed minority person in violence and that it is the interaction between isolation and feelings of powerlessness (or racial dissatisfaction) that is crucial for predicting violence.

A final attempt at unification involves the cumulative effect of all three of our predictive variables upon violence. Since it was noted that each of the three predictive variables has some effect upon violence (either independently or for specific subgroups), it seemed logical that the combined effect of the three would produce a high violence propensity. Conceptually, a combination of these variables could be seen as ideal types of the alienated and non-alienated Negro. Accordingly, Table 3 arranges the data into these ideal-type combinations.

Table 3–Percentage willing to use violence, by the combined effect of social contact, powerlessness, and racial dissatisfaction

	Not Willing (%)	*Willing (%)*	*Total (%)*
Ideal-type alienated (low contact, high powerlessness, and high dissatisfaction)	35	65	100 (N = 51)
Middles in alienation	76	24	100 (N = 147)
Ideal-type non-alienated (high contact, low powerlessness, and low dissatisfaction)	88	12	100 (N = 107)

NOTE.–$x^2 = 49.37; P < .001$ (2 d.f.).

The group at the top of the table represents the one most detached from society—individuals who are isolated and high in attitudes of powerlessness and dissatisfaction. The group at the bottom of the table is the most involved in the society; these people have intimate white contact, feelings of control, and greater satisfaction with racial conditions. The middle group is made up of those with different combinations of high and low detachment. Note the dramatic difference in willingness to use violence between the "ideal-type" alienated group (65 per cent willing) and the group most bound to society (only 12 per cent willing). The "middles" in alienation display a score in violence between these extremes.

SPURIOUSNESS

It is possible that the relationship between our predictive variables and violence is due to an intercorrelation with other relevant variables. For example, social class should be related both to violence and to our isolation-alienation measures. In addition, we could expect a greater propensity toward violence in geographical areas where an extreme breakdown of legal controls occurred, such as the South Central and Watts areas (in contrast to the Crenshaw area, where no rioting took place). In such segregated ghettos, violence may have been defined by the inhabitants as a legitimate expression, given their intolerable living conditions, a group definition that could override any effects of isolation or alienation upon violence. In short, it seems essential to control our isolation-alienation variables by an index of social class and by ghetto area.[27]

Because of the rather small violent group, it is necessary to examine our predictive variables separately in this analysis of controls. Table 4 presents the original relationship between each of the independent variables and violence, controlled by two areas of residence: the South Central-Watts area, at the heart of the curfew zone (where violence occurred), and the Crenshaw area, on the periphery (or outside) of the curfew zone (where violent action was rare). In addition, Table 4 includes a control for education, as a measure of social class.[28]

When the ghetto residence of the respondent is held constant, it appears that our independent variables are important in their own right. Education (social class), however, proved to be a more powerful control variable. Among the college educated, only isolation persists as a predictor of violence; powerlessness and racial dissatisfaction virtually drop out. Yet each variable has a very strong

[27] Age was also considered as a control variable but was dropped when it was discovered that age was not correlated with violence or the independent variables. The r's ranged from .04 to .09.

[28] For this sample, education was believed to be superior to other indexes of class. It is an index that is freer (than either occupation or income) from the societal restrictions and discrimination that Negroes face. Also, it was discovered that Negro occupations in the more deprived ghetto areas were not comparable to the same occupations listed in standardized scales, such as the North-Hatt or Bogue scales.

effect upon violence among the high school (lower-class) group. In other words, we do not have an instance of spuriousness, where predictive variables are explained away in both partials, but another set of interaction effects—attitudes of powerlessness and dissatisfaction are predictors of violence only among lower-class respondents. These results may be interpreted in several ways. Persons higher in the class structure may have a considerable amount to lose, in terms of occupational prestige and acceptance in white society, by endorsing extreme methods. The college educated (middle class) may be unwilling to risk their position, regardless of feelings of powerlessness and dissatisfaction. These results may further indicate that middle-class norms favoring diplomacy and the use of democratic channels (as opposed to direct aggression) are overriding any tendency toward violence.[29] An extension of this interpretation is that middle-class Negroes may be activists, but non-violent activists, in the civil rights movement. Thus, class norms may be contouring resentment into more organized forms of protest.

Table 4—Percentage willing to use violence by contact, powerlessness, and racial dissatisfaction, controlling for two geographical areas and education

	Neighborhood		Education	
Independent Variables	South Central– Watts	Crenshaw	Low (High School or Less)	High (Some College)
Low contact	53** (N = 62)	33** (N = 45)	52** (N = 77)	24* (N = 33)
High contact	27 (N = 83)	10 (N = 109)	26 (N = 86)	10 (N = 105)
Low powerlessness	22** (N = 73)	11* (N = 88)	19** (N = 67)	14 (N = 93)
High powerlessness	55 (N = 77)	25 (N = 68)	51 (N = 100)	18 (N = 45)
Low dissatisfaction	26** (N = 81)	12** (N = 130)	22** (N = 96)	12 (N = 114)
High dissatisfaction	53 (N = 68)	39 (N = 28)	59 (N = 73)	17 (N = 24)

$* P < .05.$ $** P < .01.$

NOTE.—Interaction χ^2 between contact and neighborhood: P is not significant. Interaction χ^2 between powerlessness and neighborhood: $P < .02$. Interaction χ^2 between dissatisfaction and neighborhood: P is not significant. Interaction χ^2 between contact and education: P is not significant. Interaction χ^2 between powerlessness and education: $P < .02$. Interaction χ^2 between dissatisfaction and education: $.05 < P < .10$.

CONCLUSIONS

In an attempt to locate the Negro participant in violence, we find that isolated Negroes and Negroes with intense feelings of powerlessness and dissatisfaction are more prone to violent action than those who are less alienated. In addition, isolation has its strongest effect upon violence when individuals feel powerless to

[29] For a discussion of class norms, see Lipset, *op. cit.*

control events in the society or when racial dissatisfaction is intensely felt. For those with higher expectations of control or with greater satisfaction regarding racial treatment, isolation has a much smaller and nonsignificant effect (though in the predicted direction) upon violence. That is, a weak tie with the majority group, per se, appeared insufficient to explain wide-scale participation in extreme action. This study indicates that it is the interaction between a weak bond and a feeling of powerlessness (or dissatisfaction) that is crucial to violent participation.

Viewed another way, the combined or tandem effect of all three predictive variables produces an important profile of the most violence-prone individuals. Negroes who are isolated, who feel powerless, and who voice a strong disaffection because of discrimination appear to be an extremely volatile group, with 65 per cent of this stratum willing to use violence (as contrasted to only 12 per cent of the "combined lows" in alienation).

Ghetto area and education were introduced as controls. Each independent variable (taken separately) retained some significant effect upon violence in two geographical areas (dealing with proximity to the Watts violence) and among the less educated respondents. Powerlessness and dissatisfaction, however, had no effect upon violence among the college educated. Several interpretations of this finding were explored.

Applying our findings to the context of the Negro revolt of the last fifteen years, we note an important distinction between the non-violent civil rights activists and the violence-prone group introduced in this study. Suggestive (but non-conclusive) evidence indicates that the participants in organized civil rights protests are more likely to be middle class in origin, to hold considerable optimism for equal rights, and to have greater communication with the majority —this represents a group with "rising expectations" for full equality.[30] In contrast, this study located a very different population—one whose members are intensely dissatisfied, feel powerless to change their position, and have minimum commitment to the larger society. These Negroes have lost faith in the leaders and institutions of the community and presumably have little hope for improvement through organized protest. For them, violence is a means of communicating with white society; anger can be expressed, control exerted—if only for a brief period.

---

[30]See Ruth Searles and J. Allen Williams, Jr., Negro College Students' Participation in Sit-ins, *Social Forces,* **XL**, pp. 215-220, 1962; H. Edward Ransford, "Negro Participation in Civil Rights Activity and Violence (unpublished Ph.D. dissertation, University of California, Los Angeles, 1966); and Pearl M. Gore and Jullian B. Rotter, A Personality Correlate of Social Action, *Journal of Personality,* **XXXVII**, pp. 58-64, 1963.

PART FIVE

Taking On the Fuzz:

Do Liberals Challenge Police or Make Their Job Impossible?

For a variety of reasons, American society is poorly equipped today to keep civil speaking up from being transformed into uncivil acting out. We look here at one interlocking set of such reasons. Police already seem overburdened with their traditional role of combating crime, and are held in such low esteem by many liberal intellectuals that involvement by the law is often the key stimulus that escalates civil demonstrations into disturbances. Moreover, there is some danger that unofficial groups will develop to supply the perceived lack of law and order. Hence the concern here with whether liberals challenge police to do a more effective and humane job, or whether today's liberals increase social instability so much as to make it impossible for the police to do the necessary job under today's particularly demanding conditions.

Specifically, this section has three foci. First, the sources of tension between liberals and police will be catalogued. Second, the extent of our problems with crime will be sketched. Third, attention will be given to disturbing signs that significant numbers of people feel that police and defense activities cannot be trusted to civil and military authorities. Specifically, we focus on:

Liberals and Police: are cops id or superego?

Criminals, Crime, and Police: who is the victim of what, and how many times?

Thunder from the Right: saving the republic or changing its character?

A. A BASIC DILEMMA

All societies give more or less emphasis to two broad ways of looking at life, and the existing balance between these two views at any point in time in any society tells much about the quality of life in it. One view may be described as idealistic, of viewing people and society as they might be at their best. The second may be described as pessimistic, of responding to people and society so that they cannot be at their worst. The latter view implies a concept of man that emphasizes toughness in action in specific cases, authority, and skepticism about man's ability to perfect himself. The idealistic view tends toward comprehensiveness of thought, defines broader boundaries for permissible behavior, and implies a great belief in the perfectability of man.

Since man's intellectual beginnings, political philosophies have stressed the two views, often recommending some balance, but sometimes going to one extreme or the other. The *Federalist Papers*, for example, built upon a balanced notion. Men as conceived in the *Papers* are not angels, so they cannot do without some structures for governance. But neither are men such varlets that they must be ministered unto by a powerful state lest things inevitably and early get out of hand. Consequently, in the *Federalist* tradition, men must play a critical role in controlling the structures that control them. Totalitarian states rest on a more pessimistic view of man—at least until he is converted into the perfect citizen in some remote future.

A basic determinant of the quality of governance inheres in the balance between the two broad views of man. Rousseau tackled that question head on. A citizen can be truly free only as he himself controls his own behavior, he noted, which can occur only under very special circumstances. Hence the delicious irony that man is born free but is everywhere in bondage in varying degrees. The degree of that bondage will depend in essential ways on the balance between the idealistic and pessimistic views of man in the prevailing philosophy of governance.

We look here at a modern form of the contrast of the idealistic and pessimistic views: the tension between liberals and the police. Not all liberals are idealists, in our sense, nor are all police pessimists. Both sides get plenty of support from various quarters. But liberals and police are major actors in a major conflict in our society, and the differences between the two can be arresting, to risk a bad pun. Moreover, the quality of the balance achieved between the two will in significant ways affect the quality of American life.

Let us take as a basic position that various mixes of the idealistic and pessimistic views are appropriate in the well run society, given changing times and problems. Too much of the pessimistic view, for example, and a police state could emerge. Too much of the idealistic view, on the other hand, and a truly just society might be immobilized in the face of attacking barbarians. Given that some balance of the two views is appropriate, however, most of the vital questions remained unanswered. What balance is appropriate at a particular point in time? And how does a society effectively shift that balance when the conditions change? These are puzzling questions, worthy of the best in man.

Two points are clear amidst all the ambiguity. First, a society can be said to be reworking its balance of the two views when—like today—their proponents challenge one another. This challenging is vital in a nonauthoritarian society. Indeed, it may be a basic process for innovation in a changing environment. However, more or less serious risks are involved. A society can skid past an appropriate balance if too optimistic a view seriously shakes it, which then encourages a suppressive overreaction.

Second, both promise and peril are implicit in a society reworking its balance of the two views of man. The promise, of course, is a more humane society. The peril is an accelerating polarization, occurring when both sides plead their cases so strongly that they become too far apart to engage in meaningful dialogue toward constructive change. Evidences abound, unfortunately. Consider only two signs of this polarization:

> "All over the U.S.A. the John Birchers, the Minutemen, the States Righters, the Nazis and Ku Klux Klanners are arming and training for total warfare against our people. . . . The Afroamerican hasn't got a chance in the U.S.A. unless he organizes to defend himself." Quoted in Harold Cruse, "The Crisis of the Negro Intellectual," pp. 385-386, Morrow, New York, 1967.
> "We have taken off the kid gloves with these elements who cause riots." Police Chief of Tampa, Florida.

It is easy to see how such sentiments can help accelerate polarization and encourage violence.

The danger of skidding beyond a workable balance of optimism/pessimism in our dominant view of man is particularly serious in the case of today's liberals and police. Members of the two groups not only tend to differ in their operating views of man, but they have many other reasons for thinking and feeling about themselves as very different kinds of people. Police tend to anticipate the worst, are likely to respond to individual cases, are probably of lower socio-economic status, and have less education. Liberals are more likely to take a longer range, optimistic view, to see themselves as having higher socio-economic status, and they will tend to have more education.

Our interest is in whether different concepts of man, reinforced by disparities between liberals and police, will help or hinder adaptation to evolving social demands. Our guiding questions are perhaps too dramatic, but they convey a real sense of the basic issue. Are liberals effectively challenging the police, thereby encouraging a more just society? Or are liberals so insistent that they encourage crime and the criminal? Alternatively, are police so zealous in serving the existing order that they inhibit the development and testing of new forms of social life or political expression?

B. LIBERALS AND POLICE:
ARE COPS ID OR SUPEREGO?

There is no question that the police today feel themselves one-down and defensive. "Many police," says Seymour Lipset, "have consciously come to look upon themselves as an oppressed minority, subject to the same kinds of prejudices as other minorities." Respect for the police has never been especially high in America,[1] but the current social ills of our society have cast an even darker pall over their status. The signs are unmistakable. "Pig" has become the new slang for "fuzz," which was bad enough. One of the more popular hippie buttons reads: "Beware! Your Police are Armed and Dangerous." Most people smile sardonically at that.

The police have been under attack in the public and scholarly presses, as well as in the streets and the courts. Research on civil strife has found the police playing the roles both of precipitator and victim of prejudice and violence. For example, the *Walker Report* which investigated the riots that marred the Democratic National Convention of 1968 produced the most damning indictment of police behavior in modern times. ". . . On the part of the police," the *Report* notes, "there was enough wild club swinging, enough cries of hatred, enough gratuitous beating to make the conclusion inescapable that individual policemen, and lots of them, committed violent acts far in excess of the requisite force for crowd dispersal or arrest. To read dispassionately the hundreds of statements describing at first hand the events . . . is to become convinced of the presence of what can only be called a *police riot*."[2]

Police often serve as a scapegoat for the frustrations of the oppressed. The policeman serving as a representative of the law also serves as the "tangible target for grievances against shortcomings throughout that system: against assembly-line justice in teeming lower courts; against wide disparities in sentences; against antiquated correctional facilities; against the basic inequities imposed by the system on the poor . . . ."[3] Being a scapegoat encourages police to prejudice and

[1] A large number of surveys have included occupational prestige scales. Generally the occupation of policeman is ranked about the middle range. See J.J. Preiss and H.J. Ehrlich, "An Examination of Role Theory: The Case of the State Police," p. 125, University of Nebraska Press, Lincoln, Nebraska, 1966. For a more extensive discussion of the police as agents of the political system, see David Easton and Jack Dennis, "Children In The Political System," pp. 294-303, McGraw-Hill Book Company, New York, 1969.

[2] "Report of the National Advisory Commission on Civil Disorders," p. 299, Bantam Books Inc., New York, 1968.

[3] Daniel Walker, Rights In Conflict, A Report to the National Commission on the Causes and Prevention of Violence, Prepared by the Chicago Study Team to the National Commission on the Causes and Prevention of Violence, p. 5, Bantam Books Inc., New York, 1968.

violence, of course, which in turn encourages further scapegoating. The process is nasty and circular.

The liberal intellectuals, to use the best of a collection of possible terms, have contributed massively to the disrepute in which the police find themselves today. The cumulative picture of the police in much research is numbing, for example. Scholarly research has unfavorably compared the average policeman to the general middle-class population. That composite policeman is undereducated, unprofessional, bigoted, authoritarian, pugnacious, and suspicious of human nature. The negative attitudes of liberals in part rest on such research, and in part those attitudes extend that research to this contemporary *reductio ad absurdum*: All cops are fascist pigs.

This broad characterization of the dominant liberal view can be supported briefly. In summary, liberals see police at their worst as a kind of institutional and insidious id reflecting the evil in man. To this point novelist and poet Nelson Algren in "Down with Cops" argued in an article not reprinted here that the average American does not really want to improve the police because "the cop is no more than the instrument which fulfills us; no more than the extension of our own vindictiveness." Through the police, in other words, each of us works out his biases and grievances against society. The 'Cop Mentality,' he argues, illustrates an evil buried in all of us.[4] At their best, liberals tend to see police as a kind of conscience or superego of the establishment, altogether too interested in suppressing and harassing innovative minorities with different manners or morals or concepts of economic organization. Police, in contrast, should spend more of their time attempting to curb galloping crime rates. Seymour Lipset sketches the case in "Why Cops Hate Liberals—and Vice Versa," an article reprinted in this section. Lipset describes why liberals and cops often view each other with acrimony, and how the police are spurred by their frustration and alienation to pursue right wing politics.

The resulting load on the police is a trying one. Since the public has long accepted the policeman's lot as one of long hours, hard work, low pay, and little prestige, attacks from any quarter, and especially from liberal intellectuals, tend to generate searing defensiveness. And that defensiveness may trigger overreaction in the streets when police are forced to maintain civil order as well as to fight crime.

C. CRIMINALS, CRIME, AND POLICE: WHO IS THE VICTIM OF WHAT, AND HOW MANY TIMES?

Whether the criticism by liberal intellectuals helps or hinders the police is perhaps a moot point, but there is no question that the police have their hands full in dealing with their traditional mission—managing crime and criminals. The rise

[4] Nelson Algren, Down With Cops, *Saturday Evening Post*, pp. 10-14, **238**, no. 21, October 23, 1965.

of crime in American society has been so dramatic that it has been a major emphasis in the last three contests for the presidency. FBI figures show an overall rise in crime of 88 percent since 1960, and that may significantly understate the case.

Increases in crime have triggered major legislative reactions. For example, President Johnson placed more emphasis on curbing crime and its causes than any other president. In one year, 1968, he recommended a dozen pieces of legislation designed to fight crime. Johnson believed that to control crime, the conditions of poverty would have to be erased. He also believed that the ultimate responsibility for crime control had to rest with local units of government such as cities and towns. Consequently, in 1965 Congress enacted his Law Enforcement Assistance Act which provided funds for work by local governments on new methods of crime control and law enforcement. In 1968, Congress passed the Omnibus Crime Control and Safe Streets Act, which was a revised version of a bill proposed by President Johnson. The Omnibus Crime Bill was the most comprehensive anticrime legislation in the nation's history. Its major provision was for block grants to states to be used for improving crime control. The bill also contained a watered-down gun control provision.

"The Challenge of Crime in a Free Society" summarizes much of the foundation for the legislation outlined above, a foundation developed by a commission that President Johnson had assembled to study the problem of crime in our country. The findings of the commission are disturbing. It reported that the rate of increase in crime since 1960 was even higher than the 88 percent increase reported by the FBI. The commission also emphasized that crime was more widespread in the population than commonly thought; that massive unfairness existed in the system of justice; that archaic means often were used to deal with criminal offenders; and that efforts to combat crime often were inadequate, unimaginative, and primitive. Over two hundred recommendations were made for improving these conditions. Most have not been acted upon.

How bad conditions are, and some of the reasons why they are so bad, receive detailed attention from Philip H. Ennis in "Crime, Victims, and the Police." Ennis presents data suggesting that a truly staggering volume of crime goes unreported, perhaps as much as 50 percent. He places some of the blame for the lack of reporting on unfavorable attitudes of the general public about the treatment that they expect from the police. Professor Ennis' data come from a survey taken by the National Opinion Research Center at the University of Chicago. Ten thousand households were sampled in an effort to answer such questions as:

What types of crime have the respondents been the victims of?
Who is the most likely to be the victim of crime in our society?
Why are so many crimes unreported in official statistics?
What are the attitudes of those persons surveyed toward the police?

The dissatisfaction with police reported by Ennis seems to have deep roots, as

Martin Mayer graphically describes in "The Criminal and the Law." Mayer characterizes the criminal process in action, this time from the perspective of the suspected criminal rather than the victim. Mayer details the handling of suspected felons from the moment of their arrest, and concludes that "the American way of dealing with crime and the people accused of crime is an unholy and inexcusable mess." The system of assembly-line justice is as unjust as it is typical of big city justice. Many courts allow some criminals to go free, or let many more plead guilty to reduced charges because of the lack of facilities and personnel necessary to give them a trial. This unsavory catalogue could be interminably extended.

In all the complexity, at least one point seems clear. The initial actions taken by Congress and the Courts to alleviate crime and to professionalize the police represent only meager steps toward the massive remedial actions that will be necessary to solve the problems. A public awareness that the problems exist and a conviction that they should be solved will make a great deal of difference. Many of the recommendations of the President's Commission on Crime could be acted on with little effort. The fact that only a few recommendations have been implemented implies that the public and its officials still care too little.

D. THUNDER FROM THE RIGHT: SAVING THE REPUBLIC OR CHANGING ITS CHARACTER?

Some special publics may care too much about the inadequacy of our civil authorities, however, or at least they do not always care very wisely. There are many such groups, but we will call them rightist even though they vary considerably in their style and approach. Commonly, they share the deep concern that our social and political institutions are crumbling, whether the issue be fluoridation of water, sex education in schools, or commies in government. In this sense, many people have rightist tendencies on some issues, but there is a more or less constant collection of people who find themselves on the same side of almost all issues. These groups also tend to believe that the civil and military authorities are not now adequate to do the policing and defensing necessary to preserve the Republic, whether in the urban streets or in international affairs. A few rightist interest groups seek to make up the required difference by being armed and prepared. Eric Norden's "The Paramilitary Right," is an interpretive survey of one such group, the Minutemen.

The rightist interest groups provide thunder from the right, violent and/or verbal, whose motivation is mixed. Commonly, they explain their reason-for-being as a long-overdue reaction to the liberals or leftists who have created an environment of disrespect for law or whatever. In this view, the Minutemen evolved because the Black Panthers exist. Others argue that rightists create an atmosphere of repression that encourages resistance or illegal acts by leftists. In this view, the Black Panthers are necessary because the Minutemen exist. The reality of it seems to be that a little bit of both explanations is necessary to explain the thunder from the right and the rumblings of change from the left.

The rightist behavior reflects two emphases in differing degrees. First, they have a desire in common to bring order to a society they see in chaos. The guiding assumption is that, at base, people only really want their life and property protected. Second, some rightist groups—the paramilitary right—do not seem to give much of a damn about how that order is brought about. Norden describes a number of such groups.

Distinguishing the two emphases underlying the thunder on the right is important. That people feel their life and property are threatened is an important input for our political system, and that input has to be considered in deciding on public policy. In this sense, the thunder from the right may help save the Republic from neglect of its own diversity, because it is massive feedback from some people complaining that they see their needs threatened or frustrated. Every representative political system has to give close attention to such feedback, which is the very stuff of free government. On the other hand, paramilitary groups can pervert the character of our society, imposing order at the expense of other values. In this sense, some of the thunder from the right accompanies the digging of the grave of the very institutions it professes to safeguard. No representative system can neglect such a fact.

The irony is even more subtle still. As Martin Oppenheimer sees it from his liberal left viewpoint, the establishment generally prefers to rely on the various civil authorities for law and order. In "The Ultras," Oppenheimer sketches how this preference sometimes requires putting down rightist groups. The police, the ostensible defenders of the establishment, do not always agree with this strategy. Indeed, Oppenheimer notes that police often see moderates in the establishment as "responsible for the instability of the system by refusing to let the police 'do their job'." Rightist groups in their quest for stability may, in part, weaken the major source of stability that leftist groups see as impeding social change. And from the other perspective, leftist groups in their quest for change are partially undermining that very source that seeks to deter the use of violence to inhibit change.

34

WHY COPS HATE LIBERALS
—AND VICE VERSA

Seymour Martin Lipset

There is an increasing body of evidence which suggests an affinity between police work and support for radical-right politics, particularly when linked to racial unrest. During the presidential campaign, George Wallace was unmistakably a hero to many policemen. John Harrington, the president of the Fraternal Order of Police, the largest police organization in America, with over 90,000 members and affiliates in more than 900 communities, publicly endorsed him. And Wallace has reciprocated this affection for some time. While governor of Alabama, he placed the slogan, popularized by the Birch Society, "Support Your Local Police" on the automobile license plates of the state of Alabama. During the 1964 and 1968 presidential campaigns, he frequently referred to the heroic activities of the police, and denounced the Supreme Court, and bleeding-heart liberals and intellectuals, for undermining the police efforts to maintain law and order. The police were pictured as the victims of an Establishment conspiracy to foster confrontationist forms of protest and law violation, particularly on the part of Negroes and student activists.

Similar reports concerning police support for right-wing or conservative candidates who have campaigned against civil rights and integration proposals have

Reprinted from Seymour Martin Lipset, Why Cops Hate Liberals—and Vice Versa, *Atlantic*, **223**, no. 3, pp. 76-83, March 1969.

appeared frequently in the press. Thus in 1967, Boston journalists commented on the general support for Louise Day Hicks among the police of that city. Mrs. Hicks had won her political spurs in the fight which she waged as chairman of the Boston School Committee against school integration. And when she ran for mayor, the police were seemingly among her most enthusiastic backers. In New York City, police have stood out among the constituency of the Conservative Party, an organization which also has opposed public efforts to enforce school integration. The New York Conservative Party was the one partisan group in the city to fight a civilian review board of the police department, an issue which has come up in many other communities.

Jerome Skolnick of the University of Chicago made a study of the Oakland, California, police in 1964 based on interviews with many of them. He concluded that "a Goldwater type of conservatism was the dominant political and emotional persuasion of the police." During the 1964 campaign, a broadcaster on the New York City police radio suddenly made an emotional appeal for support of Senator Goldwater. Many police called in to endorse this talk. Almost no one out in police cars that night phoned in to back Lyndon Johnson, or to complain about the use of the police radio for partisan purposes. In Los Angeles, an official order had to be issued in 1964 telling the police that they could not have bumper stickers or other campaign materials on their police cars, because of the large number who had publicly so supported Goldwater. The late chief of police of the city, William H. Parker, stated his belief that the majority of the nation's peace officers were "conservative, ultraconservative, and very right wing," a description which fits his own orientation.

There is also evidence of strong support and sympathy among the police for the John Birch Society. In 1964, John Rousselot, then national director of the Society, claimed that "substantial numbers" of its members were policemen, and a study of the national membership of the Society by Fred Grupp, a political scientist at Louisiana State, confirms this contention. Mr. Grupp sent out a questionnaire to a random sample of the Birch membership with the help of the Society and found that over 3 percent of those who reported their occupations were policemen, a figure which is over four times the proportion of police in the national labor force. In New York City in July, 1965, a reporter judged that the majority of the audience at a large rally in Town Hall sponsored by the Birch Society's Speakers Bureau wore "Patrolmen's Benevolent Association badges." The Society itself "estimates that it has five hundred members in the New York City Police Department." In Philadelphia, the mayor placed a number of police on limited duty because of their membership in the Society. In a recent interview, Richard MacEachern, head of the Boston Police Patrolmen's Association, frequently referred to Birch Society material as the source of his information concerning "The Plan" of black militants to destroy the police through use of deliberate violence.

That peace officers in high places are sympathetic with the Society may be seen in the fact that former Sheriff James Clark of Selma, Alabama, who not only played a major role in suppressing civil rights demonstrations in his city but also has been a frequent speaker for the Birch Society, was elected president of the national organization of sheriffs. While serving as chief of the Los Angeles Police Department, William H. Parker took part in the Manion Forum a right-wing radio discussion program run by Clarence Manion, a leader of the Birch Society. According to William Turner, in his book *The Police Establishment*, Louis Neese, the police chief of Trenton, New Jersey, "incorporated sections of a Birch 'Support Your Local Police' circular into a declaration of departmental policy.

All this is no new development. The identification between the police and right-wing extremism is not simply a reflection of recent tensions. During the 1930s, investigations of the Black Legion, a neofascist organization in the industrial Midwest, which engaged in terror and vigilante activities, indicated that it appealed to police. Not only did it include many patrolmen in Michigan and elsewhere, but a grand jury in Oakland County, Michigan, reported that the chief of police in Pontiac was an active member. The Legion, it should be noted, engaged in kidnapping, flogging, and even murder of suspected Communists. Father Coughlin, who was probably the most important profascist leader of the 1930s, also found heavy backing within police ranks. An investigation of his organization, the Christian Front, revealed that 407 of New York's finest belonged to it.

Gunnar Myrdal, in his classic study of the race problem in America, *An American Dilemma*, conducted in the late thirties and early forties, asserted that one of the principal sources of Ku Klux Klan activity in the South at that time came from law enforcement officers. This finding jibed with reports of the membership of the Klan during the early 1920s when it was at the height of its power, controlling politics in many Northern as well as Southern states. Klan leaders according to one account "took particular pride in emphasizing the large number of law enforcement officers . . . that had joined their order." Typical of Klan propaganda which attracted police support was the plank in the program of the Chicago Klan which called for "Supporting Officials in all Phases of Law Enforcement," a slogan close to the "Support Your Local Police" campaign waged by the Birch Society and George Wallace four decades later. According to Charles Jackson, membership lists seized in different parts of California indicated that "roughly 10 percent of the . . . policemen in practically every California city," including the chiefs of police in Los Angeles and Bakersfield and the sheriff of Los Angeles County, belonged to the Klan. In Atlanta, the home base of the organization, a study reports that "a very high percentage" of the police were members. Considerable police backing for the Klan was also reported in analyses of its operation in cities as diverse as Portland (Oregon), Tulsa, Madison, and Memphis.

Looking back through the history of religious bigotry in this country, we find that the anti-Catholic nativist American Protective Association (APA), which flourished in the early 1890s, also appears to have been supported by the police.

My own researches on this movement and its membership indicate that the police were considerably overrepresented among APA members. In Minneapolis 6.5 percent were policemen, in Sacramento 8 percent, and in San Jose 7 percent.

Although there is a general understanding that the police should be politically neutral, their role as public employees has inevitably involved them in local politics. Prior to the emergence of civil service examinations, appointment to the force was a political plum in most cities. And once a man was hired, chances for promotion often depended on access to local officeholders. In many communities, the police were part of the machine organization. The widespread pattern of toleration of corruption and the rackets which characterized urban political life until the 1940s usually depended on the cooperation, if not direct participation, of the police. Those who controlled the rackets paid special attention to municipal politics, to those who dominated city hall, in order to make sure that they would not be interfered with by the authorities.

Although machine and racketeer domination of local government is largely a thing of the past in most cities, the police are of necessity still deeply interested in local politics. High-level appointments are almost invariably made by elected officials, and those who control city politics determine police pay and working conditions. Hence, the police as individuals and as a body must be actively concerned with access to the political power structure. They must be prepared to adjust their law enforcement policies in ways which are acceptable to the political leaders.

Such assumptions would lead us to believe that police would avoid any contact with radical groups, with those who seek to change the existing structures of political power or community leadership. Thus the evidence that significant minorities of police have been moved to join or openly back right-wing and bigoted movements is particularly impressive. For every policeman who has taken part in such activities, we may assume that there were many others who sympathized, but refrained from such behavior so as to avoid endangering their job prospects. (This comment, of course, does not apply to those communities which were actually dominated by extremist movements.)

The propensity of policemen to support rightist activities derives from a number of elements in their occupational role and social background. Many of the police are not much different in their social outlook from others in the lower middle class or working class. Twenty-five years ago, Gunnar Myrdal noted that police in the South were prone to express deep-seated anti-Negro feelings in brutal actions against Negroes and thus undo "much of what Northern philanthropy and Southern state governments are trying to accomplish through education and other means." He accounted for the phenomenon as resulting from the fact that the police generally had the prejudices of the poor whites. "The average Southern policeman is a promoted poor white with a legal sanction to use a weapon. His social heritage has taught him to despise the Negroes, and he has had little education which could have changed him." A recent study of the New York City police by Arthur Niederhoffer, a former member of the Department, reports that "for the past fifteen years, during a cycle of prosperity, the bulk of police candidates has been upper lower class with a sprinkling of lower middle class; about ninety-five per cent has had no college training." In a survey of the occupations of the fathers of 12,000 recruits who graduated from the New York Police Academy, he found that more than three quarters of them were manual or service workers.

The Birch Society apart, movements of ethnic intolerance and right-wing radicalism have tended to recruit from the more conservative segments of the lower and less-educated strata. On the whole, the less education people have, the more likely they are to be intolerant of those who differ from themselves, whether in opinions, modes of culturally and morally relevant behavior, religion, ethnic background, or race. The police, who are recruited from the conservative, less-educated groups, reflect the background from which they come. John H. McNamara recently found that when he separated the New York police recruits into two status groups on the basis of their fathers' occupations, those "with fathers in the higher kill classification were less likely to feel that the leniency of courts and laws account for assaults on the police" than those who came from lower socioeconomic origins.

Once they are employed as policemen, their job experiences enhance the possibility that whatever authoritarian traits they bring from their social background will increase rather than decrease. McNamara found a sizable increase in the proportion of police recruits who resented legal restrictions on their authority or propensity to use force. At the beginning of recruit training, only 6 percent agreed with the statement "The present system of state and local laws has undermined the patrolman's authority to a dangerous extent," while 46 percent disagreed. After one year in field assignments, 25 percent of the same group of men agreed with the statement, and only 19 percent disagreed. Similar changes in attitudes occurred with respect to the proposition "If patrolmen working in tough neighborhoods had more leeway and fewer restrictions on the use of force many of the serious police problems in these neighborhoods would be greatly reduced." Fourteen percent agreed with the statement at the beginning of their career, as compared with 30 percent after one year in the field, and 39 percent among a different group of policemen who had been employed for two years.

In general, the policeman's job requires him to be suspicious of people, to prefer conventional behavior, to value toughness. A policeman must be suspicious and cynical about human behavior. As Niederhoffer points out, "He needs the intuitive ability to sense plots and conspiracies on the basis of embryonic evidence." The political counterpart of such an outlook is a monistic theory which simplifies political conflict into a black-and-white fight, and which is ready to accept a conspiratorial view of the sources of evil, terms which basically describe the outlook of extremist groups, whether of the left or right.

The propensity of police to support a radical political posture is also related to their sense of being a low-status out-group in American society. The Oakland study revealed that when police were asked to rank the most serious problems they have, the category most frequently elected was "lack of respect for the police. . . . Of the two hundred and eighty-two . . . policemen who rated the prestige police work receives from others, 70 per cent ranked it as only fair or poor." The New York City study also indicated that the majority of the police did not feel that they enjoyed the respect of the public. James Q. Wilson found that a majority of Chicago police sergeants who completed questionnaires in 1960 and 1965 felt that the public did not cooperate with or respect the police. Many articles in police journals comment on the alleged antagonism to the police voiced by the mass media. Studies of police opinion have indicated that some police conceal their occupation from their neighbors because many people do not like to associate with policemen.

If policemen judge their social worth by their incomes, they are right in rating it low. A recent article in *Fortune* reports that "the patrolman's pay in major cities now averages about $7,500 per year—33 percent less than is needed to sustain a family of four in moderate circumstances in a large city, according to the U.S. Bureau of Labor Statistics." As a result, many are forced to moonlight to earn a living. Fletcher Knebel cites an expert estimate that from a third to a half of all the patrolmen in the country have a second job. The relative socio-economic status of the police has worsened over time. Richard Wade, an urban historian at the University of Chicago, points out that the situation has changed considerably from that of fifty years ago when "policemen had an income higher than other trades and there were more applicants than there were jobs." John H. McNamara, who has studied the New York Department, concludes:

> During the Depression the department was able to recruit from a popu-
> lation which included many unemployed or low-paid college graduates. . . .
> As general economic conditions have improved, however, the job of police
> officer has become less attractive to college graduates.

In his surveys of police opinion in Chicago, Boston, and Washington, D.C., Albert J. Reiss reports that 59 percent believe that the prestige of police work is lower than it was twenty years ago. Lower police morale is not simply a function of a relative decline in income or in perceived status. The police believe their conditions of work have also worsened. Eighty percent state that "police work [is] more hazardous today than five years ago." Sixty percent believe that the way the public behaves toward the police has changed for the worse since they joined the force.

The policeman's role is particularly subject to fostering feelings of resentment against society, which flow from a typical source of radical politics, "status discrepancies." This term refers to a sociological concept which is used to describe the positions of individuals or groups who are ranked relatively high on one status attribute and low on another.

Presumably the fact of having a claim to some deference makes people indignantly resent as morally improper any evidence that they are held in low regard because of some other factor in their background or activities. In the case of the police, they are given considerable authority by society to enforce its laws and are expected to risk their lives if necessary; on the other hand, they feel they receive little prestige, and they get a relatively low salary as compared with that of other occupational groups which have much less authority.

Many police have consciously come to look upon themselves as an oppressed minority, subject to the same kind of prejudice as other minorities. Thus Chief Parker explained some of the bitterness of the police as stemming from the "shell of minorityism" within which they lived. This view was given eloquent voice in 1965 by the then New York City Police Commissioner, Michael J. Murphy: "The police officer, too, belongs to a minority group—a highly visible minority group, and is also subject to stereotyping and mass attack. Yet he, like every member of every minority, is entitled to be judged as an individual and on the basis of his individual acts, not as a group." Clearly, the police appear to be a deprived group, one which feels deep resentment about the public's lack of appreciation for the risks it takes for the community's safety. These risks are not negligible in the United States. In 1967, for example, one out of every eight policemen was assaulted. This rate is considerably higher than in any other developed democratic country.

The belief that police are rejected by the public results, as Wilson argues, in a "sense of alienation from society" which presses the police to develop their own "sub-culture" with norms which can provide them with "a basis for self-respect independent to some degree of civilian attitudes." Given the assumption of the police that they are unappreciated even by the honest middle-class citizenry, they are prone to accept a cynical view of society and its institutions, and social isolation and alienation can lead to political alienation.

The police have faced overt hostility and even contempt from spokesmen for liberal and leftist groups, racial minorities, and intellectuals generally. The only ones who appreciate their contribution to society and the risks they take are the conservatives, and particularly the extreme right. The radical left has almost invariably been hostile, the radical right friendly. It is not surprising therefore that police are more likely to be found in the ranks of the right.

In the larger context, American politics tends to press the police to support conservative or rightist politics. Liberals and leftists have been more concerned than conservatives with the legal rights of the less powerful and the under-privileged. They have tried to limit the power of the police to deal with suspects and have sought to enlarge the scope of due process. Efforts to enhance the rights of defendants, to guarantee them legal representation, to prevent the authorities from unduly pressuring those taken into police custody, have largely concerned liberals. The American Civil Liberties Union and other comparable groups have fought hard to weaken the discretionary power of the police. To many policemen, the liberals' constant struggle is to make their job more difficult, to increase the physical danger to which they are subject. Many are convinced that dangerous criminals or revolutionists are freely walking the streets because of the efforts of softhearted liberals. To police, who are constantly exposed to the seamy side of life, who view many deviants and lawbreakers as outside the protection of the law, the constant concern for the civil rights of such people makes little sense, unless it reflects moral weakness on the part of the liberals, or more dangerously, is an aspect of a plot to undermine legitimate authority. And the fact that the Supreme Court has sided with the civil-libertarian interpretations of individual rights in recent years on issues concerning police tactics in securing confessions—the use of wiretaps, and the like—constitutes evidence as to how far moral corruption has reached into high places. Reiss's survey of police opinion found that 90 percent of the police interviewed felt that the Supreme Court "has gone too far in making rules favoring and protecting criminal offenders." The liberal world, then, is perceived as an enemy, an enemy which may attack directly in demonstrations or riots, or indirectly through its pressure on the courts.

The fights over the establishment of civilian police review boards which have occurred in many cities have largely taken the form of a struggle between the liberal political forces which favor creating such checks over the power of police departments to discipline their own members and the conservatives who oppose these. In the best-publicized case, the referendum in New York City of November, 1966, to repeal the law creating such a board, the ideological lineup was clear-cut. The Patrolmen's Benevolent Association was supported in its successful efforts by the Conservative Party of New York and the John Birch Society. It was opposed by New York's liberal Republican mayor, John Lindsay, as well as by Robert Kennedy, the reform Democrats, the Liberal Party, the New York *Times*, and the New York *Post*. There can be little doubt that this struggle has helped to strengthen the police backing for the Conservative Party.

The greater willingness of police to join or back groups which have been antagonistic to religious (Catholics in the nineteenth century, Jews in the twentieth) and racial minorities also may be a function of concrete job experience, as well as of the degree of prejudice present in their social milieu. Ethnic slums characteristically have been centers of crime, violence, and vice. Most immigrant groups living in urban America in the past, as well as more recent Negro migrants, have contributed disproportionately to the ranks of criminals and racketeers. Hence, the police have often found that their experience confirmed the negative cultural stereotypes which have existed about such groups while they lived in the crowded, dirty, slum conditions. The ethnic minorities have, in fact, often appeared as sympathetic to criminals, as supporters of violence directed against the police. The ethnic slum historically has been an enemy stronghold, a place of considerable insecurity. Right-wing political groupings which define minorities or leftist radicals as conspiratorial corrupters of American morality have strongly appealed to the morally outraged police.

In evaluating the disposition of the police to participate in the radical right, it is important to note that only a minority of the police are involved in most

Police Salaries

Policemen complain, and the experts tend to agree, that police salaries are not high enough to attract college-educated or other highly-skilled persons, and that policemen are not adequately compensated for the hazards and responsibilities they are asked to accept. Painters, carpenters, electricians, mechanics, firemen, for example, tend to earn as much or more than policemen in the south and midwest and in the smaller eastern cities. Only on the west coast do policemen have a statistical edge, and it is slight.

Top 10 Cities, 500,000 or more population	Minimum Base Pay	Maximum Base Pay
San Francisco	$9,935	$10,535
Chicago	8,710	11,000
Los Angeles	8,580	10,105
Philadelphia	8,480	9,000
Seattle	8,340	9,600
San Diego	8,150	9,900
Cleveland	7,935	8.935
New York	7,930	9,380
Detroit	7,500	10,300
Houston	7,200	8,100
Top 5 Cities, 100,000-500,000		
Oakland	9,875	10,535
Berkeley	9,385	10,345
Torrance	9,240	10,190
San Jose	8,665	10,535
Fresno	8,410	9,840
Lowest 5 Cities, 500,000 or more		
San Antonio	6,000	7,200
Memphis	6,120	7,440
Kansas City	6,180	8,150
Atlanta	6,210	8,220
Boston	6,345	8,320
Lowest 5 Cities, 100,000-500,000		
Knoxville	4,500	5,700
Mobile	4,910	6,120
Little Rock	5,100	6,120
Portsmouth, Va.	5,400	6,900
Chatanooga	5,520	6,480

These statistics are minimum and maximum base pay figures for patrolmen as of January 1, 1969, except for Chicago and Philadelphia estimates, which include pay raises to take effect July 1, 1969. A retroactive pay hike, which will place them just below San Francisco in the big-city standings, is expected for New York patrolmen early in the year.

These figures do not reflect pay differentials based on longevity (which in Los Angeles, New York, Cleveland, Detroit, and Houston, for example, can increase pay rates as much as $800 annually), paid holidays (New York patrolmen get $335 to $405 extra each year), or uniform allowances. Nor do they reflect cost of living variables, which tend to reduce the apparent gap between metropolitan police salaries and the pay scale for smaller cities, particularly in the South.

communities. Most police, though relatively conservative and conventional, are normally more concerned with the politics of collective bargaining, with getting more for themselves, than with the politics of right-wing extremism. The Patrolmen's Benevolent Association is basically a trade union which seeks alliances with other labor unions, particularly those within the civil service, and with the powerful within the dominant political parties. Police have struck for higher wages, much as other groups have done. There have been occasions when they have shown sympathy for striking workers on the picket line, particularly when the workers and the police have belonged to the same ethnic groups. One of the main attractions of police work is the lifelong economic security and early pensions which it gives. In this sense, the policeman, like others from low-income backgrounds, is concerned for the expansion of the welfare state.

Like all others, the police are interested in upgrading the public image of their job. They do not like being attacked as thugs, as authoritarians, as lusting for power. Some cities have successfully sought to increase the educational level of new recruits and to have a continuing education program for those on the force. The academic quality of the courses given at police academies and colleges in various communities has been improving, and there is much that is hopeful going on.

Yet the fact remains that recent events have sorely strained the tempers of many police. Almost two thirds of the police interviewed in Reiss's study feel that "demonstrations are a main cause of violence these days." The reactions of police organizations around the country suggest that Ortega y Gasset was correct when he suggested in his book *The Revolt of the Masses*, published in 1930, that free societies would come to fear their police. He predicted that those who rely on the police to maintain order are foolish if they imagine that the police "are always going to be content to preserve ... order [as defined by government].... Inevitably they [the police] will end by themselves defining and deciding on the order they are going to impose—which, naturally, will be that which suits them best." In some cities, leaders of police organizations have openly threatened that the police will disobey orders to be permissive when dealing with black or student demonstrators. The Boston Police Patrolmen's Association has stated that the police there will enforce the law, no matter what politicians say. The president of the New York Patrolmen's Benevolent Association has announced that his members "will enforce the law 100 per cent," even when ordered not to do so.

This "rebellion of the police" is a response to their being faced with "confrontation tactics" by student and black radical militants. New Left radicals and black nationalists openly advocate confrontation tactics. They seek deliberately to inflame the police so as to enrage them into engaging in various forms of brutality. Stokely Carmichael has declared that a demonstration which does not result in police action against the participants is a failure. The events at Chicago during the Democratic Convention constitute the best recent example of the way in which a major police force can completely lose its head when faced by a confrontationist demonstration.[1] Some black and white New Radicals openly declare that the killing of police in the ghetto area is not murder, that it is an inherent form of self-defense. But police have been shot at and occasionally killed in ambush.

The current tensions between the police and New Left student and black nationalist radicals probably involve the most extreme example of deliberate provocation which the police have ever faced. The tactics of the campus-based opposition rouse the most deep-seated feelings of class resentment. Most policemen are conservative, conventional, upwardly mobile working-class supporters of the American Way, who aspire for a better life for their families. Many of them seek to send their children to college. To find the scions of the upper middle class in the best universities denouncing them as "pigs," hurling insults which involve use of the most aggressive sexual language, such as "Up against the wall, Mother F—," throwing bricks and bags of feces at them, is much more difficult to accept than any other situation which they have faced. Police understand as normal the problems of dealing with crime or vice. They may resent violence stemming from minority ghettos, but this, too, is understandable and part of police work. But to take provocative behavior from youths who are socially and economically much better off than they and their children is more than the average policeman can tolerate.

The deliberate effort to bait and provoke the police by contemporary New Left radicals is rather new in the history of leftist movements. The American Socialist Party in its early history actually pointed to the police department as a

---

[1] Ironically, the Chicago police force has been one of the few major ones which had made real efforts to adjust to changing conditions. William Turner's recent book, "The Police Establishment," states that close to 25 percent of the force is Negro, a proportion far above that of New York and Los Angeles. It also deliberately lowered the height requirements "to make more Puerto Ricans eligible." Although, as Turner documents, there has been considerable tension between the Chicago police and the black community, a study of the attitudes of Negroes in four cities by Gary Marx in his "Protest and Prejudice" reported that the percentage of adult Negroes answering "very well" or "fairly well" to the question of how they thought the police treated Negroes in their city was 64 percent in Chicago, 56 percent in New York, 53 percent in Atlanta, and 31 percent in Birmingham. In spite of the fact that the Chicago Police Department has been in the lead in adapting its recruitment policies to the new climate of race relations, in a study of three cities Reiss found that police in the Windy City were much less likely than those in Boston or Washington, D.C., to blame "civil rights groups" for arousing the public against the police. These comparative data also indicate that the morale of the Chicago police was higher than that of those in Boston and Washington. Over half of the Chicago police interviewed believe that the public rate the prestige of police higher than twenty years ago, while only a fifth of those in the Eastern cities have this opinion. "Chicago police officers are considerably more likely to advise both their sons and other young men to consider a career as a police officer" than are those in the other communities. George O'Connor, the director of professional standards for the International Association of Chiefs of Police, has rated the Chicago department "the best equipped, best-administered police force in the United States." Given such data, it is likely that Tom Hayden, one of the leaders of the Chicago demonstrations, is right in his contention that the brutal reaction of the Chicago police could have occurred in most other cities.

good example of the way the government could provide needed services efficiently. The Communists, of course, never described the police in this fashion, but in the twenties, European Communists concerned with attaining power rather than with symbolic demonstrations defined the police, like the rank and file of the military, as exploited working-class groups who should either be converted to the revolution or at least be neutralized. They directed propaganda to the self-interests of the police, calling on them to refuse to serve the interests of the ruling class during strikes or demonstrations. The European left has often sought to organize the police in trade unions, although it is, of course, also true that they have had an ambivalent attitude toward them. The police have been involved in brutal suppression of left-wing and trade-union demonstrations in Europe, which have made them the target of left-wing criticism and counter-violence. Nevertheless, the left there remembers that the police come from proletarian origins. During the May, 1968, student demonstrations and strikes in Italy, a leading Communist intellectual, Pier Paolo Pasolini, told the New Left students that in a conflict between them and the police, he stood with the police: "Your faces are those of sons of good families, and I hate you as I hate your fathers. The good breeding comes through. . . . Yesterday when you had your battle in the Valle Giulia with the police, my sympathies were with the police, because they are the sons of the poor" (quoted from the *Corriere della Sera* by Melvin Lasky in the August issue of *Encounter*).

Given the interest shown in the welfare of the police by sections of the European left, their membership in trade unions, and their working-class origins, it is not surprising that the political behavior of European police has been more ambivalent than that of their American compeers. On various occasions, segments of the police in Europe have shown sympathy for left and working-class forces, particularly where they have been serving under leftist governments for some time. This was true in Social Democratic Berlin and Prussia generally before 1932, in Vienna before 1934, and in parts of Republican Spain before 1936. The ambivalent attitudes of the police have shown up most recently in France, where a number of police unions issued statements after the May, 1968, events, denying responsibility for use of force against student demonstrators. The police organizations wanted it known that the government, not the police, was responsible for the vigor of the actions taken.

It is doubtful that the American New Left students will ever come to see the police in a sympathetic light, as exploited, insecure, alienated members of the underprivileged classes. As members of the first leftist youth movement which is unaffiliated with any adult party, they are unconcerned with the consequences of their actions on the political strength of the larger left-wing movement. To a large extent, their provocative efforts reflect the biases of the educated upper middle class. Lacking a theory of society and any concern for the complexities of the "road to power" which have characterized the revolutionary Marxist movement, they are prepared to alienate the police, as well as conventional working-class opinion, in order to provoke police brutality, which in turn will validate their total rejection of all social institutions. Hence, we may expect a continuation of the vicious circle of confrontation and police terror tactics.

Liberal moderates properly react to this situation by demanding that the police act toward deviant behavior much as all other professionals do, that they have no more right to react aggressively toward provocative acts than psychiatrists faced by maniacal and dangerous patients, that no matter what extremists do, the police should not lose their self-control. Such a policy is easy to advocate; it is difficult to carry out.

Furthermore, it ignores the fact that most of the police are "working-class" professionals, not the products of postgraduate education. As James Q. Wilson points out, "This means they bring to the job some of the focal concerns of working-class men—a preoccupation with maintaining self-respect, proving one's masculinity, 'not taking any crap,' and not being 'taken in.' Having to rely on personal qualities rather than on formal routines ... means that the officer's behavior will depend crucially on how much deference he is shown, on how manageable the situation seems to be, and on what the participants in it seem to 'deserve.' " If society wants police to behave like psychiatrists, then it must be willing to treat and train them like psychiatrists rather than like pariahs engaged in dirty work. At present, it treats their job like a semiskilled position which requires, at best, a few weeks' training. Norman Kassoff of the research staff of the International Association of Chiefs of Police has compared the legal minimum training requirements for various occupations in the different American states. Calculated in terms of hours, the median minimums are 11,000 for physicians, 5000 for embalmers, 4000 for barbers, 1200 for beauticians, and less than 200 for policemen. The vast majority of policemen begin carrying guns and enforcing the law with less than five weeks' training of any kind.

The new tensions have increased the old conflict between the police and the liberals. For it must be said that liberals are prejudiced against police, much as many white police are biased against Negroes. Most liberals are ready to assume that all charges of police brutality are true. They tend to refuse to give the police the benefit of any doubt. They rarely denounce the extreme black groups and left radicals for their confrontationist efforts. They do not face up to the need for tactics to deal with deliberate incitement to mob violence. If the liberal and intellectual communities are to have any impact on the police, if they are to play any role in reducing the growing political alienation of many police, they must show some recognition that the police force is also composed of human beings, seeking to earn a living. They must be willing to engage in a dialogue with the police concerning their problems.

35

THE CHALLENGE OF CRIME IN A FREE SOCIETY

President's Commission on Crime

This report is about crime in America—about those who commit it, about those who are its victims, and about what can be done to reduce it.

The report is the work of 19 commissioners, 63 staff members, 175 consultants, and hundreds of advisers. The commissioners, staff, consultants, and advisers come from every part of America and represent a broad range of opinion and profession.

In the process of developing the findings and recommendations of the report the Commission called three national conferences, conducted five national surveys, held hundreds of meetings, and interviewed tens of thousands of persons.

The report makes more than 200 specific recommendations—concrete steps the Commission believes can lead to a safer and more just society. These recommendations call for a greatly increased effort on the part of the Federal Government, the States, the counties, the cities, civic organizations, religious institutions, business groups, and individual citizens. They call for basic changes in the operations of police, schools, prosecutors, employment agencies, defenders, social workers, prisons, housing authorities, and probation and parole officers.

Reprinted from the Report of the President's Commission on Crime, U.S. Government Printing Office, Washington, D.C., 1967.

But the recommendations are more than just a list of new procedures, new tactics, and new techniques. They are a call for a revolution in the way America thinks about crime.

Many Americans take comfort in the view that crime is the vice of a handful of people. This view is inaccurate. In the United States today, one boy in six is referred to the juvenile court. A Commission survey shows that in 1965 more than two million Americans were received in prisons or juvenile training schools, or placed on probation. Another Commission study suggests that about 40 percent of all male children now living in the United States will be arrested for a nontraffic offense during their lives. An independent survey of 1,700 persons found that 91 percent of the sample admitted they had committed acts for which they might have received jail or prison sentences.

Many Americans also think of crime as a very narrow range of behavior. It is not. An enormous variety of acts make up the "crime problem." Crime is not just a tough teenager snatching a lady's purse. It is a professional thief stealing cars "on order." It is a well-heeled loan shark taking over a previously legitimate business for organized crime. It is a polite young man who suddenly and inexplicably murders his family. It is a corporation executive conspiring with competitors to keep prices high. No single formula, no single theory, no single generalization can explain the vast range of behavior called crime.

Many Americans think controlling crime is solely the task of the police, the courts, and correction agencies. In fact, as the Commission's report makes clear, crime cannot be controlled without the interest and participation of schools, businesses, social agencies, private groups, and individual citizens.

What, then, is America's experience with crime and how has this experience shaped the Nation's way of living? A new insight into these two questions is furnished by the Commission's National Survey of Criminal Victims. In this survey, the first of its kind conducted on such a scope 10,000 representative American households were asked about their experiences with crime, whether they reported those experiences to the police, and how those experiences affected their lives.

An important finding of the survey is that for the Nation as a whole there is far more crime than ever is reported. Burglaries occur about three times more often than they are reported to the police. Aggravated assaults and larcenies over $50 occur twice as often as they are reported. There are 50 percent more robberies than are reported. In some areas, only one-tenth of the total number of certain kinds of crimes are reported to the police. Seventy-four percent of the neighborhood commercial establishments surveyed do not report to police the thefts committed by their employees.

The existence of crime, the talk about crime, the reports of crime, and the fear of crime have eroded the basic quality of life of many Americans. A Commission study conducted in high crime areas of two large cities found that:

43 percent of the respondents say they stay off the streets at night because of their fear of crime.

35 percent say they do not speak to strangers any more because of their fear of crime.

21 percent say they use cars and cabs at night because of their fear of crime.

20 percent say they would like to move to another neighborhood because of their fear of crime.

The findings of the Commission's national survey generally support those of the local surveys. One-third of a representative sample of all Americans say it is unsafe to walk alone at night in their neighborhoods. Slightly more than one-third say they keep firearms in the house for protection against criminals. Twenty-eight percent say they keep watchdogs for the same reason.

Under any circumstance, developing an effective response to the problem of crime in America is exceedingly difficult. And because of the changes expected in the population in the next decade, in years to come it will be more difficult. Young people commit a disproportionate share of crime and the number of young people in our society is growing at a much faster rate than the total population. Although the 15- to 17-year-old age group represents only 5.4 percent of the population, it accounts for 12.8 percent of all arrests. Fifteen and sixteen year olds have the highest arrest rate in the United States. The problem in the years ahead is dramatically foretold by the fact that 23 percent of the population is 10 or under.

Despite the seriousness of the problem today and the increasing challenge in the years ahead, the central conclusion of the Commission is that a significant reduction in crime is possible if the following objectives are vigorously pursued:

First, society must seek to prevent crime before it happens by assuring all Americans a stake in the benefits and responsibilities of American life, by strengthening law enforcement, and by reducing criminal opportunities.

Second, society's aim of reducing crime would be better served if the system of criminal justice developed a far broader range of techniques with which to deal with individual offenders.

Third, the system of criminal justice must eliminate existing injustices if it is to achieve its ideals and win the respect and cooperation of all citizens.

Fourth, the system of criminal justice must attract more people and better people—police, prosecutors, judges, defense attorneys, probation and parole officers, and corrections officials with more knowledge, expertise, initiative, and integrity.

Fifth, there must be much more operational and basic research into the problems of crime and criminal administration, by those both within and without the system of criminal justice.

Sixth, the police, courts, and correctional agencies must be given substantially greater amounts of money if they are to improve their ability to control crime.

Seventh, individual citizens, civic and business organizations, religious institutions, and all levels of government must take responsibility for planning and implementing the changes that must be made in the criminal justice system if crime is to be reduced.

In terms of specific recommendations, what do these seven objectives mean?

1. PREVENTING CRIME

The prevention of crime covers a wide range of activities: Eliminating social conditions closely associated with crime; improving the ability of the criminal justice system to detect, apprehend, judge, and reintegrate into their communities those who commit crimes; and reducing the situations in which crimes are most likely to be committed.

Every effort must be made to strengthen the family, now often shattered by the grinding pressures of urban slums.

Slum schools must be given enough resources to make them as good as schools elsewhere and to enable them to compensate for the various handicaps suffered by the slum child—to rescue him from his environment.

Present efforts to combat school segregation, and the housing segregation that underlies it, must be continued and expanded.

Employment opportunities must be enlarged and young people provided with more effective vocational training and individual job counseling. Programs to create new kinds of jobs—such as probation aides, medical assistants, and teacher helpers—seem particularly promising and should be expanded.

The problem of increasing the ability of the police to detect and apprehend criminals is complicated. In one effort to find out how this objective could be achieved, the Commission conducted an analysis of 1,905 crimes reported to the Los Angeles Police Department during a recent month. The study showed the importance of identifying the perpetrator at the scene of the crime. Eighty-six percent of the crimes with named suspects were solved, but only 12 percent of the unnamed suspect crimes were solved. Another finding of the study was that there is a relationship between the speed of response and certainty of apprehension. On the average, response to emergency calls resulting in arrests was 50 percent faster than response to emergency calls not resulting in arrest. On the basis of this finding, and a cost effectiveness study to discover the best means to reduce response time, the Commission recommends an experimental program to develop computer-aided command-and-control systems for large police departments.

To insure the maximum use of such a system headquarters must have a direct link with every onduty police officer. Because large scale production would result in a substantial reduction of the cost of miniature two-way radios, the Commission recommends that the Federal Government assume leadership in initiating a development program for such equipment and that it consider guaranteeing the sale of the first production lot of perhaps 20,000 units.

Two other steps to reduce police response time are recommended:

> Police callboxes, which are locked and inconspicuous in most cities, should be left open, brightly marked, and designated "public emergency callboxes."
>
> The telephone company should develop a single police number for each metropolitan area, and eventually for the entire United States.

Improving the effectiveness of law enforcement, however, is much more than just improving police response time. For example a study in Washington, D.C, found that courtroom time for a felony defendant who pleads guilty probably totals less than 1 hour, while the median time from his initial appearance to his disposition is 4 months.

In an effort to discover how courts can best speed the process of criminal justice, the known facts about felony cases in Washington were placed in a computer and the operation of the system was simulated. After a number of possible solutions to the problem of delay were tested, it appeared that the addition of a second grand jury—which, with supporting personnel, would cost less than $50,000 a year—would result in a 25-percent reduction in the time required for the typical felony case to move from initial appearance to trial.

The application of such analysis—when combined with the Commission's recommended timetable laying out timespans for each step in the criminal process—should help court systems to ascertain their procedural bottlenecks and develop ways to eliminate them.

Another way to prevent crime is to reduce the opportunity to commit it. Many crimes would not be committed, indeed many criminal careers would not begin, if there were fewer opportunities for crime.

Auto theft is a good example. According to FBI statistics, the key had been left in the ignition or the ignition had been left unlocked in 42 percent of all stolen cars. Even in those cars taken when the ignition was locked, at least 20 percent were stolen simply by shorting the ignition with such simple devices as paper clips or tinfoil. In one city, the elimination of the unlocked "off" position on the 1965 Chevrolet resulted in 50 percent fewer of those models being stolen in 1965 than were stolen in 1964. . . .

Stricter gun controls also would reduce some kinds of crime. Here, the Commission recommends a strengthening of the Federal law governing the interstate shipment of firearms and enactment of State laws requiring the registration of all handguns, rifles, and shotguns, and prohibiting the sale or ownership of firearms by certain categories of persons—dangerous criminals, habitual drunkards, and drug addicts. After 5 years, the Commission recommends that Congress pass a Federal registration law applying to those States that have not passed their own registration laws.

2. NEW WAYS OF DEALING WITH OFFENDERS

The Commission's second objective—the development of a far broader range of alternatives for dealing with offenders—is based on the belief that, while there are some who must be completely segregated from society, there are many instances in which segregation does more harm than good. Furthermore, by concentrating the resources of the police, the courts, and correctional agencies on the smaller number of offenders who really need them, it should be possible to give all offenders more effective treatment.

A specific and important example of this principle is the Commission's recommendation that every community consider establishing a Youth Services Bureau, a community-based center to which juveniles could be referred by the police, the courts, parents, schools, and social agencies for counseling, education, work, or recreation programs and job placement.

The Youth Services Bureau—an agency to handle many troubled and troublesome young people outside the criminal system—is needed in part because society has failed to give the juvenile court the resources that would allow it to function as its founders hoped it would. In a recent survey of juvenile court judges, for example, 83 percent said no psychologist or psychiatrist was available to their courts on a regular basis and one-third said they did not have probation officers or social workers. Even where there are probation officers, the Commission found, the average officer supervises 76 probationers, more than double the recommended caseload.

The California Youth Authority for the last 5 years has been conducting a controlled experiment to determine the effectiveness of another kind of alternative treatment program for juveniles. There, after initial screening, convicted juvenile delinquents are assigned on a random basis to either an experimental group or a control group. Those in the experimental group are returned to the community and receive intensive individual counseling, group counseling, group therapy, and family counseling. Those in the control group are assigned to California's regular institutional treatment program. The findings so far: 28 percent of the experimental group have had their paroles revoked, compared with 52 percent in the control group. Furthermore, the community treatment program is less expensive than institutional treatment.

To make community-based treatment possible for both adults and juveniles, the Commission recommends the development of an entirely new kind of correctional institution: located close to population centers; maintaining close relations with schools, employers, and universities; housing as few as 50 inmates; serving as a classification center, as the center for various kinds of community programs and as a port of reentry to the community for those difficult and dangerous offenders who have required treatment in facilities with tighter custody.

Such institutions would be useful in the operation of programs—strongly recommended by the Commission—that permit selected inmates to work or study in the community during the day and return to control at night, and programs that permit long-term inmates to become adjusted to society gradually rather than being discharged directly from maximum security institutions to the streets.

Another aspect of the Commission's conviction that different offenders with different problems should be treated in different ways, is its recommendation about the handling of public drunkenness, which, in 1965, accounted for one out of every three arrests in America. The great number of these arrests—some 2 million—burdens the police, clogs the lower courts and crowds the penal institutions. The Commission therefore recommends that communities develop civil detoxification units and comprehensive aftercare programs, and that with the development of such programs, drunkenness, not accompanied by other unlawful conduct, should not be a criminal offense.

Similarly, the Commission recommends the expanded use of civil commitment for drug addicts.

3. ELIMINATING UNFAIRNESS

The third objective is to eliminate injustices so that the system of criminal justice can win the respect and cooperation of all citizens. Our society must give the police, the courts, and correctional agencies the resources and the mandate to provide fair and dignified treatment for all.

The Commission found overwhelming evidence of institutional shortcomings in almost every part of the United States.

A survey of the lower court operations in a number of large American cities found cramped and noisy courtrooms, undignified and perfunctory procedures, badly trained personnel overwhelmed by enormous caseloads. In short, the Commission *found assembly line justice.*

The Commission found that in at least three States, justices of the peace are paid only if they convict and collect a fee from the defendant, a practice held unconstitutional by the Supreme Court 40 years ago.

The Commission found that approximately one-fourth of the 400,000 children detained in 1965—for a variety of causes but including truancy, smoking, and running away from home—were held in adult jails and lockups, often with hardened criminals.

In addition to the creation of new kinds of institutions—such as the Youth Services Bureau and the small, community-based correctional centers—the Commission recommends several important procedural changes. It recommends counsel at various points in the criminal process.

For juveniles, the Commission recommends providing counsel whenever coercive action is a possibility.

For adults, the Commission recommends providing counsel to any criminal defendant who faces a significant penalty—excluding traffic and similar petty charges—if he cannot afford to provide counsel for himself.

In connection with this recommendation, the Commission asks each State to finance regular, statewide assigned counsel and defender systems for the indigent.

Counsel also should be provided in parole and probation revocation hearings.

Another kind of broad procedural change that the Commission recommends is that every State, county, and local jurisdiction provide judicial officers with sufficient information about individual defendants to permit the release without money bail of those who can be safely released.

In addition to eliminating the injustice of holding persons charged with a crime merely because they cannot afford bail, this recommendation also would save a good deal of money. New York City alone, for example, spends approximately $10 million a year holding persons who have not yet been found guilty of any crime.

Besides institutional injustices, the Commission found that while the great majority of criminal justice and law enforcement personnel perform their duties with fairness and understanding, even under the most trying circumstances, some take advantage of their official positions and act in a callous, corrupt, or brutal manner.

Injustice will not yield to simple solutions. Overcoming it requires a wide variety of remedies including improved methods of selecting personnel, the massive infusion of additional funds, the revamping of existing procedures and the adoption of more effective internal and external controls.

The relations between the police and urban poor deserve special mention. Here the Commission recommends that every large department—especially in communities with substantial minority populations—should have community-relations machinery consisting of a headquarters planning and supervising unit and precinct units to carry out recommended programs. Effective citizen advisory committees should be established in minority group neighborhoods. All departments with substantial minority populations should make special efforts to recruit minority group officers and to deploy and promote them fairly. They should have rigorous internal investigation units to examine complaints of misconduct. The Commission believes it is of the utmost importance to insure that complaints of unfair treatment are fairly dealt with.

Fair treatment of every individual—fair in fact and also perceived to be fair by those affected—is an essential element of justice and a principal objective of the American criminal justice system.

4. PERSONNEL

The fourth objective is that higher levels of knowledge, expertise, and integrity be achieved by police, judges, prosecutors, defense attorneys, and correctional authorities so that the system of criminal justice can improve its ability to control crime.

The Commission found one obstacle to recruiting better police officers was the standard requirement that all candidates—regardless of qualifications—begin their careers at the lowest level and normally remain at this level from 2 to 5 years before being eligible for promotion. Thus, a college graduate must enter a department at the same rank and pay and perform the same tasks as a person who enters with only a high school diploma or less.

The Commission recommends that police departments give up single entry and establish three levels at which candidates may begin their police careers. The Commission calls these three levels the "community service officer," the "police officer," and the "police agent."

This division, in addition to providing an entry place for the better educated, also would permit police departments to tap the special knowledge, skills, and understanding of those brought up in the slums.

The community service officer would be a uniformed but unarmed member of the police department. Two of his major responsibilities would be to maintain close relations with juveniles in the area where he works and to be especially alert to crime-breeding conditions that other city agencies had not dealt with. Typically, the CSO might be under 21, might not be required to meet conventional education requirements, and might work out of a store-front office. Serving as an apprentice policeman—a substitute for the police cadet—the CSO would work as a member of a team with the police officer and police agent.

The police officer would respond to calls for service, perform routine patrol, render emergency services, make preliminary investigations, and enforce traffic regulations. In order to qualify as a police officer at the present time, a candidate should possess a high school diploma and should demonstrate a capacity for college work.

The police agent would do whatever police jobs were most complicated, most sensitive, and most demanding. He might be a specialist in police community-relations or juvenile delinquency. He might be in uniform patrolling a high-crime neighborhood. He might have staff duties. To become a police agent would require at least 2 years of college work and preferably a baccalaureate degree in the liberal arts or social sciences.

As an ultimate goal, the Commission recommends that all police personnel with general enforcement powers have baccalaureate degrees.

While candidates could enter the police service at any one of the three levels, they also could work their way up through the different categories as they met the basic education and other requirements.

In many jurisdictions there is a critical need for additional police personnel. Studies by the Commission indicate a recruiting need of 50,000 policemen in 1967 just to fill positions already authorized. In order to increase police effectiveness, additional staff specialists will be required, and when the community service officers are added manpower needs will be even greater.

The Commission also recommends that every State establish a commission on police standards to set minimum recruiting and training standards and to provide financial and technical assistance for local police departments.

In order to improve the quality of judges, prosecutors, and defense attorneys, the Commission recommends a variety of steps: Taking the selection of judges out of partisan politics; the more regular use of seminars, conferences, and institutes to train sitting judges; the establishment of judicial commissions to excuse physically or mentally incapacitated judges from their duties without public humiliation; the general abolition of part-time district attorneys and assistant district attorneys; and a broad range of measures to develop a greatly enlarged and better trained pool of defense attorneys.

In the correctional system there is a critical shortage of probation and parole officers, teachers, caseworkers, vocational instructors, and group workers. The need for major manpower increases in this area was made clear by the findings from the Commissions national corrections survey:

> Less than 3 percent of all personnel working in local jails and institutions devote their time to treatment and training.
> Eleven States do not offer any kind of probation services for adult misdemeanants, six offer only the barest fragments of such services, and most States offer them on a spotty basis. Two-thirds of all State adult felony probationers are in caseloads of over 100 persons.

To meet the requirements of both the correctional agencies and the courts, the Commission has found an immediate need to double the Nation's pool of juvenile probation officers, triple the number of probation officers working with adult felons, and increase sevenfold the number of officers working with misdemeanants.

Another area with a critical need for large numbers of expert criminal justice officers is the complex one of controlling organized crime. Here, the Commission recommends that prosecutors and police in every State and city where organized crime is known to, or may, exist develop special organized crime units.

5. RESEARCH

The fifth objective is that every segment of the system of criminal justice devote a significant part of its resources for research to insure the development of new and effective methods of controlling crime.

The Commission found that little research is being conducted into such matters as the economic impact of crime; the effects on crime of increasing or decreasing criminal sanctions; possible methods for improving the effectiveness of various procedures of the police, courts, and correctional agencies.

Organized crime is another area in which almost no research has been conducted. The Commission found that the only group with any significant knowledge about this problem was law enforcement officials. Those in other disciplines—social scientists, economists and lawyers, for example—have not until recently considered the possibility of research projects on organized crime. . . .

6. MONEY

Sixth, the police, the courts, and correctional agencies will require substantially more money if they are to control crime better.

Almost all of the specific recommendations made by the Commission will involve increased budgets. Substantially higher salaries must be offered to attract top-flight candidates to the system of criminal justice. For example, the median annual salary for a patrolman in a large city today is $5,300. Typically, the maximum salary is something less than $1,000 above the starting salary. The Commission believes the most important change that can be made in police salary scales is to increase maximums sharply. An FBI agent, for example, starts at $8,421 a year and if he serves long and well enough can reach $16,905 a year without being promoted to a supervisory position. The Commission is aware that reaching such figures immediately is not possible in many cities, but it believes that there should be a large range from minimum to maximum everywhere.

The Commission also recommends new kinds of programs that will require additional funds: Youth Services Bureaus, greatly enlarged misdemeanant probation services and increased levels of research, for example. . . .

7. RESPONSIBILITY FOR CHANGE

Seventh, individual citizens, social-service agencies, universities, religious institutions, civic and business groups, and all kinds of governmental agencies at all levels must become involved in planning and executing changes in the criminal justice system.

The Commission is convinced that the financial and technical assistance program it proposes can and should be only a small part of the national effort to develop a more effective and fair response to crime.

In March of 1966, President Johnson asked the Attorney General to invite each Governor to form a State committee on criminal administration. The response to this request has been encouraging; more than two-thirds of the States already have such committees or have indicated they intend to form them.

The Commission recommends that in every State and city there should be an agency, or one or more officials, with specific responsibility for planning improvements in criminal administration and encouraging their implementation. . . .

36

CRIME, VICTIMS, AND THE POLICE

Phillip H. Ennis

"A skid row drunk lying in a gutter is crime. So is the killing of an unfaithful wife. A Cosa Nostra conspiracy to bribe public officials is crime. So is a strong-arm robbery. . . ." So states the report of the President's Commission on Law Enforcement and Administration of Justice, commonly known as the Crime Commission report, in pointing out the diversity of crime. Our recent investigation at Chicago's National Opinion Research Center reveals that Americans are also frequent prey to incidents which may not fall firmly within the jurisdiction of criminal law, but which still leave the ordinary citizen with a strong sense of victimization—consumer frauds, landlord-tenant violations, and injury or property damage due to someone else's negligent driving.

With the aid of a new research method for estimating national crime rates the Crime Commission study has now confirmed what many have claimed all along—that the rates for a wide range of personal crimes and property offenses are considerably higher than previous figures would indicate. Traditional studies have relied on the police blotter for information. The present research, devised and carried out by the National Opinion Research Center (NORC), tried a survey approach instead. Taking a random sample of 10,000 households during the summer of 1965, we asked people what crimes had been committed against them during the preceding year. The results—roughly 2,100 verified incidents—

Reprinted from Phillip H. Ennis, Crime, Victims, and the Police, *Transaction,* 4, no. 7, pp. 36-44, June 1967.

indicated that as many as half of the people interviewed were victims of offenses which they did not report to the police.

This finding raised several questions. How much did this very high incidence of unreported offenses alter the picture presented by the standard measures, notably the FBI's Uniform Crime Reports (UCR) index, based only on reported incidents? What was the situation with minor offenses, those not considered in the UCR index? What sorts of crimes tended to go unreported? And why did so many victims fail to contact the authorities? These were some of the issues we attempted to probe.

THE UNKNOWN VICTIMS

More than 20 percent of the households surveyed were criminally victimized during the preceding year. This figure includes about *twice as much* major crime as reported by the UCR index. The incidence of minor crimes—simple assaults, petty larcenies, malicious mischiefs, frauds, and so on—is even greater. According to our research, these are at least twice as frequent as major crimes. The UCR index includes seven major crimes, so the proliferation of petty offenses not taken into account by the index makes the discrepancy between that index and the real crime picture even greater than a consideration of major offenses alone would indicate.

Table I compares our figures with the UCR rates for the seven major crimes upon which the index is based—homicide, forcible rape, robbery, aggravated assault, burglary, larceny (over $50), and auto theft. The homicide rate projected by the survey is very close to the UCR rate—not surprising since murder is the crime most likely to be discovered and reported.

The survey estimate of the car theft rate is puzzlingly low. This could be because people report their cars "stolen" to the police and then find that they themselves have "misplaced" the car or that someone else has merely "borrowed" it. They may either forget the incident when interviewed or be too embarrassed to mention it. The relatively high rate of auto thefts reported to the police confirms other studies which show people are more likely to notify the police in this case than they are if they are victims of most other crimes. It may also indicate that people think the police can or will do more about a car theft than about many other offenses.

The startling frequency of reported forcible rape, four times that of the UCR index, underscores the peculiar nature of this crime. It occurs very often among people who know each other—at the extreme, estranged husband and wife—and there appears to be some stigma attached to the victim. Yet among the cases discovered in the survey, too few to be statistically reliable, most were reported to the police. Do the police tend to downgrade the offense into an assault or a minor sex case or put it into some miscellaneous category? This is a well-known practice for certain other kinds of crime.

Table I—Estimated Rates of Major Crimes: 1965-1966

Crime	NORC sample: estimated rate per 100,000	Uniform Crime Reports, 1965: individual or residential rates per 100,000
Homicide	3.0	5.1
Forcible rape	42.5	11.6
Robbery	94.0	61.4*
Aggravated assault	218.3	106.6
Burglary	949.1	296.6*
Larceny ($50+)	606.5	267.4*
Car theft	206.2	226.0†
Total	2,119.6	974.7

*The 1965 Uniform Crime Reports show for burglary and larcenies the number of residential and individual crimes. The overall rate per 100,000 population is therefore reduced by the proportion of these crimes that occurred to individuals. Since all robberies to individuals were included in the NORC sample regardless of whether the victim was acting as an individual or as part of an organization, the *total* UCR figure was used for comparison.

†The reduction of the UCR auto theft rate by 10 percent is based on the figures of the Automobile Manufacturers Association, showing that 10 percent of all cars are owned by leasing-rental agencies and private and governmental fleets. The Chicago Police Department's auto theft personnel confirmed that about 7-10 percent of stolen cars recovered were from fleet, rental, and other non-individually owned sources.

To what extent is crime concentrated in the urban environment? To what extent are there regional differences in crime rates? And to what extent are the poor, and especially Negroes, more or less likely to be victims of crime? Behind these questions lie alternative remedial measures, measures which range from city planning and antipoverty programs to the training and organization of police departments and the allocation of their resources throughout the nation.

THE WILD, WILD WEST

The NORC findings presented . . . give an overview of the crime rates for central cities in metropolitan areas, for their suburban environs, and for nonmetropolitan areas in the four main regions of the country. . . . crime rate (per 100,000 population) for serious crimes against the person (homicide, rape, robbery, and aggravated assault) and serious crimes against property (burglary, larceny over $50, and vehicle theft).

The myth of the wild West is borne out by our figures. Its present crime rate, for both property and personal crimes, is higher than that of any other region of the country. The West has almost twice the rates of the Northeast for all three types of communities. The South, in contrast, does not appear to have the high rate of violent crime that is sometimes alleged.

As one moves from the central city to the suburbs and out into the smaller towns and rural areas, the crime rates decline, but much more drastically for crimes against the person than for property crimes. The metropolitan center has a violent crime rate about *five times* as high as the smaller city and rural areas, but a property crime rate only *twice* as high.

Evidently the city is a more dangerous place than the suburbs or a small town. Yet these figures require some qualification: About 40 percent of the aggravated assaults and rapes (constituting most of the serious crimes against the person) take place *within* the victim's home; and about 45 percent of all the serious crimes against the person are committed by someone familiar to the victim. Random "crime in the streets" by strangers is clearly *not* the main picture that emerges from these figures, even in the urban setting.

Who are the victims? Among lower income groups (under $6,000 per year) Negroes are almost twice as likely as whites to be victims of serious crimes of violence but only very slightly more likely to be victims of property crimes. Our figures show that, per 100,000 population, an estimated 748 low-income Negroes per year will be victims of criminal violence and 1,927 victims of property offenses, whereas the numbers for whites in the same income bracket are 402 and 1,829. The situation is exactly reversed for upper income groups. The wealthier Negro is not much more likely than the white to be a victim of a violent crime, but he is considerably more likely to have property stolen. His chances of losing property are 3,024 in 100,000, whereas the figure is only 1,765 for whites in the same income bracket. Burglary is the most common property crime against more affluent Negroes. The implication is that ghetto neighborhoods in which poor and richer Negroes live side by side make the latter more vulnerable to property losses than are higher income whites, who can live in more economically homogeneous areas.

Despite the fact then that per capita offense rates are generally acknowledged to be higher among Negroes than among whites, the incidence of whites being victimized by Negroes—an image frequently conjured up by the specter of "crime in the streets"—is relatively infrequent. Negroes tend instead to commit offenses against members of their own race. The same is true of whites. Further, to the extent that crime is interracial at all, Negroes are more likely to be victims of white offenders than vice versa. Our figures show that only 12 percent of the offenses against whites in our sample were committed by nonwhites, whereas 19 percent of the nonwhite victims reported that the persons who committed offenses against them were white.

WHO CALLS THE POLICE?

What happens when a person is victimized? How often are law enforcement and judicial authorities involved? What changes occur in the victim's attitude and behavior as a result of the incident?

If the "right thing" to do is to call the police when you have been a victim of a crime, and there is considerable pressure to do just that, why is it that half the victimizations were not reported to the police?

The more serious the crime, the more likely it is to be reported: 65 percent of the aggravated assaults in our sample were reported to the police, but only 46 percent of the simple assaults; 60 percent of the grand larcenies, but only 37 percent of the petty larcenies. Insurance recovery also appears to play a role in the very high rate of reported auto thefts (89 percent) and reported victimizations that are the result of automobile negligence (71 percent). Victims of offenses at the border of the criminal law apparently do not think the police should be involved. Only 10 percent of the consumer fraud victims called the police, whereas 26 percent of the ordinary fraud victims (mainly those of bad checks) did so.

Those victims who said they did not notify the police were asked why. Their reasons fell into four fairly distinct categories. The first was the belief that the incident was not a police matter. These victims (34 percent) did not want the offender to be harmed by the police or thought that the incident was a private, not a criminal, affair. Two percent of the nonreporting victims feared reprisal, either physically from the offender's friends or economically from cancellation of or increases in rates of insurance. Nine percent did not want to take the time or trouble to get involved with the police, did not know whether they should call the police, or were too confused to do so. Finally, a substantial 55 percent of the nonreporting victims failed to notify the authorities because of their attitudes toward police effectiveness. These people believed the police could not do anything about the incident, would not catch the offenders, or would not want to be bothered.

The distribution of these four types of reasons for failure to notify police varies by type of crime and by the social characteristics of the victim, but two points are clear. First, there is strong resistance to invoking the law enforcement process even in matters that are clearly criminal. Second, there is considerable skepticism as to the effectiveness of police action.

THE ATTRITION OF JUSTICE

A clue to this skepticism lies in the events which follow a call to the police. All the victims who reported an offense were asked how the police reacted and how far the case proceeded up the judicial ladder—arrest, trial, sentencing, and so forth. We have simplified the process into six stages:

Given a "real" victimization, the police were or were not notified.

Once notified, the police either came to the scene of the victimization (or in some other way acknowledged the event) or failed to do so.

Once they arrived, the police did or did not regard the incident as a crime.

Regarding the matter as a crime, the police did or did not make an arrest.

Once an arrest was made, there was or was not a trial (including plea of guilty).

The outcome of the trial was to free the suspect (or punish him "too leniently") or to find him guilty and give him the "proper" punishment. . . .

Failure of the police to heed a call and their rejection of the incident as a crime account for a large proportion of this attrition. Also noteworthy are the low arrest and trial rates. Once the offender is brought to trial, however, the outcome appears more balanced. About half the offenders were treated too leniently in the victim's view, but the other half were convicted and given "proper" punishment.

SATISFACTION AND REVENGE

How do the victims feel about this truncated legal process? Do they feel that the situation is their own fault and accept it, or are they dissatisfied with the relatively frequent failure of the police to apprehend the offender? When the victims were asked their feelings about the outcome of the incident, only 18 percent said they were very satisfied; another 19 percent were somewhat satisfied; 24 percent were somewhat dissatisfied; and 35 percent were very dissatisfied (4 percent gave no answer).

The level of satisfaction was closely related to how far the case went judicially. (See Table II.) People who did not call the police at all were the most dissatisfied. If they called and the police did not come, about the same percentage were very dissatisfied; but peculiarly, there were more who reported that they were satisfied. An arrest lowered the dissatisfaction level, but the dramatic differences appeared when the offender was brought to trial. If he was acquitted or given too lenient a penalty (in the victim's view), dissatisfaction ran high; if he was convicted and given the "proper" penalty, the victim was generally quite pleased. This suggests that the ordinary citizen's sense of justice includes a vengeful element—a desire for punishment over and above monetary compensation for loss. Advocates of rehabilitation rather than retribution for criminals might well take such public sentiments into account.

Table II—Degree of Satisfaction With Outcome of Offense

Disposition of case	Very satisfied	Somewhat satisfied	Somewhat dissatisfied	Very dissatisfied
No notification of police	13%	18%	28%	41%
Police did not respond to notification	22	22	18	38
Police did not consider incident a crime	24	26	24	26
Crime, but no arrest	20	23	27	30
Arrest, but no trial	33	21	22	24
Acquittal or too lenient penalty	17	13	26	44
Conviction and "proper" penalty	60	16	12	12

Quite independent of the judicial outcome of the case is its impact on the daily life and feelings of the victim and his family. Slightly more than 40 percent of the victims reported increased suspicion and distrustfulness along with intensified personal and household security measures. It appears that it is the unpredictability of the event and the sense of invasion by strangers rather than the seriousness of the crime that engenders this mistrust. With these strong feelings and the frequent lack of knowledge about the identity of the offender, victimization may well exacerbate existing prejudice against the groups typically blamed for social disorder and crime.

POLICE POPULARITY POLL

How does the public feel about the police? The survey asked all the crime victims and a comparably large sample of nonvictims a series of questions probing their attitudes on how well the local police do their job, how respectful they are toward the citizenry, and how honest they are. Items concerning the limits of police authority and exploring the functions of the police were also included.

Several conclusions emerged. Upper income groups are consistently more favorable in their evaluation of the police and are more in favor of augmenting their power than those with lower incomes. Negroes at all income levels show strong negative attitudes toward the police. (See Tables III and IV.)

Table III shows rather clearly that Negroes, regardless of income, estimate police effectiveness lower than whites do, with Negro women being even more critical than Negro men of the job the police are doing. Furthermore, Negroes show a smaller shift in attitude with increasing income than do whites, who are more favorable in their opinion of police effectiveness as their income rises.

Table III—Positive Opinions On Local Police Effectiveness

(Percentage who think police do an excellent or good job in enforcing the law)

	White		Nonwhite	
Sex	Less than $6,000	$6,000 or more	Less than $6,000	$6,000 or more
Male	67%	72%	54%	56%
Female	66	74	39	43

Table IV shows that Negroes are also sharply more critical than whites are of police honesty. Here there are no income differences in attitude among white males. Women at higher income levels, both white and Negro, appear to be relatively less suspicious of police honesty. It is difficult to say how much these attitude differences are attributable to actual experience with police corruption and how much they express degrees of general hostility to the police. In either case the results indicate a more negative attitude toward the police among Negroes than among whites.

Table IV—Opinions On The Honesty Of Neighborhood Police

| | Males | | | |
| | White | | Nonwhite | |
Police are . . .	Less than $6,000	$6,000 or more	Less than $6,000	$6,000 or more
Almost all honest	65%	67%	33%	33%
Most honest, few corrupt	24	26	47	41
Almost all corrupt	3	1	9	19
Don't know	8	6	11	7

| | Females | | | |
| | White | | Nonwhite | |
Police are . . .	Less than $6,000	$6,000 or more	Less than $6,000	$6,000 or more
Almost all honest	57%	65%	24%	35%
Most honest, few corrupt	27	29	54	49
Almost all corrupt	2	0	10	4
Don't know	14	6	12	12

The next question probed a more personal attitude toward the police—their respectfulness toward "people like yourself." Almost 14 percent of the Negroes answered that it was "not so good." Less than 3 percent of the whites chose this response. This represents a much more critical attitude by Negroes than by whites, with hardly any differences by sex or income. There is some tendency, however, for very low income people of both races and sexes to feel that the police are not sufficiently respectful to them.

One further conclusion is more tentative. It appears that there is no *one* underlying attitude toward the police. The police have many and sometimes only slightly related jobs to do in society. For example, they have a role both in suppressing organized gambling and in maintaining civil order. Most people (73 percent) feel the police should stop gambling even though it brings a good deal of money into the community. A significant minority (21 percent) feel the police should act only on complaints, and only 2 percent said the police should not interfere with gambling at all. With respect to police control of demonstrations for civil and political rights, on the other hand, a slight majority (54 percent) say police should not interfere if the protests are peaceful; 40 percent say police should stop all demonstrations; and 3 percent feel demonstrations should be allowed under any and all circumstances. Negroes are much more permissive about demonstrations than whites, and somewhat more permissive about gambling. Among lower income Negroes there is a significant relation between permissiveness on gambling and a strong prodemonstration attitude. But whites show no such consistent attitudes on the two issues. They tend to favor police intervention in gambling but not in rights demonstrations.

A more dramatic example of discontinuities in attitudes toward police has to do with limitations on their power. A national cross-section of citizens was asked:

"Recently some cities have added civilian review boards to their police departments. Some people say such boards offer the public needed protection against the police, and others say these boards are unnecessary and would interfere with good police work and morale. In general, would you be in favor of civilian review boards or opposed to them?"

In favor	45%
Opposed	35
Don't know	20

"Do you favor giving the police more power to question people, do you think they have enough power already, or would you like to see some of their power to question people curtailed?"

Police should have more power	52%
Have enough power already	43
Should curtail power	5

"The police sometimes have a hard time deciding if there is enough evidence to arrest a suspect. In general, do you think it is better for them to risk arresting an innocent person rather than letting the criminal get away, or is it better for them to be really sure they are getting the right person before they make an arrest?"

Risk arresting innocent	42%
Be really sure	58

"The Supreme Court has recently ruled that in criminal cases the police may not question a suspect without his lawyer being present, unless the suspect agrees to be questioned without a lawyer. Are you in favor of this Supreme Court decision or opposed to it?"

In favor	65%
Opposed	35

The significance of these results is their lack of consensus. On none of the questions is there overwhelming agreement or disagreement. Opinions are split almost in half, with the exception that hardly anyone is in favor of curtailing present police powers. The advocates of extending police authority in questioning suspects are almost balanced by those who think the police have enough power to do their job. Further, there is lack of internal agreement on the specific facets of the question. Being in favor of a civilian review board does not necessarily make a person support the Supreme Court decision on interrogation of suspects. Nor does a preference for having the police risk arresting the innocent rather than letting a criminal go free strongly predict being in favor of granting more power to the police in questioning people.

It is not clear why attitudes toward the police are so scattered. Perhaps police power is too new an issue on the national scene to have its components hammered into a clear and cohesive whole. Local variations in police practices may also blur the situation. It appears we are only at the beginning of a long process of relocating the police in the political spectrum.

As the federal presence in local law enforcement enlarges, both the shape of crime and the nature of law enforcement itself will change. Accurate crime statistics will be essential in monitoring these changes and in evaluating the worth of new programs designed to protect the public from the growing threat of invasion and victimization by criminal acts.

37

THE CRIMINAL AND THE LAW

Martin Mayer

... The American way of dealing with crime and the people accused of crime is an unholy and inexcusable mess. Even those who disagree with what the Supreme Court has been trying to do about the mess—and most lawyers and judges, plus all policemen, *do* disagree with the Court—can't find much to say for the system as it works today.

We don't even know how bad it is. We don't know how many crimes there are (the FBI Uniform Crime Reports depend on a lot of guesswork by the police and don't cover the whole country). We don't know how many people are arrested. The courts in all but a handful of states don't keep good enough records to tell us how many people are formally charged with crime each year—the best guess, after eliminating the speeders, drunks, prostitutes, gamblers and shoplifters, is about 700,000, more than half of them juveniles. We don't have the vaguest notion of what the courts do with the juveniles; that's kept secret by law. Of the grown-ups accused in court, we *think* about two thirds plead guilty.

A team of investigators from the University of Chicago, who worked for a year putting together the information, estimates that a decade ago there were about 55,000 jury trials in the country. Some of those jury trials were for offenses not many people would call "crimes"—among the jury trials turned up

Reprinted from Martin Mayer, The Criminal and the Law, *Saturday Evening Post,* **240**, no. 3, pp. 25-27, 70-78, February 11, 1967.

by the Chicago professors was one for installing a kitchen appliance without a license and another for illegally keeping a mud turtle. In some of the Southern and Western states you're entitled to a jury trial before you can be fined for being drunk and disorderly. Probably about 40,000 of the jury trials deal with real crimes, which means that only about one eighth of the adults who are charged even ask for that "due process of law" which is supposed to be the glory of the American legal system. In the big cities, where the big problems are, the proportion is much lower—in Manhattan only three percent of the felony indictments (the most serious crimes) lead to jury trials; and for misdemeanors (the less serious crimes), New York doesn't have jury trials at all.

We think—again, we don't know—that about 70 percent of those who stand trial are convicted by a jury. What happens to the 225,000 or so who plead guilty and the 25,000 or so who are convicted after trial is another mystery. Apparently, about 140,000 a year go to prison. Most of them have been in the jug before; nobody knows what proportion of the nation's crimes are committed by people who are already experienced at crime, but there's no question that the police keep catching the same criminals. The criminologists believe that about two thirds of the people sent to prison for the first time dislike the experience enough to go straight later, while one third become recruits to the large and growing cadre of habitual criminals.

The reason we don't know much is that for all our talk about crime and criminals, we really don't care. "To us," Nicholas deB. Katzenbach wrote in the *American Bar Association Journal* shortly before his resignation as Attorney General, "the system of criminal justice is largely invisible because we have no contact with it." We hire policemen and prosecuting attorneys and judges, and ask them to "stop" crime and to punish what they can't stop. Most of the people involved in the system are involved in it every day, and it looks more or less all right to them because they're used to it; anyway, they're so busy taking care of today's problems that they can't take much time to wonder what finally happened to yesterday's.

About the only people who must visit the criminal justice system but don't live there are the judges in the courts of appeals, who occasionally review some of the convictions in the relatively few jury trials. Recently, a number of these judges, especially (but not exclusively) those on the Supreme Court, have become increasingly disturbed by what they see when they visit. In a series of opinions over the last 10 years, the Supreme Court has insisted that defendants are entitled to help from lawyers both before and after trial, that the D.A. may not use against them evidence illegally seized by the police, and that juries may not hear confessions wheedled out of suspects during interrogations in station-house back rooms.

How much difference these rulings will make, nobody knows. The courts never see anything but the part of the iceberg that shows—and the Supreme Court sees only a tiny ragged edge of that, because it's only the hard cases that come for final appeal to Washington. Angry opponents of the Court's decisions can point to some dozens (perhaps hundreds) of undoubted thieves, murderers and rapists who have had to be released because their recent convictions—or the cases being prepared against them—had been based on evidence that the police gathered in ways the Court no longer permits. But these defeats for justice—and it should be remembered that justice is defeated when a guilty man goes free as well as when an innocent man is convicted—may be merely a temporary result of changing the rules in the middle of the game. . . .

To understand why the Court wants to change today's system, and why it will be hard to change, you have to look at the system fairly closely. About the best place to start is New York's Part 1-A, a Manhattan courtroom which since January 11 has been on a "we-never-close" basis, seven days a week, to give everybody a little more time to process the business.

Part 1-A is an arraignment court—a court to which prisoners are brought by the police who have arrested them, so that a judge may learn the charge the State expects to prove, hear the prospective defendant's lawyer if there is one and assign one if there isn't, set or deny bail or release with orders to return on a certain day.

The court is a large, squarish room with a high ceiling. The walls are wood-paneled to a height of about seven feet; dark fixtures hang down from the geometrically ornamented ceiling and give an even, just-bright-enough light, not influenced by what comes through the dirty northern windows, which face another wing of the building. Before January 11, suspected felons passed through 1-A at the rate of one every five minutes; now there will be 10 minutes or so for each case. Most cases are adjourned for one reason or another; a few are disposed of; a few are assigned to trial.

The courtroom has four entrances. At the rear, a pair of heavy doors covered in leather swing soundlessly into the center aisle of a public area, full of long, dark-wood benches, which occupies about three quarters of the room. The public end is separated from the business end by a hip-high, dark-wood barrier. Into the working part of the court open three small doors, one at the spectators' left for the lawyers and court attendants and two straight ahead. One of these leads to the judge's chambers and one to the shallow pens where suspects, eight or nine to a cell, await their moment in court. Lawyers interview their clients, often for the first time, through the bars.

Both parts of the courtroom seethe with humanity. In the public area sit several hundred people—those of the accused felons who are out on bail or "on recognizance," their friends and families, complaining witnesses, some police-men, some lawyers. There is a great deal of motion along the rows of seats and up and down the center and both the side aisles. A buzz rises from the area, though many, perhaps most, sit dumbly and incuriously. People are not allowed to read in courtrooms, and the proceedings up front are only partly audible—and rarely comprehensible—in the rear.

Judge Simon Silver, looking quite small, as judges usually do in black robes, sits on a chair behind a very long desk on a platform raised perhaps 18 inches off the courtroom floor. Behind him are flags and a gilded motto: N GOD WE TRUST (the "I" had fallen off). Below the judge, at a long table, sit assorted clerks and probation officers. Over by the lawyers' door is a small desk and some chairs for the young Legal Aid lawyers, three or four of them, who will represent about three fifths of the defendants. Backed against the wooden barrier is a sometimes empty, sometimes crowded row of wooden armchairs, for the individually retained lawyers. On the wall at the spectators' right are more chairs for policemen, chatting, lounging, waiting to lead their catch to the bar. The Assistant District Attorney, a very young lawyer with protruding eyes and a glum expression, stands at a lectern before the judge's platform. In dead center, facing the public area, a uniformed policeman, known in the lingo of the court as "the bridgeman," pulls a folder from the clerk's table and calls out in a stentorian voice:

"Docket Numbers Twelve Hundred Fifty and Fifty-One, Defendants Michael and Mary. . ."

A young couple comes from the public area to the railing before the bridgeman. They are accompanied by a policeman, who talks to the D.A.

"Do you waive the reading of the charge?" the D.A. asks. There is confusion at the center; their lawyer isn't present. At the lawyers' row one rather shabbily dressed older man says to a younger colleague: "If you're not here, you get murdered. If you are here, you get murdered."

Michael and Mary have returned to their seats, to await their lawyer. A burly white man is at the railing, waiting while his lawyer and the policeman talk with the D.A. The D.A. says, "Your Honor, there's a motion to reduce this charge to assault in the third degree. I have no objection." The case is set for trial; the judge asks, "Would you rather have a three-judge court or a one-judge court?"

A statutory-rape case: a small, thin, Puerto Rican boy, a pregnant girl who looks about 13, and her mother. The D.A. says, "We agreed to a rather long adjournment to give the parties an opportunity to get married. I request a *final* adjournment." These statutory-rape cases are not meant to be prosecuted—they simply enable the State to act as a substitute father, pulling the shotgun out from behind the door.

The Puerto Ricans leave. A white man in a ragged tweed jacket, the stuffing coming out the bottom, takes their place. He stole $64 worth of jewelry from Macy's; the charge is reduced from grand larceny (a felony) to petit larceny (a misdemeanor), and he pleads guilty. The judge browses through some papers—the man's "pedigree sheets," a confidential report—and says, "Four months."

"Your Honor, I have a wife and four children—nobody else takes care of them."

"You should have thought of that before." The judge looks down at the flimsy carbons. "You had a year suspended a few months ago. By rights, I should give you that. Instead, I gave you four months. I think I was pretty generous."

Next a very pale, flabby, middle-aged man in a suit, white shirt and tie comes up with a policeman holding his elbow. He has laid his hands on a child on the

Staten Island ferry. The District Attorney asks $10,000 bail: "He's on parole from a life sentence for rape in Maryland."

His lawyer objects: "It's academic, anyway—but he turned himself in."

The D.A. says again, "He's on a life sentence."

The judge shakes his head. "*He came in*."

"Yes, Your Honor," says the D.A.

The judge sets $500 bail, and the man goes off to jail, to await trial (or return to Maryland); an out-of-towner, he is a bad risk for the bail bondsman.

A tall, broad-shouldered young man comes up with a girl: charge of felonious assault. He and the girl talk with the D.A. The judge interrupts:

"Where's your lawyer?"

The man shakes his head.

"Do you want to go back to jail?"

"No."

"Then get a lawyer—you're on bail, you can afford a lawyer."

But the girl with him is the girl he beat up. The D.A. says, "The People will consent to a reduction to third-degree assault."

The girl speaks to the D.A. even more earnestly, and he shrugs his shoulders. The complaint is dismissed, and the boy and girl go off arm in arm.

A young Negro comes up, grinning, the arresting officer with him, and the D.A. puts the arresting officer in the witness chair. An oath is administered, and the D.A. asks, "Officer, did you arrest this defendant in possession of what you believed to be stolen property?" He did; the man could give no convincing explanation of why he was walking down the street at night carrying a television set and four suits of clothes; but nobody had reported a burglary, and the Legal Aid lawyers were raising hell about holding a man against whom no complainant had appeared. In Britain, the circumstances and the man's inability to explain them would have constituted a crime; not in America. The purpose of the detective's testimony is to put these circumstances on record, to prevent any possible suit for false arrest. The charge is dismissed.

A ratty little colored man comes in from the pens, and a detective in plain clothes is put on the stand. The case is felonious assault—a knifing—and the victim is in critical condition in the hospital. The D.A., leafing through a folder—he never heard of the case until 30 seconds before—requests that the man be held without bail: "I should like to point out to Your Honor that there is a fifty-fifty chance the complainant witness will not survive."

At the lawyers' row is an overdressed, overpowdered lady of 50 or so, in a bulging red blouse and a wide-brimmed hat. She mutters, "Now, that's an adverse comment. He could say, 'there's a fifty-fifty chance the complainant witness *will* survive.' He has a negative attitude."

Farther along the row, another lawyer is saying, "*You* got troubles—there are two defendants and a policeman I can't find."

This is not a pleasant place to work. "You'll notice that a criminal lawyer never wears a hat," says one of them. "You know why? It's because if you put a hat down anywhere in a criminal court building, somebody steals it."

"The problem with being a defense lawyer is that it's like giving your life to the Boston Red Sox," says James Vorenberg, director of the National Crime Commission, and before that a Harvard professor who used to take his children to root for the home team. "You always lose."

Discussions of criminal procedure in America normally start with a sonorous statement to the effect that all men are presumed innocent until proven guilty. Unfortunately, an abstract "presumption of innocence" cannot long survive the experience of the courts. "No one who has been indicted and formally charged with a crime is really presumed innocent by anyone but his friends or well-wishers, or somebody who happens to know that the government was wrong," the late Charles P. Curtis once wrote.

The best of horror stories is that of the innocent man convicted of a crime, and among the most popular of entertainments is the murder which the police have the deuce of a time solving. Both situations are real, too, they happen. But their incidence is statistically invisible in each year's 300,000-odd serious criminal cases where an adult is arraigned before a judge. Substantially more than 95 percent of these defendants have unquestionably done *something* for which they could properly be punished by law—simple, if not necessarily felonious, assault; possession, if not necessarily sale, of narcotics—and about 80 percent will in fact be convicted.

In the great majority of cases, the presumption of innocence is not put to the test in court. Of those arrested on a serious criminal charge, more people are cleared and released by the police themselves than by the entire legal process of arraignment, preliminary hearing, indictment by the grand jury (where this custom exists), and trial. A defendant's next best chance is to persuade the D.A. not to prosecute; six or seven times as many people are released between arraignment and trial as are acquitted after a trial. A good proportion of these will be defendants (like our young man whose girl decided she wanted him even though he had beaten her to a pulp) who have never troubled to deny the charges against them—but for one reason or another it seemed impolitic for the prosecutor to proceed. Of the cases where the prosecutor does decide to press charges, something over 95 percent (in Manhattan, the figure runs about 99 percent) result in conviction by guilty plea or verdict.

"The sad fact is that the cops don't go around arresting people indiscriminately," says the New York defense attorney Harris Steinberg, a sober, deeply thoughtful man who came into the criminal field largely because there were no other jobs in the late '30's for young Jewish graduates of the Harvard Law School. "And the district attorneys don't go around indicting people indiscriminately."

Nobody is trained at a law school—or prepared by the culture—to operate as a defense lawyer in a system of criminal law like ours. It is a true paradox (though probably an inevitable one) that a period when the Supreme Court is insisting on ever-widening representation by lawyers in the criminal process should also be a period when the traditional and popular function of the lawyer in the criminal courts has almost disappeared.

Almost—but not quite. "I have sympathy for these people; they're my clients," Steinberg says. "And there's a great deal the lawyer can do. A man may have had a stroke or a heart attack—he doesn't think it has anything to do with his stealing the money, but I may know the D.A. has a policy of not indicting someone it may kill. A man may not know that the person who will testify against him is an accomplice whose testimony has to be corroborated, and that it isn't. He may not know the statute of limitations has run."

After a brawl in a bar the police will bring in and book the man who's still standing up—and he may regard himself as guilty, because he knifed somebody. But he may have a valid claim of self-defense. A boy who was part of a criminal group but didn't directly do anything may not have committed any crime, even though he identifies with others who are guilty, and the police have brought him in. He needs a lawyer to tell him he is clear.

Basically, however, the criminal defense lawyer, like lawyers in many different areas of the profession, works as a negotiator for his client. The aim of the negotiations is to trade a plea of guilty for a reduction in the seriousness of the charge and/or the promise of a light sentence. "Plea bargaining," as this process is called, has no legal standing, but it is the central phenomenon of our system of criminal justice.

"Maybe the most common crime in America," says a New York lawyer who takes occasional court-assigned criminal cases, "is the perjury of the defendant who swears before the judge that he hasn't been promised anything in return for his plea of guilty." It is not that the judges do not know what has been going on—normally, they do, and may even have been consulted—but that without such a statement in open court a convict may later take the option of appealing for a new trial on the grounds that his guilty plea was induced. A few weeks ago, the first report from the A.B.A. minimum standards project, by a committee headed by Justice Walter Schaefer of the Illinois Supreme Court, called on the courts to recognize plea bargaining as wholly legitimate, and to find ways by which judges can promote and control this negotiated justice.

As Judge Henry T. Lummus of Massachusetts once wrote, "The fact is that a criminal court can operate only by inducing the great mass of actually guilty defendants to plead guilty, paying in leniency the price for the pleas." More than 600 people are arraigned every day in the seven "parts" of the Manhattan criminal courts; and there are fewer than a hundred lawyers in the district attorney's office. If even one percent of these 600 arraignments were actually to proceed to a full-fledged trial, the system would break down instantly. On a smaller scale, the same situation holds everywhere. A Midwestern prosecuting attorney told an investigator from the American Bar Foundation that "All *any* defense lawyer has to do to get a reduced charge is to request a jury trial."

Sometimes the prosecutor is not, in fact, paying much for the plea. In a rape case, for example, conviction may be hard to get because of the girl's intense reluctance to testify; reduction to an assault charge in return for a guilty plea may be the State's best result. The stiff mandatory sentences for burglary, which frighten defendants, make convictions much harder to obtain, because juries don't like to slap people in jail for 10 years just because they broke into a house; reduction of the charge to breaking-and-entering, at a year or two, makes the prosecutor's life easier. Some of the State's evidence may have been illegally seized by the police, and would not be admissible in court; or the State's witnesses may have criminal records, which gives a jury pause.

For the man who committed the crime and believes he will be convicted (and a guilty man must be highly experienced and sophisticated to give himself much chance of acquittal), even fairly small favors may seem desirable: there is a big difference between 18 months in jail and three years. The offer is particularly attractive when it involves reducing the charge to a misdemeanor rather than a felony, because felony convictions may involve the loss of citizenship rights, down to and including the right to hold a driver's license—and because some "recidivist" statutes demand life imprisonment after a third or fourth felony conviction. The importance of this factor was demonstrated in a recent study of city criminal courts, in which between 50 and 90-plus percent of all cases were disposed of by guilty pleas—except in Las Vegas, where the District Attorney did not have the right to reduce charges to misdemeanors, and only 20 percent of accused felons "copped out."

What the lawyer normally seeks for his client in a criminal situation, then, is not vindication and acquittal, but a conviction followed by a suspended sentence or immediate parole. At the Los Angeles Public Defender's office (in its own way a civilized place, where the management supplies newspapers and magazines and people take a number and sit on an upholstered theater seat rather than a wood bench while waiting for a lawyer), a young assistant bursts in on an interview to tell his boss, gleefully, "You know what Rosy did to my man? Reduced it to simple assault, and let him off with time served. . . ."

In the vast majority of cases the negotiation of these pleas is the real contribution the criminal lawyer makes to his client. Some judges will not accept naive guilty pleas to charges like armed robbery and nighttime breaking-and-entering, which are *always* reduced on negotiation (the reduction from armed to unarmed robbery is known as "swallowing the gun"). But there is no question that a lawyer can make a better deal than a defendant can. . . .

38

THE PARAMILITARY RIGHT

Eric Norden

". . . See the old man at the corner where you buy your papers? He may have a silencer-equipped pistol under his coat. That extra fountain pen in the pocket of the insurance salesman that calls on you might be a cyanide gas gun. What about your milkman? Arsenic works slow but sure. Your automobile mechanic may stay up nights studying booby traps. These patriots are not going to let you take their freedom away from them. They have learned the silent knife, the strangler's cord, the target rifle that hits sparrows at 200 yards. Only their leaders restrain them. Traitors beware! Even now the cross hairs are on the back of your necks."

. . .

Despite their early public image as gun-happy but relatively harmless kooks— "the first World War Three buffs," as one observer dubbed them—the Minutemen in recent years have evinced a tendency to translate their threats into action. Senator J. William Fulbright, the bête noire of the ultraright ever since his exposure of General Edwin A. Walker's indoctrination of his troops with Birchite propaganda in 1961, has received hundreds of threats from Minutemen and their supporters. In 1962, one fanatic Minuteman put aside his pen and reached for his rifle. The plot to assassinate Fulbright was the brain child of "John Morris," the *nom de guerre* of a Dallas Minuteman activist and former

Reprinted from Eric Norden, The Paramilitary Right, *Playboy,* **16,** no. 6, pp. 102-104, 146, 242-264, June 1969.

recruiter for George Lincoln Rockwell's American Nazi Party, who was convinced that the systematic liquidation of leading liberals could "purify" the country, terrorize the opposition and enable the paramilitary right to "gain control of the Government." Morris persuaded a number of fellow Minutemen in Kansas City that Fulbright would make an ideal first victim. A former aide to DePugh, Jerry Milton Brooks—nicknamed "the Rabbi" because of his virulent anti-Semitism—claims that "Morris' plan was to knock off Fulbright during one of his speaking tours in Arkansas. One Kansas City Minuteman put up the money for Morris and another loaned him a 1952 Buick to get to Little Rock. A Texas man was supposed to hire a private plane and fly him out of the state after Fulbright was zapped."

According to Brooks, "Morris purchased a rifle with a telescopic sight; but on the day he was to depart for Little Rock, news of the plot leaked to DePugh, who blew his top. At this stage, he was still preaching his principle of deliberate delay, which means all the emphasis is on recruiting and propaganda and stockpiling arms, so you don't zap anybody till the outfit's ready to function fully underground. DePugh met Morris on a bridge in Lexington, Missouri, and told him he had to call off the plan because, whether it succeeded or failed, all that would happen was that the authorities would be sicked onto the Minutemen. DePugh made it clear that if Morris went ahead, he'd be the one who'd end up six feet under. The poor guy panicked and beat it out to Oklahoma."

DePugh has since denied that there was ever a serious plan to take Fulbright's life, but admits having "talked" with Morris. "The whole thing was blown up out of all proportion," he asserts, adding: "But just because I've exercised a restraining influence in the past, that doesn't mean I'll always do so. There is *no* act too brutal or illegal for us to take if it will help save this country from communism—including assassination. There'll be a lot of dead s.o.b.s before this fight is over. . . ."

Brooks, who blew the whistle on the cyanide plot in Kansas City's U.S. District Court during DePugh's trial for violation of the National Firearms Act— and who is now hiding out in the Alaskan tundra to escape his former comrades' retribution—believes that the Minutemen are biding their time for a fresh attack on the UN, with or without cyanide gas. "That place is a symbol of everything they hate," he explained to a journalist. "They're bound to take another crack at it someday."

Real or imagined Communists—in and out of the UN—have been a favorable target of Minuteman terrorist attacks in recent years. In the predawn hours of October 30, 1966, 19 heavily armed Minutemen, divided into three bands, were intercepted by staked-out police (tipped by an FBI informant) as they zeroed in on left-wing camps in a three-state area. Targets of the coordinated forays were Camp Webatuck at Wingdale, New York, where fire bombs with detonators had already been set in place; Camp Midvale in New Jersey; and a pacifist community at Voluntown, Connecticut, established by the New England Committee for Nonviolent Action. According to Queens district attorney Nat Hentel, who helped coordinate the roundup, the Minutemen, disguised as hunters, intended to burn the camps to the ground—along with their inhabitants. A state police official added, "I don't know what they thought they were going to accomplish, but they had plenty of hardware available to get the job done."

As the Minutemen were being herded into custody, raids on secret munitions bunkers and basement arms caches by 110 state, county and city police officers netted a huge arsenal of Minuteman combat matériel: 1,000,000 rounds of rifle and small-arms ammunition, chemicals for preparing bomb detonators, considerable radio equipment—including 30 walkie-talkies and shortwave sets tuned to police bands—125 single-shot and automatic rifles, 10 dynamite bombs, 5 mortars, 12 .30-caliber machine guns, 25 pistols, 240 knives (hunting, throwing, cleaver and machete), 1 bazooka, 3 grenade launchers, 6 hand grenades and 50 80-millimeter mortar shells. For good measure, there was even a crossbow replete with curare-tipped arrows. . . .

The paramilitary activists had even succeeded in infiltrating the state police. Hentel announced in the aftermath of the raids that for two years, an unnamed state policeman—one of three state troopers comprising a Minuteman "action squad"—had looted heavy weapons from armories for the organization and had tipped off Minuteman leaders on pending state and Federal investigations. According to Hentel, the trooper had also served as an organizer for the Minutemen and had recruited National Guardsmen as possible leaders of Minutemen cells. The three state policemen were subsequently cashiered, but no criminal action was taken against them.

The Minutemen arrested in the raids were drawn from a cross section of lower-middle-class America; in addition to the state troopers, there were a cabdriver, a gardener, a subway conductor, a fireman, a mechanic, a plasterer, a truck driver, a heavy-equipment operator, a draftsman, several small businessmen, a horse groom and two milkmen. Most were respectable family men in their late 20s or early 30s, known to their neighbors as solid, church-going pillars of the community—but they inhabited a world far removed from the P.T.A. and the Rotary Club. One of the milkmen, nicknamed "Nathan Hale" because of the inscription *liberty or death* on the stock of one of his semiautomatic rifles, carefully stored highly volatile plastic bombs in the refrigerator. . . .

In the aftermath of the roundup, a high New York City official revealed to *The Washington Post* that if the orchestrated raids on the leftist camps had proved successful, the Minutemen's next move was to have been an assassination attempt on former CORE leader James Farmer, marked for death as a "top black Red." Hentel adds that during the raids, hundreds of copies of a forged pamphlet, purportedly issued by a black nationalist group, was discovered in the Bellmore, Long Island, home of Minuteman leader William Garrett. The leaflets—which Hentel characterized as part of a plot to foment racial violence—had been thrown from speeding cars in racially tense areas of Queens and Long Island, urging Negroes "to kill white devils and have the white women for our pleasure." Hentel feels that a racial conflict was only narrowly averted through the cooperation of local newspapers and radio stations, which clamped a news blackout on the incident. William H. Booth, chairman of the New York City

Commission on Human Rights, contends that there was a "tie-in" between the Minutemen and rumored attacks on whites by Negroes that led to racial disturbances in the East New York, Bushwick, Lafayette, Bensonhurst-Gravesend and South Ozone Park areas of the city in 1966.

The raids put a temporary crimp in Minuteman plans, but they failed to break the back of the organization, even in the New York/New England area. In June 1967, five New York City Minutemen organized an assassination attempt against Hebert Aptheker, director of the American Institute of Marxist Studies and a member of the national committee of the U.S. Communist Party, whose Brooklyn campaign headquarters had already been the target of an abortive Minuteman fire-bombing. The conspirators this time planted a homemade pipe bomb on the roof of the Allerton Community and Social Center in the Bronx, directly above an upstairs room where Aptheker was scheduled to address an audience on Marxist dialectics. Due to a defective timing mechanism, the bomb exploded after the meeting, shattering a skylight above the speaker's stand and causing considerable damage to the empty auditorium. The Minutemen plotters were swiftly apprehended and their leader was sentenced to two years in prison; his four codefendants—one of them the owner of a Bronx sporting-goods shop— were let off with lighter sentences.

The six Minutemen who launched a second attack on the pacifist encampment at Voluntown late last summer fared no better. Once again, FBI infiltrators in their ranks had tipped off local authorities—but this time the warning almost came too late. State troopers, alerted by Federal agents to the impending raid, had stationed themselves in force at the entrance to the 40-acre farm two miles north on Route 165, but the Minutemen slipped through the cordon and surprised two women residents of the camp outside the main farmhouse. (None of the pacifists had been apprised by police of their danger.) According to one of the women, the six masked Minutemen, dressed in combat fatigues and carrying rifles with fixed bayonets, "spoke quietly, moved quietly and seemed very self-assured." The Minutemen shoved the women inside the farmhouse, bound them securely and taped their eyes and mouths, before setting forth to ransack the ground floor.

The scenario was abruptly interrupted by the belated arrival of the state troopers. The Minutemen opened fire and a brief gun battle ensued before they threw down their weapons and surrendered. Six people were shot in the melee— one state trooper, four raiders and one of the women residents, who was wounded in the hip when a trooper's shotgun discharged as he side-stepped a Minuteman's bayonet thrust. The six men were charged with conspiracy to commit arson and assault with intent to kill. One of them was identified as chairman of his home town's Wallace for President organization; another served as cochairman of the Wallace campaign in Norwich, Connecticut.

Minuteman chief DePugh invariably denies responsibility for such terrorist raids and claims they are carried out by local leaders without his approval. But in recent years, DePugh has encountered his own share of difficulties with the law. He was sentenced to four years' imprisonment for violations between May 1963 and August 1966 of the National Firearms Act, which makes it illegal to possess unregistered automatic weapons; he is appealing the conviction. And on March 4, 1968, a Federal Grand Jury in Seattle indicted DePugh and his chief aide, Walter Patrick Peyson, on charges of masterminding a conspiracy to dynamite the police and power stations in Redmond, Washington, as a diversionary tactic preparatory to robbing the town's three banks—all part of a bizarre plan to swell Minuteman coffers in the tradition of the early Bolshevik terrorists. Redmond's chief of police reports that the FBI knew of the conspiracy in advance.

Most such Minuteman plots have so far been aborted—or so it seems. As one Minuteman activist in Pennsylvania told a newsman: "Sure, some of the guys get caught. That's all in the game. But there are a lot of bombings—and murders—in this country that never get solved; and after the first day, you never read anything about it in the papers. We're not happy about all these convictions, but it's still just the visible tip of the iceberg."

In response to the burgeoning of Minuteman violence—reported and unreported—the legislatures of New York and California, two states that rank high in Minuteman activity, have already passed legislation outlawing all paramilitary organizations. . . .

Congressional pressure for a Federal crackdown on the Minutemen has continued, with some effect. The FBI and the Treasury Department have stepped up their efforts to infiltrate the group and nip its lethal plots. Local, city and state police, who initially treated the Minutemen as a bad joke, have also grown increasingly concerned—as demonstrated by the spiraling arrest rate of Minutemen for terrorist attacks and for illegal possession of weapons. The latter charge constitutes the Minutemen's Achilles' heel. . . .

But despite the surveillance of Federal, state and local police, the Minutemen's organizational effectiveness has not been appreciably impaired. Agents and informants of the FBI and the Treasury Department have succeeded in penetrating many Minutemen cadres, but the organization is structured according to the Communist Party's "cell" system. Members of one unit do not know the identity of any other Minutemen, even though they might live halfway down the block; hydralike, the group is thus able to survive the lopping off of one or more local units. Minutemen are also exhaustively trained in the techniques of clandestine intelligence and security. According to the California attorney general's report, "The Minuteman organization is designed to function as a secret underground network, and its routine operations in these times of peace are conducted along the lines of a training program for the hostilities to come. Each member is assigned a number that becomes his identification in all communications; he is warned about the use of the telephone in contacting headquarters; he is advised in the use of mail drops; he is warned to use two envelopes in organization correspondence and to place an opaque material between the inner and outer envelopes, to prevent the letter from being read by means of infrared cameras; and he is instructed to employ a wide variety of stratagems and devices as security measures." Secrecy, for the Minuteman, is a way of life—to such an extent that even the national leadership does not know the membership figures.

"I don't even know the members' names," says DePugh. "All we ask is the name and address of a unit leader—and this can be a pseudonym. I have no way of knowing exactly how many members we have, except that each group is supposed to have a minimum of five and maximum of fifteen. So I strike an average eight." DePugh's most recent estimate: 25,000 "hard-core" members, fully trained and armed, plus approximately 65,000 supporters and recruits undergoing instruction and indoctrination. "Only a relatively small percentage of these will ever become 'secure' members and be incorporated into the unit chain of command," DePugh explains. "We make a real effort to weed out all the weak links in advance; we're looking for quality, not quantity; one man ready to give his life is worth fifty who'll crack when the heat is on. That's why I reject three out of every four membership applications at the very outset." Other estimates range from an improbable low of 500 (from J. Edgar Hoover, who derides the group as a "paper organization," despite the attention it receives from his agents) to an equally improbable high of 100,000 (by a fervent Minuteman in Kansas City). Most law-enforcement officials and informed journalists believe the organization has between 5000 and 10,000 members and 30,000 to 40,000 supporters, but the "activist" percentage remains in doubt. . . .

We've got hundreds of bunkers . . . all over the country," Roy Frankhouser reported, "all of them packed with machine guns, mortars and automatic weapons—and that's in addition to the caches of arms we wrap in plastic and bury underground. Our men do twenty-four-hour guard duty in shifts over each bunker to ensure security. When D day comes, we won't be in the streets with popguns."

"When *will* D day come?" I asked.

Frankhouser shrugged. "Who knows?" he replied. "But one thing is certain: For the first time since Huey Long, the stage is set for the rise of an American brand of fascism. Not that right-wingers can take any credit for it. The race riots have done our work for us; the black nationalists are our biggest recruiting agents; I wish there were a *hundred* Stokely Carmichaels and Rap Browns. After each Watts, each Detroit, we get thousands of new backlash members—and best of all, a big slice of them are disgruntled cops and National Guardsmen. Multiply those figures in light of what's going to happen in the big cities over the next three or four summers and you've really got the makings of a revolutionary situation. Under those circumstances, anything and everything is possible— including a right-wing takeover."

"Have Minutemen been involved in inciting the race riots?" I asked.

"You mean shooting at both sides to heat things up?" He smiled. "Not yet. Right now we can afford to just stand back on the side lines and pick up the pieces; we're the inheritors of social bankruptcy, you might say. And the same holds true for the black nationalists; after each bloody riot they get a lot of uncommitted niggers going over to their side. It's sort of a symbiotic situation. Let them shoot the Jews on their list, we'll shoot the Jews on ours, and then we can shoot each other!. . .

"Look at Germany and Italy," he said. "When the people see their society dissolving into chaos, when they're threatened on every side by riots and violence and economic convulsion, they'll turn to any force tough enough and ruthless enough to impose order. That's what most people really want, you know—*order*. Not abstractions like freedom and equality and justice. That's all right for the fat times, but when the pinch is on, they want their property and their lives protected and they don't give a damn how it's done or who does it. That's why we're working and organizing now—not to take over tomorrow or the next day, which would be impossible, but to be ready when the time comes, and even a small, tight-knit and well-trained nucleus of men can play a role all out of proportion to its numbers. It only takes one wolf to terrorize a herd of sheep, you know. Cigarette?"

I declined. "The first thing we've got to do," he continued, "is disassociate ourselves from old-fogy conservatives like the John Birch Society. We've got to develop a radical revolutionary program that will appeal to the workingman on the two levels where he really lives—bread-and-butter issues and race. We've got to convince the worker that he's being economically oppressed by the powers-that-be and only we can save him. It's the carrot and the stick, in a sense; the niggers and the fear they breed are the stick, and the carrot is the promise of not only the assurance of safety from them but all the economic advantages we can deliver. We're really entering a fantastically exciting age—an age of race war, where the color of your skin is your uniform. . . ."

"Hitler had the Jews; we've got the niggers. We have to put our main stress on the nigger question, of course, because that's what preoccupies the masses—but we're not forgetting the Jew. If the Jews knew what was coming—and believe me, it's coming as surely as the dawn—they'd realize that what's going to happen in America will make Nazi Germany look like a Sunday-school picnic. We'll build better gas chambers, and more of them, and this time there won't be any refugees. The average American has only a thin veneer of civilization separating him from the savage, you know—far less of a veneer than the Germans had. When that's stripped away and he really goes wild, when this thing really explodes, there'll be a rope hanging over the lamppost for every Jew and nigger in America. Jesus, I'd hate to be in their shoes! But you remember what Napoleon said about revolutions—you can't make an omelet without breaking eggs."

He paused and seemed to brood for a few seconds.

"Of course, there are some good Jews, you know, Jews like Dan Burros, who was a friend of mine. Yeah, print that some of my best friends are Jews. Dan Burros was one of the most patriotic, dedicated Americans you'll ever meet in your life."

Frankhouser fell silent. Burros was a fanatic American Nazi who served as Rockwell's lieutenant for years, then resigned in 1962 to edit a magazine called *Kill!* and finally became a Klan leader. He had rushed into Frankhouser's house in October 1965 brandishing an issue of *The New York Times* that exposed his Jewish ancestry, snatched a loaded pistol from the wall and blown his brains out. . . .

The basic question remains: Can DePugh and his Minutemen really do what they say? The answer seems to be that they cannot by themselves—but they are not alone. Other paramilitary groups are burgeoning across the country under the stimulus of growing racial unrest. Some of these are left, and some black, such as the Black Panthers. But there is little doubt that the largest and most organized groups cluster around DePugh's end of the political spectrum. He is on particularly close terms with the Reverend Kenneth Goff of Englewood, Colorado, leader of the Soldiers of the Cross, an organization of between 3000 and 12,000 members, operating primarily in California and the Southwest. Goff, who graduated from the Communist Party to Gerald L.K. Smith's Christian Anti-Communist Crusade and went into the witch-hunting business on his own several years ago, blends Protestant fundamentalism and anti-Semitism (his oft-repeated theme is that "The United Nations is as Jewish as Coney Island") with judo, karate, *savate*, torture, mutilation and such desert survival techniques as the eating of toads and grasshoppers.

Another group on good fraternal terms with the Minutemen—and with Goff's outfit—is the California Rangers, commanded by Colonel William P. Gale, U.S. Army (Ret.), who organized Philippine guerrilla forces against the Japanese in World War Two as an aide to General Douglas MacArthur. Gale views the Communists as tools of "the international Jewish conspiracy: You got your nigger Jews, you got your Asiatic Jews and you got your white Jews. They're all Jews and they're all the offspring of the Devil." The colonel's favorite aphorism is, "Turn a nigger inside out and you've got a Jew"; and he contends that Adolf Hitler's reputation as a war criminal is all a misunderstanding: "I can show you top-secret documents that prove the six million Jews Hitler was supposed to have killed are right here in America. And if we run them out of here, they'll go down to South America and start screaming about how we burned them in gas chambers. I've got two ovens ready for them now."

The Rangers are one component of an intricate network of religio-paramilitary groups operating in California and the Southwest. A report by the California attorney general reveals that the Rangers "have intimate connections with the Ku Klux Klan, the National States Rights Party, the Christian Defense League and the Church of Jesus Christ—Christian, in addition to the Minutemen. The Church of Jesus Christ—Christian, founded in 1946, has blossomed into a string of affluent parishes from California to Florida. Its founder, the Reverend Dr. Wesley Swift of Lancaster, California, reaches over 1,000,000 listeners with his weekly radio broadcasts, which artfully blend racism and evangelism. His subordinates faithfully carry out their concept of the Christian mission: The Reverend Oren Potito, minister of the sect's St. Petersburg, Florida, parish and representative of its Eastern Conference, was arrested in Oxford, Mississippi, in October 1962 while organizing demonstrations against the admission of James Meredith to the University of Mississippi; police confiscated a small cache of firearms in his car. The church's most charismatic preacher is the Reverend Connie Lynch, a peripatetic anti-Negro demagog who wears a Confederate flag as a vest. Also a member of the Ku Klux Klan and the Minutemen, Lynch was the chief organizer of the bloody anti-Negro riots in St. Augustine in 1964, and in 1966 he traveled to Chicago to help George Lincoln Rockwell whip up whites against Negro open-housing demonstrators.

Informally linked to both Swift and DePugh is the National States Rights Party, with headquarters in Savannah, Georgia, and next to the Minutemen, the largest paramilitary organization in the nation. The N.S.R.P. has chapters in every state of the Union, but refuses to release its membership figures; a conservative estimate is 2000 members and 8000 to 12,000 active sympathizers. The party was formed in 1958 by Dr. Edward R. Fields, a chiropractor—who had previously initiated an "Anti-Jew Week" in the course of which he plastered the windows of Jewish-owned shops with anti-Semitic stickers—and Jesse B. Stoner, an attorney whose prior ventures into politics were as kleagle of the K.K.K. in Chattanooga and founder of the short-lived Stoner Christian Anti-Jewish Party, which advocated making Judaism a capital offense. His subsequent activities include legal representation of James Earl Ray, the convicted killer of Dr. Martin Luther King. Membership in the N.S.R.P. is, predictably, restricted to "white Christian Americans," and the Negro is described in the party organ as "a higher form of gorilla."

This rabid racist group was initially political in orientation and contested local elections—running on a platform of deportation for America's entire Jewish and Negro populations—in several Southern states. But by 1960, Fields reconstructed the party along paramilitary lines: A party uniform (white shirt, black tie, black trousers and arm bands emblazoned with thunderbolt insignia reminiscent of the Nazi SS emblem) was designed, arms were stockpiled and strict military discipline imposed on all members.

N.S.R.P. activists have been involved in a number of terrorist attacks on Negroes and Jews. The party first broke into the news on October 12, 1958, when a dynamite blast destroyed a Jewish synagogue in Atlanta; five men were arrested and tried for the crime, all of them N.S.R.P. members. In 1963—the same year the party launched a "Fire Your Nigger" campaign to drive more Negroes out of the South—a scuffle erupted in San Bernardino, California, between uniformed N.S.R.P. pickets and high school students, during which one of the storm troopers shot and wounded a student. On September 15, 1963, Birmingham's 16th Street Baptist Church was shattered by a dynamite blast during Sunday services, and four Negro children died. An N.S.R.P. member was arrested in connection with the bombing, charged with illegal possession of dynamite and—in the absence of conclusive eyewitness evidence placing him at the scene— sentenced to six months in prison. After an N.S.R.P. rally in Anniston, Alabama, in late 1965, in which speakers urged patriots to drive "the nigger out of the white man's streets," one of the galvanized party sympathizers in the audience took off in his car with two friends and fatally shot the first Negro he saw.

In recent years, the National States Rights Party has solidified its links with other right-wing paramilitary organizations—including the Minutemen—and urged its members to increase their stockpiles of weapons. The N.S.R.P. is still relatively small, but growing—and so is its potential for violence. Its membership reflects considerable cross-pollination with the Klan and the Minutemen, but its leaders fail to exercise even the comparative verbal restraint of the preunderground DePugh. The California Senate Fact-Finding Committee on Un-American Activities has warned that "This organization is . . . more potentially dangerous than any of the American Nazi groups."

The Ku Klux Klan, despite its long record of violence, has not until recently become a genuine paramilitary organization. The Klan has traditionally been an instrument of local terrorism rather than national revolution. Its murders, beatings and tortures have generally been carried out as vigilante acts of vengeance against "uppity" Negroes and real or imagined white traitors to the "Southern way of life," rather than as part of an orchestrated program of subversion. But all that is changing.

Today there are over a dozen Klans functioning across the country. According to political historian George Thayer, "Each one guards its individuality most jealously, refusing to subordinate itself to any one man's rule. The current strength of all Klans together is estimated to be from 50,000 to 100,000, with an additional 1,000,000 sympathisers." The largest and most violent Klan—and the one most closely linked to the Minutemen—is the United Klans of America, run with an iron hand by Robert Shelton of Tuscaloosa, Alabama. Shelton's Klans have at least 40,000 members—some estimates run as high as 85,000—scattered through 48 states, including Pennsylvania, New York, New Jersey, Illinois, Delaware, Ohio, Wisconsin, Nebraska and Indiana. (Pennsylvania Grand Dragon Roy Frankhouser, Jr., claims—possibly with some truth—that there are currently more Kluxers in Wisconsin than in South Carolina.)

Under Shelton's leadership, the Klans have adopted a distinctly paramilitary orientation. Large caches of arms, including automatic weapons, have been stockpiled across the country; Klan "military committees" have been established to teach members the techniques of guerrila warfare; "rifle clubs" and "sportsmen's clubs" have been established as fronts; and Klansmen are instructed by Shelton to join the National Rifle Association, thus allowing them to buy Government-subsidized ammunition at low prices. Klansmen have been holding more and more field exercises, Minutemen style, where members are taught sniper and rapid-fire shooting and instructed in mortar firing and the construction and handling of dynamite, fuses, Molotov cocktails and booby traps. (A recent Klan exercise taught trainees how to sabotage radio stations and power plants.) One paramilitary Klan group—Nacirema, Inc.—is even alleged to specialize in assassination. Its members are composed of the elite of Klan toughs, and are exhaustively trained in the tactics of terrorism and sabotage. The "VIP Security Guard," an organization of bodyguards for Klan rallies, outfitted in white helmets and gray shirts and slacks, is also reportedly being enlarged into a well-armed private police force. . . .

The Minutemen are among the symptoms, not the causes, of the malaise that afflicts America, a mirror in which to view the worst side of our society and ourselves before it's too late—if we care to look.

39

THE ULTRAS

Martin Oppenheimer

In general, police represent the "military wing" of a "two-war" strategy. In many localities and at the national level, Establishment thinking continues to prefer "law and order" under its own auspices, rather than the erratic social controls imposed by ultra-rightist groups. Symptomatic of this preference was the police defense of a pacifist camp in Connecticut against an armed Minuteman attack in August 1968; similar police actions against plans of Minutemen and, in the South, the Klan had taken place before. Establishment political figures today continue largely to espouse a viewpoint opposed to extra-legal methods because such methods undermine the stability of the system.

The police wing of the establishment itself does not always share this perspective, however. More and more, it would seem, police see the moderate wing of the establishment as being partly, or largely, responsible for the instability of the system by refusing to let the police "do their job," that is, apply police powers rigorously to minority ethnic and leftist political groups. Attacks on the Supreme Court are part of this approach. Hence, rather than representing one wing of a "reform" strategy, police sometimes become a part of an outright ultra-rightist repression strategy. The repression of the California Black Panthers suggests such a variation, although this normally takes the form of citizen vigilante action. It is not difficult to see how this can lead to a perception of the

Reprinted from Martin Oppenheimer, "The Urban Guerrilla," pp. 161-164, Quadrangle Books, Chicago, 1969.

police as an occupying force. "If white America is the mother country and black America is the colony, then the white police of Oakland are not police at all, but occupation troops . . . then the question of [Huey] Newton's [Panther minister of defense, convicted of manslaughter] guilt or innocence according to white law is really irrelevant: he is a political prisoner charged with defending the integrity of his people. . . ."

There is a time when law enforcement agencies no longer enforce the law against the ultra-right, or against proto-counter-revolutionaries. In many communities that time is fast approaching. The facts are evident on every hand: "Parallel to the rise of the new Radical Right since 1960 . . . there has been a sharp increase in the interest shown in weaponry, military tactics, 'self-defense,' . . . stimulated . . . by the rise of 'guerrilla' bands such as the Minutemen . . . ." Domestic arms production for private use is now about two million rifles and shotguns per year, and almost 600,000 handguns, and imports add another 1.2 million units. Private white groups, arising partly in response to the threats they perceive from black insurgency, as well as from the failure of the police to "enforce" the laws (as these groups see it), are growing in number. In Detroit, for example, six organizations issued a joint call urging citizens to defend their homes against "armed terrorists"; the head of one of them has also helped break up civil rights demonstrations and disrupt interfaith church services. Reverend Albert Cleage, a leading Detroit Black Nationalist, responded to such activities this way: "The ranges of the shooting clubs are packed; the city is way behind in processing gun registrations. So, naturally, any black man who can get hold of a gun is getting hold of it."

Many law enforcement agencies are infiltrated by the right and work hand-in-glove with it, by no means exclusively in the South, as the Panther case suggests. Law agencies throughout the country, up to the federal level, have been harassing not only militant black groups but more conventional direct-action civil rights groups, as well as left-wing groups, for years. In such an atmosphere rightist terror groups become bolder and begin to operate more freely to subvert the rights of others. Germany in the 1920's offers a classic case of such subversion; observers have pointed to a disquieting parallel in this country, in this era of political assassinations. (To speak of locally controlled gun legislation under such circumstances is to disarm the left and the black militants, preventing them from using armed defense as a deterrent to rightist terrorism—and leaves the ultra-right untouched.)

Hate activity has always been in long supply on the American political scene. Anonymous telephone calls, poison-pen letters, disruption of meetings, attempts at character assassination, blacklists, and the like are not new. But while it is not easy to make comparisons, rightist activity probably has not been so widespread since the uncertain times of the 1930's as it is today. A recent letter published in a respectable newspaper is an indication of the depth of this attitude:

Like millions of others, stunned, shocked, and appalled by the recent tragedy, one wonders "who is next," and too, when will the obvious (if drastic) steps be taken to deport all deportable Communists and to put Red fellow travelers and their like in concentration camps or under strict surveillance?

Not even the most naive or knavish can now deny that both the late President Kennedy and his brother Robert were murdered by Red rats. If the lawfully constituted authorities lack the courage and common sense to act (and but fast) an alarmed, outraged and long suffering populace might. Let's stand up and be counted, and "if that be treason, make the most of it."

Small wonder that Rap Brown has reportedly called for white leftists to bring him guns, and if they couldn't do that, give money to somebody who *can* buy a gun.